'THE FRENCH DISEASE'

The

FRENCH DISEASE

THE CATHOLIC CHURCH
AND IRISH RADICALISM, 1790-1800

DÁIRE KEOGH

FOUR COURTS PRESS

Published by
FOUR COURTS PRESS LTD
Kill Lane, Blackrock, Co. Dublin.

© Dáire Keogh 1993

ISBN 1-85182-132-5

Printed in Ireland
by Betaprint

For my parents,
Cora and Peter

Preface

I would like to express my thanks to all those who have helped me in the preparation of this book. Firstly, I acknowledge my sincere gratitude to Dr David Dickson, who supervised the earlier dissertation upon which this book is based, for his direction and generous assistance and from whom I learned so much.

I would also like to thank Professor F. X. Martin and Mr James McGuire, who introduced me to the period, and Dr Thomas Bartlett, Fr Hugh Fenning, Dr James Kelly, Dr Marianne Elliott, Professor Maurice O'Connell and Professor Emmet Larkin for reading and commenting on draft chapters. Others, too, provided valuable inspiration, particularly Professor Aidan Clarke, Professor Louis Cullen, Mr Séamus McPhillips and Dr Conor Cruise O'Brien. Especial thanks to Dr Kevin Whelan whose help has been invaluable and to whom I owe so much.

I am very grateful for the assistance of the professional staffs of the following libraries and archives: the National Library of Ireland, the National Archives, Dublin, the Dublin Diocesan Archives, the Library of Trinity College, Dublin, the Royal Irish Academy, the archives of St Patrick's College, Maynooth, the archives of Propaganda Fide and the archives of the English College Rome. I am grateful too, for permission to reproduce illustrations from the Bibliothèque Nationale, Paris and the National Archives, the National Library and the National Gallery of Ireland.

Thanks must also go to Clodagh Keogh, for her selection of illustrations, to Jarlath Hayes for the cover design, to Matthew Stout for help with formatting, and to Brian MacDonald for his invaluable assistance in the preparation of the final text. Finally, I would like to thank Michael Adams and Martin Healy of Four Courts Press for their patience and encouragement.

Contents

Illustrations

Abbreviations

A.P.F.	Archives of Propaganda Fide
B.N.L.	*Belfast News Letter*
C.D.A.	Cashel Diocesan Archives
Cork .Gaz.	*Cork Gazette*
D.D.A.	Dublin Diocesan Archives
Clare Jn.	*Clare Journal*
D.E.P.	*Dublin Evening Post*
Ennis Chron.	*Ennis Chronicle*
F.D.J.	*Faulkner's Dublin Journal*
Fr. Jn	*Freeman's Journal*
Hib.Jn.	*Hibernian Journal*
H.O. 100	Home Office, Ireland
IE.R.	*Irish Ecclesiastical Record*
I.H.S.	*Irish Historical Studies*
Lim.Chron.	*Limerick Chronicle*
Morn. Post.	*Morning Post*
Reb. Papers	Rebellion Papers
Rep. Novum	*Reportorium Novum*
N. Star.	*Northern Star*
S.N.L.	*Saunders News Letter*

CHAPTER ONE

Winter's End

There has been a revival of interest in eighteenth-century Ireland in recent years and few aspects of the period have received the measure of attention devoted to the Catholic community. A great deal of recent work has been focused on the penal laws; the traditionally accepted image of Catholics smarting under unrelenting persecution has gradually given way to a more complex picture of a resilient community, not merely adapting to their situation but displaying creativity and confidence in the face of varying degrees of opposition.

The nature of Church history has changed considerably; historians place increasing emphasis on social and economic contexts, while the very definition of 'Church' has greatly broadened since the Second Vatican Council. Both these developments have led to the publication of many fine regional studies of the Catholic Church, but the national synthesis remains unwritten. The ambitious project to record a *History of Irish Catholicism* died following the publication of a number of valuable fascicles, while the years since the Council have also witnessed the demise of *Reportorium Novum* and the *Irish Ecclesiastical Record*, the latter arguably the richest (if often eccentric) font of Irish Church history. *Archivium Hibernicum* and *Collectanea Hibernica* have published invaluable source material, but diocesan histories and episcopal biographies remain neglected. Patrick Corish has written two excellent reflective studies but, with the exception of Fr Hugh Fenning's work on the Dominicans, no systematic attempt has been made to chart the history of the Irish Church in the eighteenth century.[1]

It is possible, nevertheless, to trace the emergence of the modern Tridentine Church in Ireland in the final decades of the eighteenth century. Former emphasis on the impact of the penal laws on the Church obscured the reality of 'endurance and emergence', and spawned the images contained in Daniel Corkery's emotive *Hidden Ireland*.[2] Recent scholarship has re-examined the impact of these laws, and the work of Cullen, Bartlett and Connolly all point to a more realistic assessment of the effects of the penal code.[3] Connolly argues that far from being a systematic 'code', the penal legislation against Catholics was, in fact, 'a rag bag of measures enacted piecemeal over half a century in response to a variety of immediate pressures and grievances'.[4] The laws, he has argued, stemmed from the deep insecurity felt by Irish Protestants in the wake of the Williamite wars; the Protestant nation owed its very life to the destruction of Catholic power or as Protestant Archbishop of Dublin, William King put it, 'either they or we must be ruined'.[5]

Bartlett's succinct historiographical study of the penal laws concluded that the main problem associated with the conventional wisdom is that there is none.[6] Since the early eighteenth century, there has been no consensus amongst historians on such questions as the purpose of the laws or the degree to which they were enforced. Many of the old accounts dealing with the laws were understandably partisan. Bartlett examines Richard Mant's justification of them, based on William King's correspondence, as 'statutes protective of the Protestants', while R. H. Murray asserted that the laws were inspired 'by fear of the political influences of the papacy'. Against these Church of Ireland clergymen, Bartlett contrasts the work of two priests: L. F. Renehan, who rejected the existence of any Catholic threat, and W. P. Burke who believed that the laws were conceived 'not in fear, but in vengeance and in unbridled licence of triumph'.[7]

The purpose of the laws is equally unclear. Lecky believed that the 'code' was intended to ensure that Catholics would never again aspire 'to rise to the level of their oppressors'. For Burke, their intention was to 'pauperise, degrade and enfeeble' Ireland.[8] Certainly, the 1704 Act 'to prevent the further growth of popery' (2 Anne, c. 6) represented a formidable challenge to Catholic landowners. This Act reflected Protestant insecurity and was intended to accomplish the destruction of the Catholic landed interest which the Treaty of Limerick had left largely intact.[9] Its provisions prohibited a Catholic from buying land or leasing it for more than thirty one years; leases of the permitted length had to be held at a prohibitive rent of at least two-thirds of the yearly value. The notorious gavelling clause demanded the division of the estate on the death of the proprietor, unless the eldest son conformed to the Established Church, in which case he would inherit the entire estate; if the son conformed during the father's lifetime, the father became his 'tenant for life'.

Under the impact of this legislation, Catholic landownership was greatly reduced. In 1703 Catholics held an estimated fourteen percent of the land, while Arthur Young believed the figure had fallen to five percent by 1776. This

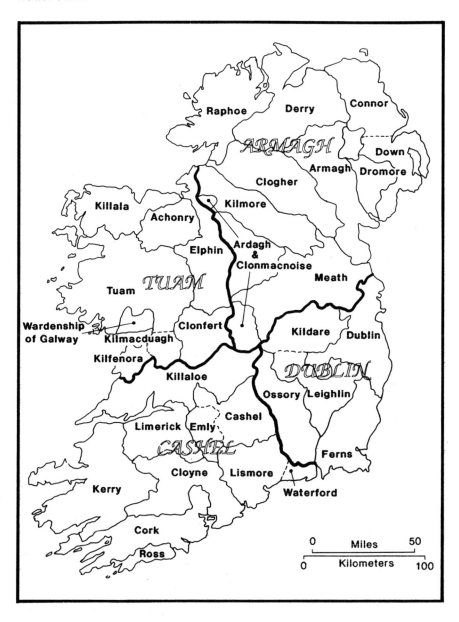

Fig. 1 Map of the dioceses of Ireland

dramatic reduction in Catholic fortunes has traditionally been accepted as evidence of the success of the penal laws, but these figures need qualification; there were marked regional variations in the application of the legislation and there were many ways in which penalties could be avoided. Cullen has emphasised the degree to which Catholics relied on trustees; conformity was often nominal and there existed a large 'convert interest' of landowning families like the Brownes and the Dalys with Catholic relatives and sympathies.[10] Distinction must also be made between ownership and leasehold. The period after 1700 witnessed the emergence of a new class of substantial tenant farmers; when their property in the form of leaseholds and livestock is considered, Wakefield believed that the personal property owned by Catholics may have amounted to half the total by the end of the eighteenth century. Catholics also came to possess economic strength in the commercial and professional middle classes, particularly in Munster and Leinster.[11]

As with the economic restrictions, the purpose of the religious aspects of the 'penal code' remain uncertain, though the impact of the legislation has been overstated. Writing in the 1950s, R. E. Burns argued that the laws intended that 'the whole nation would be Protestant', whereas Maureen Wall believed that mass conversion was never intended but that, on the contrary, preservation of the *status quo* best served the Protestant interest.[12] Measures against clerics and worship were contained in the Banishment Act of 1697 (9 William III, c.I), the 1704 Act 'to prevent the further growth of popery' and the Registration Act of the same year (2 Anne, c.7).

Had the terms of the 'Act for banishing all Papists exercising any ecclesiastical jurisdiction, and all regulars of the popish clergy out of the kingdom' been strenuously implemented, the Catholic clergy in Ireland would have been eliminated in time; there could be no ordinations without bishops, and the entry of priests from abroad was forbidden. 424 regular priests were transported in 1698, mainly to France. Many more remained in Ireland, passing themselves off as secular clergy, while others returned once the initial commotion had died down. The position of the Catholic hierarchy in 1698 was already extremely weak. There were no more than eight bishops in the country and three of these left voluntarily under the terms of the Act.[13]

Parish clergy were not affected by these laws but in 1704 they were compelled to appear before the court of sessions, register their name, address, age, parish, date and place of ordination and the name of the ordaining prelate. Priests were confined to their own county, forbidden from keeping a curate, and obliged to present two securities of £50 to guarantee their 'good behaviour'. The Act, under which 1,089 priests registered, had the effect of granting legal recognition to the Catholic diocesan clergy and far from leading to the extinction of the Church, the terms of the act facilitated its re-emergence. Priests were free to say Mass and administer the sacraments, churches remained open, and the act contained sufficient loopholes to allow for creative exploitation, often with the collusion of a compliant magistracy. Many regulars–members of religious orders–registered as diocesan clergy and bishops as parish priests, so that by Queen Anne's death in 1714 there were fourteen bishops in Ireland. Attempts were made in 1709 (8 Anne, c.3) to extract an oath of abjuration from the diocesan clergy, but a mere thirty-three priests complied, although Bishop Hugh MacMahon of Clogher, in his *relatio status* of 1714, declared that as a consequence of the oath, 'the open practice of religion either ceased entirely or was considerably curtailed according as the persecution varied in intensity'.[14]

The returns made in the 1731 'Report on the state of popery' reflect the failure of the laws; clerical numbers had risen, Mass houses continued to be built and a rudimentary educational system was in place.[15] There were, indeed, incidents of priest hunting and cases of transportation but, by and large, attempts to implement the penal laws in the early decades of the eighteenth century were sporadic, with the Church in Ulster suffering most. The laws remained on the statute book and hung in suspended animation over the heads of the Catholic clergy to be revived at moments of international crisis or perceived domestic threat, as in the years 1715, 1720, 1745, and during the war of the Austrian Succession (1740-48) or the Seven Years' War (1756-63). Luke Gardiner, the younger, described the position in a speech to the Irish House of Commons in 1782, when he said that 'papists were safe from penal laws so long as the generous and merciful disposition of their countrymen disdained to put them into execution'.[16]

I

By the accession of George III in 1760, the Hanoverian dynasty was secure on the throne. The refusal of the Holy See to recognise Charles Edward, on the death of the Old Pretender in 1766, marked the end of the Stuart cause and removed a great deal of suspicion of Catholic loyalty. Rogers, in his history of Catholic Emancipation, traced the rise of the Irish Church 'from the catacombs' to the 1760s; more recently, Whelan has placed the 'Tridentine surge' in the following decade.[17] Certainly, contemporary travellers such as Arthur Young and Thomas Campbell, were struck by the vitality of the Catholic Church in the 1770s.[18]

Fig. 2 *Extract from a poetic dialogue between Death and a person, transcribed from a Gaelic manuscript c.1745, by John Carpenter, Archbishop of Dublin 1770-86 (N.L.I.).*

Estimates of clerical numbers are incomplete, the most comprehensive figures being those from the 1731 'Report on the state of popery' and the returns of the hierarchy to Castlereagh's enquiries in December 1800.[19] In 1731, it was estimated that there were 1,445 priests and curates in Ireland of which 700 were assumed to have been regulars. Seventy years later, the number of priests had risen to 1,800, of whom 400 were regulars. It was frequently claimed in the first half of the eighteenth century that the population could not support large numbers of clergy, but such complaints may have been activated by the diocesan clergy in their propaganda battle against the encroachment of the regulars. In Ulster, Bishop MacMahon attributed the shortage of priests there 'not so much to a scarcity of vocations ... but rather [to] ... economic factors'.[20]

By 1800, however, there was a universal complaint amongst bishops of a shortage of priests. The figures for that year must be adjusted to allow for the large numbers of clerics forced to return to Ireland during the revolutionary crisis of the 1790s.[21] The shortage of 1795-1812 was caused by the closure of foreign colleges, especially in Paris. Nevertheless, Connolly's analysis of the available figures points to a decreasing clergy:people ratio; the population of Ireland increased by about eighty-eight percent between 1731 and 1800, whereas the numbers of priests rose by a mere twelve percent. This translates roughly to one priest for every 1,587 Catholics in 1731, and one to every 2,676 at the end of the century.[22]

Priestly formation varied and there was no set pattern which aspirants followed. Clerical students required a classical education which was frequently provided by the local schoolmaster. Candidates often lived for a number of years with their parish priest, serving what can be described as an apprenticeship, after which they would present a letter of recommendation to the bishop. Many, though not all, students were ordained before travelling to the continental colleges to commence their theological studies. This practice of ordaining theologically untrained young men gave rise to many abuses in the Church and was the source of heated debate throughout the eighteenth century. Attempts were made to stem the practice, but to no avail; one memorandum dating from mid-century, prepared for the Cardinal Protector, was critical of these clerics returning to Ireland 'to convert heretics who know more theology than they do themselves'.[23] In spite of criticism, the practice continued until about 1815, but bishops made efforts to improve the quality of candidates.

The Cashel statutes of 1782 laid down that all aspirants be called and examined for several years prior to ordination, while Bishop Philip MacDavett of Derry reported to Rome in 1791 that he ordained only those whom he had strictly examined.[24] Prior to the foundation of Maynooth in 1795, there was little alternative but to ordain many candidates; continental education was expensive, scholarships were few and students had to be supported by their families. This expense meant that clerics came from families ranging from the modestly comfortable to the well off.[25] Early ordination, however, allowed poorer students to survive on Mass stipends, but this weakened the discipline of the Church. Many Irish priests chose to remain in France as *curés* or chaplains, and the traits of the maverick or 'giddy' priests of the 1798 rebellion were often attributed to contamination by this process.

The dislocation caused by the penal laws undoubtedly led to a weakening of institutional structures within the Church, but Connolly's view that the Irish Church of the eighteenth century was 'characterised by a general laxity of internal discipline, reflecting both the absence of effective control and a certain religious zeal', needs qualification.[26] Many abuses did exist, of course, such as those recorded in the early visitations of Bishop Sweetman in Ferns in the 1750s, and the similar shortcomings recorded on Patrick Plunket's first tour of his diocese thirty years later.[28] At Oldcastle, County Meath , Plunket reported

> Neither order nor decency about the altar. The altar steps too low. The priest cannot properly convey his words when he stands almost on a level with the people. It is a shame that there should be but one set of altar linen and one rusty suit of vestments in such a considerable parish. A black pewter chalice, greatly impaired, is absolutely unfit for the celebration of the divine mysteries, and must be dishonourable to a respectable congregation.

In almost every parish he visited, Plunket complained of the poor quality of the vestments and sacred vessels and of the irregularity of the sanctuary. Of greater concern to him were the heterodox liturgical practices of priests who failed to preach on Sundays and were ignorant of the decrees of the Council of Trent. At the parish of Turin, Plunket wryly commented that 'every face seemed to wear visible marks of dissatisfaction at the pastor's unpastoral conduct'.[28]

Plunket's dissatisfaction, and the demands he made upon his clergy, reflect the renewed vigour of the episcopacy in the later eighteenth century. Throughout the country, the younger bishops engaged in regular visitations of their dioceses; many parishes were visited annually and complaints were carefully investigated. The ignorance of the laity was a cause of grave concern and Mass attendance was low. Congregations showed little respect and it was common for bishops to refuse confirmation on account of poor preparation.[29] The emphasis placed on catechisis is reflected in recurring references to such work in almost every *relatio status* in the period between 1782 and 1803, while the Confraternity of Christian Doctrine was established in most dioceses to assist in this task.[30] A considerable amount of religious and devotional material was printed for an eager readership; by 1782, Archbishop James Butler's 'General Catechism' had gone through eleven editions since its publication in 1775.[31] Greater devotion to the Eucharist was promoted by the Archconfraternity of the Blessed Sacrament, and sodalities of the rosary and scapular, introduced by the regulars in the 1720s, were widely established. These provided opportunities for association which would be exploited by the political radicals in the 1790s.

Episcopal efforts were made to regulate religious practice. Plunket's visitation diary for 1780 reveals that many parishes followed incomplete liturgical calendars; in 1775, Dr John Carpenter, Archbishop of Dublin, employed John Morris to print a new missal containing the feasts of all the Irish saints. Plunket recommended this missal–believed by Carpenter to have been the first printed in these islands–to his clergy.[32] The keeping of parochial registers began in earnest and renewed attempts were made to stem the abuses the hierarchy associated with 'patterns' and wakes, which activities formed a major feature of religious and social life for the laity in late eighteenth-century Ireland.

The most energetic and reforming bishops convened diocesan conferences, through which they endeavoured to renew their clergy. One day conferences were held between the months of April and October in many dioceses and fines were imposed on those absent without cause. Bishop John Troy revived the conferences in Kilkenny in 1780 and this provided a model which many of his confrères copied. Troy chose a theme for each year, and the surviving Dublin plan for 1790 reflects his meticulous approach; the theological ignorance of many of his clergy is inferred:

January:	Paschal communion–can it be deferred?
February:	Viaticum for children and Mass stipends.
March:	Why hear Mass, the altar and vestments.
April:	The ceremony of the mass, its language, can it be said in the vernacular?
June:	Penance, what is it? Is it necessary, is it a true sacrament of the New Law?
July:	Matter for penance and contrition.

August: Sacramental confession.
September: Is contrition necessary only for mortal sins?
October: The minister of penance.
November: Reserved cases, who has faculties to absolve them?
December: The sign of confession.[33]

Troy's allocation of one conference to a discussion of stipends reflects his concern at the controversy surrounding the fees demanded by priests for their ministrations. The Whiteboy movement had originally opposed tithe payment to the Church of Ireland but, in 1785-6 attempts were made in Munster to regulate Catholic stipends and dues, and maximum rates were set out. Easter and Christmas dues were put at one British shilling, the maximum marriage due, a crown. The Munster bishops met in Cork in the summer of 1786 to discuss the crisis and issued a surprisingly conciliatory statement which acknowledged abuses, laid down acceptable rates, and forbade priests to 'bargain mercenarily for their dues, nor ever to withhold from their people the sacraments on pretence of their dues not being paid to them'.[34]

Troy had taken a severe line against the Whiteboys since their first appearance in Ossory; Rightboys were excommunicated in October 1779 and again in 1784, and in August 1786 he closed the chapels in Kilkenny City to prevent oaths being administered. Nevertheless, Troy examined the question of stipends and issued regulations to his priests to be observed under pain of suspension. The official offerings ranged from 11s $4\frac{1}{2}$d to 2s $8\frac{1}{2}$d for marriages, from 5s 5d to 2s $8\frac{1}{2}$d for requiem Mass, 1s 1d from the wealthy for anointings, and 2s 2d from such as could afford it, for baptisms. Easter and Christmas dues were set at 1s 1d from those that could afford it, but no dues were to be demanded from the 'real poor'.[35]

Protests largely subsided after this, but Ó Fearghail has detailed the experience of Fr Butler, parish priest of Thomastown who was 'visited' by Rightboys in November 1789. The armed men shot at the chapel and, with cross-cut saws, demolished the gallery, benches and altar rails. Undeterred by the experience, the priest accepted £5. 18s. 7d for a wedding ten days later![36]

Clerical incomes varied through the country. The best insight is provided by the returns made to Castlereagh in 1800, but it is not always clear whether these estimates are derived from 'stated contributions', i.e. Christmas and Easter dues, or if they included 'voluntary oblations'.[37] The average income for parish priests in 1800 was £65, but this excluded the cost of keeping a curate which amounted to £10. Incomes reportedly varied from as much as £300 in the diocese of Kildare and Leighlin to a mere £25 in the wardenship of Galway. In

*Fig. 3   James Butler II,
Archbishop of Cashel
1774-91*

1805, Theobald McKenna ranged the average salary from between £30 and
£50 in Ulster to a high of £200 in Munster 'on account of a great liberality in
paying for marriages'.[38]

These incomes compared favourably with the monetary earnings of the
more prominent lay members of the parish, as large farmers of around 150
acres had a cash income of only £50 while the smaller 'middlemen' could earn
between £100 and £200.[39] Added to this, the clergy enjoyed many gifts, while
their duties involved receiving extensive hospitality; the 1800 returns declared
that 'in general, they dine nearly half the year in private families'.[40] This close
link between priests and people, and their total dependence on the laity for
support, had many advantages. However, abuses were also attributed to this
situation; complaints were made of their drunkenness and disreputable frater-
nisation with the lower orders.

The Catholic laity exhibited similar generosity in their willingness to
finance the spate of chapel building which characterised the last quarter of the
eighteenth century. The re-emergence of Catholicism was uneven in geographical terms. Broadly, it began in mid-Munster/south Leinster and perco-
lated only slowly into Ulster/north Connacht. Contrary to the received image,
Catholicism as an institutional force was more firmly entrenched in the richer
areas, the upper social classes and the town. This regional pattern was reflected

in the building of new churches.[41] The older chapels had become symbols of backwardness in the eyes of the hierarchy and the Catholic middle class. They expressed their confidence and aspirations through a massive programme of church building which continued into the late nineteenth century.[42] In 1766 Alexander McAuley commented on the changes in Ulster:

> till within these few years, there was scarce a Mass house to be seen in the northern counties of Ulster. Now Mass houses are spreading over most parts of the country. Convents, till of late were hid in corners. Now they are openly avowed in the very metropolis. From the Revolution till a few years ago, Mass houses were little huts in remote and obscure places. Now they are sumptuous buildings in the most public and conspicuous places.[43]

'Sumptuous' was certainly an exaggeration, but few contemporaries failed to be impressed by the material improvement of chapel buildings. The penal chapels of the seventeenth and eighteenth centuries were rudimentary and the descriptions contained in Archbishop James Butler's visitation books reflect the material poverty of the Church in the 1750s.[44] The older rural chapel was generally between fifty and sixty feet long and half as wide, with a mud floor and low thatched roof. It was a barn-like structure, with whitewashed mud or stone walls, a window on either side of a simple raised altar and one door at the back of the chapel. There were no galleries or furnishings, congregations stood or knelt during Mass, and the chapel was almost without decoration, apart from a crucifix behind the altar.[45]

The penal Mass house, *teach an phobail*, was the focal point of the community, serving as church, school and meeting place; on occasion it was used for threshing corn. The new churches, or barn chapels of the late penal years, were grander in scale, built of stone and with a pitched, slated roof; steeples and bells were, however, still forbidden under the penal laws. From the barn plan, they evolved to an L-shape and the more common cruciform plan. Floors were generally flagged, and galleries, often with pews, accommodated the larger congregations.[46] The chapels remained simple in their decoration, but efforts were made to improve the sanctuary, the altar and the quality of vestments and altar plate.

The level of building is recorded in the episcopal *relationes status* sent to Rome. In Munster, where church building proceeded faster than elsewhere, Bishop Matthew McKenna built eleven new chapels in Cloyne in the ten years after 1775 and James Butler II spent one thousand guineas building a house and improving the church in Thurles. Francis Moylan boasted that the churches of Tralee and Killarney, which he had built, surpassed any Protestant church in the diocese in size and workmanship.[47] The scale of the cathedrals in Waterford (1793) and Cork (1799) spoke volumes about Catholic confidence and pretensions. More than this, the new cathedrals were a witness to the re-emergence of the Catholic hierarchy. Episcopal communications in the early decades of the century were sourced *'in loco refugii nostri'* but, though penal legislation was still in place until the early 1790s, the bishops now addressed their flocks from their seat, often conspicuously re-established in the principal town of the diocese.

Ireland's twenty-six dioceses were divided between four metropolitan provinces–Armagh, Dublin, Cashel and Tuam–and each diocese was administered by a bishop assisted by a vicar general or vicar forane. Most dioceses had a chapter, the members of which had parochial duties and served merely to elect a vicar capitular to administer a vacant diocese. Provincial synods were resumed in Tuam in 1752, Cashel in 1775 and Armagh in 1779, but the first meeting of the metropolitans did not take place until November 1788 when the four archbishops spent a week together in Dublin. Relations with Rome were conducted through Propaganda Fide; the Congregation communicated either directly with the Irish bishops or through the nuncio in Brussels.

In theory, the archbishops had authority over their suffragans, but this counted for little in practice, due to the dissipation of metropolitan authority in the eighteenth century. Combined with this, years of continental experience and familiarity with the government of the Church inclined individual bishops to refer disputes directly to Rome. They regularly employed agents in Rome to act on their behalf, and the scope of their activity may be seen in the extensive correspondence between John Troy and his agent, Luke Concanen O.P.[48] The services of an agent were vital, particularly as episcopal appointments often became complicated and acrimonious.

In theory, prelates were appointed by postulation to Propaganda by individual bishops seeking a coadjutor, or by provincial bishops and diocesan clergy in the case of a vacant see. Postulations often included more than one name and the Sacred Congregation investigated the suitability of candidates, making enquiries of metropolitans and other relevant parties. Until the death of 'James III' in 1766, the Stuarts enjoyed a right of nomination to Irish sees, but the passing of this privilege made the Irish hierarchy one of the most independent episcopacies in Europe.[49] Outside pressure was, however, still brought to bear to secure the appointment of 'suitable candidates'. The ongoing secular/regular dispute often decided the outcome; on other occa-

A N

A C T

F O R

The Relief of His Majesty's Subjects of this Kingdom, profeffing the Popifh Religion.

D U B L I N :

Printed by the Executors of DAVID HAY, Affignee of the late BOULTER GRIERSON, Printer to the King's Moft Excellent Majefty, 1778.

Fig. 4 Title page of 1778 Relief Act (N.L.I.)

sions, the Gallican card was played. John Troy enjoyed considerable influence at Propaganda until the death of Cardinal Stefano Borgia in 1804.

A bishop enjoyed scant financial rewards; in 1800 the average episcopal income (derived from the bishops' mensal parishes) was £300; Cork topped the scale at £350, but the bishop of Kilfenora and Kilmacduagh earned a mere £100.[50] Because of the modest rewards, an independent income was desirable; James Butler (Cashel, 1774-91), Dominic Bellew (Killala, 1779-1812) and Michael Peter MacMahon (Killaloe, 1765-1807), all came from prominent landed families which could readily support them, while the remaining bishops came from the prosperous classes of middlemen and merchants.

I I

Despite the growing sense of corporate identity, visible in the last quarter of the eighteenth century, it would be wrong to exaggerate the unity of the hierarchy. Divisions remained, and the Munster bishops, led by James Butler II, Archbishop of Cashel from 1774 until his early death in 1791, formed a definite party, exhibiting what their opponents believed were Gallican tendencies. Butler frequently referred to 'our national Church' in his correspondence, though his behaviour did not tend to schism, but merely reflected the complexity of Irish life. 'Gallican' was a tag used loosely in Ireland, bearing little resemblance to the rampant variety in France.

Educated at St Omer and consecrated at the early age of thirty-one, the archbishop displayed, above all, an antipathy towards the friars–despite his claims to the contrary–attempting to prevent their appointment to the hierarchy. The regulars tended not to be educated in France and, consequently, they were more ultramontane than their secular colleagues. This fact complicated the ongoing secular/regular dispute, giving credibility to suggestions of Gallicanism among certain prelates.

The debate surrounding the Test Oath of 1774 marked the height of the Gallican controversy in Ireland. The oath derived largely from the efforts of the Church of Ireland Earl-Bishop of Derry, Frederick Augustus Hervey, and it was based on a conviction (argued by Ormond a century before) that such a declaration would sharpen Catholic divisions.[51] Hervey travelled widely on the continent and experience had taught him that while 'the Protestants have universally concluded that every R[oman] Catholic is a papist', there were in reality two strains of Catholicism, Romans and Gallicans. Irish Catholics were, he believed, predominantly Gallican, and the bishop's intention was to induce a schism amongst these factions.[52] Hervey actively canvassed a proposed oath in Britain and amongst Irish clerics in France.

He won enthusiastic support from Dr Dower, the superior of the Irish College at Toulouse, but while Lord Kenmare expressed similar sentiments, he predicted clerical opposition.[53] In an effort to win the approval of the Catholic Committee, the Earl-Bishop enlisted the assistance of the highly respected Charles O'Conor, one of its founding members, suggesting that he draw up a suitable declaration. Welcoming the opportunity to express its civil principles, the Committee framed a declaration in February 1774, but the heads of a bill introduced to the Irish House of Commons bore little resemblance to their formula. O'Conor was aghast at the alterations, particularly the articles concerning papal power. Similar reservations were expressed at a meeting of the Committee on 3 May, but confirmation of the orthodoxy of the oath by Dr John Carpenter, Archbishop of Dublin (1770-86), allowed its unaltered passage through parliament, and the oath received the royal assent in June 1774, the same month as the Quebec Act.[54]

Reaction to the oath sharply divided the Committee and the Catholic hierarchy. In spite of his ruling, Archbishop John Carpenter and Bishop Thomas Burke of Ossory became the foremost critics of the oath in opposition to James Butler and the Munster faction. Provinces, too, were divided; Dr James O'Keeffe of Kildare and Leighlin broke ranks with his archbishop and sided with the jurors. In search of moral justification, Butler submitted the oath to the judgement of the theologians at Douai and Paris who confirmed its orthodoxy. Armed with their response, he assembled his suffragans at Cork on 15 July 1775, whence a declaration was issued that the oath contained nothing contrary to Catholic principles.

A week later, in a bizarre manoeuvre, Butler attempted to convene a meeting of bishops in Kilkenny, in an effort to convince Dr Burke to delete the objectionable passages from his *Supplementum Hiberniae Dominicanae*. Burke vehemently objected and threatened to excommunicate the bishops if they remained twenty four hours in his diocese. Dr Nicholas Sweetman of Ferns turned back at New Ross and the Munster bishops adjourned to Thurles where, with the exception of the Dominican Michael Peter MacMahon, they issued a public condemnation of Burke's *Hibernia Dominicana* and its 1772 supplement containing embarrassing confidential Roman objections to a draft oath suggested in 1768.[55] By December 1775, O'Keeffe of Kildare and all of the Munster bishops, except for MacMahon, had taken the oath.[56]

Dr Carpenter and the non-jurors continued to press Propaganda for a condemnation of the oath. Rome expressed serious reservations; the faithful were to be discouraged from taking it but, fearing anti-Catholic reaction, the Congregation stopped short of public condemnation. Butler informed Rome of the peculiarities of the Irish situation; the implications of the Whiteboy disturbances, the suspicion of Catholics in government circles, and the need for an explicit declaration of principles. Again, Propaganda declined to condemn the oath, but it did issue a stark rebuke to Butler and the Munster faction, castigating them for exceeding their authority by accepting the oath without reference to 'the sovereign pontiff'.[57] Anxious to refute charges of Gallicanism, Butler wrote an apologetic letter to Cardinal Castelli, containing profound expressions of loyalty to Rome:

> as our devotion to the Holy See is profound, so is our sorrow at these reports of our disrespect. As for myself, who might, had I chosen it, have enjoyed comfort in the world, and who, in the Church which I serve at my own expense, have only care and labours and anxiety–why should I barter my heavenly reward, my only desire and hope, for any courtly favour, vain novelties, or temporal gain? No, Eminence, my constant prayer is that God may take away that life He has given me before I become a stumbling block to my people or a scandal to my religion. But while with His favour I enjoy it, my sole ambition shall be to promote his glory, and the salvation of my flock, adhering to the faith and the Chair of Peter till my latest breath.[58]

The sudden death of Dr Burke in the autumn of 1776 marked a critical juncture for the Church in Ireland. Burke had been in the vanguard of opposition to the oath and it might have been presumed his demise would lead to an accommodation of sorts between the two sides. On the contrary, the choice of successor in Ossory rekindled debate and, once again, the 'Gallican' and 'papist' tags were employed to obscure the more fundamental secular/ regular nature of the dispute. The vicar general of the diocese, Patrick Molloy, was the favoured candidate of the Ossory clergy, and his nomination was supported by no fewer than nine bishops. Molloy, however, was tainted by his acceptance of the 'Herveyan Test', and Propaganda chose John Thomas Troy, the third Dominican bishop of Ossory in the eighteenth century. The appointment of a friar-bishop at this late date was unusual and it would be thirty years before it would happen again.[59]

Butler was greatly angered by Troy's appointment and warned Rome of 'the evils that could well befall the Catholics if our government officials are now persuaded that the Roman Curia confers bishoprics in this kingdom on those who are little motivated in their loyalty to either King or country'.[60] Butler's letter contrasted strongly with the tone of his *apologia* of the previous September, but Troy–who had been absent from Ireland for twenty one years– was, in fact, an unknown quantity. He was to demonstrate a rare quality of diplomatic skill in combining loyalty to King and Pope without compromise.

III

Troy returned to Ireland 'freighted with the prerogative doctrines of the Court of Rome'.[61] Before long, he established himself at the head of the Irish hierarchy and for almost forty years oversaw the Romanisation of Irish Catholicism, a process universally attributed to Cardinal Cullen. James Butler's Roman agent, Valentine Bodkin, believed that Troy had been chosen by Stefano Borgia of Propaganda to 'execute the commands of the Sacred Congregation at all times and to give them the requisite information' from Ireland.[62] Troy's adherence to this mandate was unfailing, but he was never merely a 'Roman hack'. His experience and knowledge of Vatican politics, the tutelage received from his predecessor and mentor, Thomas Burke, and the lessons learned as Master of San Clemente equipped him for his task. A shrewd diplomat, he often practiced a subtle economy of truth. Above all, Troy was pragmatic. In affairs of state, he sought to represent Catholics as dutiful subjects but he jealously guarded the independence of the Church and the sole right of the hierarchy in the management of its affairs. In many respects, his motto might have been to 'render unto Caesar. . .'.

As well as his appointment to the Diocese of Ossory, Troy's nomination as apostolic delegate to Armagh was a matter of concern to the 'Munster faction' within the hierarchy. The appointment of Archbishop James Butler's former Roman agent, Dominic Bellew, as parish priest of Dundalk in 1772, in preference to local candidates, had precipitated a crisis in the Diocese of Armagh. This led to bitter divisions and the suspension of Archbishop Anthony Blake (1704-87) for non-residence, neglect and financial irregularities.[63] Troy tried to reconcile the parties; Blake was restored and Peter Markey, the Armagh Chapter's choice, was given the parish of Dundalk. Not to be outdone, Blake petitioned Rome for a co-adjutor, nominating Dominic Bellew as the most suitable candidate. The Chapter protested to Propaganda, predicting 'certain ruin' if Blake's wish was granted, but Bellew's timely nomination as Bishop of Killala in December 1779 averted further conflict. Embittered by these events, Bellew remained a vocal critic of Troy until his death in 1812.[64]

The Bishop of Meath, Patrick Plunket, was, in turn, named as candidate for the co-adjutorship. Plunket (1738-1827) was one of the ablest members of the hierarchy. Having studied at the college of Trente-Trois in Paris, he beame superior of the Lombard College and professor of theology at the prestigious College of Navarre, before returning to Ireland as bishop in 1779 after an absence of twenty seven years.[65] In January 1781, James Butler informed him that it was 'pretty certain ... [he] was the prelate selected to be an angel of peace to [Armagh] that long distracted diocese'.[66] The Archbishop's congratulations, however, were premature, for Plunket's publication of the government fasts for the success of the King's armies, in a pastoral in February 1781, aroused suspicions of Gallicanism and ruled out his appointment.

The nuncio in Brussels, Ignatzio Busca, was particularly concerned at Plunket's reference to the Test Oath of 1774 which 'contracted a peculiar obligation of co-operating with the liberality, the wisdom and benevolence of their rulers'. Busca requested confirmation of the pastoral from Dr Carpenter. Leonardo Antonelli regarded Plunket's behaviour as 'reprehensible', and Troy assured his rejection for the co-adjutorship by identifying Plunket along with James Butler as 'the present heads of the Gallican party in this kingdom'.[67]

Troy's actions in Armagh heightened his unpopularity, and his appointment as administrator of that diocese on the sudden retirement of Blake in April 1781, brought the bishops of Munster and Ulster together in opposition to the Dominican. Butler expressed concern at the manner in which the primate was 'suspended and deposed', citing the alarm it would cause every prelate of the kingdom if 'suspensions be sent as "lettres de cachets" are in France'.[68] Above all, his critics feared that Troy would be transferred to Armagh. It was this which prompted the Ulster bishops' protest to Rome, opposing him on the grounds that he was a regular, from a distant diocese, and unpopular with the government.[69] Rome rebutted this attack on 'the learned and able' Dr. Troy but, in the event, the co-adjutorship went to Richard O'Reilly, the Roman educated co-adjutor Bishop of Kildare and Leighlin.[70]

In spite of these institutional differences, the bishops were united in their fundamental concern for the welfare of the Irish Church. After they got to know each other, Butler and Troy enjoyed 'a great friendship', no doubt based on a common zeal for change.[71] In their respective dioceses, they attempted to implement the instructions of the Council of Trent, and both sought to improve their clergy, the quality of worship and the instruction of the faithful. This was facilitated by the fact that the political climate in Ireland was changing rapidly, and the passing of Gardiner's Relief Act in 1778 provided an opportunity to end the Test Oath controversy.

Debate still surrounds the motivation behind Gardiner's legislation. Enlightenment ideas, an European decline in 'popery', the activities of the 'patriots' at home and a growth in religious toleration, have been cited to account for the relief measures. Recent writing, however, tends to support the view that the importance of toleration has been overstated. Dismantling the received view has left no conclusive alternative but, Irish relief is increasingly interpreted in the broader imperial context, of the Quebec 'relief' of 1774 and the outbreak of hostilities in the American colonies with the consequent need to recruit Irish Catholic soldiers.[72]

The initiative seems to have come from London and the legislation was modelled on Sir George Saville's 1778 Act, which had given relief to England's Catholics. The Irish bill offered more limited concessions, dealing almost exclusively with landed property: it allowed Catholics to purchase land on equal terms with Protestants, and the notorious gavelling law was removed. Opposition to the measures was led by the anti-Catholic George Ogle and Hercules Langford Rowley, and a series of amendments further limited the scope of the legislation, jeopardising the passage of the entire bill. In the final analysis, the significance of the bill lay not so much in its content as in its principles, which Edmund Burke confidently predicted would 'extend further' in time.[73] Forty years later, in the wake of O'Connell's 'revolution', Thomas Wyse vindicated Burke's confidence, arguing that Gardiner's Relief Act 'was the first step which really emancipated'.[74]

Troy remained aloof from any public comment on the progress of the legislation. Whereas James Butler and the Munster bishops added their names to a list headed by Lords Trimleston, Fingall, Gormanston and Kenmare in a loyal Catholic address to the King in April 1778, Troy, by contrast, urged 'patience and silence'.[75] Their differences, however, were based more on style than substance. Troy's views on Catholic relief had presumably been sounded by the Castle: in consequent hope of concession, he broke ranks with Dr Carpenter, publishing the government fasts and denouncing the 'specious notions of liberty and illusive expectations of sovereignty' of the American colonists. Significantly, Troy assured his archbishop that his actions had been taken without 'any uncanonical ... connection' with the juring bishops of Munster.[76] The eventual ratification of the relief bill demanded a suitable public demonstration of gratitude; in August, Dr Carpenter issued a pastoral calling the faithful to fidelity and allegiance to 'his most sacred majesty', while Troy accepted the Test Oath, arguing that 'it contains nothing against the defined articles of Faith or Morals and seems now required as the condition *sine qua non* of our establishment in this kingdom'. Dr Carpenter and many

Fig. 5 Bookplate of John Troy, Bishop of Ossory 1776-86

others have reconciled it to their conscience, particularly as the Court of Rome, though pressed for a decision on the subject, always declined it.[77]

The 1778 relief measures left intact all the restrictions on the Catholic clergy and worship, but the momentum for change was still in place. With the initiative coming from London, Catholic loyalty proved a trump card in the face of increasing Volunteer pressure on the administration. The Catholic Committee, dominated by an aristocratic faction, played no role in securing the concessions of 1778, so that Troy, by opening communication with the Castle, was peculiarly well placed to regulate the form of future relief meaures.

The complex development and debate on the Catholic question in the aftermath of the 1778 legislation has been examined by O'Flaherty and Bartlett. Their work illustrates the formative influence of Troy, whose guiding ambition remained the removal of disabilities without compromising the independence of the hierarchy.[78] Attempts by Charles O'Hara, M.P. for Sligo, to introduce further relief measures in 1779 stumbled on this hurdle. Luke Gardiner presented the heads of O'Hara's bill to Troy, who was goaded into action by provisions to exclude the regular clergy from Ireland. Assuming the role of general-secretary of the episcopacy, Troy quickly marshalled opposition to these provisions. He circulated the bishops, calling on them to nominate two prelates to represent each province on a sitting committee to be assembled in Dublin.

Reaction from the provinces echoed Troy's concern. He confessed to Butler that the bishops 'all dislike the intended bill and desire nothing more than being put on the footing of the English clergy'.[79] Butler shared Troy's anxiety, agreeing that O'Hara's proposals would damage the Church, but the unity of the hierarchy was jeopardised by rumours passed to Troy by an un-named Protestant peer, that a remonstrance, calling for the banishment or secularisation of the regular clergy, had been submitted to members of parliament by the Munster bishops. The rumour was denied by Butler.[80]

Troy conducted discreet negotiations with Gardiner and by the first meeting of the sitting committee on 12 November, he was in a position to assure the bishops that O'Hara's bill would be replaced by 'a less complicated and more agreeable' substitute. Perhaps more significantly, Gardiner assured the bishop that no bill would be forwarded without consultation with the Catholic hierarchy.[81] While Troy shared with James Butler his hopes for a total repeal of the penal laws before Easter 1780, the bitterness roused by the Gordon Riots blighted the prospect of imminent relief.[82] Only the escalation of Volunteering and 'patriot' attempts to secure free trade and legislative independence forced the administration to re-enter the 'race for the Catholic'. The heads of a bill were introduced to the Irish Commons by John Dillon, in Gardiner's absence, on 5 February 1782.[83]

Gardiner's second relief bill was much more sweeping than the first. The remaining disabilities relating to land were removed and the secular clergy were freed to perform ecclesiastical functions, though they were still prohibited from assuming ecclesiastical rank or titles, or to minister in a church with a steeple or bell. A prohibition was placed on the future entry of members of religious orders into Ireland but, except for an obligation to take the Test Oath, no measures were to be taken against the regulars already in the country. The bill also allowed the establishment of Catholic schools, on receipt of a licence from the Protestant ordinary, but endowment of such schools was forbidden. Troy undoubtedly regretted the restrictions on the regular clergy, but comparison with the persecution envisaged in O'Hara's proposals of 1779 may have softened the blow. In any event, the prohibition was merely the re-enactment of an existing statute which had long been in disuse.

Of even greater concern to the hierarchy in 1782 were the unsuccessful proposals of John Hely-Hutchinson, Provost of Trinity College, concerning the education of clerics. The Provost sought to provide a domestic education for candidates for the priesthood, thus ending the system of continental education which had been a particular source of Protestant suspicion. Hely-Hutchinson recommended that clerics should receive a liberal education at Trinity College, sponsored and supervised by the government. There would be provision for a Catholic faculty of theology and he hoped that promotion to the Catholic hierarchy would, ultimately, be conditional on a domestic education.[84] Lord Kenmare reported Hely-Hutchinson's educational proposals to Edmund Burke whose response, later published as a pamphlet, contained a succinct and authorative rejection of the proposals and a justification of the Tridentine ordinances requiring exclusive clerical education.[85] In any event, a decision was taken to postpone the education question until August and Hely-Hutchinson's proposals were never taken further.

The determination of the hierarchy to oppose government interference in Catholic education was again manifested in their opposition to Orde's education plan in 1787.[86] A proposal to confer on the King the right of nomination to Irish sees again highlighted the underlying divisions within the Irish episcopacy. The origin of the initiative is uncertain but James Butler believed it lay with the Irish House of Commons Speaker, Edward Pery, and the Church of Ireland Archbishops of Cashel and Armagh, Charles Agar and Richard Robinson. Troy first received news of the proposal from Bishop MacMahon of Killaloe who had been informed of the development by Bishop Moylan of Kerry.[88] According to MacMahon, Butler had initially opposed the move but, in an attempt to allay Ascendancy fears of foreign interference, now accepted changes which would have allowed the metropolitan final say in the choice of bishops.

Butler's proposals enjoyed the support of Bishops Moylan, Egan and Plunket. Conway of Limerick opposed the change, while MacMahon believed that Butler's intention was to prevent the ordination of regular bishops. Troy opposed any alteration in the traditional practice of episcopal appointments and strongly rejected the right of any group of prelates to speak on matters which, he asserted, should be treated between the King and the Pope through their ministers in Brussels. Determined to defend the papal prerogative, he condemned the attempts of a small group of members of parliament to 'frighten us into improper concessions'.[88] Troy informed the internuncio at Brussels of these ominous developments; Busca expressed total opposition to the proposals and, at Troy's suggestion, informed Alleyne Fitzherbert, the British minister in the city, of his objections. Continuing his diplomatic assault on the proposals, Troy met with John Burke, the M.P. who had first raised the suggestion in the Irish House of Commons, and dissuaded him from introducing the objectionable clause into Gardiner's bill.[89]

The easy passage of the 1782 Relief Act through parliament brought an effective end to the penal laws in so far as they had restricted Catholic worship in Ireland for almost a century. Certain of the civil disabilities were still in place–the major professions and political rights were withheld–but these were not of primary concern to the hierarchy, whose priority remained the strengthening of the Catholic Church as an institution. The events of 1778-82 had seen unprecedented political activity by the episcopacy, activity which illustrated the ongoing factional divide amongst the bishops. Debate on Gardiner's bill had exposed the ongoing secular/regular conflict, and the apparent willingness of the 'Munster faction' to concede to political pressure reflected a residual lack of self-confidence amongst sections of the hierarchy.

Such actions may well have been due to the peculiarities of the Irish situation but, contrasted with the resilience and determination of Troy, it was not difficult to see how the Gallican tag could be applied to the Munster bishops. Troy's opposition secured the independence of the hierarchy, while his resolute refusal to compromise on the papal prerogative was the first salvo in a long battle ahead. His role in these critical debates secured his position at the head of the Irish hierarchy; his was the opinion sought by Gardiner and his associates framing relief legislation and it was he, the bishop of Ossory, that led the defence of Roman interests. It was not surprising, then, that he was Rome's choice to succeed John Carpenter as Archbishop of Dublin in 1786.

The great era of relief witnessed changes in the Catholic mind which presented an enormous challenge to the renewed hierarchy. Out-of-doors politics became a primary cause of alarm, as the Whiteboys and later Rightboys disturbed the peace. Beginning in protest against the enclosures of common land in Tipperary in 1761, the 'levelling' of the Whiteboys eventually spread through much of Munster and south Leinster where they opposed high rents, evictions and, above all, tithes.[90] Attempts were made in the 1760s to represent Whiteboyism as part of a wider Jacobite or popish plot; a number of priests were arrested and the judicial murder of Fr Nicholas Sheehy at Clonmel in 1766 became the *cause célèbre* of the eighteenth century.

The bishops of Munster denounced the Whiteboys in a series of pastorals in the 1760s. In 1774 the Archbishop of Cashel, James Butler II, took matters further, organising the people of Ballyragget in a league–sworn at their chapel by a justice of the peace–to defend their landlord, Robert Butler, brother of the archbishop himself.[91] At the height of the disturbances in 1775, the Bishops of Ferns (July), Ossory (Sept. and twice in 1779) and Kildare and Leighlin (Oct.), denounced and excommunicated the Whiteboys for 'drawing on us and our holy religion, the odium of our mild government'.[92] The partial admission of

Catholics to the political nation in 1778 and 1782 highlighted for Troy the need for gratitude and responsibility and, with the outbreak of renewed agrarian disorder in 1784, he repeated his excommunication, cursing the Whiteboys to

> everlasting Hell ... When they shall be judged, may they be condemned ... may their posterity be cut off in one generation. Let their children be carried about as vagabonds and beg and let them be cast out of their dwellings. May the usurers search all their substance and let strangers plunder their labours. May there be none to help them, nor none to pity their fatherless offspring. May their names be blotted out ... let their memory perish from the earth. Let all the congregation say Amen, Amen, Amen.[93]

Attempts by the Rightboys to regulate dues in 1786 increased tension, and the hierarchy became alarmed at the ineffectiveness of their pastorals and excommunications. Chapels became the favoured place for Rightboy meetings and oath swearings. In Limerick they threatened to shut the chapels if priests refused them the sacraments. In the neighbouring diocese of Killaloe, Bishop MacMahon's attempts to calm Castleconnel resulted in an exodus from the chapel, as the people 'would not listen to a word from him'. All of this, Bishop Conway of Limerick believed, illustrated how close the province came 'to a total overthrow of religion'.[94] Troy could derive some solace from the warm approbation his efforts received from the Duke of Rutland and Thomas Orde in 1784; and from Lord Lutterel, commander-in-chief in Munster, in 1786. However, in early 1787, 'Black Jack' Fitzgibbon, later Earl of Clare, attempted to introduce a bill 'to prevent tumultuous risings' which contained a clause ordering the destruction of any chapel in which an illegal oath had been sworn.[95] Catholic relief had been hard won, but it had been given not as a right, but as an indulgence. The implications of Fitzgibbon's threats were all too clear for the hierarchy.

The remaining disabilities may have been of little concern to the hierarchy, but the laity increasingly hoped for total relief. Catholic interests had been represented since the 1760s by the Catholic Committee but, under its largely aristocratic leadership, it had confined itself to occasional addresses of loyalty. More recently, it had been absorbed in the quarterage dispute, and the relief measures of 1778 and 1782 owed little to its activity. The election of a new general committee of Catholics in 1781, however, reduced the influence of Kenmare and the old guard. The renewed Committee received overtures from both reformers and administration in their contest for Catholic support.

Throughout, the hierarchy advocated Edmund Burke's advice of 1779, that the Catholics should show themselves dutiful subjects to the crown; 'in general keep yourselves quiet ... [and] intermeddle as little as possible with the parties that divide the state'.[96] Troy was particularly concerned at attempts by Hervey to represent himself as the protector of the Catholic interest and urged the Earl-Bishop's correspondent, Dungannon priest, James Dillon, to adopt 'from prudential circumstances' a neutral stance on the issue of parliamentary reform.[97]

In any event, the reformers were sharply divided on the Catholic question and the prominent position of the Ascendancy troika of Foster, Beresford and Fitzgibbon in the administration made early concession unlikely. Nevertheless, George Ogle's communication to the Volunteer Convention in November 1783 of an address purporting to be from 'a Roman Catholic peer' disavowing Catholic intentions of claiming further relief prompted an immediate response from the Catholic body. An emergency session of the Committee refuted the content of Ogle's communication and expressed eagerness for the removal of their 'shackles'. More importantly, the body declared that it alone was 'the medium through which the voice of the Roman Catholics of Ireland has been conveyed'.[98] This bold declaration of confidence and authority reflected the distance travelled since the Committee had humbly submitted the Test Oath formula to Dr Carpenter for his approval in 1774, while the challenge to the aristocratic faction was prophetic of the 1791 split. Combined with these changes, the activities of the Rightboys produced a potentially lethal cocktail, awaiting ignition. In 1789 the minute book of the Catholic Committee contained a sole entry, a loyal address celebrating King George III's return to health; events in France of the same year, however, would change irrevocably the character of the Catholic community.[99]

CHAPTER TWO

'The French Disease'

The French Revolution cast a long shadow over Ireland in the 1790s and throughout the decade the country fell beneath the Gallic spell. While for Tone and the reformers the revolution represented the morning star of liberty to Ireland, the great majority of the Catholic clergy saw it as the incarnation of all that was anathema to Christianity. Thomas Hussey, chaplain to the Spanish Ambassador in London, summed up these sentiments in August 1790 when he attributed the changing temper of Irish Catholics to what he called 'the French disease'.[1]

As the decade progressed, the hierarchy grew stronger in their condemnation of the revolutionary system, invariably referred to as a 'malady' or 'contagion'. Inspiration for their tirade derived from the experience of the Church on the continent. Through an extensive network of continental contacts, the bishops were continually informed about the plight of the Church in Europe. From 1793 onwards, the situation became particularly acute, as Britain entered on a war footing with France. In these circumstances, it was unthinkable that Irish Catholics would ally themselves with the French or, indeed, embrace the levelling principles of the revolution. Haunted by images of the suffering Church in Europe, the Irish bishops exerted all their energies to prevent this happening.[2]

I

The revolution led to a massive rending of the religious fabric of France. Yet, even amongst the deists and atheists of the Enlightenment, few could have forseen the sensational rupture between Church and state at the calling of the States-General in 1789. The *cahiers de doléances* of the Third Estate reflected a desire for radical reform of the Church, but their grievances were largely centred on matters of finance. Many shared the Enlightenment principle of a *religion utile,* reflected in support for the humble parish priest and hostility to the religious orders and over-endowed higher clergy. At no point, however, did the spokesmen of the Third Estate attack the Catholic religion as such, or question its central role in the activities of the State.[3]

Many of the *cahiers* of the First Estate suggest that the parish clergy, at least, were prepared to accept the reforms demanded. They resented the privileges of the hierarchy and regular clergy and saw in reform a possibility of extending their own power. The *curés* envisaged a reformed Church in which they would be all powerful. Each diocese would be governed, not by a bishop, but a synod, while priests would have an enhanced role within society, regulating religious practice, education and social behaviour. In short, Gibson comments that 'their programme was one for a clerical Utopia, with Catholicism as the sole religion and its parish clergy in full control of not only religious but also social life'.[4]

There were 192 *curés* amongst the 303 members of the First Estate present at Versailles and their dominance was crucial in the decision taken on 19 June to join with the Third Estate. That *révolte des curés* was essential to the successful establishment of the revolution but there were divisions within the ranks of the *curés*; 35 per cent of their number voted against the motion while it was supported by almost twenty per cent of the upper clergy. A financial crisis in France had been the primary reason for calling the States-General and, in an effort to raise revenue, the National Assembly nationalised Church property. The Assembly then proceeded to abolish tithes, thereby ending the traditional source of clerical income. There was provision for compensation but, when the abolition was enacted a week later, the Church received no reparations for loss of tithe income of one hundred million livres a year.

In place of tithes, the act contained provision for the payment of salaries to priests and the running expenses of the Church, but included in these costs were the charitable works of the clergy. The state's adoption of responsibility for the poor established a principle which threatened the jealously guarded local prestige of the *curés*, but the clergy offered no resistance to this development, nor did they oppose the Assembly's decision, prompted by Talleyrand, to declare Church property part of the *biens nationaux*. A similar passivity met the decrees of February 1790, which abolished religious orders. The first signs of a rift between the revolution and the *curés* appeared in April 1790, when the Assembly rejected a proposal that Catholicism be declared the state religion.

Utopian fantasies faded fast, and the decisive split came on 12 July 1790 with the adoption of the 'Civil Constitution of the Clergy'. The constitution addressed many of the grievances of the *curés*, expressed in the *cahiers*; ecclesiastical sinecures were abolished, bishops were required to have served fifteen years as curés, absenteeism was forbidden and episcopal salaries were fixed at 12,000 livres. Curés were to receive a salary of at least 1,200 livres and bishops were compelled to govern their diocese in consultation with a council of curés. The constitution adapted the organisation of the Church to the administrative framework of local government; old diocesan boundaries were redrawn to correspond with the new Departmental structure, reducing the number of dioceses from 135 to 83. The attempt to extend democracy to all aspects of government was also applied to the Church. Clergy were no longer to be appointed but elected; bishops by departmental electors and curés by those in the districts.

To all intents and purposes, the Church in France had been nationalised and bishops and priests became 'ecclesiastical public functionaries'. The curés had sought to curb the power of the aristocratic episcopate; they intended that the Church be governed by a synod of priests, but they had never contemplated the election of bishops and priests by laymen. At issue was the question of authority; the conflict between clericalised religion and the principle of popular sovereignty.[5] The National Assembly, representing the nation, was determined to extend the sovereignty of the people to the Church and there could be no negotiation nor compromise on that principle. The Gallican lawyers drawing the constitution had no intention of consulting the Pope, nor would they call a national synod, since the existing episcopate was totally aristocratic in its composition. The revolution, itself an ecclesia with its own moral code and doctrine of civil rebirth, had assumed responsibility for the religious life of its people.[6]

II

The crucial rupture between Church and state came in November 1790, following the decision of the Assembly to add an oath to the Civil Constitution. This marked the end of national unity and the beginning of civil war; it was 'the point at which the revolution "went wrong"'.[7] The oath became a referendum, both on the revolution and the Tridentine model of Catholicism: the clergy divided between constitutionnels and réfractaires, revolutionaries and coun-ter-revolutionaries. Not surprisingly, only seven bishops accepted the oath, described as 'the sacrament of the revolution'; this included three bishops in partibus and the non-believers Talleyrand and Loménie de Brienne. Just over half of the lower clergy subscribed to the oath, but there were striking regional differences. In fact, the map of clerical reaction to the oath was remarkably similar to the map of religious practice in late twentieth-century France. In the Var, the figure was almost 100 per cent, but only 10 per cent in the Vendée or Bas-Rhin.[8] The rector of the Scots College at Douai noted that of the 'numerous clergy' of the town, only two had complied and taken 'the vile oath', and that one of these had become bishop of the department. Analysis of the motivation of almost 60,000 clerics is a formidable task, but Timothy Tackett's monumental study of reaction to the clerical oath shows a complex scenario in which rejection of the oath reflected opposition to the revolution, social background, theological formation or defence of local independence. Any, or all, of these factors determined clerical behaviour in 1791. The bishops chose to leave France but the majority of the refractory clergy remained, their presence leading to bitter conflict between themselves and the *constitutionnels*.[9]

Reaction of the Irish clergy in France to the oath revealed a similar complexity. Recent studies by Loupés on the Irish clergy in Bordeaux during the revolution shows that they were equally divided on the issue, with nine jurors (seven parish priests and two curates) and nine non-jurors (eight parish priests and one curate). This is in marked contrast with what might have been expected from clerics educated for a mission under a strict Tridentine system and with a keen sense of the universal Church. Yet, there was no great difference in the divide amongst the Irish and native French clergy; there were 59 per cent jurors among the clergy of the Gironde as a whole. Commenting on the difficulty in analysing the lines of division between the jurors and refractory clergy, Loupés believes that these Irish priests do not 'lend themselves readily to patterns devised by historians to account for the responses'.[10] Age, superiority, wealth, family ties, length of time in the ministry in France; none of these factors define the opposing groups. A similar difficulty, however, is also faced in drawing the line dividing the Irish lay community in France; no simple analysis can account for their acceptance or rejection of the revolution.[11]

There was, nevertheless, a tendency in the Irish newspapers to portray the juring clergy in less than favourable terms. The pro-revolutionary *Cork Gazette*, which devoted considerable attention to French news, reported the persecution of the non-juring clergy of Amiens in June 1791. There, the constitutional bishop was at the head of a society called 'the Devil's Club', while the non-juring clergy were deprived of benifices. These had been given to 'others of loose morals and no principles'.[12] Shortly after this, the same newspaper carried a report of satisfaction amongst the lower clergy at the improvement in their financial position, resulting from the regulations of the Assembly. In consequence, the constitutional clergy 'preach vehemently in favour of the Rights of Man', and their efforts contributed to the stability of the new government.[13]

Pius VI's response to the Civil Constitution, *Quod aliquantum*, published 10 March 1791, was an assault on the very principles of the revolution. The Pope perceived the intention of the constitution as the destruction of religion in France. The constitutional Church was declared schismatical, all juring clergy were suspended and the ordination of new state bishops was condemned as sacrilegious. The bull inextricably linked the cause of the refractory Church and counter-revolution, highlighting the anti-clericalism of the revolution, and Louis XVI's justification of his flight on religious grounds. A concerted purge of the refractory clergy began in May 1792, following the outbreak of France's war with Austria, with the expulsion of non-jurors denounced by twenty active citizens. All *réfractaires* were ordered to leave France on 26 August; failure to do so resulted in deportation to French Guiana, the 'dry guillotine'. Between 30,000 and 40,000 priests left France, carrying into exile lurid accounts of the persecution of the Church, confirming Pius VI's condemnation of the revolution and fuelling counter-revolutionary sentiment throughout Europe.[14]

III

The experiences of the Irish priests in France, their correspondence, and the accounts they carried home with them, had enormous influence in shaping clerical opposition towards the revolution. In July 1791, Charles Kearney, rector of the Irish College in Paris, wrote to Bishop Patrick Plunket of Meath, informing him of the 'evil influence of our famous revolution'. In its dismal description of the Church in revolutionary France, Kearney's letter is typical:

> religion lost–impiety triumphing–the Sees occupied by schismatics, immoral, irregularly consecrated bishops–the true ones dispersed, persecuted, outlawed, parishes abandoned to wolves–the true pastors obliged to hide themselves–the churches deserted–everything, in a word, that hell can invent put into execution to discourage the faithful and absolutely overturn religion.[15]

The already chaotic political situation became increasingly volatile and a great deal of anger was directed against the foreign clergy as the French suffered defeats in the early stages of the war. The King had previously afforded the clergy some degree of protection but, as the Jacobins gained control of the Assembly, even this support was removed. In any event, the monarchy was abolished in August 1792 and the majority of the Irish refractory clergy left France following the decree of exile. Once more, the newspapers carried extensive coverage of the difficulties suffered by priests as they attempted to leave France.

These trials did not necessarily determine the behaviour of many of those priests in the years ahead. Indeed, quite a significant proportion of the clerics later implicated in United Irish activity had witnessed the events of the revolution first hand and some had themselves been assaulted. Ironically, in the wake of the rebellion of 1798, Leonard McNally attributed the inspiration of the rising to the influence of schoolmasters and priests, and he singled out the clerics expelled from France as having been the most active in promoting sedition.[16] Valentine Derry recalled meeting an Armagh priest, Fr James O'Coigley, shortly after his return to Ireland in 1790. O'Coigley gave Derry the 'most satisfactory account of the causes and commencement of the revolution [he] had obtained from any quarter'. The priest, he believed, was 'not then a friend to the French Revolution'.

In fact, O'Coigley had run many risks and narrowly escaped being lanternised by the mob at the outbreak of the revolution. He 'refused positively' to accept the oath, choosing to return and 'die in any manner' in Ireland rather than swear against his conscience He went on to play a prominent role in the 'uniting business' and was executed in 1798 for his part in an United Irish mission to France.[17] Fr Mogue Kearns, a curate from the Duffry, County Wexford, had actually been hung from a lamp post, which fortunately bent under his weight so that his feet could touch the ground![18] Another Wexford priest, and later United Irishman, Fr Michael Murphy escaped a similar fate at Bordeaux, yet Musgrave commented that he had afterwards 'manifested a strong predilection for the principles of that nation and a desire to join them, should they land in Ireland'.[19]

The decrees of the National Assembly had serious implications for the discipline of the Church, not only in France, but throughout Europe. The French Church had become schismatic, the appointment of bishops was now conducted by election and priestly celibacy had been abolished. Such developments represented precedents which the Irish bishops were anxious to avoid. In 1792, a priest of the Dublin diocese, Robert McEvoy, married and justified his action by an appeal to the decrees of the Franch National Assembly. McEvoy's marriage met with immediate condemnation from Archbishop Troy, who regarded his appeal to the Assembly as ominous. Reeling from the humiliation of being identified with the losing side in the bitter split in the

Catholic Committee, Troy was anxious to firmly establish his spiritual authority in advance of the Catholic Convention.

McEvoy was excommunicated on 29 September 1792, and the notice of excommunication read in every church of the diocese on the following Sunday.[20] The Paris sansculottes had massacred three bishops and 220 priests in that month and Troy's pastoral contained a blistering attack on the progress of the revolution in France. There is no doubt, however, but that his address was intended as a warning to Irish radicals contemplating a similar policy. Troy described McEvoy's appeal to the National Assembly as:

> ridiculous and absurd in the extreme, as all decrees and proceedings of that assembly relative to the Church were apparently designed and, without doubt, uniformly tend to establish the dominion of a selfish and intolerant philosophy, the parent of infidelity, on the ruins of religion. Hence: the propagation of errors against the Catholic faith, the profanation, pillage and prostration of churches, the usurpation of ecclesiastical authority by unprincipled and mercenary intruders, the debasement and persecution of orthodox clergy, the suppression of religious institutions, the total subversion of ecclesiastical discipline, and other innumerable most fatal, but necessary, consequences of the infidel system, which the enemies of religion have long been endeavouring to establish.[21]

Significantly, Troy had this pastoral reprinted in the aftermath of the 1798 Rebellion, when sectarian polemic was at its height. He wanted to illustrate the swift and decisive measures that had been taken by the Irish episcopacy to stem the flow of the 'dismal consequences' which had erupted from the French Revolution.

IV

1793 saw a further deterioration in relations between the Church and the French Revolution. Louis XVI was executed on 21 January, an anti-revolutionary insurrection broke out in the Vendée in March and refractory clergy were prominent amongst the counter-revolutionaries. The Jacobins took power on 2 June and embarked on a programme of deChristianisation. The assault was extended to the constitutional clergy; churches were closed, clerics pressurised to resign their ministry and, by the spring of 1794, Mass was celebrated in only 150 French parishes.[22]

The advent of war between Britain and France, in February 1793, introduced a novel turn in relations between the British government and the Church. Uniquely, the interests of the Church and the government now coincided and the fate of both seemed intertwined. O'Donoghue has commented on the irony of a situation where less than twenty years since the beginning of the dismantling of the penal laws, the British government should be seen by the hierarchy as the saviour of Christendom.[23] On 18 September 1793, the National Assembly ordered the arrest of all citizens of foreign powers in France. This decree against the 'enemies of the revolution' resulted in an exodus of the remaining priests. Many of these went to England where they joined an already large group of emigré clergy; in London alone there were 1,500 French priests in August 1793. Contemporaries commented on the welcome received by these refugees and such accounts, reported widely in the press, strengthened the bond of gratitude between the Church and the British government.

The presence of the emigrés, recounting their doleful tales, also contributed to a change in British attitudes towards Catholicism and a decline in the fear of popery. Abbé Paul MacPherson, Scots agent in Rome, described the scene in London at the end of August 1793:

> I was astonished at the attention and civility shown to them at London. Nor is less regard paid to them at Dover where, if you were to judge of the inhabitants by the people you see on the streets, you would think the one half were French priests. Not only is no insult offered to them, but everyone of every rank pays them the greatest attention. Generous Britain, Heaven must reward such eminent charity. They pass and repass between Dover and Ostend without paying a farthing. Government pays their freight; the English passengers if there be any, [share] their victuals, if not, the honest Tars–'damn their eyes, would they allow a poor French priest to pay for a meal or two'.[24]

The English government provided accommodation for the clergy and an allowance of £2 per week for a priest and £10 for a bishop.[25] A number of these priests made their way to Ireland, where some of their number staffed the newly founded Catholic academies and seminaries; at Carlow there were two French Sulpicians and, in Maynooth, Abbé Andre Darré of Auch and Abbé Pierre Justin Delort of Bordeaux formed part of a wider societé d' emigrés.

In their battle against domestic radicalism, the Irish bishops were eager to stress this new sympathetic relationship between the Church and the King's government. Throughout the 1790s, gratitude and loyalty to King George became a recurrent theme in pastoral addresses. In stark contrast to the rhetoric of the radicals, the concessions of Catholic relief were invariably attributed to 'His Majesty's bounty' and the embarrassing memories of the penal era were played down. Ironically, Thomas Hussey, Bishop of Waterford and Lismore, whose celebrated pastoral of 1797 was castigated for reviving the memories of past sufferings, took this to an extreme in a sermon delivered in London in May 1798. In a stylised reflection on the renewed relationship between Britain and the Holy See, Hussey created an elaborate image of an unbroken friendship between Pius VI and George III. Referring to the period of the King's 'illness' in 1789, Hussey declared that though communication between the two courts had been interrupted for over two hundred years, and though Rome was the only part of the world to which the King was restricted by law from sending a public message:

> the Supreme Pastor, well knowing that no political difference, nor even a difference of religion and creed can break the gentle chain of charity, ordered as fervent supplications to be offered up in that city for His Majesty's recovery as could be displayed in the cathedral of his own metropolis; and Rome saw with astonishment and joy her altars surrounded by pious votaries for the recovery of a king, between whom and them an impolitic wall of separation had been raised for some centuries past.[26]

There were visible signs of this *rapprochment* between the Holy See and London. In November 1791, King George's son, Prince Augustus, visited Rome and received an enthusiastic welcome to the city. The loyalist *Faulkner's Dublin Journal* gave a full account of the meetings between the Prince and the various clerics in Rome. Augustus was described as the first Protestant prince to have been offered apartments in the Apostolic Palace, or to have received the public congratulations of the clergy.[27] During this visit, the prince met with the last of the Stuart pretenders, the Cardinal Duke of York, a meeting symbolising the definitive acceptance of the House of Hanover by Rome and the end of the Jacobite cause.

On a diplomatic level, links were strengthened by the activity of Sir John Cox Hippisley in Rome and the arrival of Monsignor Charles Erskine in London in 1793. Erskine had been despatched to London by Pius VI, but Dr Douglas, the Vicar Apostolic of London, having consulted with Grenville, opposed his appointment as nuncio and Erskine acted as unofficial representative instead.[28] Erskine was frequently received at court, where, according to Troy, he was well received. Troy was convinced that Erskine's presence would lead to new political and commercial relations between 'these kingdoms and the papal states'.[29] Erskine announced that he had been commissioned by Pius VI to assure the King that he would use the utmost influence amongst the Catholics to inspire 'veneration for, and fidelity to so benevolent a sovereign'.[30]

Throughout the 1790s, and often working closely with the administration, Erskine exerted his influence upon the Irish hierarchy, urging them at every instance to oppose any manifestation of the French malady. Troy's Roman agent and fellow Dominican, Luke Concanen, expressed concern at the possible reaction to Erskine's arrival. Concanen dreaded Erskine's appearance in either Dublin or London and was convinced that it would serve only to 'alarm the opposition party and give room to our enemies for many sharp and satirical publications'.[31] Nevertheless, in spite of the hierarchy's continued resentment at Erskine's presence, he was to be of considerable use to the bishops in the wake of the rebellion of 1798 as Troy sought to combat the representation of the rebellion as a 'popish plot'.

The Irish mission had long depended on the continental colleges for the education of the clergy; at the outbreak of the French Revolution there were four hundred Irish clerics in colleges throughout Europe. With the suppression of the continental seminaries in the course of the revolution, the Irish episcopacy became acutely aware of the need to provide alternative priestly formation. The urgency of the situation required immediate action, especially as many of the clerics returning from France had brought with them a 'strong tincture of that destructive, republican spirit which [had] desolated the Church in that unhappy nation'.[32] This corruption was not confined to France and, reflecting the spirit of the Roman Colleges, Cardinal Livizzani urged Troy that only subordinate, docile boys should be sent to Rome.[33]

Early in 1793, Cardinal Antonelli, Prefect of Propaganda Fide, instructed Troy to raise the issue at the next meeting of the bishops. The bishops faced many difficulties in their attempt to establish a suitable domestic seminary, but through perseverance and shrewd negotiations, Troy overcame the weight of history and the constitutional and moral barriers in his path. Almost single handedly, he engineered the foundation of Maynooth College, the establishment of which effectively marked an end to the penal restrictions on the practice of the Catholic faith. The opening of the Royal College at Maynooth in 1795, was greeted with great relief by the Irish hierarchy, not least from its first president Thomas Hussey, who described the college as 'the salvation of Ireland from Jacobinism and anarchy'.[34]

Fig. 6 Execution of Louis XVI (N.L.I.)

Archbishop Troy had an extensive international correspondence, through which he monitored the fate of the Church. The French Revolution had taken its toll everywhere: even from America, Troy received alarming reports and these combined to strengthen the archbishop's resolve to oppose the spread of the 'French disease' in Ireland. In July 1794, Bishop John Carroll of Baltimore–the first Catholic bishop in the United States–informed Troy that 'the decency of religious service had been disturbed' by the profaneness of the numerous 'French democrats' who had arrived there from the West Indies.[35] Troy took every measure necessary to oppose such democrats in Ireland; exploiting the opportunities offered by a receptive media, he published pastorals and promoted anti-revolutionary publications. In particular, he welcomed the printing by Fitzpatrick in Dublin of the Abbé Barruel's *Persecution of the French Clergy,* which *Faulkner's Dublin Journal* believed contained more to be learned of French politics than any other publication written since the revolution. Troy expected 'much good from this interesting publication'. Many similar tracts were reprinted in Dublin; these included the melancholy *Retractions* of the constitutional bishop of Mont-Blanc, the printing of which reflected the determination of the hierarchy to harness the potential of the printed word in their battle against French principles.[36]

French attacks on the papal states accentuated the already acute anxiety of the Irish hierarchy, and the bishops came under pressure from Rome to maintain their vigilance against the common enemy. In February 1795, as French armies threatened Rome, Antonelli wrote to the Irish bishops, urging them to impress the need for loyalty and civil obedience in the various dioceses of Ireland.[37] This lengthy missive was the strongest and fullest attack on the French system received by the hierarchy from Rome and it was to provide much of the inspiration for their own attacks against sedition in Ireland. It spoke of the 'viciously inclined multitude' adopting revolutionary ideas and lamented the spread of the 'infection' to such an extent 'as to taint almost the universal commonwealth'. The letter denounced:

> these partisans [who] seem to place the excellency of man and his ultimate wishes in liberty, licentiousness in throwing off all reverence, [before] all awe of magistracy and even God Himself. But what havoc and destruction, both to Christian and civil society have sprung from the pretext of liberty with no other view than to pull asunder the sweet yoke of Christ, to loosen the reins to their own wanton passions and to shake the foundations of all sovereignty and government.

The Irish bishops were reminded of the vigorous exertions which would be necessary if they were to preserve their flocks from the 'incursions and voracious assaults of ravenous wolves'. Antonelli singled out Troy's 1793 pastoral *On The Duties of Christian Citizens* for praise, informing the bishops how 'very sensible' Pius VI had been to the Archbishop's earnest assault on error. The bishops were instructed to rescue the Church from any 'imputation of suspicion of disloyalty'. Great gratitude was expressed to King George III for his protection of the Pope and his 'unshakable piety and munificience' in receiving French *emigrés*. Reflecting a keen awareness of Irish affairs, no doubt due to J. C. Hippisley's presence in Rome, Antonelli concluded by reminding the prelates of their debt to the King who had removed an oppressive yoke and endowed Irish Catholics with many privileges. There was also the hope that the administration of the 'most excellent new viceroy [Fitzwilliam]' would remove the existing restrictions, placing them on a level with other subjects.

Once Napoleon Bonaparte had occupied Milan, he demanded a withdrawal of the Pope's condemnation of the revolution and Civil Constitution. Pius VI rejected these demands in the spring of 1796, but the French invaded the papal states and the subsequent peace terms forced the Pope to recognise the Republic. Irish newspapers reported the recognition contained in *Pastoralis sollicitudo* (5 July 1796), which the *Dublin Journal* described as 'in many respects remarkable'. Though the terms of the brief failed to satisfy the French Directory, the *Journal* believed that the French would rejoice in the Pope's call to Catholics to submit to government.[38]

A spate of anxious letters to Dublin from Luke Concanen, informed Troy of the fate of Rome. Anxiety was mounting amongst Irish clerics there and the general populace was gripped with terror and consternation since news arrived of an imminent French assault on the holy city. It was rumoured that Napoleon intended to plunder Rome and carry the Pope and the Curia to Paris as victims of the guillotine. Concanen reported the relief brought to the city by the arrival of a courier 'crying out through the streets, pace, pace'.[39] The following week, Concanen informed Troy of the presence of a number of 'desperate' Jacobins in Rome and the discovery of a 'dire' conspiracy to plunder and burn the city and then kill the Pope, cardinals and clergy.

As tension in the city mounted, visions of the Virgin were reported and thousands flocked to see the various miraculous apparitions throughout the city. Concanen commented on an immense crowd gathered at the basilica of the SS Apostoli to see the Madonna dell Archetto.[40] This phenomonen marked the heightened religious sensitivity which the revolution unleashed throughout Europe; in the Vendée the first sign of tension was marked by the appearance of the Virgin in Saint-Lauret-de-la-Plaine. In Italy, in particular, miracles were often explicitly counter-revolutionary. At Lecce, in Puglia, locals marked the foundation of the Neapolitan Republic by planting a tree of liberty. However, the statue of St. Oronzo in the piazza turned its head dissapprovingly. Locals then tore down the tree, fearing their patron would leave the town, and marched through the streets chanting 'Viva S. Oronzo!, Viva il Re!'.[41]

Images of misery painted in the newspapers and the loyal prints, reminded Catholics that their worst situation was preferable to the best that could be hoped for under French dominion. The *Dublin Journal* gave accounts of all the countries in Europe where the French had made 'fraternal visits' and, in a phrase later borrowed by Troy, declared that the 'fruit of the Tree of Liberty is poisonous in its core'. The Tree of Liberty, like the tree in the Garden, would indeed bring knowledge–knowledge of being plunged into irretrievable perdition.[42] Accounts were published of the ghastly excesses of the French armies, reports which were widely believed and were utilised by counter-revolutionary propagandists. The reforming *Dublin Morning Post* failed to be swayed by these tales of woe and printed an irreverent exhortation to the Pope in August 1796:

> The French are deists–devils downright devils.
> In heavenly wheat accursed destructive weevils!
> Abominations! Atheists to a man.
> Rogues that convert the finest flour to bran,
> In vice's drunken cup forever guzzling,
> Just like hogs in mud uncleanly nuzzling.
>
> Heir of St Peter, kindle thy ire,
> And bid France feel thy Apostolic fire,
> Think of that quantity of sacred wood,
> Thy treasuries can launch into the flood,
> What ships the holy manger can create,
> At least a dozen of the largest rate,
> And lo enough of St Martha's hair,
> To rig a dozen mighty ships of war,
> Our Saviour's pan spoon, that a world adores,
> Would make a hundred thousand pairs of oars.

If the progress of the French armies on the continent alarmed the Irish hierarchy, the appearance of the French fleet off Bantry in December 1796 heightened their francophobia. Images of the Napoleonic armies threatening the papal states may have roused their anxiety, but the advent of Lazare Hoche's army of 14,500 men and 41,644 stand of arms prompted a rush of pastorals condemning the French and associated Irish radicalism.[44] On Christmas Day, Bishop Francis Moylan of Cork, whose brothers had fought alongside George Washington, issued a pastoral calling the Catholics to loyalty to King and government, and pointed to the 'irreparable ruin, desolation and destruction occasioned by French Fraternity'. Moylan held up to his congregation the fate of Flanders, Italy, Holland and Germany, all basking in French liberty. The bishop warned his flock against the 'specious treachery of the French' and called on them to 'range under the banners of true Irish loyalty'.[45] Moylan's address was widely welcomed in loyalist circles; Robert Day, M.P. and chairman of the Grand Jury of Dublin, described it as 'breathing a spirit of peace and loyalty worthy of an apostle'. Regardless of every personal consideration, Moylan had not 'balanced between duty and danger', nor lost a moment in giving battle to an atheistical enemy.[46] W. J. MacNeven, however, dismissed the pastoral as 'a pious fraud'.[47]

16 February 1797 was set aside as a day of solemn thanksgiving for the deliverance of the kingdom from French invasion. On that day, a solemn High Mass and *Te Deum* were celebrated at Francis Street Chapel. Dr Moylan officiated at the altar, and many of the other bishops were in attendance, including O'Reilly of Armagh, Plunket of Meath, Delaney of Kildare and Leighlin, Teahan of Kerry and Hussey of Waterford.[48] The sermon, preached by Archbishop Troy to a congregation of up to 3,000, was a fierce broadside directed at the French Revolution; Troy's passion was no doubt fuelled by the images contained in Concanen's letters, which O'Donoghue has compared to Burke's *Reflections* in their severity.[49]

The Archbishop of Dublin spoke of the 'sad and frightful picture France exhibited to an amazed world'.[50] 'Liberty and Equality', he asked, 'what deceits have not been practiced, what crimes have not been perpetrated under sanctioned abuse and misapplication of these magical sounds?'. In a recurrent theme, he drew pictures of the consequences of the confusion of the *rights* and *duties* of man:

> To these detestable and destructive systems we are to ascribe the sophistical theory of abstract but impracticable *rights* of man, and the uniform silence on his *duties* to God studiously observed by the constitution framers and revolutionary dictators of France. *Hence*: their malevolence to pious institutions, their incessant and atrocious persecu-

tion of the faithful ministers of religion: *hence*, their veneration for the putrid and moundering remains of their infamous preceptors and associates, avowed atheists and libertines, which they triumphantly enshrined in the most august and magnificent edifice in Paris raised to the worship of the living God, and since converted to a pagan Pantheon: *hence*, the prostration of churches, their profanation of sacred vessels and ornaments; the robbery, the imprisonment, the transportation, the massacre of the orthodox clergy ... *Hence*: the emigration of myriads of honourable and respectable Frenchmen of every description, preferring exile and beggary to irreligion and disloyalty: *hence*, the indefinite number of others who have perished in prisons, or on scaffolds or by the daggers of hired assassins: *hence*, the execrable murder of their lawful Sovereign, the most benevolent of Monarchs, by the sentence of a self created and incompetent tribunal, which usurped and combined the functions of judges, jurors and accusers: *hence*, their sword of hatred to Royalty, the annual festival to commemorate the horrid deed and the triumph of regicide; as if kingly government wisely administered were essentially incompatible with the social rights and the happiness of subjects: *hence*, their choice of wild ungovernable democracy as most congenial to their licentious principles and to their formal declaration that insurrection is a sacred duty: *hence*, the introduction of manners the most profligate and abandoned, the most savage and ferocious, which have barbarised a people heretofore humane and polite.[51]

This was not, Troy assured his congregation, a fanciful or exaggerated description of the innumerable evils from which Ireland had been spared. It was, rather, a true picture of the shattered state of France and the countries infected by French fraternity. This simple reflection, the archbishop was convinced, should be sufficient to put them on their guard against attempts to woo them from attachment to the King or obedience to their superiors. 'Do not then', he warned, 'approach the rotten tree of French Liberty if you desire to live'. Despite its shining foliage, it bore 'forbidden fruit, fair to the eye, but deadly to those who taste it'. In the same month, the Dominican bishop of Killaloe directed a severe attack at the French in his Lenten pastoral. MacMahon, whose French aristocratic relations had suffered at the hands of the revolutionaries, condemned 'the destructive ravages of a furious, blood thirsty foe', and attributed the saving storms at Bantry to divine providence.[52]

The Cork Franciscan and veteran pamphleteer, Arthur O'Leary, delivered a blistering attack on the French revolutionary system during a service of thanksgiving at St Patrick's Chapel, Sutton Street, London.[53] He spoke of the sun quitting the skies to avoid the spectacle of France and he compared the National Convention there to Milton's Pandemonium 'where the infernal peers sat in council to deliberate on the means of destroying the King of Heaven'. History gave witness to gloomy instances of patricides plotting the death of their father, but only in modern France could be seen a sacrifice with son the priest and father the victim! 'In the obscurity of the night, so favourable for the works of darkness, the Jacobins met in a spacious church, converted into a club room, for debating on murder and politics'. There a French republican appeared, holding a bloody head–'behold my father's head which I cut off for not subscribing to our glorious constitution; and lo! the sacrifice every true republican should make to liberty'. Apart from the florid literary style, O'Leary's sermon is particularly interesting in that it reflects a view from outside the hierarchy. He was, however, unrepresentative, given his many previous political involvements and it was widely believed that O'Leary received a government pension.[54]

Throughout 1797 and '98, the fate of the Pope was particularly critical; dispatches from Rome made deep impressions on the Irish bishops, particularly upon Troy who had spent over twenty years there. The Irish newspapers also followed the progress of the Italian campaign, with the radical prints showing little sympathy for the Pope's sufferings. The Peace of Tolentino in February 1797, a full account of which was carried in the *Ennis Chronicle*, extracted a vast indemnity from the papal states. While Luke Concanen lamented that the museum of Paris 'will be the finest that ever existed', the *Dublin Morning Post* slyly credited Pius VI with possessing 'the providence of a Churchman' in remitting £600,000 to England. There was little doubt, the paper believed, but that the Pope would soon take shelter with the Defender of the Faith [George III].[55] Alluding to the rhetoric of salvation and providence used in the pastorals of the Irish bishops, following the failure of the Bantry expedition, the same paper thought it 'very remarkable' that neither storm, nor earthquake, hurricane nor tornado had halted Bonaparte's march on Rome.[56]

Arthur O'Connor's *Press* carried similar pieces, as part of a campaign to counter the effects of propaganda in the hierarchy and loyalist prints. The *Press* reported widely from the continent, correcting the negative representations of republican Europe. On the contrary, the paper pointed to the joy of the liberated Europeans, in contrast to 'the miseries to which the slaves of the Pope are subjected'.[57] In January 1798, the *Press* carried a long report of the health of the French Church, in an attempt to refute the 'government journals.[which have] abused the French so often on the score of religion, and evidently for the

*Fig. 7 Lazare Hoche
(N.L.I.)*

purpose of exasperating the Roman Catholics of Ireland against them, as destroyers of the Catholic Church'.[58]

By July 1797, most of Italy had fallen to the French and republics had been established on the French line. Many of these republics had, indeed, outdone the French in matters of religion, much to the alarm of Luke Concanen. In the Cisalpine Republic, the Bishop of Comacchio had been refused entry to his diocese because he had not been elected by the people. This had also been the case in Genoa, where the *Press* reported that religion had been abolished and that new-born babies were carried to the Tree of Liberty.[59] The French finally entered Rome in February 1798 and Concanen, in a series of letters to Troy, dated 'the 1st year of the Roman Republic', refers to 'a happy and free people', now that the 'Old Tyrant' had been banished and the Tree of Liberty planted on the Capital. The Pope and the cardinals had been sent out of the city to Siena, but would probably finish up in Paris. As for the Irish Colleges in the City, Concanen held out little hope. The religious houses were quartered by French troops and Minerva stabled 250 horses; 'a pleasant scene for the sons of true liberty'.

The worst fears of the Irish clerics in Rome were soon realised with the suppression of the priories and the banishment of up to 2,000 foreign priests and friars in May.[60] With the Pope sent off, 'a poor fugitive priest through the world',[61] Charles Erskine quickly condemned the action of the French and declared that they had 'given their last proof of their hatred for Christ's Church and their determined intention to destroy it by laying their hands upon the Supreme Pastor'.[62] He directed that the collect *Pro Pontifice* be said in every parish and that prayers be said for the safe delivery of the Pope from the hands of the persecutors, not only of the Catholic religion but, of all Christianity. 'Who knows', Erskine concluded, 'but by exciting in the people a sense of devotion they might also be recalled from that precipice, in which I hear with horror they are plunging themselves'.

This was the reality of the situation. The 'French disease' had brought the institutional Church in Europe to her knees and yet the Catholic Irish seemed to have embraced French principles. Throughout the 1790s, the continental crisis had exercised a huge influence on the minds of the Irish hierarchy and it is against this background that the bishops' reactionary stance must be interpreted. The destruction of the Church in Europe had brought home to them the reality of the French Revolution, not in abstract terms, nor lofty notions of 'liberty', but in images of a Church laid low, particularly in Italy by the onslaught of a 'second Atilla, more ferocious than the Hun, his predecessor'.[63] The continental crisis sharpened the sensitivity of the hierarchy to the potential of the growing politicisation in Ireland and also provided images of misery for their pastorals in which they urged loyalty and obedience to the laws. The continental crisis, too, brought a convergence of interests between the Church and the government, and this novel situation provided the atmosphere in which the hierarchy could pursue their deferential campaign for relief.

Amongst the lower clergy, however, affairs in Europe failed to bring about any such consensus of opinion, and observers noted a shift in their political stance. Sir Richard Musgrave, a biased, if occasionally astute, commentator, noted this change, declaring that it struck him how

> the horrors which people had felt at the cruelties and barbarities committed by the French republicans began to abate in the minds of the Roman Catholics in the beginning of the year 1793 and that they continued to wear away gradually until the rebellion broke out.[64]

Many, like James O'Coigley, had been brought round 'with the majority of the Irish nation ... by calumny, false suspicion, prejudice and unjust persecution'.[65] William MacNeven reported to the French Directory in 1796 that Irish 'priests had ceased to be alarmed by the calumnies circulated respecting the irreligion of the French', and had adopted the principles of the people upon whom they depended. They were, he believed, 'generally good republicans who had rendered great, though discreet, service in propagating the United system'.[66] Against the background of European developments, it was unthinkable that this should be happening in Ireland; every effort was made by the hierarchy to stem the spread of the French contagion in Ireland.

CHAPTER THREE

The Radical Challenge 1790–1793

In examining the Church's reaction to radicalism in the 1790s, it has become axiomatic to divide the decade into two halves, taking the failed Fitzwilliam viceroyalty as the dividing line. While this division may be too neat, it does provide an adequate framework for an analysis of the decade. With Fitzwilliam's recall, hopes for emancipation were definitively dashed and constitutional politics offered no further scope for the removal of remaining Catholic disabilities. Against this stymied parliamentary background, the drift from reform towards an underground revolutionary position was accelerated. Ironically, however, the failure of the relief bill of 1795 and the arrival of Camden as lord lieutenant guaranteed the success of the bishops' scheme for a national Irish seminary. With the Royal College firmly established, the hierarchy appeared satisfied, vacating the political arena and adopting the mantle of steady loyalism.

This 1795 divide, while affording a workable framework, simplifies the complexity of the decade, blurring a proper understanding of the period. In many respects the markers had already been laid down with Hobart's Relief Act and the subsequent Convention Act of 1793. From that time the Catholic position seemed became increasingly polarised, with a majority of the clergy and laity opting for the opposing sides in the ensuing political conflict.

I

Under the influence of the French Revolution, Ireland witnessed an unprecedented period of politicisation in the 1790s, a process not confined to the realm of 'high politics' but one which transformed the whole of society. In this situation where, according to Samuel McSkimmin's often quoted observation, 'every illiterate bumpkin considered himself a consummate politician', the

French revolution soon became the test of every man's political creed.[1] It was inevitable that the Catholic Committee would fall under this revolutionary spell; from early 1790 it adopted a more aggressive stance, deciding to press for the repeal of the remaining penal laws.[2] The Committee underwent a further transformation with its decision to extend the scope of elections to the general committee. This election of members by ballot effectively terminated the existing aristocratic domination of the Committee; a new radicalised leadership emerged from among the Catholic middle class, with many subsequent United Irishmen amongst their number.

This radicalisation of the Committee had not gone unnoticed by the Catholic clergy. In August 1790 Thomas Hussey, chaplain to the Spanish ambassador in London, commented to Richard Burke on the changing temper of Irish Catholics. Hussey may, at times, have lacked diplomacy, but his intuitions were sharp. In the event of a war with France, further relief for Catholics would be unavoidable. It was absurd, he argued, to wait until necessity compelled what true policy should offer voluntarily. Besides, Hussey was convinced that the Irish Catholics under the influence of French revolutionary principles would no longer tolerate their situation 'without their resisting or even complaining'.[3]

Archbishop Troy saw the progress of the 'French disease' in a more sinister light and became particularly alarmed at the possible consequences of this new radicalism for religion. In June 1789, the English Catholic Committee had drawn up an oath in the form of a declaration of their civil principles, attempting to allay Protestant fears concerning further concessions to Catholics. This notorious 'Protestation' had met with immediate condemnation of the four Vicars Apostolic in England who saw in it schismatic tendencies and a confusion of temporal and spiritual powers.[4] The Irish bishops, too, condemned the oath which James Butler of Cashel described as 'fraught with principles most dangerous to religion'.[5]

Troy feared that a similar oath would be demanded from Irish Catholics in the event of future relief measure and sought to define what he regarded as the preserve of the hierarchy. While acknowledging the competency of the Committee in the realm of temporal and political concerns, he claimed for the bishops an exclusive and inherent right 'to judge on all points of religious doctrine'. In the unfortunate event of a similar oath being proposed to Irish Catholics as 'the absolute price' of further indulgence, Troy insisted that it not be adopted without the approval of the hierarchy.[6] The archbishop's adamant stance on this issue reflected his anxiety at the growing independence of the radicalised Committee, and represented an attempt to stem developments proceeding along French lines; there the National Assembly was moving closer towards the Civil Constitution which would declare all papal jurisdiction at an end, in effect nationalising the Church.

Troy's fears were not without foundation, and the fluctuating links between radical Catholics and Presbyterians confirmed his anxiety.[7] Samuel Barber's celebration of revolutionary France as a 'happy country! where rights of men are sacred, no Bastille to imprison the body, nor religious establishment to shackle the soul. Every citizen as free as the thoughts of man', hardly squared with the archbishop's appraisal of the situation there.[8] That Presbyterians should reach out to Catholics was not an altogether new departure and the failure of the Volunteers illustrated that no reform movement could be successful unless it addressed the Catholic issue. Tone's *Argument on behalf of the Catholics of Ireland* sought to bring this home to Ulster Presbyterians in the conviction that, as Burrowes had argued six years earlier, the Catholics also 'live in a period of liberation–[and] have caught the love of freedom from yourselves'.[9]

Presbyterian and Catholic radicalism merged in the foundation of the United Irishmen in late 1791; nevertheless, a significant segment of Presbyterian opinion remained to be convinced of this transformation in its ancient enemy and sectarianism continued to blight the growth of any popular union. The radicals attempted to dispel these prejudices and Fr. James O'Coigley's mission to the Presbyterians of Antrim and Down fits into this context.[10] In his autobiography, O'Coigley describes his efforts to 'combat many deep rooted prejudices on both sides' between 1791 and '93. In a telling admission, he comments that his 'success would have been comparatively trifling, had it not been for the spirited exertions of that truly, respectable, virtuous and enlightened body, the dissenters of the county of Antrim, but chiefly and in particular those of Belfast'.[11] MacNeven, writing in the wake of the rebellion and union, gave a stylised account of O'Coigley's journey amongst 'the Covenanters' of Antrim and Down:

> [O'Coigley] was introduced as a fellow labourer in the common cause. The affection which those poor men showed to one whom, shortly before, they would perhaps have regarded as a demon, was truly astonishing. Intelligence was dispatched to every part, they crowded to receive and caress him, but when they learned that this Romish priest was so sincere a lover of liberty, as to have been actually fighting at the capture of the Bastille, their joy was almost extravagant.[12]

The alarm in Government circles at this novel alliance was immense, Grenville declaring that there was 'no evil' he would not prophecy if it were to take place.[13] O'Coigley, well aware of the government's opposition, claimed that it was 'of great utility to the Irish government that such religious disputes should exist between the Dissenters and Catholics'. Leading gentlemen had sought to convince him it would be easier to mix oil and water than to bring the two parties together.[14] Significantly, the Presbyterian radical, Rev. William Steel Dickson, made similar claims in his recollections, describing how a government faction in 1792 had propagated notions of Catholic inability to 'enjoy' let alone 'bear liberty' in order to defeat the prospects of Catholic emancipation.[15]

The Catholic hierarchy shared the Castle's anxiety at the growing ties with the radical Dissenters. Cardinal Antonelli had been informed of events in Ireland by Fr Charles O'Conor of Belanagare, and the Prefect instructed the bishops of Ireland to take appropriate measures to halt any junction with the Presbyterians.[16] Antonelli wrongly assumed that the hierarchy had it in their power to manipulate their flock's political principles. However, by the end of 1791 the pace of change in Ireland had accelerated beyond their control. The formation of the Catholic Society in October of that year brought divisions within the Committee to a head, illustrating the essential difference between the radical members–McKenna, Braughall, Keogh and company–and the old guard, the former seeking total enfranchisement as a right while the aristocratic party were content with a dutiful appeal for relief.

The composition of the Catholic Society was never clear; Westmorland believed that it contained 'fifty or sixty of the most violent agitators'; it was also rumoured to contain up to twenty priests.[17] The Society reflected the mood of the more advanced Catholics of the Committee; McKenna's *Declaration,* calling for a total repeal of the penal laws, received a warm response, with William Knox informing Thomas Jefferson that at subsequent meetings of Catholics, they resolved to remain no longer in an 'excluded state'.[18] Significantly, the *Declaration* was couched in similar rhetoric to the addresses of the newly founded United Irishmen, speaking of a spirit of harmony and sentiments of affection between Irishmen. The loyal prints quickly responded to the *Declaration*, with *Faulkner's Dublin Journal* seeing in it 'unnecessary truths mixed with rank falsehoods, which affects a tone of manliness, and falls in other parts into a style of slavish cunning: which professes loyalty in words, yet seems bursting with a suppressed republicanism'.[19]

The government decided to fight the Committee on the issue of McKenna's pamphlet. Chief Secretary Hobart met four members of the Committee

(Edward Byrne, Randal McDonnell, John Roche and D.T. O'Brien), on 26 November 1791 and demanded a disavowal of the *Declaration* under threat of refusing further concessions to Catholics. Despite Byrne's attempt to stress the independent nature of the Catholic Society, the delegation would not reject the principles enunciated in the pamphlet. Although they rightly saw the critical nature of their predicament, their response reflected the confidence of the renewed Catholic Committee; Hobart was informed that while the *Declaration* was not the act of the Committee, 'unfortunately for us it contained truths as to our situation which we could not disavow and, should we even attempt to condemn its publications or the authors of it, divisions and a paper war would be the inevitable consequence'.[20]

Troy was quick to respond to the growing crisis. Anxious to distance the Catholic body from any imputation of disloyalty, he wrote to Major Hobart. Adopting a Burkean line, Troy argued that if the Catholics were given a share in the franchise they would fall more under the influence of their natural leaders, the clergy and gentry. With their own positions secured, these leaders would in turn become more resistant to radical influences. Unlike Burke, however, Troy would never have accepted any alliance with the dissenters, even if it was to defeat them at a later stage.[21] In fact, Troy outlined for Hobart the dangers of the dissenting influence on Catholics and spoke of episcopal appointment of parish priests being rejected in some country places along French lines under the 'encouragement and connivance of Protestant gentlemen'.[22] Troy outlined the injustice of Catholics being dispossessed of their lands in order to make Protestant freeholders. He also cited instances of Catholics voting at elections under the guise of Protestants and, in a reflection of his subtle diplomacy, declared that 'the most loyal and conscientious Catholics wish the right to suffrage at country elections to be communicated to respectable freeholders of their persuasion'.

Despite pressure from Hobart, the Catholic Committee pressed on with its demands for repeal, voting 90 to 17 in favour of the petition which it had been intended to present in the previous session. Appended to this petition were the resolutions adopted at the Rotunda convention in 1783.[23] This rejection of Kenmare's proposed declaration of unconditional loyalty led to his secession–and that of the old guard–from the Committee.[24] Sixty-eight of the seceders, led by Kenmare, Fingall, Gormanston and Troy, presented an independent address to the Lord Lieutenant on 27 December in 'order to prevent misrepresentation or misconceptions' of their sentiments.[25] In their petition, the seceders–described by Smyth as 'supreme practitioners of the traditional and ineffectual strategy of supplication'–offered the past as a pledge of their future good conduct and looked with 'respectful confidence' to the government for a further extension of its favours.[26] The petitioners did not presume to point out the measure or extent to which such repeal should be carried, but left the same to the 'wisdom and discretion of the legislature'.

The secession resulted in a deep rupture within the Catholic body. Kenmare was formally expelled from the Committee; it condemned the 'insidious and servile address calculated to divide the Catholics of Ireland and eventually to defeat their just application for relief from the grievous oppressions under which they have for so long laboured'.[27] Battle lines were now drawn for the ensuing conflict between Kenmarites and the advanced Dublin leadership, with the Catholic community becoming polarised in their loyalty as both sides sought support for their stance. Troy attempted to rally the hierarchy to his side.[28] He wrote to Bishop Moylan of Cork explaining his reasons for signing the address; despite the flattery and intimidation used to deter him, he felt that it was absolutely necessary to step forward in a decided manner at a time when Catholic loyalty was under question, and in the face of 'the most extravagant levelling principles being avowed by 'some infatuated people'. Though confident the storm would soon cease, he was determined to stand firm, otherwise the clergy would 'become obnoxious and be reputed the authors of sedition'. Troy was content with his decision, but admitted to having many vindictive persons to deal with who, in 'the genuine spirit of intolerance', had already threatened him with the consequence of his action. He requested that Moylan would relay his sentiments to the remaining Munster bishops.[29]

Given Kenmare's influence in the south-west, Troy was certain of a favourable response from Bishop Teahan of Kerry (1787-1797); a loyal address, inspired by Kenmare and the bishop was, indeed, promptly published by the Catholics of County Kerry. They declared their opposition to writings and associations which might possibly sow 'the seeds of discontent and impatience among the lower class of their persuasion', and pledged their unshaken loyalty, perfect submission to the laws, and dutiful attachment to the King and his government. The address rejected every act tending toward faction or commotion and humbly begged 'a relaxation of the penal statutes, made in angry times against them'.[30]

The Leinster bishops also presented loyal addresses but none of these received significant popular support. Bishop Daniel Delaney's address mustered only forty-two signatures in Carlow, while James Lanigan could only garner a mere sixty-three in Kilkenny. The Bishop of Ferns, James Caulfield was especially opposed to radical Catholic politics; his chagrin on receiving only eleven signatures from a congregation of over two hundred can be easily imagined. This followed a challenge to the address by Edward Hay and James Devereux, whom the bishop regarded as a 'young hot-headed libertine'.[31] Nevertheless, Caulfield can hardly have been surprised; in November 1791 he had informed Troy of the epidemical 'frenzy for levelling' in Wexford and the 'diabolical Jacobin spirit' of the Committee which he feared would ruin the Church in Ireland.[32] The paltry Wexford address was never presented and the only other bishop to sign a petition was Thomas Costelloe of Clonfert (1786-1831).[33]

The northern bishops retained their composure, remaining aloof throughout the crisis. Dr Plunket of Meath, however, criticised Troy's decision to side with the aristocratic faction. He was concerned that the division in the Catholic ranks had resulted in 'no small amusement of a host of foes'. Plunket, who had spent twenty seven years in France and led the Gallican party in the Irish Church since the death of James Butler in July 1791, believed that had some compromise or adjournment taken place 'we should be more respectable at the moment'.[34]

Troy had obviously hoped for a unanimous response from the hierarchy but, in this, his judgement was faulty. The secession had only illustrated the deep divisions within the Catholic body and highlighted the hierarchy's delicate claim on the loyalty of their flock. A resolution of the Catholic Committee on 15 January 1792 criticised the seceders for their attempt to 'form divisions and to disseminate discord' amongst the Catholics. More ominously for the hierarchy, the seceders were castigated for attempting to 'seduce the Roman Catholic clergy from the laity, and to set them at variance which, by converting the ministers of the Gospel into instruments of oppression, tends to vitiate the purest source of confidence, to weaken the closest bonds of society, and to endanger the very being of religion in the minds of the people'.[35] The implication was simple, either the clergy joined with the people, or the people would act alone.

I I

The events of 1791 had brought the country to a new level of political awareness. The Kenmarite secession and the subsequent collapse in their support resulted in a full scale mobilisation of political opinion in the country. The pace of change swept the clergy into a difficult position, seeking simultaneously to stand by the people in their demand for further relief, while remaining ostentatiously loyal to the government. Within the Catholic body, the balance of power had visibly shifted from what Burke called 'the dozen or score of old gentlemen', to the new radicalised leadership.[36] Moreover, motivated by the need for recruits to the British army, London now appeared ready 'to play the Catholic game' and some form of relief seemed inevitable.[37]

The Dublin administration came under increasing pressure from Pitt's government, in particular from Henry Dundas, to grant concessions to the Irish similar to those already enjoyed by English Catholics.[38] Westmorland opposed any gestures to Catholics and saw in Pitt's proposals a threat to the whole establishment of a country where 'everyman held his estate by the dispossession of a Catholic'.[39] Echoing Duigenan, Ogle and the conservative ultras, he argued that if a man had the right to vote, had he not a greater right to have his property restored to him?[40] The Catholic Committee, however, was confident that the London government would manage the progress of a relief bill through all stages in Dublin. The arrival of Richard Burke sent rumours flying through Dublin that relief was inevitable and the Committee asserted in a manifesto that 'they had the FIRST AUTHORITY for saying that the application would have infinite weight'.[41]

On 25 January 1792, Sir Hercules Langrishe introduced what was essentially a government bill in the Irish House of Commons which granted limited relief for Catholics.[42] Although the bill stopped far short of the Committee's demands for admission to petty or grand juries, freedom to serve in the county magistracies and a share of the county franchise, sufficient concessions were made to turn the parliamentary debate into an anti-Catholic tirade.[43] While the relief bill was carried, a petition from the Catholic Committee suffered a humiliating rejection, 208 votes to 25, and a petition in favour of Catholic relief signed by over 600 citizens of Belfast met with a similar fate.

The parliamentary session generated a seething resentment within the Catholic community, but Richard Burke also identified the effects of these attacks upon the Committee and the Presbyterians. Burke spoke of 'Catholic and Dissenter turned adrift together' hand and hand, forming what Thomas Addis Emmet later described as 'a community of insult'.[44] Although Richard Burke believed that this marriage was not complete, every attempt was being made to couple the two parties. The toasts at a United Irish dinner in Belfast on 19 April reflect this, as glasses were raised to Tom Paine and the Rights of Man, Napper Tandy and the Rights of the Subject, Wolfe Tone and Reform of Parliament, while 'the Catholic parish priest had proposed religion without priestcraft'.[45] There was particular resentment amongst the Catholic Committee at the insults hurled in their direction and the attempts made by the ultras in parliament to discredit their body. The Committee members were insultingly dismissed as 'shop keepers and shop lifters'; Duigenan referred to them

Fig. 8 John Keogh (N.G.I.)

as 'men of very low and mean parentage'; loyal prints attacked the right of this 'small popish faction' to speak for the Catholics.[46] Tone, in particular, reacted strongly to the depiction of the Committee as a 'rabble of obscure porter-drinking mechanicks' meeting in 'holes and corners', 'considering themselves the representatives of a Catholic body who disavowed and despised them'.[47]

These attacks placed the Committee on the defensive, but resentment quickly gave way to anger. Initially, the Committee sought to clear itself from any imputation of disloyalty and on 4 February outlined the limits of its demands.[48] In the following month, conscious of its English predecessor, it issued what was in effect an Irish 'Protestation', demonstrating that the principles of Catholicism were in no way incompatible with the duties of citizens or 'repugnant to liberty, whether political, civil or religious'.[49] The declaration answered many of the attacks levelled at Catholics during the parliamentary debates, renouncing such concepts as the deposing power of the Pope, his infallibility, his civil authority outside the papal states, and the breaking of faith with heretics. The Committee also renounced all interests in forfeited estates and declared that, should Catholics be restored to the elective franchise, they would not use that privilege 'to disturb and weaken the establishment of the Protestant religion or Protestant government' in the country.[50] Nevertheless, the day the declaration was adopted, the altered mood of the Committee was reflected in the decision taken to print and distribute at cost 10,000 copies of Burke's *Letter*, Tone's *Argument* and other pro-Catholic tracts.[51]

The Committee decided to muster the assistance of the clergy to secure maximum support for the declaration. Troy quickly rallied to its assistance and, together with his senior clergy–described by D'Alton as the 'Dublin Chapter'– promptly signed the declaration.[52] Troy acted independently of the hierarchy and his conciliatory response reflected a desire to bring his isolation from the Committee to an end.[53] The mood in Ireland had changed considerably since the secession and Catholic opinion was now firmly behind the Committee. Besides, Troy was no doubt aware of criticism that the bishops appeared to be more concerned to support government than to attend to the suffering of their people.[54] Troy urged his suffragans to subscribe to the declaration, but its importance was lost on some of their number. Daniel Delaney, perhaps the mildest of the Leinster bishops, compared the declaration to a maidservant denying for the twelfth time that she had taken her mistress's silver spoon. There was a degree of truth in this, since a number of similar declarations had been made in the course of the eighteenth century.[55]

The Committee's success in obtaining so many signatures to the declaration was largely due to its effective marshalling of the clergy throughout the country. Smyth has described the opposition of the parish priest of Duleek, County Meath, to the declaration as 'far from typical' but there is little doubt that the clergy were in many cases intimidated into supporting the venture against their own judgement.[56] James Caulfield complained to Troy of the violent and sullen mood of the people of Wexford, declaring that it was 'a happy epoch indeed when the people, the puppies, the rabble dictate'. Caulfield believed the radicals planned 'to give the clergy nothing if they do not come into their measures', while John Keogh confided to Thomas Hussey that 'the people seem well inclined to give them [the non-co-operating clergy] the French cure'.[57]

A similar ambiguity surrounds the clergy's support for the Catholic Convention. Certainly Troy had not convinced the Committee of his commitment to their policy, and was still regarded with suspicion by the leadership. In March 1792 he was seen leaving the Castle and Randal McDonnell later called on him to ascertain the nature of his conversation with Major Hobart. Caulfield, aware that Troy was to be questioned, tipped him off, warning the archbishop that 'if you do not acquit yourself with candour, you should be laid aside'.[58] Troy was again called on by the Committee to lend his support to the election of regional delegates to the Convention. After several conferences, he demonstrated his intentions 'beyond a possibility of doubt' and wrote to all the bishops of Ireland requesting their assistance in the plan.[59]

In spite of their differences, the Committee wished to harness the support of the clergy, and the published plan for the Convention included an appeal for clerical co-operation. The appeal, however, was diplomatically drafted and aimed to exploit the fears of the hierarchy to maximum advantage:

> Every endeavour should be used to cultivate and improve the friendship of our clergy. The clergy and laity, having but one interest, should have but one mind, and should therefore mutually combine their talents, their opinions and their exertions in order to effectuate our common emancipation. This union of sentiments and design, this interchange of counsel and of aid, will serve to strengthen the bonds of common friendship and will be the best security against innovation in matters which relate to religion.[60]

In a veiled threat, the bishops were assured that by such co-operation, 'will the clergy secure to themselves that influence over the laity of their own persuasion, which it is useful that a good clergy should have'. The Committee sent a number of the Dublin leaders to the country to canvas episcopal support. John Keogh was particularly active in converting the hierarchy to the cause of the Convention. Tone and Keogh travelled together to Ulster in July 1792; Tone's diary for 18 July records him winning episcopal support at Newry and Downpatrick, and the following day at Drogheda. On 9 August the two dined in Drogheda with all the northern prelates, apart from Maguire of Kilmore.[61] In the Province of Armagh, they found a natural ally in Plunket, and Tone singled him out for praise, believing 'he would be a credit to any situation'.[62]

Tone credits Keogh with bringing round the six Munster bishops. Reports reaching London, however, described Keogh interrupting an episcopal conference at Thurles, threatening the assembled prelates with a revival of Whiteboy tactics of withholding dues and collections unless they lent their support to the Committee.[63] Keogh's letter to Thomas Bray, Archbishop of Cashel (1792-1820), reflected no such tension and referred to the 'union of efforts and sentiments in the clergy and laity, so essential to our happiness'. He spoke of the respectful attachment which had always characterised the relations between priest and people in Ireland and assured Bray that in these dispositions 'the Committee will be zealous to set the example'.[64]

Included with this letter were copies of the plan for the election of delegates, presumably the ones referred to by Tone in his diary entry for 1 August–'busy all day folding papers for the Munster bishops. Damn all bishops. Gog [Keogh] not quite right on that point. Thinks them a good thing. Nonsense!'[65] In the same letter, Keogh informed Bray of his mission to the north and of alarming symptoms there of 'poor Catholics' being forced into contests with 'bigoted Protestants'.[66] Despite the 'wicked designs of certain people', the delegates of the Committee, in conjunction with the bishops, had used every effort to prevent disorder. Lack of episcopal records for Ulster make it difficult to verify Keogh's claims.[67]

Forkhill in County Armagh had been the scene of the mutilations in 1791 of the local Protestant schoolmaster Alexander Barkley and his wife. This incident stimulated much loyalist propaganda and the sectarian temperature ran high in the summer of 1792.[68] These differences were not helped by the fact that the local curate, Fr Cullen, was believed to have been involved in the mutilations and was apparently dismissed by his bishop on instructions from government.[69] It was against this background, and within the context of the elections to the Convention of 1792, that 'John Byrne' published his *Impartial Account of the late disturbances in the County of Armagh*,[70] which concluded with an account of the attack on Barkley.[71]

The Committee had scored a major coup in winning the support of the Catholic clergy for their planned Convention and the huge response to the Declaration and election of delegates had spectacularly repulsed the 'shopkeeper and shoplifter' jibe. The tone of Catholic meetings became increasingly assertive. A meeting of Limerick Catholics, under the chairmanship of the prominent merchant Francis Arthur, lamented the 'degraded state in which our children stand', declaring that 'we are taxed without being represented, and bound by laws to which we have not given consent'.[72] Such rhetoric, and a host of chapel meetings assembled on the instructions of the Committee, did little to sooth episcopal or loyalist anxieties. The acerbic Richard Musgrave described the clergy as never failing to inspire their flocks 'with admiration of the Gallic nation and with the most inveterate hatred towards the English', pointing to the active agitation of James O'Coigley amongst the Defenders and afterwards amongst the United Irishmen.[73] The parallels between the French National Assembly and the proposed Convention were only too obvious. The Roscommon Grand Jury pointed to the 'anarchy and tumult' which had come from the French Assembly, and their Donegal colleagues, while declaring 'tenderness' for Catholics, stated their determination to 'maintain at the hazard of everything dear to them the Protestant interest of Ireland'.[74]

Popular support for the Committee placed the clergy in an impossible situation. Edmund Burke's advice to Francis Moylan summed up their dilemma. He urged minimal involvement in the Committee business, while at the same time advising the hierarchy to avoid any suggestion of opposition to the aspirations of the Catholic laity.[75] Such advice afforded Moylan little consolation, given the mood of the Catholics of his own city, as reflected in the toasts at a Catholic dinner in October 1792. According to the *Cork Gazette*, a radical if racy newspaper, the toasts included; His Holiness the Pope, Edmund Burke and Maria [sic] Antoinette, Cardinal York, Catholic ascendancy, The Sub-Committee, Confusion to Protestant Bigotry and the Elective Franchise to the Sans Culottes.[76]

For the most part, the hierarchy tried to walk this tightrope, and the surviving episcopal correspondence reflects their deep felt tensions and discomfort. Bishop Laurence Nihell of Kilmacduagh (1783-95) had several applications made to him to become involved in the elections in Ennis. He refused, considering it a political matter and noting the alarm concerning the whole business in government circles. Nevertheless, he chaired the meeting held to sign the Declaration, but once that was completed, he withdrew and gave the chair to a lay man. The other prelates of Connaught were, according to Nihell, 'equally reserved as to the parochial meetings'.[77] Bishop William Egan of

Waterford and Lismore, though wishing the Committee success in gaining the elective franchise, believed that the active support of the clergy might work against the cause, rekindling the kind of acrimony present during the 1792 parliamentary session.[78]

At the same time, there was a growing fear amongst the hierarchy that their prudential low-key approach had failed to stem the spread of Jacobinism. Troy's anxiety was reflected in his muscle-flexing excommunication of Fr Robert McEvoy in September 1792, and his condemnation of the decrees of the Assembly concerning religion as universally tending to 'establish the dominion of a selfish intolerant philosophy'.[79] Teahan of Kerry, who obviously fell strongly under Kenmare's influence, shared Troy's concern and condemned what he saw as the 'open and avowed attachment of the Committee to the cause of French anarchy and irreligion'. This unbridled spirit had given rise to 'a contempt for authority amongst the illiterate and a mistaken notion of liberality which sought to shake off restraints of every kind'.[80]

The was similar anxiety amongst the western bishops: Tone described Boetius Egan of Tuam as 'flinching', while the Bishop of Killala, Dominic Bellew, became alarmed at the potential of the Committee, suggesting that the hierarchy be given greater authority within the body as a whole. 'Damned kind' was Tone's response, while a furious John Keogh 'now began to think the Catholic bishops were all scoundrels'.[81] Keogh later condemned the bishops as 'old men used to bend to power, mistaking all attempts at liberty as in some way connected with the murderers in France'.[82] Still, memories of the Kenmare split were too recent in the bishops' minds to allow for any precipitate behaviour and the general spirit in the episcopacy favoured a united stance with the Committee.[83]

III

Troy and Moylan attended the Convention in December 1792, despite having previously decided against taking any part in the proceedings. Troy confessed to Thomas Bray that he had been compelled to attend by a misrepresentation of his motives for staying away.[84] His initial apprehensions were quickly allayed by the sustained applause that welcomed the two prelates to the Tailors' Hall, where they were placed on either side of the chairman. The two returned to the Convention on 8 December when the petition, already approved and signed by the delegates, was read aloud. Significantly, the petition was presented to the bishops as a *fait accompli* and read merely for their 'information' with no implication that their approval was being sought by the Committee. Nevertheless, Moylan and Troy signed the petition on behalf of the prelates and clergy of Ireland, in a tacit acknowledgement of the supremacy of the Committee within the Catholic body.

Again reflecting flexibility in his position, Troy regarded the petition as 'perfectly unexceptionable' and delivered an inspiring speech to the assembly in which he proclaimed the bishops and clergy 'second to no description of Catholics [in the demand] for their emancipation'. Troy concluded his address to great bursts of applause by declaring the determination of the clergy to rise or fall with the people.[85] Troy's usually sharp political perceptions had obviously been blunted by his euphoric reception at the Convention; he naively attributed the delegate's decision to petition the King directly to a 'diffidence in the Castle'.[86] In this, he underestimated opposition to the Convention; loyalists regarded the direct appeal to the King as an insulting usurpation of the legitimate power of the Irish government. The reception of the Convention's delegates by the King, and their discussions with Henry Dundas, represented a further affront and kindled loyalist ire prior to the debate on Hobart's relief bill.

The hierarchy had been tainted by their association with the Committee and participation in the 'Back Lane Parliament'. Indeed, the whole Convention was represented as a papist assembly which the co-operation of the Catholic clergy had made possible. The influential role of many United Irishmen within the Committee also disturbed Protestant sensitivities, while Troy's promise to 'rise or fall' with the Committee placed him inextricably at their head. The temper of the country, too, was at fever pitch; loyalist indignation had been greatly roused and their prints analysed in detail the implications of the Convention. From Wexford, the *Dublin Journal* reported a growing divide in the town, reflected in the reaction to James Edward Devereux's election to the Convention:

> Mr Devereux who was lately elected a representative for the town of Wexford in the popish parliament which is now sitting in this town under the very nose of government was, upon his election, immediately chaired round that town, in all the parade of a legitimate representative of the county. This however had its effect upon the Protestant mind, for we learn that the Mayor and Corporation are to have a meeting to instruct their representatives in Parliament. George Ogle and the Protestant interest is the favourite toast.[87]

In the marathon Commons' debate which followed the introduction of Hobart's relief bill, the 'Protestant interest' was to the fore, and the anti-Catholic rhetoric which had characterised the 1792 session was revived with even greater ferocity. Alarmed by this development, the bishops sought to emphasise their loyalty to the King and constitution. In particular, they attempted to distance themselves from any suggestion of support for the Defenders arising from the House of Lords enquiry into Defenderism. Conscious that further relief might be endangered by such accusations, the four metropolitans issued a pastoral in January 1793 in which they denounced the 'seditious and misguided wretches of every religious denomination', as 'enemies of God and man, the outcasts of society and a disgrace to Christianity'. Stressing the connection between obedience and relief, the bishops urged their flock to avoid 'idle assemblies' and every appearance of riot.

No doubt conscious that the pastoral would be closely monitored by the ultras, prayers were requested that God would assist both houses of parliament in their deliberations. It was hoped the members would be moved to display 'consummate wisdom and liberality, for the advantage of the kingdom, and the relief and happiness of His Majesty's subjects'.[88] Bishop MacMahon of Killaloe echoed these sentiments in a similar address in April 1793 calling his flock to 'allegiance, loyalty and gratitude'.[89] Troy developed these themes with customary zeal in his *Pastoral on the Duties of Christian Citizens* in which he addressed arguments raised by Foster, Fitzgibbon and the ultras.[90] Published in February 1793, the pastoral was an attempt to counter the black propaganda levelled at the Church and aimed to remove any remaining doubts about Catholic loyalty to the King and constitution. The scope of the pastoral was wide and Troy dealt with the issues of papal infallibility and temporal jurisdiction, the deposing power of the Pope and so on. The pastoral contained a strong definition of Catholic social teaching and, in the face of the current levelling principles, Troy reminded his readers that social inequality was an inevitable part of life. The bishop acknowledged that there were abuses in society, but added that protests against these 'should always be loyal and decorous'.

Troy was particularly frank in his response to accusations that Catholics, favouring arbitrary government, were unfit to participate in a free constitution. He traced a long line through history, pointing to full Catholic participation in governments of every description. Far from being unreliable, the very principles of their faith made Catholics, by nature, loyal and dutiful subjects; the Church had always taught obedience to constituted authority, whether the government be aristocratic of democratic. Catholics were indeed fit to enjoy the benefits of a free constitution, and this was evinced by the example of modern republics established by them.

Once again, Troy's independent stance brought a barrage of criticism from a variety of sources. The intended conciliatory effect of the pastoral was destroyed by the anger it arose in both houses of parliament. In the Commons, Duigenan was particularly critical describing the pastoral as 'a political tract, containing arguments not a little hostile to the established constitution in Church and state'. In the upper house, Bishop Charles Agar and Lord Clare took exception to Troy's reference to the Catholics as 'an enslaved people'.[91] It appeared to many that Troy was advocating republican government, while the very reference to 'citizens' in the title of the pastoral had ominous overtones.

Within the Catholic Committee, too, the pastoral was greeted with no small degree of resentment. Anthony Thompson, the Committee member for Thurles, lamented that it was deficient in political perspective; by resurrecting 'controversial material long confined to the dormitory' it had provided ammunition to their enemies. Thompson's remarks are significant since he represented a moderate voice within the Committee. His comments reflected disappointment rather than criticism, since he acknowledged to Thomas Bray that no man possessed 'more enthusiasm for our liberation than Dr. Troy', nor had anyone exhibited more zeal in the cause.[92]

Troy was conscious that his *Instructions* had been widely misrepresented. In the second edition of the pastoral, published in April 1793, he attempted to remove any ambiguity from the text by singling out the British constitution for specific approval.[93] This edition received a much more favourable response than the first and Troy was greatly pleased by the compliments paid by many leading Protestants, including Lord Donoughmore and Bishop Thomas Stopford of Cork, private secretary to the lord lieutenant. The other Catholic prelates also expressed their unanimous approval of the pastoral, but the greatest comfort to the archbishop was the changing reaction from within the Committee: he noted that 'the sudden clamour raised against it by some of our own giddy people, before they even had read it, has totally subsided'.[94]

Despite Troy's confidence, the revisions to the *Instructions* failed to quell the suspicions of the ultras; as Anthony Thompson had predicted, the pastoral resulted in the revival of many of the age-old accusations against Catholics.[95] Within the Commons, Patrick Duigenan spoke for two hours on one occasion delivering a virulent attack on the pernicious principles of Catholicism. Pamphlets appeared in Dublin pointing to the contradictions between the contents of the pastoral and the Catholic Committee's Declaration of the previous year which Troy and the Dublin clergy had signed.[96] This commotion raised by Duigenan left Major Hobart with no choice but to attach a new oath to his relief bill, as he deemed it 'essential to the security of the Protestant establishment that such tenets should be clearly disavowed'.[97] This development can hardly have been welcomed by Troy, who must have questioned the wisdom of publishing the pastoral in the first place. His efforts to rescue Catholics from any suggestion of disloyalty had completely backfired and he was now placed in the compromising position of having to accept an oath based on the Committee's *Declaration*. Given the opposition of the hierarchy to the Protestation of the English Catholics, there can be little doubt of their reluctance to accept an Irish equivalent.

Troy immediately embarked on an exercise in damage limitation and sought clarification of the exact implications of the oath. In particular, he was concerned by its final clause in which Catholics vowed not to disturb or weaken the establishment of the Protestant religion or government. Seeking assurances from Hobart and 'several Lords and Commoners', Troy was told that this clause was confined to the exercise of the bill. In all other respects, Catholics were free to act as before; nothing more was intended by the article but to weaken 'by disturbance'. Convinced of this, the archbishop and his clergy were amongst the first to subscribe to the oath on 31 May 1793.[98]

Despite these assurances from the Castle, Troy's action damaged his credibility in the eyes of the Holy See. Cardinal Antonelli interpreted the vow not to 'weaken or disturb the Protestant religion' as a resignation of the duty to preach Catholic doctrine; how else could converts be made? Troy responded to these accusations, emphasising for Rome the basis of Protestant insecurity, founded on the memory of 1641 and 1688. Archbishop O'Reilly of Armagh justified the oath on the grounds that the admission of Catholics to the franchise had heightened Protestant fears; the clause represented nothing more than an attempt by government to allay this anxiety. There was no question of the oath limiting the religious liberty of the Church, since religious disabilities had been removed by the earlier relief measures.

Propaganda rejected these arguments and a meeting of the Congregation in June 1794 severely censured the oath. These objections were communicated by Antonelli to the Irish bishops, but the cardinal's naive reading of the situation was reflected in the contradiction of his call to loyalty to the crown, while at the same time condemning the oath.[99] Troy's reputation had been tarnished by his independent action on the issue. Valentine Bodkin reported that he had 'lost much of his credit and vogue' in Rome. However, through skillful diplomacy, Troy rescued his integrity. By withholding publication of

*Fig. 9 Delegates of the Catholic Committee present their petition
to King George III (N.L.I.)*

Antonelli's letter, he avoided undesirable public comment in Ireland while, in a reply to Propaganda in February 1795 he outlined the peculiar nature of Irish society which had warranted his actions. When Antonelli was replaced as prefect of Propaganda Fide by Cardinal Gerdil in the spring of 1795, Rome expressed no further objections to the oath.[100]

IV

News that Hobart's relief bill had received the royal assent on 9 April brought euphoria to Dublin and a great illumination was planned to mark the occasion. One observer described how 'Dublin [was] now as a noon day, every bell is chiming, every heart delighted'.[101] This joy, however, soon receded as Catholics contemplated what had been withheld by the bill. The concessions were indeed significant, but partial relief failed to satisfy Catholic demands for total emancipation and the notion of a share in the franchise without parliamentary representation made little sense. As John Foster warned 'it is vain to imagine that admission to the elective franchise does not draw with it the right of representation'.[102] Tone aptly described their anger when he declared that if the Catholics deserved what had been granted, they also deserved what had been withheld.[103]

The acrimony which marked the bill's passage through the Irish parliament deprived it of its conciliatory effect and served to fuel Catholic resentment. The combination of these factors led to a growing polarisation within the Catholic community and, as the Committee dissolved itself many of the radicals naturally drifted towards the United Irishmen. Disaffection was widespread in the wake of the 1793 parliamentary session. Edmund Burke complained to Grattan of the 'mutinous spirit' which he believed had become 'the very constitution of the lower part' of his compatriots. This burgeoning support for republicanism was also commented upon by Musgrave who noted that the general horror at the barbarities of the French republicans began to abate in the minds of Catholics from early in 1793. This is borne out by Troy's decision to postpone his intended office following Louis XVI's execution. Indeed, Troy wondered if it was wise to hold the service at all considering the scandalous objections made to it by 'our own people' in Dublin.[104]

By the summer of 1793, Catholic agitation had taken on a life of its own and the clergy were unable to exercise control over the course of events. There was a rise in Defenderism and a number of attacks upon priests who were compiling names for the militia ballots. The bishops came under greater pressure from Rome to call their flock back to a sense of duty.[105] The previous two years had brought the country to an unprecedented level of politicisation and few Catholics can have avoided being caught up in the political frenzy. The Church played an important role in this development in that the Catholic Committee had harnessed its organisational resources as a vehicle to implement its programme. Just as the old reform congress of 1784 had failed because the High Sheriffs in the counties were unwilling to co-operate in the election of delegates, so the Catholic Convention of 1792 had been a success precisely because the Committee had used parish structures and the clergy in building a broadly democratic and representative Convention.

The role of parish meetings throughout 1792 gave the impression of a powerful Church, one capable of exerting real influence over its members. This power was, however, illusory; the fleeting and erratic efforts of Dr Troy in particular reflect the delicate nature of the bond between priest and people. In reality the clergy could at best motivate a *willing* flock and the threats made to various bishops by Keogh, Devereux and the more radical Committee members reflect the new-found confidence of the laity, manipulating the real fears of the clergy. The Kenmare secession had illustrated for Troy the limitations of episcopal influence and his confused reaction to events throughout 1792 and '93 represented his attempts to respond to this changing relationship. While Troy and his confrères identified this new situation, both the Roman and Castle authorities failed to acknowledge this shift. Despite information to the contrary, the Castle authorities continued to presume that the hierarchy was in a position to regulate the behaviour of Irish Catholics. The Archbishop of Dublin made no attempt to correct the Castle's mistaken perception, but exploited it to the advantage of the hierarchy.

CHAPTER FOUR

The Royal College [1]

The dramatic events of the first quarter of the 1790s resulted in deep divisions within the Catholic body. The Irish political landscape had been transformed under the impact of events in France, and the Catholic community had become polarised in its response to the revolution. The Catholic Convention, however, presented an image of unity which belied this reality, and Troy's stated determination to rise or fall with the people completed the illusion. The presence of bishops at the Convention and the manner in which the Catholic Committee had successfully exploited Church structures, convinced government of the desirability of exerting greater influence over Irish Catholicism. A power struggle developed, with the Irish bishops resisting any measure of state control over the Church. This conflict was further complicated by the presence of lay radicals, reluctant to surrender the novel influence that they had exercised on the Church during the heady days of the Convention.

I

Heated debate on Hobart's relief bill in 1793 raised, once again, the vexed question of government control over the Catholic Church in Ireland. The Catholic clergy's reliance on their flocks for financial support was identified by many M.P.s as the central cause of their unreliability; the proposed solution to this dependence was the introduction of a provision for the clergy. Some suggested that the *regium donum* paid by the Crown to Presbyterian ministers since 1672 be extended to Catholics, but Thomas Lewis O'Beirne developed a far more ambitious plan, involving both state provision and an extension of government control over episcopal appointments.

O'Beirne, a convert from Catholicism, had been a clerical student at the Lombard College in Paris. He served as private secretary to the Duke of Portland during his Viceroyalty in 1782, when he had first suggested state payment to Catholic clergymen.[2] O'Beirne was convinced that such a measure would make the clergy independent of the laity and bring 'their bishops more in contact with the government'.[3] Rumours about the imminent introduction of a pension for the clergy abounded in the autumn of 1792. While the Catholic Committee was reported to favour such a scheme, there was general alarm among the hierarchy.[4] The bishops opposed any possible crown veto, sharing Edmund Burke's suspicions of Westmorland and any plan designed to separate priests and people.[5]

Archbishop Troy learned of the proposed provision in April 1793 from the Marquis of Waterford, who informed him of the intention of Lord Tyrone to introduce such a measure in the House of Commons. This placed Troy in an unenviable dilemma; while he utterly opposed such a scheme, he did not wish to antagonise his adversaries by renewed conflict. Troy believed that the plan would destroy the confidence of Catholics in their clergy. He foresaw the enormous calamities likely to result from any such move–pensions would lead many priests to indigence and a lack of zeal, and government provision would be taken by the laity as an excuse to contribute nothing towards the maintenance of their clergy. This would leave the clergy materially poorer than before; but, more ominously, it would lead to 'a chain of patronage in government to bishoprics and parishes'.[6]

Lord Dillon confirmed Troy's worst fears when he confided that the King would nominate Catholic bishops once an establishment for the clergy was fixed. Troy fiercely opposed these principles, reminding Dillon that no changes could take place without papal permission. Troy dreaded 'great evils' if these projects were executed and derived little solace from his belief that many of the 'inferior clergy, without reflecting', viewed them 'in a very favourable light'.[7] Patrick Plunket of Meath, who had been O'Beirne's superior at the Lombard College, expressed similar opposition to the scheme, while Francis Moylan feared that pensions would make the lower clergy independent of their bishops unless the money was 'immediately under the control' of the prelates. In short, the hierarchy believed that the plan was designed to render the Church dependent on the treasury.[8]

The bishops moved swiftly to protect their interests. Moylan suggested that Bishop Egan of Waterford should obtain the heads of the proposed bill before the Earl of Tyrone introduced it in parliament. Unlike Egan, whose friendship with the Marquis of Waterford ideally placed him to head off the manoeuvre, Moylan believed that Troy did not have 'sufficient weight with government to be much attended to'.[9] By implication, it would appear that his confrères believed that Troy had not as yet rehabilitated himself in Castle circles

Fig. 10 Admission ticket of Richard McCormick to Catholic Committee meeting, Tailors' Hall, April 1793 (Nat. Archives)

following publication of his pastoral *Duties*. Depite such reservations, the Archbishop met the Marquis and convinced him of the scheme's dangers. Far from improving the loyalty of the people, the measures would, he warned, convert them to 'become Presbyterians, or Methodists, or politicians'.[10] The Marquis agreed that the measure needed further consideration and the bill was deferred, much to Troy's relief. However, the issue would raise its head again during the Fitzwilliam Viceroyalty.

The question of Catholic education was also of great concern to the hierarcy, as the revolution's progress had almost completely destroyed the network of Irish colleges in France. Troy, however, looked on events on the continent with encouragement and cherished unrealistic hopes of a restoration in France. In that event, he remained to be convinced of the value of domestic clerical education, given the restrictions likely to be placed on episcopal plans. 'Nothing but absolute necessity', he declared 'would reconcile me to it, as I think it almost impossible to render it as useful as we wish'.[11] As immediate hopes of a restoration faded, the desirability of Irish-based seminary education became increasingly obvious. There was general acceptance of the potential danger posed by the return to Ireland of young clerics, supposedly imbued with destructive democratic principles. Edmund Burke was especially alarmed, and believed that a solution to the education question was 'not only expedient, but of absolute necessity for the order, civilisation, peace and security of the kingdom'.[12] Two major obstacles, however, frustrated the bishops' plans: amendments inserted in the 1793 relief act, and the renewed interest of the Catholic Committee in the education question.

The passage of Hobart's relief bill through parliament was marked by anti-Catholic rhetoric similar to that which characterised the 1792 session. The difference now was that the assertiveness of the Catholic Convention had given greater credibility to the fears of the ultras. Apart from Hobart's controversial oath, Fitzgibbon introduced an amendment in the Lords which ruled out the possibility of any institutions being exclusively for Catholic education and also subjecting any future colleges to supervision by Dublin University. This development threatened the bishops' hopes of establishing seminaries in Ireland.

Richard O'Reilly condemned Fitzgibbon's 'wicked clause' which, he believed, destroyed the possibility of any advance in the area of clerical education under the bill.[13] The aged Bishop of Limerick, Denis Conway, expressed disbelief that parliament would hinder the foundation of a college exclusively for Catholic education when clearly no other would be fit for the instruction of the clergy.[14] Troy himself declared that the restrictions in the bill made it 'useless, at least as far as it regards clerical education'. He was convinced that the timing of Fitzgibbon's amendment was critical since opposition to this new clause would jeopardise passage of the entire relief bill.[15]

The Catholic Committee had also taken up the education question and this generated even thornier difficulties for the bishops. While the Committee had dissolved itself in April 1793, one of its final acts was the establishment of a sub-committee to advance the cause of Catholic education. The new sub-committee reflected the emerging radicalism of the Catholic body, with at least three of their number, John Keogh, Richard McCormick and John Sweetman, becoming influential United Irish members at a later stage.[16]

The bishops had little respect for the sub-committee and were not inclined to have any dealings with it. James Caulfield disparagingly referred to the seven members as 'your secret committee', while Troy regretted their independent stance, believing that it was 'neither prudent nor decorous [of the Committee] to exclude or not to mention the clergy'.[17] At the heart of the misunderstanding and mutual suspicion which characterised relations between the bishops and the newly formed sub-committee, lay the failure of both parties to appreciate their respective aims; the bishops sought to establish seminaries for clerical formation while the laity aimed at something closer to a university.[18] In this respect, Fitzgibbon's subjection of any future colleges to Dublin University caused the sub-committee little concern, neither were they worried by the 1793 amendments which ruled out the possibility of exclusively Catholic colleges.

Troy was cynical about the sub-committee's intentions, condemning equally their ignorance of 'the nature of the ecclesiastical spirit' and their neglect of the practical observances of the Church. He believed that Edmund Burke had a far deeper grasp of the issues involved in clerical education, when he outlined the necessary conditions for the formation of a celibate clergy in his *Letter to Lord Kenmare* of 1782, a response to Hely Hutchinson's speech in the Irish House of Commons advocating clerical education within the university.[19] Burke stressed the unique character of seminary formation, and drew the distinction between the content of clerical and classical lay education. He declared that even if a Catholic cleric were possessed of such a classical foundation:

> they [would] soon lose them in the painful course of professional and parochial duties; but they must have all the knowledge and, what is to them more important than the knowledge, the discipline necessary to those duties. All modes of education, conducted by those whose minds are cast in another mould, as I may say, and whose original ways of thinking are formed upon the reverse pattern, must be then not only useless but mischievous.[20]

Thomas Orde's 1787 educational plans had also contained proposals for clerical formation at Trinity College and these met with equally vigorous episcopal opposition; Boetius Egan of Tuam described the proposals as 'a deep laid and hostile plan against the interests of the Catholic religion'.[21] In 1793 Burke counselled the hierarchy to minimise contact with those who were not convinced of the need for exclusive clerical management of any future seminaries, declaring that 'they who would trouble this natural order of things, on account of the poor squabble of religious parties and divisions are either stark mad, or doing the work of the atheistical faction which are at present making havoc in the world'.[22] The nervous Caulfield was concerned that episcopal contact with the sub-committee would be misunderstood in government circles and that the bishops might appear to have taken up the cause of parliamentary reform.[23]

The prelates, however, could not afford to be seen to have dismissed the approaches of the sub-committee out of hand, and both groups met in April 1793. At this meeting the sub-committee outlined its proposals for the establishment of a system which would accommodate both clerical and lay students, including non-Catholics. The proposed college would be under the joint management of clergy and laity and would be funded by subscriptions raised amongst the laity.[24] Thomas Addis Emmet's subsequent account of this meeting is in stark contrast to the record of the proceedings given to Thomas Bray by Troy. Emmet described how the sub-committee's scheme received the 'most decided approbation' of the 'majority' of the prelates. In Troy's account, he and Richard O'Reilly were the only bishops present and they both disapproved of the proposals. The archbishop's version of the transactions would seem to be borne out by Wolfe Tone who condemned the prelates as ignorant bigots for their rejection of the plan.[25] Tone's enthusiasm for the establishment of seminaries is ironic in that he recommended the measure as the best means of altering the conservatism of the clergy and bringing them around to reform. 'In this light', he wrote, 'as in ten thousand others, the revolution was of infinite service to Ireland ... This education business appears to me of infinite importance for a thousand reasons'.[26]

Meetings of the hierarchy were necessary to advance their plans but the bishops were anxious to maintain a low profile given the reaction the Convention had aroused in the previous year.[27] James Caulfield was particularly concerned that a full meeting of the hierarchy in the spring of 1793 might be misrepresented as the bishops forming a House of Lords, just as the Committee had had a Back Lane Parliament.[28] For similar reasons, Boetius Egan of Tuam opposed any meeting of the hierarchy during the parliamentary session. Richard O'Reilly of Armagh believed that a meeting should take place, but he felt that an archbishop and one suffragan would be sufficient representation for each province. Troy favoured a 'thin and late meeting' of the prelates as most acceptable to the government.[29] In the interim, he agreed to meet with Hobart to ascertain the government's educational proposals.[30]

Troy met with the Chief Secretary in November 1793 and in a later memorandum outlined for him the crucial nature of the education question. The Irish Church was facing a critical shortage of priests: despite hopes of a counter-revolution in France, it was unlikely that funds could be recovered to re-establish Irish colleges there. Besides, Troy warned that the licentious principles which had infested France might survive any restoration: it would, therefore, be unwise to expose clerical youth to the danger of 'imbibing seditious maxims' which they might later propagate in Ireland.[31] The archbishop confidently stressed the social responsibility of the clergy, particularly since Catholics had been restored to the franchise. In this novel situation, he argued the advantages which could be wrought by a well educated and disciplined clergy, pointing to clerical exertions against disaffection and sedition during the previous summer. Adopting a Burkean line, Troy argued that an educated clergy was essential 'for the support of His Majesty's government and the maintenance of good order, both of which ... would be endangered if the Roman Catholic people were deprived of their religious instructors'.

The archbishop's memorandum reflects careful and shrewd preparation and a determination to avoid ambiguity on the issue of Catholic education. He outlined the necessary conditions for the establishment and management of any future seminaries. It was essential, he argued, that any such colleges should be 'exclusively clerical ... and subject only to their ecclesiastical superiors'. Troy was aware that this would require the alteration of Fitzgibbon's amendment to the 1793 Relief Act, and the removal of the prohibition on the endowment of Catholic schools contained in the Relief Act of 1782. With this in mind, the archbishop informed Hobart that no scheme could be realised without 'some annual pecuniary aid from government'.

Encouraged by government reactions, Troy met his fellow archbishops as well as Bishops Moylan, Caulfield, Plunket, Teahan and Bellew. Together, they drew up ambitious plans for the establishment of diocesan and provincial seminaries and decided to pursue the issue of clerical education with greater vigour. They addressed the first of a series of queries to the Attorney General, Arthur Wolfe, concerning the exact position of Catholics under the 1793 Relief Act.[32] In particular, the episcopacy sought clarification on the ability of Catholics 'to bequeath, grant or apply money for the endowment of schools, academies or other places of education'.[33] The bishops approached Edmund Burke in the hope of enlisting his support for their project. Burke was convinced of the value of their scheme, but believed that the bishops' plans required 'management and co-operation upon both sides of the water'. He recommended his son Richard and Thomas Hussey, 'the ablest man of business and the best clergyman' he knew, for this purpose.[34] Richard Burke was as ineffectual in the Maynooth business as he had earlier been as agent of the Catholic Committee, but Edmund himself devoted great energy to the seminary question.

The Attorney General's reply to the bishops' queries can hardly have given their plans much encouragement: while he acknowledged the ability of Catholics to educate their youth, he believed that the laws precluded the endowment of schools and seminaries.[35] There was, however, the possibility that such endowments could be permitted by means of a special royal licence. Sackville Hamilton, under-Secretary at the Castle, advised Troy that such a licence could be obtained by a memorial to the Crown.[36] The bishops immediately acted on this suggestion and Dr McKenna was instructed to draw up a suitable memorial for presentation to the Lord Lieutenant.

Accompanied by several other members of the hierarchy, Troy met with Westmorland in December 1793 and presented an address of loyalty to the King. Despite the Lord Lieutenant's known antipathy to the Catholic cause, Troy was pleased with the tenor of the meeting and was confident that the government would soon meet all the bishops' educational needs except for the provision of funds.[37] The meeting with Westmorland marked a new departure in relations between the Irish Church and the Castle administration. The significance of the event was not lost on the archbishop himself; he informed Luke Concanen that this had been the first time in over a century that such a conference had taken place between a Viceroy and the Catholic hierarchy.[38] Anxious to build upon this new relationship, Troy met Edward Cooke in late December, inviting the Secretary to report to him 'the names of such clergymen as he might have reason to complain of in future'.[39]

Communication with the Castle served only to deepen suspicions of the hierarchy harboured by the Catholic Committee, particularly as the bishops kept their planned meeting with Westmorland secret from the Committee members whom they had recently met.[40] All of this contributed to the 'Castlelick Clergy' jibes which had been predicted by Burke and gave an impression of constant meddling by the administration and the hierarchy in each others affairs.[41] Quite unmoved by these accusations, and equally unconcerned about the possible wrath of the Committee, Troy explained to Concanen that the bishops had chosen this course of action:

> not only in order to dispose government in our favour, but particularly in order to declare and clarify our true feelings at a time, unfortunately, when many of our people are acting foolishly and raving about a chimerical liberty and the false pretended rights of man. I have been pleased to find this government extremely satisfied with our conduct. Some democrats will raise a racket; but ... [we] are equally indifferent to their praise or censure. We are neither aristocrats nor democrats in the modern acceptance of party language. We have spoken as bishops, without taking notice of any party.[42]

The bishops were not to be deterred from their chosen course: pleased to learn that their address of loyalty presented to the Lord Lieutenant had been 'received in a most gracious manner' by King George, they proceeded with their planned memorial requesting a royal licence for the endowment of Catholic colleges.[43]

The memorial was couched in the same language as Troy's memorandum to Major Hobart of the previous November, placing a similar emphasis on the mutual advantage to Church and state of the establishment of domestic seminaries.[44] Condemning the 'profligate principles of rebellion and atheism' propagated in France, the bishops stressed their unwillingness to expose Irish youth to the contagious dangers of sedition and infidelity. Nor would they risk the introduction to Ireland of 'the pernicious maxims of a licentious philosophy' which infected returning clerics might carry with them. They emphasised the utility of a properly educated and disciplined clergy who would not only instruct Catholics in the precepts of Christianity, but would also inculcate 'obedience to the laws and veneration for his Majesty's royal person and government'.

The memorial stressed the particular nature of priestly formation, especially the need for strict ecclesiastical discipline, without which the cleric might become a 'very dangerous member of society'. Stressing the unsuitability of Trinity College, the bishops requested permission to establish Catholic seminaries where young men might be prepared for the priesthood under 'ecclesiastical superiors of their own communion'. Ever conscious of the great financial expense involved in establishing educational institutions, the memorialists expressed their hope that the plan might 'appear to His Majesty as a subject not unworthy of his royal consideration and bounty'. Despite the memorial's urgent tone and Troy's grim warning that the 'Protestant establishment would not long survive' the destruction of the Catholic religion, Westmorland failed to be convinced: it was almost nine months before he passed on the memorial to the Sergeant and Solicitor Generals for their opinion.[45]

By this time, however, the situation had been dramatically transformed by the formation of Pitt's new coalition with the Portland Whigs in summer 1794. Westmorland's administration in Dublin was now in its last days. Indeed one of the last acts of the Viceroyalty was a reply delivered by Sackville Hamilton in January 1795 to the bishops' memorial in which the Secretary curtly declared the seminary proposals impossible, owing to the terms of the 1793 Relief Act. This was in spite of assurances given by the Lord Lieutenant to Kenmare in January 1794 that the bishops' plan met with his complete approbation.[46] Hamilton's response reflected the characteristic hostility of the old regime to the Catholic claims for relief.[47]

I I

The imminent arrival of a new Viceroy, Earl Fitzwilliam, generated widespread euphoria in Ireland and the populace was hastened into an orchestrated rush as Catholic addresses of welcome were drawn up to place before him. In general, the hierarchy shared the hopes of the people, but there was a degree of uncertainty as to the most appropriate means of expressing their sentiments. Still reluctant to appear at the head of calls for reform, Dr Troy sought advice from Thomas Bray. In particular the Archbishop of Dublin was adamant that he would not sign any address unless 'all parties be united' behind it, and he wondered whether a separate address on behalf of the prelates might not be prudent.[48]

Lay Catholics shared none of Troy's reservations; on 23 December a meeting of the Catholics of Dublin appointed a committee of nine which immediately set about petitioning the new Lord Lieutenant for the total repeal of the remaining penal laws. In Dublin, New Year's Day 1795 was set aside for this purpose and the petition was to be signed in the various city chapels. The radical *Morning Post* commented on the Dublin petition that 'it cannot be doubted that every well meaning Catholic will come forward with the firmness and moderation which the occasion requires'. In a possible reference to the archbishop and the more conservative elements of the Catholic community, the paper remarked; 'so far no directions have been given to the jobbers and sycophants belonging to the Castle, to the contrary'.[49]

Thomas Braughall and the more radical Catholics set about canvassing support for the petition and attempted to enlist the help of the clergy as they had done with the Convention three years previously. This time, however, clerical assistance was much more forthcoming: among the first to respond to the invitation was Bishop Patrick Plunket of Meath. Plunket had sided with the liberals in the Committee split following Kenmare's secession in 1791. It was to be expected then that he would give the 1795 petition his support. Writing to Thomas Braughall in January 1795 he declared:

> I am of your opinion that it [the petition] will derive great weight and consequence from the unanimity with which each county and principal town will make it their own. I have recommended it with energy from

my altar and signed it in a most public manner. My two assistants followed my example and I am writing to the vicars of this diocese to exert themselves in promoting the signatures in their respective districts.[50]

Before long the nation's prints were filled with the loyal addresses of Catholics from every corner of the country, many bearing the signatures of the local bishop and clergy. Amongst these were the primate Richard O'Reilly, John Cruise (Ardagh), John Young (Limerick), Hugh O'Reilly (Clogher), Daniel Delaney (Kildare and Leighlin), Patrick Plunket (Meath), Boetius Egan (Tuam), Dominic Bellew (Killala), James Dillon (Raphoe) and Francis Moylan (Cork). It does not appear as if Troy signed the Dublin petition of 1 January 1795 but, by the end of January the Catholic petitions were so numerous that Henry Grattan declared that they would 'reach from College Green to Holyhead'.[51]

Great hopes were placed in the new Viceroy and Ireland appeared on the brink of a new era. Within days of his arrival, the Lord Lieutenant initiated a series of sweeping changes, dismissing John Beresford as chief revenue commissioner and Arthur Wolfe as Attorney General. The radical press celebrated these assaults on the junto, praising Fitzwilliam for dislodging the 'hydra of persecution from its den, the Castle'.[52] The bishops shared the popular perception of the Earl holding out the olive branch and lost no time in gathering themselves in Dublin to prepare a new submission on the seminary question. The first of these meetings took place in January at the Augustinian Priory in John's Lane. The changing atmosphere is reflected by the fact that no fewer than eighteen bishops were present, making this by far the largest meeting of the hierarchy for over a hundred years.[53]

These meetings continued for over five weeks and the newspapers followed proceedings with great interest. The *Morning Post*, the most radical and anti-clerical of the Dublin prints, described their importance, and shared Henry Grattan's belief in the need for government support for a Catholic seminary, an 'object so important and so interesting to the morals and conduct of a rising generation'.[54] The bishops were confident their plan would win the support of this new benevolent regime. Fitzwilliam was, after all, a disciple of their greatest ally, Edmund Burke, who had spent the preceeding months preparing the ground on both sides of the water. He persuaded the Duke of Portland to send Thomas Hussey to Ireland and convinced Henry Grattan of the necessity of domestic seminaries.[55] Fitzwilliam, however, did not confine his interest in Catholic affairs to education, and the bishops were once again confronted by

*Fig. 11   Edmund Burke
                (N.G.I.)*

the prospect of a royal veto on episcopal nominations and state pensioning of their clergy.

In December 1794, Thomas Hussey warned of the imminent introduction into the Irish House of Commons of a bill to establish a provision for Catholic clergy. Hussey repeated many of the fears sounded by the bishops in the previous years, but he was confident that the move would be resisted as it had been in 1792.[56] Troy was particularly anxious to avert the establishment of a royal veto over episcopal appointments; he saw an ominous precedent in the concession of a similar veto to George III in Corsica. He wrote to Luke Concanen in September 1794, urging him to impress on Propaganda the dire consequences for the Irish Church if the nomination of bishops and 'other delicate matters should be dependent on heretics and on a Protestant government'.[57] Again, in January 1795 the archbishop wrote to Cardinal Antonelli about rumours of a proposed veto. Troy was unsure of the veracity of these reports, but expressed the conviction of the entire hierarchy that the plan would be 'absolutely destructive' to the Irish Church and requested that any such overtures be resisted by the Holy See.[58]

The Cardinal's response was hardly that hoped for by the archbishop: Without referring to Troy's warnings, Antonelli reminded the bishops of the 'esteem and gratitude' of the Pope towards King George, and called on the Irish prelates to instill loyalty and obedience in their flocks.[59] This letter is a perfect reflection of the bizarre twist which the French Revolution had brought to relations between Rome and the Court of St James. Dependent as the papal states were on the efforts of British armies, the Roman authorities were obliged, through a mixture of guile and gratitude, to urge Irish Catholics to obedience. It is this curious relationship which makes sense of the oscillating directives from Rome during this time and later, especially in 1808-15, simultaneously urging obedience to the crown and the laws while reprimanding the hierarchy for its willingness to accept the various loyal oaths proposed by the Dublin government.

Once again, Thomas Lewis O'Beirne, notoriously ambitious and by now Bishop of Ossory and chaplain to the Lord Lieutenant, was to the fore in recommending the establishment of a provision for the clergy and a royal veto.[60] Some form of veto appeared inevitable: despite their opposition to the principle of state interference, the prelates believed little could be gained from opposing the government's plan. Hussey reported a proposed scheme in January 1795 which allowed the clergy elect their candidates, but the final choice would be made by government from a panel of three names submitted to them.[61] At a meeting of the hierarchy in Dublin on 17 February, the bishops discussed these proposals and agreed that any royal veto ought to be resisted *in limine*. However, when they formulated their position to be presented to the Holy See, they advised the Pope 'not to agree to His Majesty's nomination if it can be avoided'. If it was unavoidable, the King was to be allowed nominate one of three names 'to be recommended by the respective Provincial Bishops'[62]

This certainly represented a weakening of the bishops' total opposition to the proposals and reflects a sense amongst the hierarchy in early 1795 that their unrestricted independence would have to be sacrificed as part of the price to be paid for total emancipation. In the field of clerical education, however, the bishops were adamant that no concessions would be made. Asked if they could 'agree to the appointment of President or Professors in the intended Colleges by government, parliament or any lay authority; and if not, what degree of interference on the part of any of these is admissible?', the bishops replied negatively and declared that 'no interference is admissible'.[63] The prelates were decisive that there would be no outside meddling in the affairs of the proposed college which, they believed, would entirely defeat the purpose of its foundation.

In particular, they were concerned by the renewed activity of the lay sub-committee and rumours that government intended the college to be open to lay and clerical youth. Thomas Bray was angered by 'the gentlemen Catholic managers' who were using every means at their disposal to pressure the administration into allowing them a 'joint superintendence with the bishops' over the college in the area of professorial appointments and management of funds. Bray resented this interference into what he called 'our business', and insisted on the prelates' exclusive rights in the management of the proposed seminaries. How 'this contest' with the laity would end was, he believed, impossible to forsee but the bishops were determined to 'proceed with all possible secrecy, caution and moderation'.[64]

The bishops' letter of 2 February seeking Grattan's support for their scheme contained no reference to the sub-committee. Instead they mentioned their discussions with 'our principal laity', most probably the Kenmareites, with whom they had always concurred and declared that they would continue to act with them 'in forwarding every salutary measure for the advantage of our entire body'. In what is most probably a reply to this appeal, Grattan referred to differences between the bishops and the Catholic Committee and the latter's objections to the prelates' plans for the college but hoped that this disagreement would be 'settled to all your satisfaction'.[65] The bishops were determined to proceed with caution on the education question. It was expected that the bill to establish seminaries would follow the general emancipation bill and it was understood that the planned college depended on the success of Grattan's bill.[66] As events unfurled, however, this was not to be the case and the failure of the emancipation bill actually facilitated the prompt establishment of the Royal College.

Fitzwilliam's great plan for Ireland and his all-out war on Jacobinism, particularly his proposed yeomanry, depended upon Catholic emancipation. Although Fitzwilliam had made no reference to his plans to repeal remaining Catholic disabilities in his speech from the throne of 22 January, poor communications with London convinced him that the cabinet there approved of his proposals. The Viceroy was quite unaware of opposition to emancipation in Whitehall and the pressure being applied by Pitt to halt the proposed repeal which King George believed amounted to 'the total change of the principles of government which have been followed by every administration in the kingdom since the abdication of King James II'.[67] Henry Grattan introduced a relief bill in the House of Commons on 12 February. The immediate adverse reaction to this signalled that the Lord Lieutenant's administration was doomed.

Believing that the Viceroy was moving too fast, the Duke of Portland instructed Fitzwilliam to abandon the emancipation bill and to proceed instead with the planned seminaries and provision for the clergy. These measures, the duke was convinced, would be more effective than total emancipation and with these assurances of the 'good intentions of government', 'all ideas of further concessions might ... be laid aside'.[68] A week later an angry Fitzwilliam was recalled from Dublin, plunging the country into crisis. Thomas Hussey, who broke the news to Burke, was dumbfounded and described the country as being on 'the brink of civil war'.[69] He could not understand how 'the spirit of this nation [could] bear that the most popular and virtuous Viceroy that ever came to this country should be removed'.[70] Neither could the Viceroy understand the reservations in Whitehall concerning emancipation. Fitzwilliam believed that the country was now ripe for rebellion. Referring to the jacobinical principles of the Catholics, he believed that they lacked 'but a cause and a leader and the Castle is furnishing both'.[71]

The Castle prints interpreted events quite differently, attributing Fitzwilliam's recall not to the emancipation bill, but to his abrupt dismissal of 'His Majesty's most confidential and faithful servants'. These removals, the *Dublin Journal* argued, were not on account of any charge of incapacity or misconduct, but rather 'for the mere purpose of giving their employments to His Excellency's family [the Ponsonbys] and friends [Henry Grattan]'.[72] Burke, so long a champion of the Catholic cause, had encouraged Fitzwilliam to make this assault on the junto, but he had urged the Lord Lieutenant to avoid the emancipation question which, he was convinced, would weaken the new administration and restore the very faction he had hoped to oust.[73] Nevertheless, whatever the cause of the Viceroy's demise, the feeling amongst the Catholic body was one of disgust and the title of a political skit, 'The sense of a loyal and insulted nation' published in the *Morning Post* aptly captured their mood.[74]

Despite Portland's claims to the contrary in his letter to Fitzwilliam on 16 February, little had come of discussions on the educational question at the time of the recall, except that there would be just one college and that the grant of £4,000 would be less than half that expected by the bishops.[75] Hussey feared that the planned college would now suffer the same fate as the relief bill, but was greatly relieved when the duke requested him to stay on in Dublin until his plans would be brought to a conclusion.[76] Indeed Portland requested Earl Camden, the new Viceroy, to proceed with the instructions contained in his letter to Fitzwilliam of 16 February, namely completion of the educational proposals and establishment of a provision for the clergy.[77] Although he had expressed no such reservations towards Fitzwilliam's plan, Burke advised Hussey to reject any degree of interference in Church affairs and above all to resist a veto and 'Castle choices'.[78] He was not opposed to government possessing such powers *per se* but he saw only disastrous consequences in the hands of a hostile junto.

Camden immediately tackled the seminary question. Both London and Dublin were anxious to remove the anti-Catholic tag from the administration; the proposed seminary was seen as a final concession and an adequate substitute for emancipation. Within three weeks of his arrival in Dublin, Camden's Chief Secretary, Thomas Pelham, introduced a bill to the Commons on 24 April 1795 establishing the Royal College .[79] The Catholic bishops had reservations about the scheme, however, particularly the admission of outside interference in the proposed college. Edmund Burke too, dreaded any role for the junto in the college's affairs, urging the bishops to 'trust to God's good providence, and the contribution of your own people, for the education of your clergy [rather] than to put into the hands of your known, avowed, and implacable enemies–into the hands of those, who make it their merit and their boast, that they are your enemies, the very foundations of your morals and your religion'.[80]

With this in mind, Hussey proposed to Camden that the college be established by charter from the King and that the power of superintendence and visitation would rest not with the local Protestant ordinary, but rather with 'persons amongst the highest orders of the clergy of the R.C. persuasion'.[81] The Viceroy rejected this suggestion, believing it gave too much credence to the notion of an establishment for the Catholic clergy and proceeded with his own plans for the college.[82] Under this scheme, the it was to be governed by a board of twenty-one trustees which would include the Chancellor and three Chief Justices. The trustees would be responsible for drawing up the statutes of the College and for internal discipline, with the Chancellor and chief justices as ex-officio members of the board acting as visitors. The inclusion of 'Black Jack' Fitzgibbon and the chief justices as trustees created a sense of alarm in Catholic circles: many shared Burke's view that not alone were all benefits of the college lost, but that 'a more mischievous project never was set on foot' in Ireland.[83]

Troy would certainly have preferred if the judges had not been included as trustees, but regarded their presence as a necessary evil. He was, however, satisfied that the internal regulation of the college would be left to the bishops.[84] With skill and diplomacy, the archbishop had successfully brought the new administration, particularly Pelham, around to accepting almost totally his model for the Royal College. Subjection to Trinity College had been resisted, as had outside involvement in the appointment of the president and professors. He had compromised by accepting four Protestant and six lay

Catholics trustees, but the presence of ten bishops and the president on the board assured effective clerical control of the College.

III

The seminary bill had a swift passage through parliament and received the royal assent on 5 June 1795. Debate on the bill was unusually muted. Patrick Duigenan later commented that the measure had been carried 'with little notice or discussion' and the debate was not even recorded in the *Parliamentary Register*.[85] Undoubtedly the 'conciliatory mood' of the new regime assisted the bill's passage; so did the death the previous autumn of the Provost of Trinity, Hely Hutchinson, removing much colour which otherwise would certainly have characterised the debate. He had long been parliament's strongest opponent of segregated colleges and Lecky lamented that in his passing 'the nation. ... lost, in a most critical moment, the wisest and ablest advocate of liberal education'.[86] There was minor opposition to the bill in the Lords. Charles Agar, Archbishop of Cashel, attempted once again to affix the Catholic *Declaration* of 1792 to the oath, but Hussey successfully circumvented these proposals by quiet approaches to the Castle.[87] Significantly, all real opposition to the bill came from outside of parliament.

Fitzwilliam's recall had polarised political opinion in Dublin and Grattan observed that 'never was a time in which the opposition here were more completely backed by the nation, Protestants and Catholics united'.[88] Camden's arrival had brought riots to the Dublin streets but, in time these protests gave way to more sophisticated opposition. Portland had urged Camden to rally the friends of government and to conciliate the Catholics. To this end, the new Viceroy offered the seminary bill, but his offer seemed derisory to the Catholic body under the circumstances.[89] Edward Tighe M.P. observed that the college bill was no more than 'a sop to the Roman Catholic clergy by way of compensation' for the emancipation bill which was now doomed.[90]

The leading members of the Catholic Committee were determined not to let this insult pass without protest. Tempers were running high and, following their Francis Street meeting on 9 April, Edmund Burke complained that the proceedings had been 'wholly Jacobinical' in tone and that talk of separation reflected 'foolish language, adopted from the United Irishmen'.[91] There was also resentment amongst Committee members that their education plans had been usurped by the bishops, and it was decided by the sub-committee to present a petition to parliament in opposition to the education bill.

Fig. 12 Maynooth College

The petition was brought before the house by Henry Grattan on the bill's second reading. It objected to the proposed college on two grounds; first was the power given to the trustees to make all college appointments which, the petitioners believed, should 'be thrown open to examination, and should be made the rewards of superior merit, without any possibility of jobbing'. The second, and much more fundamental, objection was to the college's exclusively Roman Catholic character. The petition opposed this segregation, which was described as 'highly inexpedient, inasmuch as it tends to perpetuate that line of separation between his Majesty's subjects of different religions, which the petitioners do humbly conceive it is the interest of the country to obliterate'.[92]

Referring to this episode, Lecky declared that there was 'hardly a more striking proof of the change that [had] passed over the spirit of Irish Catholicism than is furnished by the petition'.[93] Yet, while the petition reflected both the liberal principles of the Committee and the great divide between their priorities and those of the hierarchy, it was also a strategic political move, described by Maurice O'Connell as 'more an expression of anger than a serious attempt to have the bill altered'.[94] The Grattanite party in parliament shared the Committee's frustration. They opposed the bill in the belief that its passing might smother the general sense of disappointment in the country on which they hoped to capitalise, and would tend to divide Catholic and Protestant reformers, whom they hoped to combine in the common cause.[95] Despite these objections, the bill was carried without any difficulty.

I V

On the Feast of SS Peter and Paul, 29 June 1795, Troy and seventeen bishops celebrated a solemn High Mass in Francis Street, Dublin. The intention of their 'awful, impressive and affecting' ceremony was 'by way of thanksgiving of the legislature for the late act which endowed a Roman Catholic college, and to implore the divine blessing upon his Majesty's person and government'.[96] Troy had indeed much for which to be grateful. He had, after all, achieved what would have been considered impossible a year earlier–the establishment of an autonomous college under exclusive episcopal superintendence.

The first meeting of the trustees in Fitzgibbon's chambers in the House of Lords presented quite a different spectacle but, with the exception of their attendance at this initial meeting–which decided merely to invite tenders for land and buildings–and one more the following month, the Protestant trustees took no part in the government of the college. However, possible embarrassment at Fitzgibbon's presence at this meeting may be reflected in the almost total obliteration of his name from the minutes of the trustees' meetings.[97] The Catholic lay trustees (Lords Fingall, Kenmare and Gormanston, Sir Edward Bellew, Sir Thomas French and Richard Strange) were drawn from amongst the Catholic Committee seceders of 1791-2 and presented no challenge to episcopal authority.

The absence of any members of the old sub-committee reflects the rupture which had occurred in the Catholic body. In many respects, the hierarchy had been less than honest in their relations with the lay Catholics. Since the sub-committee had first expressed their concern for the education question, the bishops had not been frank with them. Throughout 1793 and '94 they had met with the sub-committee, but all this time they had kept them in the dark about their ongoing discussions with Major Hobart and the Castle. The sub-committee had been led to believe that the bishops supported their plan for one thriving national college, only to discover otherwise.

In the recriminations which followed the establishment of the Royal College, it was suggested that the hierarchy had exploited the prospect of a college under the control of radical Catholics as a bargaining tool to frighten government into assenting to their own scheme. Thomas Addis Emmet, reflecting much later on the events, believed that such a plan was infinitely more attractive to the Castle authorities who could make it 'subservient to every purpose which the government wish'.[98] Troy was conscious of the anger amongst the sub-committee at how events had unfolded; at one stage he contemplated including Edward Byrne amongst the trustees 'for peace sake'. However, the fact that Byrne signed the petition against the college bill ruled out this possibility.[99]

The Fitzwilliam episode had wrought an enormous change in the standing of the Catholic hierarchy. The bishops undoubtedly shared the general despondency at the Viceroy's recall and the fate of his relief bill but, had it passed, they would certainly have had to suffer the imposition of a veto and provision for the clergy which the Viceroy had proposed. The arrival of Camden spared the hierarchy this crisis, and the eagerness of the new Lord Lieutenant to conciliate leading Catholics greatly aided the realisation of their educational plans, without any of the compromises which they had feared necessary only a few months earlier. For this, the bishops owed a particular debt of gratitude to Thomas Pelham, Chief Secretary at the Castle, who had consulted closely with them throughout the period. Fitzgibbon, by then Earl of Clare and himself a trustee of the college, later grumbled that 'Lord Pelham and Doctor Troy had contrived the college between them'.[100] This hierarchy's gratitude is reflected in Troy's congratulatory note to Pelham on his elevation to the peerage in 1801. The archbishop spoke of his 'fostering hand by which the college at Maynooth had been raised and protected'. On another occasion, Francis Moylan referred to Pelham as 'the cornerstone' of the College.[101]

In many respects, the education crisis contributed to the formation of a national episcopal conference in Ireland and the emergence of a greater sense of unity amongst the bishops. The political activity of the Catholic Committee surrounding the Convention had certainly increased communication between the bishops at both provincial and inter-provincial levels, but the sheer scale of the meetings at John's Lane, in preparation for the bishops education submission in January 1795, represented a significant development in the process. The quarterly Maynooth trustees meetings would in future serve as episcopal conferences, and the experience gained in the negotiations prior to the foundation of the college proved invaluable, especially in the negotiations on the Act of Union.

A renewed sense of identity and newly established relations with the Castle buoyed up spirits amongst the hierarchy, and this confidence is reflected in the growing tendency of bishops to use episcopal titles. This confidence did not go unnoticed. On receipt of a letter from Coppinger of Cloyne bearing episcopal arms, Edmund Burke urged the bishops to avoid such ostentatious displays while, Duigenan protested in the Commons that many of the loyal petitions in 1795 were signed by 'persons assuming the titles of Roman Catholic bishops and archbishops, in direct contradiction and defiance of the laws which they profess'. With these objections in mind, Michael Daly wrote to Thomas Bray from Lisbon in June 1795 and apologised for his failure to address the archbishop as his 'station in life entitles', on account of the noise of 'some scoundrels in parliament'.[102]

More than any one, Archbishop Troy was responsible for this effective marshalling of the Irish hierarchy. He had succeeded in bringing his confrères together to face the crisis of clerical education and, in so doing, confirmed his position at the head of the Irish Church. Despite the prominent role he played throughout negotiations with the administration, he shrewdly involved his fellow bishops at all levels of the discussions. He pointed out to Bray the necessity of episcopal meetings 'in order that no bishop may hereafter complain that the important business of clerical education was regulated without his concurrence or consent'.[103] Nevertheless, Maynooth remains a monument to Troy's perseverance, and its foundation greatly enhanced his standing and reputation in the eyes of both the Irish Church and the Holy See.[104] With the Catholic Committee becoming more and more submerged within the United Irishmen, the Archbishop became to all intents and purposes the public leader and acknowledged voice of Irish Catholics.

Maynooth College, however, had not been established without cost to the hierarchy; above all, the bishops' reputations had been sullied by their Castle courtship. The popular perception of the college as a sop in place of general emancipation survived; as Edmund Burke had predicted, constant meddling of the bishops and clergy with the Castle had set them at variance with their own body.[105] Grattan too, in the debate on his ill-fated relief bill, referred to the establishment of Maynooth and condemned government for its use of the clergy in order to 'pervert religion into an instrument against liberty'.[106] In this scenario Troy was the villain of the piece, having accepted the government thirty pieces of silver–a grant of £8,000 per annum. Troy was undaunted by these jibes. He had achieved the object of his efforts, the establishment of an autonomous national seminary; he now turned to face his next challenge, the crisis of disaffection and Defenderism.

CHAPTER FIVE

Gathering Pace 1795-1798

By the summer of 1795 the pace of events in Ireland had altered the priorities of the Catholic Committee and the importance of education paled into insignificance when compared to the question of general emancipation. The previous year had seen their hopes for a repeal of remaining Catholic disabilities dashed. Dublin Castle firmly opposed any repeal measures and the British government, faced with a crisis of management in Ireland, was no longer willing to play the Catholic game. The present constitution offered little hope of further relief to Catholics who increasingly looked towards the United Irishmen and to France for their salvation.[1] Thomas Hussey identified this frustration, warning Edmund Burke that not alone was emancipation at stake in 1795, but the greater question of whether Britain meant 'to retain Ireland'.[2] The Catholic hierarchy, however, emerged from the Fitzwilliam debacle greatly strengthened. Anxious lest its achievements be endangered by the rash behaviour of the Catholic masses, the bishops felt they had little choice but to adopt a course of steady loyalism. In the years from 1795 to 1800, apparently impervious to the very real sufferings of their people, they preached unquestioning loyalty and obedience, very often in the face of draconian government measures.

I

By the spring of 1795, Defenderism had spread beyond Armagh and symptoms of disaffection were to be found in fourteen counties of Ulster, north Leinster and Connaught.[3] Daily reports reached the capital of unrest in the countryside and the papers were filled with accounts of what the *Dublin Journal* described as the 'alarming depredations committed by the Defenders'.[4] The recall of Fitzwilliam added to this tension, and the *Northern Star* declared that the rejection of the Catholic bill had given 'the insurgents a plea for disaffection'.[5] The new Lord Lieutenant, Camden, was puzzled by the Defenders whose curious mixture of the traditional agrarian movement and sophisticated radicalism eluded all attempted definitions. Violence continued to spread and ominous reports of an alliance between the Defenders and the United Irishmen determined Camden to take whatever actions were necessary to halt what he called 'the government of terror'.[6]

The apparently sectarian character of Defenderism did not go unnoticed by the press. Loyalist prints were quick to draw incriminating connections between the Catholic question and Defender violence. Commenting on the Catholic address in February 1795, the *Dublin Journal* declared that the alarming state of the country 'required the serious and immediate considera- tion of the government' and concluded that 'the power of their clergy over them gave us expectation that these disturbances would be quickly terminated'.[7] Troy was conscious of such criticism and was angered by the aggressive tone of the Catholic Committee in the face of the impending defeat of the Catholic bill. In a strong letter to Bishop Plunket, of Meath, he railed against 'our philosophical orators in Francis Street [who] have injured a good cause', commenting that 'friends and enemies equally condemned their violent proceedings'.[8]

Compromised by the actions and declarations of the meeting in Francis Street chapel on 9 April, Troy was convinced that the 'Catholic body was sound and ought not suffer for the intemperance of self-created leaders', Keogh, Sweetman and Lewins.[9] In the House of Commons debate on the Catholic bill some weeks later, the speeches of the 'Francis Street orators' and the United Irish ideas of the Committee were held up as justification for refusing further relief.[10] Marcus Beresford informed his father that 'the debate degenerated into abuse of the Catholics, and attempts to connect them, through Tone, with United Irishmen, Jackson and treason'.[11]

Links between Catholicism and the Defenders were a continuing source of acute embarrassment to Troy as he was anxious to emphasise the essential loyalty of Catholics. He was greatly angered in July 1795 by the highly publicised arrest in Kildare of the schoolmaster Lawrence O'Connor, a freemason and leader of the Meath Defenders. O'Connor, arrested while swearing the country people to be true to the French, was tried for high treason in September 1795.[12] Schoolmasters often served as local leaders amongst the Defenders, but the fact that O'Connor served as occasional parish clerk in Agher, County Meath, particularly disturbed Troy who complained to Bishop Plunket:

this connection between the parish priest and O'Connor furnishes much matter of speculation to all. It is easy to conjecture what our enemies may, and what even our friends do actually say. The latter regret the connection much, and remark that O'Connor as a schoolmaster and clerk, was in some degree an official man in the confidence of the priest who could not be entirely ignorant of his principles. Hence they censure the priest in employing such a person in any capacity instead of endeavouring to banish him from the parish.

Troy concluded by stressing for Dr Plunket the need for greater caution so that similar scandals might be avoided in the future.[13] The Bishop of Meath, in turn, referred the case to Lord Fingall who recommended that an enquiry be made into O'Connor's behaviour from the priest in question, Father John Cregan, pastor of Summerhill. Fingall, however, criticised attempts to attribute the current disturbances to popery when, in fact, they had their 'origin in French principles and irreligion'. It was absurd, he argued, for the government to give 'a legal establishment and encouragement' to Catholicism while at the same time throwing 'out hints and foul unfounded aspersions on its ministers and all who profess it'. The government, he believed, ought to be called on to put a stop to 'the snarlings and illiberal insinuations of its own really most prejudiced servants'.[14]

Referred to by Fingall as 'our zealous friend in town', Troy was feeling increasingly pressurised to take strong action against the Defenders and he showed little inclination to criticise government policy. In an effort to deflect criticism, the clergy refused to attend O'Connor at his execution or administer the sacraments to him.[15] He was hanged at Naas in September while Lord Camden was in the town, in a gruesome display which reflected the administration's reliance on exemplary terror as the only means of containing Defenderism. O'Connor's body was disemboweled, quartered and his head placed on a pole over Naas gaol on the specific instructions of the Lord Lieutenant; however, such brutality merely added to the cult which quickly developed around the dead leader.[16]

Apart from the disturbed state of Ireland, Troy received daily reports recounting the sorry state of Italy and the havoc being inflicted there by the advancing French armies. The Irish bishops were urged by Rome to recall their flock to a sense of duty and peaceable behaviour in the face of severe and furious attacks 'against the most sacred precepts of Christian religion and Catholic faith'.[17] Troy published a pastoral condemning the Defenders, similar to the one he had issued in Ossory in 1784 against the Whiteboys.[18] He attacked the progress of Defenderism which, he said, had been marked by 'disorder and plunder and not unfrequently, by bloodshed'. Declaring his hate and abhorrence of 'every proceeding of persons associated under the title of *Defenders*,' the archbishop denounced their acts as 'contrary to the laws of God and the Church'. He referred to 'those unhappy *Defenders* and other similar delinquents ... a disgrace to Christianity, and outcasts of Society'. Defender oaths were in no way binding, but as 'bonds of iniquity' were 'unlawful, sinful, wicked and damnable'. Troy cautioned his flock against the 'insidious arts of designing men' and their attempts to 'subvert the orderly subordination established by divine providence for the preservation and happiness of society'.

Lamenting the fact that his previous instructions appeared to have fallen on deaf ears, Troy denounced the 'many who, ceasing to be Christians, obscure and dishonour the bright name of Roman Catholic, which they affect to retain'. No doubt sensitive to the bitterness harboured by many of the radical laity in the wake of the Fitzwilliam/Maynooth episode, he attacked the attempts of the Defenders to discredit the clergy 'whom they represent to the unthinking multitude, as insensible to the distresses of the poor'. The archbishop also condemned the interpretation of Defender activity as 'the result of a plan devised by Roman Catholics in general to destroy the established government'. In the face of 'all these evils', and 'of delusion in some, and of obloquy in others', he announced that he was refusing the sacraments and Christian burial to all those refusing to abjure Defender oaths.

In terms of rhetoric and philosophical stance, Troy's denunciation of the Defenders differed very little from his earlier excommunication of the Whiteboys.[19] Nevertheless, what was new in 1795 was the archbishop's standpoint and the means he employed to distribute his pastoral. Troy had come a long way in his relationship with the government since first taking the oath of allegiance in March 1779. Already in frequent communication with the Castle, he decided to enlist the assistance of the administration in circulating his pastoral. This was a novel departure and it reflected a *quid pro quo* attitude, with the archbishop willing to express publicly his gratitude for the new relationship between Church and state. It is also certain that by mid-1795 he was anxious to establish his loyalty beyond doubt and, by so doing, to replace the radicals or 'self-created leaders' at the head of the Catholic community in the eyes of the administration.[20]

Troy sent a copy of his pastoral to Robert Marshall at Dublin Castle, expressing a desire that it should be circulated as widely as possible through the newspapers 'and otherwise as Mr Pelham shall think expedient', in an effort to make it more effective.[21] The archbishop's servant had dropped copies of the address in the newspaper offices, but Troy could not be certain of a favourable response. He requested Marshall to make no reference to his sending the pastorals to the offices, should he make representation to the various editors. Declaring that he had published the excommunication without any contact with the Castle, Troy added that it was 'by no means necessary and perhaps inexpedient'. He was certain the well disposed of every communion would 'not be displeased' but, as to the approbation or censure of others, the archbishop was 'perfectly indifferent'.

Thomas Pelham acknowledged the pastoral and informed Troy that the Lord Lieutenant had read the address and 'expressed himself in terms of the warmest approbation'.[22] Troy was overjoyed at the positive response of the administration, declaring that 'the most humble have ever highly valued the approbation of estimable characters'.[23] He continued:

> In writing and publishing the exhortation ... I conceive myself complying with what I owe to the religion I teach and to the society of which I am a member. Both are dishonoured and injured by riot and disorder. It is the duty of every man to oppose the abettors of either and to vindicate the principles he avows from calumny.

Troy must also have been consoled by the compliments paid to him by Charles Erskine. Lamenting the unruly conduct of the Defenders, he expressed his 'greatest regard' for Pelham and his confidence that Troy, by his 'co-operation with government, by preaching, by admonition and instruction of the ignorant and misled', would recall the people to their senses. Erskine was pleased to be able to confirm for Pope Pius VI what he already knew; that the flock committed to Troy's care 'shall not be exposed to diminution or infection'.[24] Further comfort for Troy came from Bishop John Carroll of Baltimore, who praised his efforts in 'these perilous and perplexing circumstances'. That some had impeached Troy's conduct was not surprising, for Carroll knew that it was harder 'for a good man to resist the heated zeal of impetuous, though well meaning, advocates of a good cause than to quell violence of impiety or open persecution'.[25]

The radical *Morning Post* had no such garlands to offer the archbishop: scoffing at Troy's 'power of saving and damning whom he pleases', it ironically lamented the fate of the Defenders, 'hanged by the laws here and damned by Dr Troy hereafter'.[26] A similar cynicism for such episcopal ordinances was reflected in Leonard McNally's celebrated report to the Castle in September 1795:

> A contempt for their clergy universally prevails, deism is daily super-
> seding bigotry and every man who can read or can hear and understands
> what is read to him begins in religion, as in politics, to think for himself.
> This is evident not only from the declarations of the peasants, and the
> oaths of the Defenders, now administering in every part of this kingdom,
> but from the ridicule and laughter which they have all with very few
> exceptions thrown upon the address, drawn up by Archbishop Troy, and
> publicly read from altars by priests. The address which a few years ago
> would operate with terrors of thunder on an Irish congregation of
> Catholics is now scoffed at in the chapels and reprobated in private.
> Excommunication has lost its terrors, and no wonder when Christianity
> hourly declines, and I do apprehend that the priests at the altar and the
> priests in private houses hold and preach very different doctrines and
> should a serious commotion take place I am convinced that Doctor Troy,
> so far from finding protection in his spiritual character, would be one of
> the first sacrifices to popular cruelty and revenge.[27]

Similar sentiments were expressed by Arthur O'Connor who declared, 'ask the Catholic clergy and they will tell you that their power is declined. Ask the Protestant gentry from one end of the kingdom to the other, and they will tell you that the superstitious power of the Catholic clergy is at an end'.[28]

Undaunted by this changing atmosphere, the bishops continued to preach against Defenderism. Patrick Plunket began a visitation of Meath in late April 1795 and his diary reflects the priority attached by him to appeals for peace and loyalty. In all, Plunket records thirty six sermons in which he condemned violence and Defenderism. The bishop preached submission to the laws as an act of religion and spoke of 'the madness of the prevailing disturbances'. In September, Plunket stepped up his campaign against Defenderism and broad-ened the scope of his sermons; at Fertagh (17 September) and Clonard (21 September) he considered 'the origins of Defenders, its motives and conse-quences exposed to view, and judged by reason and religion'. He preached against drunkenness, invariably described as a cause or companion of Defenderism. On 23 August, Plunket denounced the Defenders at Mullingar, County Westmeath, which was still free from disturbance. Two days later he was approached by a Mr Reeves, on behalf of the Protestants of Mullingar, requesting a copy of his sermon with a view to having it printed. The bishop made no further reference to the sermon; it is unlikely that it was ever published.[29]

The hierarchy was in an invidious position by the end of 1795, anxious to maintain loyalty, while attempting to avoid the 'Castlelick Clergy' jibes to which Burke had earlier referred.[30] The dilemma became particularly acute in December 1795 when the bishops were obliged to lead prayers of thanksgiving for the delivery of King George from an attack made on him while on his way to open parliament. Having consulted with Bishop Moylan of Cork, Troy recommended a formula to Thomas Bray which answered the purpose of the address without 'exposing the bishops to censure or obloquy'. However, despite his reservations, Troy was certain of the desirability of receiving the attention 'of the respectable prints for public information'.[31]

The bishops continued to ingratiate themselves at the Castle and the measure of their accommodation within administration circles is reflected in the various accounts of the laying of the foundation stone at Maynooth, in April 1796. The *Dublin Journal* recorded the occasion as 'one of the most affecting scenes we ever witnessed, promising to raise in Ireland the cause of science, morality and religion'. The Royal College, the paper believed, would 'carry down to future times the liberality and patriotism of Lord Camden's administration'.[32] The students of the college, accompanied by a band, led Camden from the upper end of the town to where he laid the foundation stone; three specially written odes were then recited, in Greek, Latin and English, and the *Hibernian Journal* recorded that 'the countenances of all manifested pleasing sensations of mind at the liberality of the legislature and the government to their Roman Catholic brethern'.[33]

Patrick Plunket recorded the occasion in his diary. For him, the highlight of the day was riding back to dinner at the Castle in the Lord Lieutenant's carriage, together with Thomas Hussey and Archbishops Troy and O'Reilly.[34] News of the occasion quickly spread; writing from Rome, the Dominican John Connolly described Plunket's account of the ceremony as 'by far the most satisfactory that has been yet sent to Rome. Who could imagine, when I left Ireland nearly thirty years ago that some of our Catholic prelates were to go in 1796 in state through Dublin and to dine at the Castle?'[35]

It was not difficult in these circumstances for the Defenders and United Irishmen to portray the clergy as 'insensible to the distresses of the poor'.[36] The winter of 1795 and the first half of 1796 had seen the escalating levels of violence and the Castle decided to meet fire with fire; throughout the period 'Defender terror and official terror mirrored each other'.[37] In his recent study of the Catholic question, Bartlett devotes considerable attention to the repression meted out by the crown forces in their attempt to suppress violence and the levels to which Camden was prepared to excuse illegal activities.[38] Carhampton had been sent to Connaught to put down disturbances there, resulting from the flow of Catholic refugees from Ulster. The Lord Lieutenant turned a blind eye to the behaviour of the soldiers which might 'in some instances be carried on with a warmth which might better have been suppressed'.[39]

To bolster their armoury against disaffection, the government introduced an insurrection act in March 1796 which allowed the Lord Lieutenant to 'proclaim' areas on the request of the justices of the peace. The act gave the justices sweeping powers of search and arrest, the death penalty was specified for tendering unlawful oaths and *habeas corpus* was suspended in the following October. The excesses of government forces continued and the introduction of an indemnity act was evidence of Camden's resolve to excuse illegal acts.[40] Newspapers were filled with accounts of army cruelties which reached new heights after the establishment of the yeomanry in late 1796. Catholic resentment continued to rise as they became increasingly vulnerable on all sides; even General Lake admitted in March 1797 that 'some irregularities (though I really believe very few) may have been committed ... chiefly by the yeomanry ... whose knowledge of the country gives them an opportunity of gratifying their party spirit and private quarrels'.[41]

The hierarchy remained silent about government repression and monotonously continued to call the faithful to loyalty. Troy's Lenten pastoral in February 1796 denounced 'impiety and irreligion' and exhorted Catholics to refrain from 'cursing, swearing, from unlawful combinations and, still more, unlawful oaths whereby you engage in them'.[42] In Troy's private correspondence there is evidence of his alarm at the fate of the Armagh Catholics, but he absolved the government from direct blame, attributing responsibility to 'the supine neglect of the magistrates and prejudice of the gentry in that quarter'.[43] On another occasion, he wrote:

> the Protestant rioters in County Armagh stiling themselves Orange boys, composed principally of low Presbyterians encouraged by the connivance of Protestant magistrates, have committed such atrocious excesses against the persons and property of unarmed and unoffending Catholics in that neighbourhood as to create great discontent and alarm in the Catholic body, which only desires that offenders of every description be punished according to the laws.[44]

Lord Gosford, the Governor of Armagh, addressed a meeting of the magistrates of the county in December 1795 and Troy's description of the outrages bears many similarities to his address, thousands of copies of which were printed and distributed gratis.[45] He too referred to the 'supineess of the magistracy' and grievous oppression of the Catholics of Armagh by lawless persons.[46] The newspapers entered into polemical warfare on the causes of the disturbances, with the *Dublin Journal* denouncing the 'extraordinary and utmost energy taken by the *Dublin Evening Post* to smear the Orangemen of County Armagh' while remaining silent about the Defenders and United Irishmen.[47]

Orangemen, the paper stated, 'declare no bigotry or fanaticism, or illiberal prejudice', but were willing to live in harmony with Turk, Jew, Arab, Cherokee, even 'the Arch Devil himself ... provided the latter gentleman will behave himself properly, find security that he will cut no caper among them in the shape of a Defender, or an United Irishman'.[48] In the House of Commons, James Verner–denounced by James O'Coigley as 'a man who has done everything but what is right and just, from a common feeder and handler of gamecocks, metamorphosed into a legislator for his country'–referred to reports of seven thousand Catholics being driven from Armagh, cynically declaring that 'whatever the Roman Catholics have suffered, they have brought upon themselves'.[49]

Throughout the crisis, the hierarchy voiced no public criticism of the administration, but there are indications of unease in their private correspondence. There are also instances where the bishops made discreet representations to the Castle, but these were extremely confidential, as Troy feared they 'might become the subject of party conversation and newspaper obloquy against the government'.[50] In August 1796 Troy approached the Castle administration requesting that a confessor be admitted to see a Meath Defender named Traynor who was under sentence of death for high treason. The Archbishop of Dublin made this appeal on receipt of a letter from Plunket in which he described the 'unChristian rigour exercised at present against the unfortunate Traynor'. Troy shrewdly relayed to Cooke the Bishop of Meath's letter, in which Plunket referred to 'the prejudice and unrelenting injustice of a certain part of the public here who, in defiance of common sense and common policy, will not be persuaded that we clergy are not secret abettors of the mad and wicked system which threatens to bury religion under the ruins of civil power'.[51] In the following month the Castle approached Troy with a view to supplying a confessor for Charles Teeling, who had recently been brought from Belfast.[52]

From Beaconsfield, Edmund Burke observed events in Ireland with increasing alarm. More than anyone Burke had foreseen ghastly consequences for Ireland in the recall of Fitzwilliam, to which he responded with 'grief, shame and anguish'.[53] The interim period had served only to confirm Burke's anxiety and he frequently referred to the Camden administration as the 'junto' or the 'Directory'. Catholics, he believed, were 'treated like enemies, and as long as they are under any incapacities their persecutors are furnished with a legal pretence of scourging them upon all occasions, and they never fail to make use of it'.[54]

Burke was concerned at the draconian measures adopted by the government, believing that 'in Ireland it is plain they have thrown off all sorts of political management and even the decorous appearance of it'.[55] He saw disastrous consequence in these policies which, he was convinced, would jacobinise Ireland and lead the Catholics to 'use the only means that is left for their protection'.[56] Worried that the dissolution of the Catholic Committee in 1795 had left the Catholics without an effective voice, Burke warned Thomas Hussey that 'Catholic Defenderism ... [had become] the only restraint on Protestant Ascendancy'. He was critical of the quiescence of the hierarchy and cautioned his friend on the dangers in overstating passive obedience:

> The doctrine of passive obedience, as a doctrine, it is unquestionably right to teach; to go beyond that, is a sort of deceit and the people who are provoked by their oppressors do not readily forgive their friends, if whilst the first persecutes, the others appear to deceive them. These friends lose all power of being serviceable to that Government in whose favour they have taken an ill-considered step.[57]

While Hussey accepted the counsel of his mentor, the bishops continued to exhort their flocks to loyalty and the failed French invasion at Christmas 1796 provided them with another opportunity to rally to the side of the government. The advent of Lazare Hoche's army of 14,500 men and 41,644 stand of arms brought a rash of pastorals in condemnation of the French and the associated Irish radicalism.[58] On Christmas Day, Francis Moylan of Cork issued a blistering attack on 'the specious treachery' of the French and he called his flock to loyalty to King and government. Congregations were warned against promises of emancipation from tyranny and the restoration of lost rights . The bishop held up the fate of Flanders, Italy, Holland and Germany, all of which had fallen victim to French liberty and fraternity. In conclusion, Moylan urged his people to 'range under the banners of true Irish loyalty'.[59]

The pastoral was warmly greeted in loyalist circles; the *Dublin Journal* described it as 'an admirable address', while an anonymous pamphleteer praised the Bishop of Cork who, he claimed, 'would do honour to any Church, and adorn any situation'.[60] In January 1797 Moylan was rewarded with the freedom of Cork and Robert Day, M.P. and chairman of the Grand Jury of Dublin, addressed the Grand Jury, declaring that no panegyric could do justice to the pastoral which reflected a 'spirit of peace, loyalty and philanthropy worthy of an apostle'. The bishop had not waited until the danger of invasion had past, but exposed himself to the 'most rancorous vengeance' and displayed courage and 'striking loyalty'. In all, Day believed Moylan had 'vindicated the great Roman Catholic mass against the misconceptions of men prejudiced because uninformed and, what is more difficult, against the disaffection and criminal tardiness of certain discontented individuals of their own body'.[61] Camden also expressed his pleasure at the pastoral, a fact which the *Morning Post* believed did 'great honour to His Excellency's candour and liberality of mind'.[62] In radical circles, however, the pastoral made little impact; when W. J. MacNeven was asked about it by the Secret Committee of the House of Lords in 1798, he replied that he never heard the pastoral complained about since it was 'only a pious fraud' which 'contained a remarkable falsehood in favour of the administration'.[63]

Moylan's pastoral was followed up by a spirited address from John Young, the strong minded bishop of Limerick. Young's pastoral was read in all the chapels of his diocese in January 1797 and its principles were explained in Irish. The bishop's rhetoric was much the same as that of his confrère in Cork. Young referred to the great danger facing Ireland, with 'a ferocious enemy, inured to slaughter, rapine, and sacrilege' hovering around with the avowed purpose of destroying the peace and prosperity of the country and substituting anarchy in the place of 'good government'. The bishop called on Catholics to show their attachment to the laws and 'the mild and equitable government of his majesty'.

The present crisis gave Catholics an opportunity to demonstrate to the world that disloyalty and disaffection were not principles of the Catholic religion; on the contrary, Young reminded his congregation of their 'deepest sense of obligation' to show 'affectionate obedience' to the civil powers. A novel feature of the bishop's pastoral was his call on his flock to take arms to defend Ireland:

> Your interest and your duty call on you to join heart and hand with your other fellow-subjects, to repel their hostile attempts. If the circum-

stances of your situation in life do not admit you to repel force by force,
you still have it in your power to disappoint the expectation of the
enemy, by shewing by your conduct, a determined and unanimous
resolution of giving every assistance in your power to the executive
government of the land.

Young's pastoral was printed in full in two of the radical Dublin prints, the
Morning Post and the *Dublin Evening Post*, but neither commented on the text
or the bishop's unique call to arms.[64] The strength of his support for government in 1797 is interesting, considering Young's later determination to
maintain the independence of the clergy and his fears that the proposed clerical
pension, described by him as a 'douceur' for the Act of Union, would have dire
consequences for religion and lead to a claim of government patronage.[65]

Archbishop Troy chose the occasion of the day of solemn thanksgiving for
the delivery of the kingdom on which to preach against the French. On 16
February a solemn High Mass and a *Te Deum* were celebrated at Francis Street.
Dr Moylan officiated at the altar, and many of the bishops were in attendance.[66]
Before a congregation of almost three thousand, Troy delivered a fierce attack
on the French which was by far the longest of the pastorals in 1797 and has been
likened to Edmund Burke's *Reflections*.[67] He began by exposing the 'folly of
French principles' and the 'impious demagogues' of France who have 'destroyed everything valuable and dear to man'. They had torn up the very
foundations of society and France now presented 'a sad and frightful spectacle
to an amazed world', as did the countries 'which experienced the calamity of
French dominion or fraternity'.

Turning his attention to Ireland, Troy warned against the evil and dangers of
illegal oaths which tended to 'excite or promote rebellion'. He called his flock
to their duty which he summed up in the Petrine admonition to 'fear God and
honour the King' (1 Pet. 2:17). In a theme which would be repeated many
times, the archbishop reminded his listeners of the disabilities suffered by Irish
Catholics in the past and their 'loyal and virtuous conduct during a long and
painful trial' and expressed gratitude for the relaxation of the penal laws. Troy
made no direct references to the United Irishmen, but denounced the 'artifices
of designing and ambituous men' who addressed the Catholics 'under the mask
of friendship and [tempted] them to a violation of their duty'. This was not the
way forward, but only through a continuation of a peaceful and an exemplary
demeanour 'which attracted the first and progressive rays of illumination',
could Catholics 'expect to enjoy hereafter a brighter sunshine'. Troy received
the customary encouragement for his endeavours from Charles Erskine who

congratulated him on his pastoral and declared that the Irish Catholics were indeed 'fortunate to have at this critical period such pastors as Your Lordship'.[68]

The mood of the country was, however, greatly altered and Catholics increasingly looked, not to Troy and the other bishops but, towards the United Irishmen for their salvation. The former Dublin Catholic Committee was now indistinguishable from the United Irishmen; Burke described John Keogh as 'a franc Jacobin', adding that little divided himself and Richard McCormick from Oliver Bond and Henry Jackson.[69] Castle reports confirmed these developments. Leonard McNally reported that the successes of the French armies gave great satisfaction and that the fate of the Pope, far from being regretted, gave 'sincere pleasure to the Catholics'.[70] The *Morning Post*, which had scoffed at the fate of the Pope, now ridiculed Troy's letter which it declared 'is rightly termed a pastoral as there is sufficient wool gathering in it to show that the Doctor considered his flock to be sheep'.[71]

In the north, General Lake had begun his bloody campaign to disarm Ulster and there the strongest defence of the Catholics against the tyranny of the army was mounted by the *Northern Star*. Examples of this defence were collected in a pamphlet entitled *Truth Unmasked or Food for the Liberty* which appeared in April 1797. The pamphlet reprinted articles from the *Northern Star* and was sold in aid of the twenty thousand starving in the Liberty of Dublin.[72] Was it to raise Protestant against Catholic that the Yeomanry and militia were arrayed? Was it to support an administration which has brought the country to the verge of destruction? 'Think in time', the article reminded soldiers, 'you are Irishmen'. Lake, however, had enough of the *Northern Star* and in the same month sought permission from Dublin to 'seize and burn the whole apparatus', which he believed had done mischief beyond all imagination.[73]

United Irish proclamations denounced the persecution of Catholics and, in parliament, Henry Grattan condemned martial law and the excesses of the military. He resigned from the yeomanry in protest, as did Sir Lawrence Parsons and the Duke of Leinster in a concerted Whig manoeuvre.[74] To the great embarrassment of the government, Lord Moira also condemned the behaviour of the army in both the Irish and English Houses of Lords. James O'Coigley compared the situation in Ulster to the 'tyranny of Robespiere'. From mid-1797, the government began to employ similar tactics in Leinster and parts of Munster as reports of United Irish activity began to reach the Castle.[75] Arthur O'Connor's *Press* announced that 'the greatest part of Ireland groans under military execution, rapine conflagration and butchery rage without compassion and control'.[76] Yet, throughout this crisis the hierarchy remained silent and voiced no public protest at the suffering of the Catholic community. The bishops generally contented themselves with their traditional chorus of gratitude and loyalty to the government and monarchy. One exception to this, however, was Thomas Hussey whose denunciation of military abuses, despite his otherwise unquestionable loyal, 'strenuous and steady' royalism, led to his ostracisation and stigmatisation as 'the rebel bishop'.[77]

Thomas Hussey differed from the remainder of the hierarchy in many respects. He spent the greater part of his life outside Ireland and, even during his period as president of Maynooth and Bishop of Waterford, he continued to spend considerable time in London. Circumstances placed Hussey at the centre of a bustling political circle and his interests were very often a great deal more temporal than those of his fellow bishops. Hussey's interest in the 'Catholic question', more often than not, concerned the political implications of the various developments; he attached far greater importance to the material welfare of the Catholic community than either Troy or Plunket. This is reflected again and again in his correspondence with Edmund Burke, particularly in his shocked reaction to the recall of Fitzwilliam and the collapse of the relief bill. The freedom and social status Hussey enjoyed in London greatly altered his perspective on Catholic Ireland, and he shared none of the quiescent deference of his confrères. Perhaps it was this confidence which caused him to misread the political realities of Ireland and lead him into conflict with the establishment there.

Born in 1746 in Harristown, County Meath, into what Thomas England called 'a distinguished and respectable Irish family', Hussey was described by Edmund Burke as 'a man of birth and respectable connections in the country.[78] Having completed his studies at Seville, he was ordained to the priesthood in March 1769 and immediately appointed one of the ordinary chaplains to the Spanish ambassador in London. Fifteen years later he became principal chaplain, a position he held until his death in 1803. This appointment placed the young cleric at the centre of a lively political and intellectual circle. Few failed to be impressed by his intellect and wit; Charles Butler commented that 'he did not come into contact with many whom he did not subdue, the highest rank often sunk before him'.[79]

Before long, Hussey could count the Duke of Portland, Lord Chatham, the younger Pitt and Fox and Dr Johnson amongst his acquaintances. It was at this time, too, that Hussey became friends with Edmund Burke, a relationship that would have a profound and lasting effect upon the young cleric. In 1792 he was admitted a fellow of the Royal Society of London. Burke commented that he was 'a man well informed and conversant in the state affairs and general politics of several courts of Europe and immediately and personally habituated in some of these courts'.[80] Despite all this, the Belfast Presbyterian United Irishman, William Drennan who was admittedly prejudiced against Catholics, spoke of the 'native broadness and vulgarity of Hussey's brogue, strange that someone of the most ancient strain of Ireland and in foreign courts all his life should smack so strongly of the bogtrotter!'[81]

Hussey's society connections led him into many involvements. During the American War, a secret embassy was sent under Richard Cumberland to Spain in an effort to break the Franco-Spanish alliance. At the special request of King George III, Dr Hussey joined the delegation and, despite its failure, he made an impression at the Spanish Court. Cumberland commented that he was 'inclined to think he [Hussey] considered himself as forced upon a scene of action where he was to play his part with as much finesse and dissimulation as suited his interest or furthered his ambition'.[82] In 1793 the Spanish minister, Chevalier Azara, proposed Dr Hussey to Pius VI as intermediary between the Holy See and the British government. Sir J. C. Hippisley objected to this suggestion and succeeded in having Charles Erskine appointed instead.[83]

Hussey's political progress continued despite this setback; he increasingly concerned himself with the interests of the Catholics in both England and Ireland.[84] Not everyone shared Hussey's self-confidence; in September 1796 Francis Higgins informed Dublin Castle that 'the Roman Catholics hold a superficial opinion of Doctor Hussey as a courtly priest–if anything was to be effected, or wished to be done in the Roman Catholic Body, Dr [Arthur] O'Leary could do more with them in one hour than Hussey in seven years'. This comparison with O'Leary is significant, since the Cork priest was in the pay of the Castle and the antipathy between himself and Hussey was re-nowned.[85]

Exhibiting what Burke called 'a very rare union ... of the enlightened statesman with the ecclesiastic', Hussey argued that full Catholic emancipa-tion was not only desirable, but essential.[86] In 1790, he wrote to Richard Burke that 'should these kingdoms be involved in a war, a further toleration of the Catholics of Ireland will become unavoidable'.[87] It was absurd, he argued, to wait until necessity compelled what true policy should offer voluntarily:

> Hitherto, the Catholics of that country have proceeded with proper deference and submission to the laws, in their application for redress, notwithstanding the endeavours of neighbouring countries, suggesting to them to wrest by force and violence, what I hope they will never mention, but with moderation and temper. Sublimated, however, as

men's minds are by the French disease (as it is not improperly called), one cannot foresee what a continuation of oppressive laws may work upon the minds of the people; and those of the Irish Catholics are much altered within my own memory and they will not in future bear the lash of tyranny and oppression which I have seen inflicted upon them, without their resisting or even complaining.

When Henry Grattan introduced his relief bill in February 1795, Hussey wrote to Edmund Burke urging him to impress on London that the question of the emancipation bill 'involves another awful one–whether they mean to retain Ireland or abdicate it to a French government, or to a revolutionary system of its own intention'. In the same letter, he warned that without the emancipation bill, any attempts by the government to enlarge the army would merely fill the ranks with paper soldiers.[88] Fitzwilliam's recall, and the consequental defeat of the relief bill, astonished Hussey. 'How in the name of God', he asked, 'can the spirit of this nation bear the most popular and virtuous viceroy that ever came to this country should be removed'?[89] This, Hussey assured Edmund Burke, was not his language, but the language of the people. With his finger on the pulse of the country, he was alarmed that:

The people begin to view the interference of the British cabinet in a hostile light; they will soon consider this parliament as a court of register, to obey the dictates of a British minister. They will wish for a separation from Great Britain and the contemptible light in which they will view their own parliament will induce them to lay it in the dust and to erect a convention on the French scale in its place.

These 'mischiefs' were unavoidable, Hussey believed, if the British government continued on its course.[90] Burke cautioned Hussey and urged him to 'preserve a profound silence', leaving matters to their own 'natural operation'.

The establishment of Maynooth had been a priority for Hussey; his association with the venture began as early as 1793. In December of that year, Burke wrote to Francis Moylan, stating that the establishment of the college was 'not only expedient, but of absolute necessity for the order, civilisation, peace and security of the kingdom'.[91] He realised the difficulties involved in implementing the project and recommended his son Richard and Hussey, 'by far the ablest man of business, and the best clergyman I know', to manage the progress of the college. Moylan replied that Burke's recommendation of Richard Burke and Hussey had met with the 'fullest approbation and consent from the prelates' who recognised the ability and zeal of both men for the cause.[92]

Writing to Archbishop Bray of Cashel, Troy commented that Hussey 'can render us essential service at the Castle and elsewhere. He is independent and can speak with a firm tone to some of our own people here'.[93] Hussey's association with Maynooth met with the approval of the British government and he was the accredited representative of the Duke of Portland on the Maynooth issue during 1794-95. In March 1795, Hussey was about to return to London but he stayed in Ireland, at the duke's request, to ensure that the business of the Catholic college was not abandoned. Later that year, in June, a meeting of the Maynooth trustees appointed Hussey president of the college, apparently on the suggestion of the duke. Hussey's delight at the progress of the college was unquestionable. In November 1796, he refers to Maynooth as his 'favourite spot, this *punctum saliens* of the salvation of Ireland from Jacobinism and anarchy'. [94]

Hussey's influence now seemed boundless; this led him to espouse yet another cause, the plight of the Catholic soldier in Ireland. It was a crusade, however, which was to lead Hussey into direct conflict with the government, the result of which has been to cast a shadow over his loyalty and generally place him amongst the instigators of the rebellion of 1798. In August 1796, Hussey informed Bishop Douglas of London that Erskine had obtained for him, from Pius VI, a vicarial authority over the King's forces in Ireland. His appointment as chaplain general was officially announced on 9 August, while at the same time chaplains were appointed to each regiment of the Irish Brigade.[95] Pitt knew Hussey to be a staunch anti-Jacobin and confirmed his appointment in the belief that he would help stamp out disaffection in the army.[96] Though the appointment carried no salary, this did not lessen the chaplain general's enthusiasm in carrying out his duties.

Following his appointment, Hussey began to seek redress for what he regarded a gross injustice and evil; the practice of forcing Catholic soldiers to attend Protestant services. This problem was not new, but it had become more acute with the formation in 1793 of the Irish militia, the rank and file of which was predominantly Catholic. The issue came to a head in 1795 with the case of Private Hyland of the Irish Light Dragoons who had been sentenced by a court martial at Carrick-on-Suir to 200 lashes for refusing, on the advice of his confessor, to attend Protestant services. Hussey complained to Edmund Burke about Hyland's treatment and also raised the question with Fitzwilliam, whom he urged to issue a proclamation against such practices.[97] Burke, too became alarmed at the punishment and warned Fitzwilliam that the French war against religion could only benefit from a civil war in Ireland. Eighteen of the Irish bishops made a similar protest to the Lord Lieutenant and urged him to take the necessary corrective action.[98]

Hussey's feelings on the subject grew stronger. He attempted to meet the Viceroy or his secretary in October 1796 but they were 'too busy in settling their bargains with the orators of College Green'.[99] On every occasion when the matter was spoken of in his presence, he expressed his strongest abhorrence to the point where his 'gentle friend, the Secretary of War [William Elliott] told him that Mr Pelham felt himself much hurt by his opinions.[100] Hussey's alienation from the Castle caused him great grievance and increased his alarm for the security of Ireland. His letter to Edmund Burke on the subject reflects his conservatism and obvious aversion to revolution of any kind:

> How little does His Majesty suspect, that those upon whom he heaps honours, and powers here, are his greatest enemies and the very men who are Jacobinising the country! They are urging these cursed senti-ment throughout the country under the name of United Irishmen, this evil is extending beyond imagination ... I am terrified at what I foresee regarding my own unfortunate native country. To pass by parliament, and break the connection with Great Britain, is I am informed the plan of the United Irishmen. The wretches never consider that their griev-ances are not from England but from a junto of their own countrymen.[101]

Hussey's position was becoming more critical. He continued to receive applications for advice from several military corps and found himself forced to choose between acquiescence in oppression or perceived Jacobinism. His response was to exhort the soldiers to patience and to promise that steps would be taken to remove their grievances. For the chaplain general, this lack of redress for the soldiers was incredible; soldiers were forming associations in the camps and 'in a country not remarkable for military discipline, where this evil will end, heaven only knows'.[102] Hussey drew up a sketch of a pastoral letter which he planned to send to the chaplains of the forces. Before he published this letter, he sent a copy to Pelham to receive his approval. He received no response.

Fear of Hussey began to grow in government circles. The wisdom of his appointment as chaplain general was now under question; there was even uncertainty as to how and why the appointment had been sanctioned in the first place. Pelham believed that Hussey had behaved in such a manner as to entirely forfeit his confidence. He complained to the Duke of Portland that the chaplain general had 'thought proper to speak of government in shops and public places' concerning the treatment of Catholic soldiers and that he had shocked those of his own persuasion as much as those who were friendly to government. Hussey, Pelham informed the duke, 'was assured enough to endeavour to frighten me by alarming my private secretary' with a copy of his proposed pastoral.

Hussey was too prudent, however, to allow the copy of the pastoral out of his hands, but he did give Pelham a copy of his letter to the soldiers in general. Pelham sent on this address, 'the most inflammatory paper that bigotry could suggest,' to the duke and sought clarification on the nature of Hussey's position as chaplain general.[103] Portland replied that he had no prior knowledge of Hussey's appointment as chaplain general and that the first he had heard of it was from Hussey himself. He had informed the duke that Pius VI was about to make the appointment and had been led to believe that such an appointment from Rome was necessary in order for the chaplains of the Irish Brigade to perform their ecclesiastical function. In any case, Hussey would never have been appointed had Portland the slightest suspicion that he would make improper use of his powers. The duke comforted Pelham with the consolation that he was 'sufficiently aware of his [Hussey's] consequence to take no steps respecting him'.[104]

Edmund Burke wrote to his friend in December of the same year declaring that while he [Hussey] found himself excluded from all communications with the Castle, he could count himself lucky that he was not in Newgate. In the same letter, described by Cruise O'Brien as Burke's political testament with regard to Ireland, Hussey was warned of the dangers of holding out 'to an irritated people any hopes that we are not pretty sure of being able to realise'.[105] In the meantime, Burke advised that it would not be wise to push the issue until such time as 'the Castle shall show a greater disposition to listen to its true friends than hitherto it has done'.

Hussey's position was further complicated in December 1796 when he received notification of his appointment to the Diocese of Waterford and Lismore. That Hussey should be chosen to succeed Dr William Egan was no surprise; he was suggested for the Diocese of Cashel as early as 1791 and, in September 1796 Dr Bray wrote to Bishop Moylan of Cork recommending Hussey for Waterford adding that he 'was much esteemed by Dr Egan as the best qualified to succeed him'.[106] In Rome, Cardinal Brancadoro opposed Hussey's appointment on the grounds that he was anti-Jesuit. Fr Luke Concanen dispelled the cardinal's reservations and assured him that when 'he'd be in a higher position he'd lose such prejudices'.[107] The clergy of Waterford, too, were divided on Hussey's appointment. Bishop James Louis O'Donnel of Newfoundland wrote to Troy in January 1797, informing him of deep divisions in the diocese:

> Mr H[Thomas Hearn] expects Mr Hussey will be the bishop and hopes thereby to screw himself into the chief administration of the diocese, as he supposes he'll spend a great part of his time in London and Dublin. This I only heard from the Keating [parish priest of St John's] party who I believe justly complain against H[earn] and his adherents. I am listed with no party.[108]

In other circles, Hussey's appointment was credited to government intervention. In their resolution on the veto question in 1799, the bishops wrote that 'if ever a Catholic prelate was to be considered the virtual nominee of the Castle, Doctor Hussey himself was assuredly that individual'. If this was the case, Fitzpatrick interprets the government's action as an attempt to remove him to where it was felt he could do little harm.[109] Hussey was consecrated early in 1797 in Francis Street chapel, Dublin. The event was in stark contrast to the consecration of his predecessor, Dr Egan, who was ordained bishop by Dr Nicholas Sweetman of Ferns in a private function in the house of his brother-in-law at Taghmon, County Wexford, on Pentecost Sunday 1771.[110] Hussey also broke with recent precedent by governing his diocese from Waterford, whereas his predecessors had lived either in Carrick-on-Suir or Clonmel.

The administration's suspicion of Hussey continued to grow. Leonard McNally informed the Castle that 'many who were formerly for mild measures have joined the determined party–among these is Dr Hussey ... he will not act or appear to act with the present government, which he openly says has lost the country'. In the same letter, McNally notes that 'the public declaration of [John] Keogh's party is that there is no longer a Catholic question, but an Irish question before the nation, and that question is freedom for the nation'.[111] Hussey continued to voice his discontent with the situation in the army. In April 1797, he wrote that the incidents were so numerous in his diocese that he charged the priests to use their spiritual power to resist what he called 'this impolitic tyranny'. He told Burke that he had prepared a pastoral letter, a short one intended only as a preface to a longer one. 'I know its contents will not be acceptable to some, but I am come hither, not to flatter my enemies, but to do my duty'.[112]

Hussey's pastoral dealt with a wide spectrum of subjects, all of which aroused wrath.[113] It began with the rhetoric normally associated with the hierarchy, but very suddenly altered course, in stark contrast to the pastorals of Young, Moylan and Troy:

> In these critical and awful times, when opinions seem spreading over this island, of a novel and dangerous tendency–when the remnants of old oppressions and new principles which tend to anarchy, are struggling for victory, and which in collision may produce the ruin of religion–when a moral earthquake shakes all Europe, I felt no small affliction and alarm, upon receiving the command of the Head of the Church to preside over the Catholics of these united dioceses.[114]

It was the reference to 'the remnants of old oppression' which set the tone of the pastoral and raised such reaction. Hussey was relieved that 'no part of Ireland was more exempt from turbulence and insubordination to the laws than this district and that the memory of legal injustices and cruelties formerly practiced in this country ... is completely and happily effaced, I hope forever'.[115] This double-edged approach characterised the pastoral and gave rise to much ambiguity as the bishop continually contrasted the present and the 'forgotten' past.

Hussey warned his priests not to allow themselves to be made the instruments of the rich, who would try through them to dominate the people. 'The poor,' he reminded them, 'were always your friends. They inflexibly adhered to you ... and shared their scanty meals with you'. The rich, on the other hand, not only shut their doors against you, 'but not infrequently hunted you like wild beasts'.[116] He then instructed his priests to shun all political interference and to avoid the 'intermixing of the politics of the world with the sublime and heavenly maxims of the Catholic religion–they have not the smallest connection with each other'.[117]

If the Catholic military frequented Protestant places of worship in any of the parishes of the diocese, the priests were to teach them how 'contrary to the principles of the Catholic faith it is, externally to profess one faith and interiorly to believe another'. Such behaviour in the eyes of the world is mean, as well as odious and abominable in the sight of God.[118] The Catholic soldier ought not to be ashamed of openly professing the Catholic religion, 'the religion of Irishmen'.[119] Hussey granted the officers competence in all matters concerning the service of the King and the soldiers were duty bound to obey them. In matters regarding the service of God, however, the officers had no authority over them. He condemned abuses in the army which had alarmed the King's true friends. Such practices would Jacobinise the soldiers and, in the hour of danger, cause them to forget their duty in order to revenge their persecutors.

The bishop launched into what was perceived as an assault on the Church of Ireland, that 'small sect whom it suited to regulate its creed and form of worship according to the shape and form of government, of the limited boundaries where the sect arose, exists and dies away'. What a contrast to the Catholic religion, preached to all peoples and nations and suitable to all forms of government, monarchies or republics, aristocracies or democracies. Despotic or popular governments are not the concerns of the Catholic Church.[120] The penal laws, he argued, had made Catholics total strangers in their own land. The ruling party, 'with insolence in their looks and oppression in their hearts', had ground them down. Even the course of justice was perverted according to the prejudices and party views of the judges, while in the senate, some of the most powerful men in the land declared that they hoped to see the day when no Catholic would dare to speak to a Protestant with his hat on.[121] Yet, even in these provoking times the Catholics remained inflexibly attached to their religion and their King.

Hussey continued his discourse, noting the progress made towards dismantling the popery laws. No matter how assiduously 'a junto may raise mobs to throw obstacles against the total repeal of them, yet all their efforts must be useless'.

> The vast rock is already detached from the mountain's brow, and whoever opposed its descent and removal must be crushed by his own rash endeavours. The popery laws are on the eve of being extinguished forever and may no wicked hand ever attempt to divide this land by making religious distinctions a mask to disturb–to oppress it.[122]

The education question, too, was raised and the prelate attacked the charity schools of Waterford where, as he had explained to Burke, the established clergy wanted no catechism taught but the Protestant one. Hussey denounced these prosleytising schools and condemned the parent who would 'be so criminal as to expose his offspring to those places of education where his religious faith or morals are likely to be perverted'. He urged his priests to make their flocks aware of the honour of being accounted a member of the Catholic communion, the religion of so many kings and princes. 'Ours', he concluded, 'is a laborious but also a meritorious and honourable employment. It forms the strongest bulwark to the state, by being the best supplement to the laws which, without morals, are in vain.'[123]

Reaction to Hussey's pastoral was immediate and virtually unanimous in its hostility. At least five pamphlets appeared, all centred on the question of Hussey's liberality and the wisdom of reviving memories of past woes.[124] The purpose of the pastoral appeared questionable. Its contradictions were immediately visible, while 'the industry with which it was circulated in the metropolis evinces views different from its avowed design'.[125] The extent of interest in the pastoral may be inferred from the fact that it ran to seven editions: as one critic remarked, the pastoral became the 'talk of Dublin and was circulated freely all over the city'.[126] It was a publication of an 'extraordinary nature ... an unseasonable and very intemperate production'.[127] At very best it was a 'saucy contemptuous challenge–daring us to enter anew ... the rancorous field of controversy'.[128]

While 'breathing apparent professions of loyalty', Dr Brittle, a Castleknock clergyman, accused Hussey of dragging forward 'the remnants of old oppression in order to distract his own clergy and madden the populace'.[129] How, at such a critical point, could a Catholic bishop 'violently tear open the old rankling wounds of past centuries ... setting afloat the boiling passions of the uneasy mind ... blowing up the dying embers of discontent and kindling afresh ... the unhallowed flame of old animosity and disaffection towards their Protestant brethren?'[130] Memories of the 'mangled carcasses of the French clergy' were, surely, ample warning to 'cool the headlong ardour of an intemperate zealot?'[131] How different was Bishop Moylan, the pamphleteer asked, who, when faced with danger at his door, did not waver one instant between French equality and the happiness of the country?[132]

The pastoral's contradictions were obvious. Its call to the clergy to avoid political interference was hardly credible, coming from one who bustled in politics throughout his life. Hussey's personal wealth undermined his admonitions to the priests to separate themselves from the rich. Unique among the hierarchy, Hussey was able to live independent of his diocese; he refused the £500 per annum due to him as bishop. In the same way, he had earlier refused a salary of £100 as president of Maynooth. His instructions were, therefore, seen as ungenerous and impolitic, an attempt to 'kindle distinctions between the poor and the rich, and instructing the unthinking and untaught that the latter are their oppressors, and thus opening wide the door of democratic rage and separation'.[133] His reference to the Anglicans as an insignificant, small sect met with a similar reaction, especially at a time when 'the liberality of Protestant principles had nearly succeeded in restoring Catholic rights'.[134]

What were the Protestants to conclude from Hussey's pastoral? Did 'the same intolerant rancour still sour the breast of Irish Catholics'? 'Oh! Much injured Ulster', one pamphleteer concluded, 'these are the friends for whom you smart under the lash of martial law and outlawry'.[135] Political reaction to the pastoral was swift and stern. In the Irish House of Lords on 4 May 1797, Lord Dillon described Hussey's letter as the 'most gross and mischievous that could be penned'. It was the most inflammatory pamphlet which he ever had read and he concluded by asking what could be expected from the poor 'so long as they are made the dupes of such men as these'.[136]

The conservative firebrand Patrick Duigenan echoed Dillon's views that the pastoral tended to 'encourage the evil dispositions of the day'. He described it as 'seditious a publication as any which has appeared in modern times, provoking the Irish Romanists to insurrection'.[137] He later condemned how 'the pious Bishop most anxiously retailed every vulgar tradition of oppressive conduct during the existence of the popery code–misrepresenting everything that was true and inflaming everything that was false'.[138] Thomas Lewis O'Beirne reacted strongly to Hussey's advocacy of segregated education and declared that 'the worst enemies of Ireland could not devise a scheme more effectually calculated to keep this description of the King's subjects a distinct people forever, and to maintain eternal enmity and hatred between them and the Protestant body'.[139] He was convinced that Hussey wished to erect a spiritual wall to replace civil barriers which were being dismantled.

The response of the Catholic hierarchy was equally united in its criticism of their confrère.[140] In a letter to Bray in April 1797, Troy said of the pastoral that 'there is too much vinegar in it, not sufficiently tempered with oil'. The reference to the Lord Lieutenant and the government as a faction or junto was too pointed. 'Terms less strong and more conciliatory would be equally effectual without giving offense', he concluded.[141] Troy believed that 'moderate Catholics thought it harsh and unreasonable, calculated to irritate, to open and not to close the wounds of party'.[142] The pastoral had been republished in Dublin where, according to Troy, it 'made a great noise' and gave particular offence at the Castle. Several copies had been sent to Thomas Pelham by Protestant clergy and laity in Waterford with bitter complaints of the disturbance it had caused.

The archbishop appealed to Thomas Bray to talk with Hussey in an effort to discourage further indiscretions.[143] Writing to Luke Concanen in Rome, Troy referred to Hussey's instruction as an 'unpastoral letter'.[144] The bishops were extremely aware of the adverse Castle reaction and believed Hussey had made himself 'odious and disagreeable by his rash and fatal pastoral'.[145] In May 1797, Troy met with Pelham. Reporting on the meeting to Bishop Plunket, he wrote:

Before I could say anything more on this subject he fortunately turned the conversation to Dr Hussey, asking me if he had not gone to England? On my answering 'yes', he said that his pastoral letter was very intemperate and inflammatory, little expected from any Catholic pastor, and especially from one circumstanced as Dr Hussey is, in these times of public agitation, where every honest man should allay the ferment instead of opening the sores. I assured him that it was published without the approbation or knowledge of any of our prelates and that we considered it as unseasonable and reprehensible in its tendency. "I thought so", said he, "but am glad to hear it from you, as the contrary was surmised". He concluded on the subject by saying "Hussey is very warm, he has acted without reflection".[146]

Edmund Burke also became alarmed by the reaction to his friend's pastoral. Writing to Hussey, he declared that 'from the moment that the government who employed you betrayed you, they determined at the same time to destroy you'. The bishop had come to an open issue with them and 'they are not people to stop short in their course' he warned.[147] Burke agreed that what Hussey had done was 'perfectly agreeable to your duty as a Catholic bishop and a man of honour and spirit'. Whether the bishop's actions were prudent in 'an enslaved country', was a different question. Hussey derived great consolation from Burke's support and declared that 'such a man's praise more than overbalanced the abuse which the Irish Parliament of —— memory endeavoured to bespatter me'.[148]

Hussey's own feelings about the controversy are best described in his letter to Bishop Moylan of Cork. Thanking the bishop for his 'candid and friendly remarks' concerning his pastoral letter, Hussey expressed surprise, however, that Moylan replied as if the pastoral had touched on politics. The remainder of the letter is most revealing;

> Surely the religious grievances we have cruelly laboured under and under a part of which we still labour ... are not politick? If they said that I rip up sores already healed; no man knows better than yourself they are not healed. You remember among many other instances the cruel whipping of the soldiers of the Sligo militia a few days ago, of which you complained to the Lord Lieutenant. I infer from the noise which the pastoral letter has made, the low idea which they form of the Catholics of the country when they think it imprudent of them to complain of their religious grievances.

Your own pastoral letter, which in the hour of danger justly received the praise of Protestants of both Kingdoms—what has it produced? A declaration from the government that Catholics of Ireland should wear the remaining chains to the end of the world! What I have written does not contain, I am persuaded, a word against the laws; and if I suffer any illegal persecution—why, I am not the first Catholic who suffered it; but of this they may be assured—that I shall not suffer silently.[149]

Hussey concluded that his private affairs called him to London, but he would not leave Ireland till 'this squall is over'.

It is difficult to assess the local effects of the pastoral. To what extent the 'incendiary' aroused feelings of disaffection is unclear, but many of the Castle's correspondents attributed the disturbed state of Waterford to Hussey. Francis Higgins reported that the bishop had taken a 'very insidious part', and that in every company he railed against Lord Camden's administration and had personally abused Pelham.[150] Caesar Colclough reported in May 1797 that Wexford and the neighbouring parts of Kilkenny and Carlow were not to be depended on as 'the Ulster address [of the United Irishmen] and Dr Hussey's pastoral letter have been circulated there and it is reported everywhere that the French are coming as friends of the poor'.[151] In some cases, however, there were poor people who resented Hussey's stance, believing that it would spoil their chances of employment in Protestant households.

Sir Richard Musgrave informed the Castle that Waterford, 'this once peaceable county, escaped the contagion of these abominable principles for four years until Dr Hussey influenced the inhabitants ... by his pastoral and the sermons he preached'. From that time on, 'the lower class of people had been much agitated', and he was convinced that Hussey was employed by Fox and Grey as 'an engine to excite sedition in this kingdom'.[152] Later in 1797, the paranoid Musgrave informed Pelham that the disturbances in the county were part of a popish plot. Hussey, he believed, was behind the plot and Musgrave requested permission to intercept the bishop's correspondence with his vicar general, Thomas Hearn. He was certain that important discoveries could be made, were the letters intercepted at Waterford.[153]

In the aftermath of the controversy, it was inevitable that Hussey would come under pressure to relinquish his presidency of the Royal College. Prompted by the Castle, some of the trustees of the College tried to persuade him to resign in May 1797, but he refused. He was still president at the end of the year, but Troy wrote to Archbishop Bray of Cashel that 'he may be prevailed upon to resign'. Should diplomatic approaches fail, Troy believed he

Fig. 13 Thomas Hussey, Bishop of Waterford & Lismore 1797-1803 (N.G.I.)

could be forced to step down, since 'the duties of president and bishop were incompatible'.[154] In the following February, the Commons debate on the grant to Maynooth was a cause of great episcopal embarrassment. In a long and heated speech, Patrick Duigenan opposed the level of funding proposed for the college and abused its president, whom he described as 'a precious importation of Lord Fitzwilliam' but that 'by some fatality' Hussey had been left behind when Fitzwilliam 'and his schemes were exported'. The bishop's influence over the students at Maynooth could only be for the worse; now the country was about to become prey to priests 'turned loose' from the college. All of these, Duigenan was convinced, had 'their brains heated with the horrible opinions of Dr Hussey their founder'.[155] Eventually Hussey was dismissed as president by the trustees of Maynooth for non-residence. Amongst the bishops there was a feeling that he should also resign the diocese of Waterford & Lismore.

In 1798 Hussey requested a coadjutor, but this was refused in Rome. Luke Concanen wrote to Troy in January 1799 that he had seen a letter to Rome in which Drs Bray, Moylan, Dillon and Sughrue 'complain of his [Hussey's] non-residence, his pastoral letter and conclude requesting no coadjutor be given him, that he may renounce and be appointed Archbishop *in partibus'*.[156] Camden shared these views and suggested to the Duke of Portland that he recommend the Pope to 'recall so dangerous a man from this kingdom'.[157] In 1801, Hussey once again requested a coadjutor and suggested Dr J. B. Walsh, rector of the Irish College, Paris. This application was also refused on the grounds that Dr Walsh was regarded in London as unsuitable, due to his pro-French sentiments.[158]

Hussey had, in fact, left Ireland shortly after the publication of his pastoral and did not return until late in 1802, a few months before his death. During this period of absence, he busied himself in many enterprises, among them being his attempts to restore the Irish College in Paris which had been closed for nine years. It was also rumoured that he was assisting Cardinal Gonsalvi in the negotiations of the concordat with Napoleon![159] Despite his absence, however, the bishop maintained his interest in the affairs of the Church in Waterford, governing his diocese through Thomas Hearn.[160]

In retrospect, Hussey regretted his indiscreet pastoral. In a revealing, letter to J. B. Clinch, professor of rhetoric at Maynooth, he referred to it as 'a foolish milk and water letter'. This letter, most likely written in early 1799, reflects his continued interest in Irish affairs. Once again, he refers to the battle between the 'remnants of old oppression' and 'new opinions that lead to anarchy'.[161] However, in a letter written to Bishop Carroll of Baltimore in September 1799,

Hussey railed against the ultras and their attacks upon his pastoral, referring to their 'vomiting ... malice in such pitiful obloquy and misrepresentations'. Nevertheless, as this was 'natural in that vile and degraded country', it could give him no pain. Of more importance was the 'most unbounded elogy [sic]' of 'the friend of America–of mankind–Edmund Burke'. Significantly, Hussey informed Carroll that the radicals had expressed equal hostility to his pastoral; 'thus both sides became my enemies. God forbid that I should look for a friend in either party'.[162] Yet in spite of the treatment Hussey had received at the hands of the government, despite the criticism and questioning of his loyal principles in all quarters, he confessed to Clinch that his 'affections for his native land were not so effaced as to enable him to say with our countryman after he had gone to bed 'arrah, let the house burn away; what do I care who am only a lodger?'[163]

Hussey returned to Ireland in 1803 and died suddenly at Tramore on 11 July, having taken a fit while swimming there.[164] Even in death he managed to arouse strong feelings and his funeral became the scene of violent protest. As his remains were being brought to Waterford for burial, the proceedings were interrupted by a group of drunken soldiers returning from an Orange meeting who tried to fling his coffin into the Suir. Thomas Hearn later described to Lord Donoughmore how this mob had uttered 'the most abusive threats to cut up his remains and his friends'.[165] The riot was only quelled with the arrival of the local militia who recovered the remains and escorted the funeral on its way.[166]

Hussey was certainly no radical and his consignment to the ranks of the instigators of the 1798 rebellion is indefensible. Even the ambivalence of modern historiography is difficult to explain, considering the wealth of sources available, the most important of which is certainly the bishop's correspondence with Edmund Burke. It was this friendship which proved the greatest influence upon the bishop. Hussey has become the victim of simplification, while the odd passing reference to him reflects the sheer dearth of solid research on the role of the Catholic Church and the 1798 rebellion. Hussey was no incendiary, nor was his voice that 'of a lone, bold, slightly aristocratic man of the world'.[167] He was very much in the mould of the 'prince bishop' and in many ways he had more in common with some of the Anglican bishops than his own Roman Catholic confrères. He was essentially conservative; his views on education, obedience to the laws and his unswerving conviction of priestly competence to regulate the lives of their flocks reflect this.

The division that historiography has created between him and the remainder of the Catholic bishops is artificial. Their correspondence reflects this clearly, nowhere more so than in the candid admission of Dr Carroll of Baltimore that he had read the pastoral with 'pleasure and approbation', until he heard it was 'censured by the most intelligent'.[168] If there was disagreement, it was on the question of prudence rather than on the content of Hussey's pastoral. It is in this respect, however, that the key to understanding Hussey's position is to be found. His English and continental experience had given him a confidence which enabled him to voice his opposition to the penal laws in the strongest terms, seeking redress as a right rather than as a reward to be sought with deference. The scope of his concerns, also set him apart from his fellow bishops and these reflected his wide political interests. It is this fact which separates Hussey from the remainder of the bishops, placing him more in line with the aggressive Catholic hierarchy of the nineteenth century than with the quiescent pastors labouring under the penal laws.

Nevertheless, the Hussey affair did affect the benign relationship the bishops had enjoyed with the Castle since the beginning of the Camden administration. The loyal reputation of the prelates had been sullied by the indiscretion of one of their number and Castle paranoia reached such levels that even Troy, the steady loyalist, became the object of suspicion. Edmund Burke reported in May 1797 that the Castle runners in London were reporting that the Archbishop of Dublin had taken the United Irish oath, while almost a year later Camden still entertained suspicions about the his integrity.[169] The taint of suspicion goaded Troy into extreme exhibitions of loyalty, to the point of allowing the Castle 'improve or alter' declarations of the hierarchy's loyalty, so long as the main point was preserved, 'the exculpation of the Roman Catholic prelates'.[170]

The affair had strengthened the hand of the Castle and allowed the administration to put the bishops under pressure. Indeed, their vulnerability was acknowledged by Francis Higgins who advised Edward Cooke to request Troy to read government proclamations from the city's pulpits, a task he was confident the beleaguered bishop could not afford to refuse.[171] It was this atmosphere which prevailed in the months leading up to the final outbreak of rebellion in 1798; in this tainted air of suspicion, the bishops studiously avoided any criticism of the administration, despite their obvious policy of repression, and co-operated in the Castle game.

CHAPTER SIX

Priests, People and Popular Politicisation 1795-1798

C atholic frustration in the aftermath of the Fitzwilliam episode quickly boiled over to anger as it became obvious that the race for the Catholics was over and that the 'dark villains of the Ascendancy' intended them to be the 'hewers of wood and drawers of water in eternum'.[1] The events of the previous three years, however, had greatly altered the temper of the Catholics, and the radical politics of the Committee had given them a new confidence and resilience. The heated reaction to the Kenmare secession, the excitement of the Convention, the revolution of 1793 and the Fitzwilliam crisis had all served as a Catholic political apprenticeship: now, with entry to parliament firmly closed in their face, out-of-door politics became increasingly inviting.

I

Tone identified this change in 1794, outlining for the French government the transformation which had taken place in Ireland, particularly amongst the Catholics, who had 'within these two years received a great degree of information and manifested a proportionate degree of discontent'.[2] Sources of dissatisfaction were in no short supply, but the depth to which political awareness had filtered down through Irish society reflected the impact of the French Revolution, at home and abroad. Ireland had witnessed an unprecedented period of politicisation. The propaganda of the radicals, with its consciously popular appeal, satisfied a desire for information which, in turn, heightened the level of political awareness.[3]

The United Irishmen brought this political evangelisation to a fine art. In September 1795, Leonard McNally attributed the 'revolution in the Catholic mind' to their publications and addresses, 'written to the passions and feelings of the multitude', which 'prepared the way for Paine's politics and theology'.

In Cork, he believed, Paine's works were read by every schoolboy and 'in most houses they now supply the place of the psalter and prayer book'.[4] Public newspaper readings from the papers also became a feature throughout the country. Very often the chapel gate was the chosen venue for these readings and their effectiveness is reflected in the worried reports reaching the Castle. In May 1797 Pelham received the following account from Baltinglass, County Wicklow:

> our town is overrun with disorder by the means of a republic newspaper now done in Carlow, where every Sunday two fellows come after Mass is over and read what they please to the ignorant country people so we are afraid to stir the day after.[5]

In late 1797 there were frequent reports of 'nocturnal assemblies of ruffians' near College Green, Dublin on the nights of publication of the *Press* and by early January 1798 the newspapers had brought such disturbances to the streets that hawkers were forbidden from selling them on Sundays under threat of being taken to the Bridewell.[6] The loyal prints and pamphleteers rounded on the radical newspapers, particularly on the *Northern Star* and later the *Press*. Charles Moore, rector of Moira, published a long reflection on the state of the country in the aftermath of the rebellion in 1798, and devoted considerable attention to the influence of the press.[7] Moore's contempt is plain and he parodied the popular politicisation of the country, describing the village shopkeeper with the newspaper spread across his counter:

> fearfully wise he shakes his empty head,
> and deals out empires as he deals his thread,
> His useless scales are in the corner flung,
> And Europe's balance hangs upon his tongue.

He condemned the wide availability of the papers, which were distributed gratis in many places, and the levels to which the *Press* and *Northern Star* had used 'every species of misrepresentation and sophistry to vilify the government, to extend the union [of Catholic and Presbyterian], to shake the connection with Great Britain and induce the people to look for French assistance'. Robert Day, chairman of the Dublin Grand Jury, raised the question of the newspapers at the quarter sessions in January 1798. In a fierce attack he condemned the 'prostitution of the press' as the most deadly 'of all the calamities inflicted by this French faction'. The press had hitherto been the 'bulwark of our liberties', but it was now reduced to a 'vehicle of defamation, infidelity and a sewer of everything vile, abominable and loathsome in society'.[8] Similarly, in the aftermath of the rebellion, the report of the Secret Committee singled out the effect of the newspapers for criticism. They had, it claimed, been used by the United Irishmen to the fullest extent to excite the people and to convert local prejudice into support for their purpose.[9]

Pubs proved a favoured spot for the public reading of newspapers: one loyal pamphleteer declared that every porter house 'could boast a set of statesmen who, without the aid of education or experience, conceived themselves competent in every branch of legislative occupation'.[10] Pubs were frequently the location for meetings of the many book clubs which sprung up in the 1780s and 1790s. In Antrim and Down alone, Adams has identified sixteen such clubs in the 1790s; often these clubs provided a pretext for more radical meetings.[11] Captain MacNevin reported from Carrickfergus that the clubs were merely a cover for the United Irishmen and in March 1796 the *Dublin Journal* described them as 'in general only a sort of preparatory school to the fraternity of Defenders'.[12] In these clubs the members were regaled on a diet of Paine and other radical pamphlets. Prints were dispersed throughout the country with great industry by pedlars and dealers; Lord Ely reported the case of a carman in Enniscorthy who carried seditious papers from Dublin to Wexford and who 'harangues people in public houses against the government'.[13] Frequently, however, Catholic priests were described as the principal carriers of radical material; believing this to be the case, a search of the desks of Father Boyce, parish priest of Celbridge and of Father Andrew Ennis, parish priest of Maynooth, was ordered by the authorities, apparently in late 1797, in an unsuccessful effort to find incriminating correspondence between Dublin and Kildare.[14]

The United Irishmen also found a surrogate for their meetings in the large number of debating societies and political clubs which were to be found in Dublin. The Convention Act of 1793 made overt political activity impossible and attention was now focused on these societies and traditional associations in the city, which the radicals transformed to their purpose.[15] These clubs included the Friendly Society of Pill Lane, the Jacobin Club, the Association of Eating and Drinking Democratic Citizens, but most is known about the Telegraphic and Philanthropic societies because of the level of attention they received in the Defender trials of 1795-6. Modelled upon the *sociétés populaires* of revolutionary France, these clubs and societies performed a similar function in Dublin's political underground.[16] Robert Day warned the Dublin Grand Jury in January 1797 that treason within the city was 'kept up to delirium, and the

The PATRICIAN SOCIETY
Meet every Monday Evening, at No. 32,
Nicholas-ftreet, at 8 o'Clock.

S I R;

Should you be difpofed to devote an Hour to Relaxation
on the above Evenings, you are folicited to honor this Society
with a Preference; thus, by combining Social·Harmony with
Chriftian Charity, this ancient, laudable, and national Eftablifh-
ment will be promoted, and while we gaily fing over the jovial
Bowl, we enjoy the pleafing Senfation of wiping the Tear of
Sorrow from the Cheek of Orphan Mifery, and lay a Foundation for the future Greatnefs and Happinefs of our Country, by
extending the Benefits of Inftruction to the rifing Generation.
    OEconomy will be obferved, and the Bill called regularly at
half paft Ten.

                              WILLIAM COLE, Prefident.

☞ An extraordinary Meeting is expected on Monday May 4, 1801,
to receive the Report of the Committee appointed to audit the Accounts
of the late Prefident, a general Report on the State of the Charity will
alfo be made.

            Printed at BYRN's cheap Printing-Qffice, 3t, Effex-ftreet,

Fig. 14 Printed notice of Patrician meeting, Dublin 1801 (Nat. Archives)

infection diffused, by the committees and corresponding associations, acting
by these cheap inflammatory publications and by secret missionaries'.[17]

In a similar way, radicals turned their attention to the Church and took
advantage of the many prosletising opportunities offered by its structures. The
chapel enjoyed a unique position in Irish society and very often it was the
recognised meeting place or focal point in the village. In many areas the chapel
was the only substantial public building available to the people and it
invariably served the functions of church, school and meeting place.[18] In the
1790s the United Irishmen harnessed the great potential of the Church, which
had been illustrated so forcibly in the electioneering organised by the Catholic
Committee in the run up to the Convention.

Chapel meetings were a constant feature of both urban and rural radicalism
in the 1790s, and the level of reports reaching the Castle reflects the anxiety
which the meetings generated. In July 1796 Leonard McNally claimed that the
Defenders had originated in these parochial meetings, but his reports were
extremely vague, revealing little or nothing of a specific nature, except that a
meeting had taken place.[19] The Francis Street meetings, attended by as many
as three thousand on occasion, had always attracted a great deal of attention
because of its strategic location in the city. Francis Higgins reported regularly

on these meetings, many of which were attended by leading United Irishmen.

He reported Edward Lewins who, he claimed, had been educated for the priesthood, haranguing against the government in the chapel in January 1796. Six months later he informed the Castle of numerous meetings held in the vestry 'for the purpose of instituting a Roman Catholic Magdalen asylum'.[20] These meetings were attended by John Keogh, Hugh Hamill, McDonnell and all the Conventionists, the leaders of the United Irishmen, together with the clergy who had 'united with them'.[21] On another occasion, he reported that the charity societies were composed of United Irishmen and that they were formed with no intention other than to carry out their sedition.[22]

The large chapel congregations also provided the radicals with an opportunity to disseminate their propaganda; broadsheets were frequently pasted to chapel doors and handbills were often passed out among the Mass goers. Reports of these handbills reached the Castle from all over Ireland. Sir William Godfrey became alarmed at the disturbed state of Kerry in January 1797 and reported his troops removing seditious papers from Listoy chapel door. Again, Edward Newenham sent a copy of a long address taken from the door of the chapel at Nenagh, County Tipperary, which may reflect the United Irish use of the 'Orange bogey' amongst the Catholics. The address 'to the poor unhappy papists', contained a supposed Orange oath drawn up by the same party, containing the toast 'that the skins of the papists of Ireland may be drumheads to the yeomanry'.[23] Similar notices were placed on the doors of Protestant churches and in March 1798 the *Dublin Journal* printed one of them, allegedly found on the door of St Mary's Church Dublin which, it claimed, illustrated 'the various means used by the United Irishmen to irritate [the Catholics] ... and the Protestants against each other:

> Liberty–Erin go Braugh!
> You Protestant hereticks take notice, that Mass
> will commence in this Church by the first of May
> next. Your blood shall flow and your souls sent to
> Hell, to the devil your grandfather.[24]

No doubt alerted by John Sweetman's prominent role in fundraising for the new chapel in Clarendon Street, in April 1797 Francis Higgins, reported on a body called 'the brotherhood' which was attached to Stephen Street chapel. The group was made up of three hundred members who had assisted the Carmelites in building their new church in Clarendon Street; Higgins was convinced that 'most of the body are sworn United Irishmen'. An attempt had been made to swear one member of the confraternity and he sought the advice of the priest, only to be told 'we will not advise you, act as you think proper, we shall only say taking any oath except which a court of justice compels is unlawful, but do as you please'. Higgins recommended Cooke to approach Troy about the matter, but commented that 'Doctor Troy can be particular, you need not doubt, which shows you that the priests are not averse to the designs of the present day'.[25]

From Rush in North Dublin, Thomas Roche warned Cooke of similar meetings, which supposedly met for religious purposes but 'too frequently to disseminate their traitorous principles and to form plans for outrage'. Roche believed that the priests had formed the societies for honourable motives, but again suggested that Troy be requested to discontinue such meetings.[26] From Edenderry, Mrs Brownrigg, wife of the Marquis of Downshire's land agent, pleaded leniency for a prisoner named Kennedy, convicted at the Athy assizes for an attack on the Carberry Charter school, and declared that:

> he became a great enthusiast in a popish mania that is of late spreading itself among the lower classes in this part of the kingdom, particularly in the Defenders called the Rosary or scapular of the Blessed Lady.[27]

The rector of Lackan, James Little, in his diary recording events in Mayo during the French invasion, pointed to the use made of scapulars and confraternities by the radicals in mobilising the people; 'after undergoing the cookery of scapularism' he declared, the people were allured to feast upon 'the dish of atheistical libertinism'.[28] Certainly, United Irish infiltration of the confraternities may have been exaggerated, particularly in the anti-Catholic paranoia which gripped the country in the wake of Thomas Hussey's pastoral, but there was a definite overlap in membership and the democratic nature of the societies is also evident. This is reflected in a number of the papers seized on suspects in Dublin in the late 1790s. In June 1797 seditious papers were found on William Green by J. C. Beresford: along with 'A new song composed on board H.M. fleet', there was also a notice to attend the Grand Carmelite Fraternity in Ash Street chapel.[29]

Papers found on Father Corcoran of Church Street included a notice to attend a meeting in O'Brien's of Cork Street, which was marked 'election night'.[30] Amongst Dr Troy's papers there is an account of a meeting of a finance committee at Townsend Street Chapel, signed by Richard Passmore, whose name frequently appears amongst lists of United Irish members.[31] In the aftermath of the rebellion suspicion lingered concerning the confraternities, which Caesar Colclough believed had been very destructive in Wexford. In the west, the Archbishop of Tuam, in response to claims of the kind made by James Little, published a pastoral against scapulars which he believed had become not only objects of superstition, but had been used as banners by the rebels.[32]

Religious processions and funerals also became transformed into United Irish rallies and displays. The first symptoms of this were seen at the funeral of a freemason in Dungannon in November 1796. The funeral procession was joined by several lodges and eventually was broken up by the dragoons.[33] The first of the Dublin United Irish funerals took place in April 1797 when five thousand, including the 'Marats of Pill Lane', marched in procession behind the remains of Edward Dunn.[34] Such political funerals became commonplace in the city and they occasioned great alarm. Sir Henry Echlin reported one such occasion in Balbriggan:

> As I was returning here in the stage yesterday, I was much surprised at seeing at least 200 men on horseback, almost all cropped pass by me. I found they were going to Lusk to the funeral of a man called Wade, a tanner from Dublin. I have seldom seen such an assemblage.[35]

There were also incidents of mock funerals. At the trial of Richard Dry in Cork in September 1797, Charles Callanan testified that when a man named Fisher had shown him a sign and asked if he would go to a funeral, he had demanded to know whether it was 'a real one'. When the prosecution enquired why he had asked this question, Callanan replied, 'because I heard there was a coffin filled with stones to be buried'.[36]

The *Morning Post* reported the Castle's alarm at these funerals with no small degree of amusement, and wondered if the government would follow up its proclamation relating to funerals with rules governing the permissible attendances at weddings and christenings. The paper even suggested that, in an effort to prevent further assemblies, babies at baptism ought to be called on to renounce not only the devil, but also 'the United Irishmen and all their works'.[37] In a similar vein, the *Northern Star*, reporting on the repressive regulations concerning funerals, declared that 'in future the people must literally follow the injunction of our Saviour and let the dead bury the dead'.[38] However, these high-profile funerals attracted adverse attention from the Castle authorities and much of the cover which the confraternities and clubs had provided for the United Irishmen was now gone. Francis Higgins reported bitterness within the Society, with some blaming the Dublin Committee for the funerals and meetings in ale houses, which alerted government 'finding them under their eye'.[39] In a similar admission, another United Irishman declared, 'it was them damn funerals which opened the government's eyes'.[40]

There was also a fear in government circles that the level to which the clergy depended on the people for support was bound to expose them to contagion. It was this consideration which had made a state provision for the clergy seem so attractive to the administration throughout the 1790s, believing that a financially independent clergy would be much more effective in calling their flocks to a sense of duty. Commenting on this dependence Wakefield later noted that:

> it is necessary for them, from their abject condition, to flatter the weakness and humour the prejudices of the people, over whom they endeavour to acquire all possible influence; but I have been assured by many Roman Catholic gentlemen that, notwithstanding these endeavours, the effect is entirely reversed; over them the people have obtained a complete political ascendancy, from their daily food depending on their parishioners, their conduct must be conformable to their opinions.[41]

This same dependence was referred to by Bishop Stock and in many cases the radicals exploited the position of the clergy, threatening them with a revival of the Whiteboy tactics of withholding dues and collections unless they lent their support to the cause. Apart from mere financial necessity, however, the social links between priest and people induced certain pressures.[42] In many cases the younger curates lodged with local families where they were exposed to the politicisation which had gripped the country; Father John Murphy's biographer attributes the priest's radical formation to the influence of the United Irishman, Tom Donovan, with whom he lodged at Boolavogue.[43]

On his tour of Ireland, 1796-7, de la Tocnaye noted that the priests, pastors and curates were invited to 'dinners without end': in their submission of 1801, the bishops admitted that the priests 'in general dine nearly half the year in private families'.[44] One loyal pamphleteer questioned the reliability of the clergy and wondered if they could be depended on to speak candidly to those upon whom they depended for their subsistence. Were they in a position to urge loyalty to the government, or did they 'conform themselves to the manners of the class of people with whom they chiefly converse, and accompany them to the ale house and dram shop?'[45]

II

From the appearance of the first symptoms of the 'French disease' in Ireland, the hierarchy had taken every measure available to them to inoculate their flock and to establish beyond all doubt the loyal credentials of the Catholic Church. Yet, despite their exertions it was impossible to deflect suggestions that the lower clergy were not only involved in the radical conspiracy, but that they were to a great degree responsible for its direction. Within the hierarchy it may have been possible to sustain a united front amongst their thirty members, but loyalty proved much more difficult to maintain amongst the eighteen hundred priests in the country. Ever since the intense political activity of the Catholic Convention, the clergy had been regarded by loyalists with a considerable deal of suspicion. Escalating Defender violence in early 1796 marked the beginning of sustained attempts to implicate the clergy in the disaffection sweeping the country.

To many observers, a transformation had overtaken the clergy; William MacNeven referred to this in the aftermath of the rebellion, in his examination before the Secret Committee of the House of Lords. The priests had, he believed, ceased to be alarmed by stories of French irreligion and had 'adopted the principles of the people on whom they are dependent'. He described the priests as 'generally good republicans' who had 'rendered great service by propagating with a discreet zeal the system of the union'.[46] The anti-Catholic Leonard McNally echoed these sentiments and informed John Pollock in July 1796 that he had become convinced of what he had always suspected, that 'the original instigators' and the 'medium of dissention' had been the Catholic clergy, but that they had concealed their true identity from those they led.[47]

For some time, the hierarchy had been concerned at the alarming level of support for French principles amongst the clergy, particularly amongst those who had recently returned from the continent. This anxiety was reflected in their private correspondence; in 1794 Bishop Lawrence Nihell of Kilmacduagh and Kilfenora expressed his dissatisfaction that many of the young priests had brought from France a 'strong tincture of that destructive republican spirit'. In their many submissions to the government prior to the foundation of Maynooth, the bishops had regularly referred to this fact.[48] In the aftermath of the rebellion, Leonard McNally claimed that priests and country schoolmasters had been the principal proponents of French politics; he also believed that the most active were fugitive priests and students returning from France.[49]

Another anti-Catholic, Edward Newenham lamented the spread of 'the fanatical rage of equality' in a correspondence the wife of General Montgomery of Quebec in 1794, attributing it to priests who the people obey 'with such superstition that they are the most abject slaves to them'.[50] In August 1796, John Troy received a complaint from Captain Richard Doyle of Ballymore Eustace in County Kildare that the parish priest there, Michael Devoy, had been preaching 'French philosophy asserting that all men are born equal'. The captain, who had been a member of the Catholic Convention, could not accept this teaching since 'he had been born a gentleman'.[51] In the wake of the abortive French invasion in December 1796, reports concerning the clergy became more frequent, and Bishop Hussey's pastoral had a similar effect.

Suspicion peaked in May 1797 as numerous reports of clerical activity reached the Castle. McNally declared that the priests were 'missionaries to a man among the people' and that they were preaching that 'the deliverance of their country from English influence is a religious duty'. Francis Higgins reported that the priests in Munster and Connaught were preaching levelling principles and that they,

> have told their congregations in their sermons that the overgrown rich, who never lived in the country, but drew away all its property were protected from contributing to the work of the country, but the poor of the kingdom in their brogues and even their salt was ordered to pay high rate of tax, to save the rich.

These sermons, he declared, had made 'wonderful impressions and alterations' on the minds of both the farmers and peasantry; from Limerick, Newenham expressed great concern that the people there 'led on by their clergy will be more fatal in assassination than the north'.[52] In the same month Troy met with Thomas Pelham at the Castle; they discussed Hussey's recent pastoral and the archbishop was questioned about levels of clerical membership in the United Irishmen. When asked if it was true that many priests were associated with them, Troy replied, 'I hope not and I do not believe it'. Neither did the Chief Secretary accept the exaggerated reports of clerical membership which, he believed, emanated from the United Irishmen to give them the appearance of strength. He did, however, have positive information that many priests had been sworn in different parts of the country.[53]

Much of the information reaching the Castle, however, was of questionable value to the authorities. In many cases the reports were extremely vague and from the beginning of 1797 they became increasingly bizarre. Perhaps most famous of all, William Corbet's 1796 account of the priests of Dublin, illustrates best the strength and the weakness of the information reaching the Castle. His report is the most substantial of the returns made by an informer and its detail alone is of great value in locating Dublin's priests in the 1790s. The succession lists of the Dublin diocesan clergy provide useful confirmation, but Corbet's account allows us to locate in addition the city's regular clergy, many of whom were implicated in United Irish activity.[54] His letter is worth quoting in full.[55]

15 October 1796

Sir,

I take the liberty of enclosing the list I promised, which to the best of my judgement is accurate. The delay which occurred was unavoidable from the extensive enquiries I had to make as to their principles. Of every individual I either got a personal knowledge or information from their own friends. Amongst others I got acquainted with Leonard or Chabot. He dined at my house on Monday last with his friend Hunter and drank freely. He told me the object of the people. Belfast was to make United Irishmen of the military as fast as they were put there–and that in this they were very successful. That the Limerick Militia were to a man United Irishmen, and that a Scotch regiment sent there since of the same way of thinking and that the people there would be glad how often the military were changed the better to extend their principles. He told me also of a conversation he said you had with Nelson [Samuel Neilson?] and Rowley Osborne afterwards, and how firmly they behaved.

Under the sanction of an oath of secrecy, I have felt Hunter's pulse. I told him a gentleman I did not know to be connected with government wished me to obtain information of what was going forward, and that I was sworn not to divulge his name. If I could offer him anything confidential I am of the opinion he would be useful privately, but never publicly.

W.M. Corbet.
E. Cooke, Esq.

In Dublin there are 15 chapels, of which nine are parish chapels, and 6 friaries.

1. Liffey St. Clark, parish priest, an old man of moderate principles. Gahan, Costigan, Kenny, O'Brien, the same. Conroy, McFarland, negative, Louby, a democrat.

2. Denmark St., a friary. Gibbons, prior, McMahon, Mulcail, Lynch, Traynor, Strong, democrats. Daily, Dalton (brother to the late count of that name), Farrell, Kindelan, Neterville, of moderate principles.

3. Mary's Lane. Dixon, parish priest, Mulcail, Leonard, Gilmore, moderates. Dwyer, Farrell, Cary, democrats.(the last two remarkable for their violent principles).

4. Church St. O'Brien, prior, a democrat. Two of the name of Corcoran, moderate. Caffry, negative. Leonard, Cashell, Carey, violent democrats. (The last mentioned is in the country beyond Swords superintending the farm of his cousin who fled from Defenderism.)

5. Arran Quay. Talbot, parish priest, in a mad house. Russell pro tem adm, democratically inclined. Purcell, Merrit, Dunn, Dixon, Powell, negative.

6. Bridge St. parish priest Fitzgerald, McGinnis, Quigley, Manning, Prendergast, moderate.

7. John's lane. Gahan, prior, Gahan Junr., moderates. Fannin, Boylan, negative. Kelly, Hickey, democrats.

8. James St. Doyle, parish priest, Maguire, Madden, Callan, moderate. Curgan, Tomins, Fitzimons, negative.

9. Meath St. Sherlock, parish priest, moderate, Brady, Dignam, Carberry, negative. Dunn, Kearns, democrats.

10. Ash St. Farrell, prior. Molloy, Cassan, Reynold, democratically inclined.

11. Francis St. Dr Troy, parish priest. Hamill, Callaghan, Gerrard, Wade, Byrne, Walsh, Sheridan, Ryan, moderates.

12. Stephen St. Long, prior, Oates, Ennis, moderate. Fitzpatrick, Flyn, Ward, Reilly, democratically inclined.

13. Lazer's Hill. Maurice, parish priest. Darcy, Devine, moderates, Griffin, O'Halloran, Kelly, negative. Smyth, Barret, democrats.

14. Rosemary Lane. Murphy, parish priest, in a mad house. Betagh, pro tem, O'Brien, Byrne, Dunn, moderates. Kinshelagh, Kelly, Carberry, negative. Bergin democrat.

15. Adam and Eve's. Brady, prior. O'Brien, Byrne, Conroy, Purfield, moderate. Two Morans, democrats. McMahon of Dorset St. Nunnery, moderate. Finn, parish priest of Ringsend, a democrat. Conolly, parish priest of Butterstown [Booterstown], do.

A breakdown of the information presents a tantalising pointer to the political opinion of the Dublin clergy. 'Democrats'–a universally accepted term of support for radical principles–apparently accounted for fewer than one third of the clergy, while the percentage of 'democrats' was far higher than amongst the regular clergy than amongst the diocesan priests. This pattern is reflected in many of the other reports reaching the Castle prior to May 1798, but once the actual rebellion broke out the diocesan clergy took a far more active role. Many of the 'democrats' referred to in Corbet's account feature frequently in subsequent reports to the Castle, which may indicate that they were singled out for surveillance.

	Moderate	*Negative*	*Democrat*
Secular	38	19	13
Regular	17	3	23
Totals	55	22	36

Because the heart of the United Irish organisation in Dublin lay around Church Street and Pill Lane, the informers paid a great deal of attention to the Capuchin friary there. As Jackson's foundry became transformed into a pike-making factory, the Castle ordered a search in the spring of 1797, of the roof and floor of the chapel at Church Street and St Michan's which had been 'newly repaired, perhaps for a bad purpose'.[56] Of the friars named, Father John Carey, described by Corbet as a 'violent democrat', was the subject of most government surveillance. Carey was born in County Meath in 1747, received into the Capuchins in Vassy, France and was ordained at Dol in about 1772.[57] He attended baronial meetings at Fagan's of Pill Lane and was frequently referred to in reports as a leading United Irishmen.[58] Samuel Turner's information in 1797 described Carey as a member of the 'General Executive Committee', presumably meaning the United Irish Directory.[59] Another of the friars, Fr Caffry, labelled 'negative' by Corbet, was described by Francis Higgins as 'a violent United Irishman'. Caffry acted as secretary to a baronial meeting in his own house; Higgins referred to his violent language and described how he gloried that 'the English task masters of the Old Irish will be shortly exterminated'.[60]

Corbet, a bookseller from Bridge Street, sent a further account of the priests in Church Street to the Castle, which was bizarre in its detail.[61] He provides a vignette of the divisions which must have marked many religious communities, referring to the two Corcorans there, both of moderate principles, who were much disliked by the community on account of this. In the same house were three others he describes as 'perfect firebrands'; Carey, known as Marat 'from commonality of mind', was the most inflammatory of them and the others were Cashell and Leonard. Carey had a brother a priest in St Michan's, equally zealous in the cause of sedition. Corbet reported that the brothers met annually with a party of republicans to celebrate the death of King Charles, which they marked with a symbolic calf's head swimming in claret!

Corbet referred to several societies of republicans in Church Street of which the Careys, Cashell and Leonard were all members; one society contained eighteen priests and one layman. The most important republican society was 'the Committee' which had formerly met at Vouzden's, but which now met at the White Cross Inn, Pill Lane.[62] This society was made up of about seventy members, mostly men 'of great property', and they imitated all the forms of the Jacobin clubs in France. All, including the waiter, were addressed as 'citizen' under penalty of a fine. The club was attended by Henry Jackson, Oliver Bond and the principal merchants of Church Street and Pill Lane. There were no priests admitted to the club except Fr Leonard, known as 'Chabot' after the notorious French revolutionary Capuchin, who acted as chaplain. In Lazer's Hill (Townsend Street Chapel), Father Griffin, 'negative' in 1796, and all the priests were 'completely up' while in John's Lane the Augustinian Fathers Kelly and Kenny, 'democrats,' were very active in propagating and swearing United Irishmen.[63]

The Dominicans at Denmark Street friary received similar attention. An undated Castle report contains information from Buchanan, an apothecary in Johnston's Court, that his foreman had confessed to having been first parochial and then baronial secretary to the United Irishmen who met in Denmark Street chapel. The unnamed foreman would not, however, supply Buchanan with names as this would incriminate his brother and several of the priests there.[64] Leonard McNally made an interesting revelation about Fr McMahon, who Corbet had described as a 'democrat' in 1796. McNally reported that McMahon was at the head of a party of priests who met once or twice a week at Herbert's Tavern at the Sheds in Clontarf and that Reilly, an officer who had served for many years in Germany, was frequently with them. The informer was convinced that they were all concerned with the politics of the day, but he had found it impossible to discover their real purpose due to their caution; even the waiter had refused £100 offered by Mr Vernon for information. Significantly, the *Press* reported that the publican was taken in for interroga-

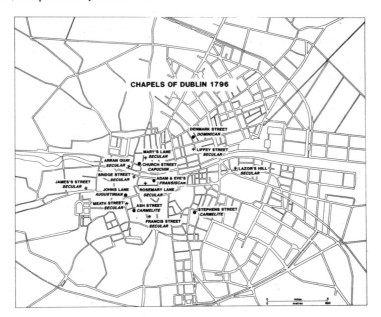

Fig. 15 Map of Dublin chapels 1796

tion in November 1797, which it claimed was for no other reason than for having his door painted green.[65]

Great suspicion surrounded meetings of priests in Dublin and the Castle runners, always anxious to discover evidence of a feared popish plot, monitored clerical gatherings throughout the city. In May 1797, when paranoia was at its height, Miles Dignam, a Grafton Street grocer and leading United Irishman, was arrested. Dignam had played an active role in the Dublin leadership and Leonard McNally reported that 'his imprisonment had alarmed many ... [and] made all cautious' and not without reason.[66] Dignam, who together with John Keogh and Henry Jackson led Edward Dunn's funeral in April 1797, was mentioned in a report to the Castle in early May when he was present at a meeting in Glasnevin; it was attended by twenty five priests, from the dioceses around Dublin, and many farmers.

Every man at this meeting was sworn and each was instructed to bring new members from their various parishes to the next meeting. The conversation at this gathering centred on a new invention, or primitive mine, described as an 'engine which, if thrown on the ground with the sharp probes out, would ruin foot and horse that might follow them unawares'. They were also to receive 'a pattern pike' from Henry Jackson, with which all those without muskets would be armed.[67] With such reports of clerical gatherings, the purpose of diocesan conferences, which had become a feature of the renewed Church in Ireland, was very often misinterpreted. In Wexford, in the wake of the rebellion, it was necessary for Bishop Caulfield to include a long section in his *Reply* explaining the nature and purpose of his monthly clerical conferences. These Ferns meetings had intentionally been held in the public house of John Rudd, a Protestant yeoman of Enniscorthy, whom the exasperated bishop declared was at least as loyal as Sir Richard Musgrave.[68]

                                         I V

Despite initial appearances, the real value of the reports reaching the Castle remained dubious. In many cases, they reflected more general anxiety than firm intelligence. The account of the clerical meeting at Glasnevin, for instance, contains remarkable detail of military preparations, but the same letter's inclusion of Grattan and Ponsonby among the United Irish Committee members reflects the desperation of the Castle informers and the sheer dearth of information in mid-1797.[69] The administration was justified in its suspicions of clerical activity amongst the United Irishmen, but the general anti-Catholic paranoia dissipated attention and the more significant of the radical priests escaped from focus. This weakness of the Castle's intelligence system is reflected in the failure to gather worthwhile evidence about Father James O'Coigley prior to his return from France at the end of 1797. Indeed it was only after O'Coigley had been identified by the Bow Street runners that the Castle authorities began to take any significant interest in the priest.

    The radical politicisation of the 1790s left few aspects of Irish life untouched and, certainly, the Catholic Church witnessed an unprecedented transformation. Gradually emerging from its endurance of the penal laws, the Church had experienced a period of rapid organisation and institutionalisation in the last decades of the eighteenth century. Despite episcopal intentions, these new structures provided the radicals of the 1790s with stems on which to graft their principles. Particularly in the wake of the 1793 Convention act, as all open fora were closed off, the radicals looked to the opportunities provided by the Church's institutions, which they expertly transformed into vehicles for their political purpose. In the frantic political activity of the period, it was impossible for the clergy to remain aloof from the concerns of the people and many of their number willingly became involved in the political process, allowing the occasions afforded by their profession to be harnessed in the cause. This was despite the strenuous exertions of the prelates. Yet, in the militant preparations which culminated in the 1798 Rebellion, only a few dozen priests sided with the United Irishmen. The vast majority adopted positions of non-involvement or of loyalty to the government. All in all, clerical participation bore little resemblance to the alarmist predictions of the Castle informers.

CHAPTER SEVEN

Rebellion

The winter of 1797-8 brought rebellion to Ireland; the level of disturbances greatly increased and chronic disaffection spread beyond Ulster into much of Leinster and parts of Munster and Connaught. Since 1796, a legislative counter attack on rebellion had been launched by the shaken authorities. Yet, despite their powerful repressive armoury and draconian military measures, the government shied away from declaring an open assault on the conspiracy. There was, however, a feeling in government circles that open conflict was not only inevitable, but necessary if the contagion was to be vented and removed once and for all.

In this sense, the administration welcomed the eventual outbreak of open rebellion, the advent of which Edward Cooke described as 'the salvation of the country'.[1] The Catholic hierarchy, on the other hand, shared none of the Castle's thirst for conflict, regarding a gradual defusion of tension as infinitely more desirable than the 'burst' the administration anticipated. Against this background of impending calamity and doom, with open rebellion in abeyance, the bishops escalated their campaign for civil obedience and spared no opportunity in attempting to recall their flock from the brink of destruction.

I

From the beginning of 1798 the bishops embarked on a full scale counter-revolutionary onslaught. For almost ten years they had waged a war of words against the 'French disease' and its associated Irish radicalism, but now there was an even greater urgency in their message and its content was increasingly blunt. It is tempting to group the various pastorals together and to view them as an unitary denunciation of the rebellion; yet, in so doing, much of their weight and original intention is lost. It is essential to view the pastorals of 1798 in a proper chronological sequence; placed in this perspective, the addresses form more of a declaration of the hierarchy's social and political philosophy than a mere ritual condemnation of rebellion.

While many of the pastorals are undated, it is possible to order them in sequence from their tenor. They reflect a great unity of purpose within the hierarchy which was, to a large degree, made possible by the foundation of the Royal College. While discussions prior to the establishment of Maynooth brought the bishops together in numbers for the first time in over a century, quarterly meetings of the trustees provided the hierarchy with a regular forum in which to discuss matters of common interest and to arrive at a common platform;[2] participation from all four provinces reflects the origins of a renewed national episcopal conference.[3] Troy's unrivalled dominance, a common fear of radicalism and this renewed sense of unity greatly facilitated the hierarchy's single-minded response to the events of 1798.

Pastoral Addresses of 1798		
Date	*Bishop*	*Diocese*
14 January	Troy	Dublin.
March	French	Elphin
6 April	Dillon	Kilmacduagh & Kilfenora.
26 April	Moylan	Cork
April	Caulfield	Ferns
22 May	Troy	Dublin [Letter to rural vicars]
27 May	Troy	Dublin.
28 May		Joint letter of Hierarchy
May/June	Coppinger	Cloyne and Ross
6 June	Young	Limerick
June	MacMahon	Killaloe
11 June		Joint letter of Munster bishops
3 July	Hussey	Waterford [Letter to Hearn]
9 July	James Lanigan	Ossory
12 July		Joint letter of Ulster bishops
Sources: Notes below		

The bishops were united in their denunciation of the disturbances in the country and the progress of the French 'contagion' in the early months of 1798, and repeatedly referred to obedience to the laws as a religious duty. In January,

Troy led a service of thanksgiving for the defeat of the Texel fleet, described by the radical *Press* as 'ecclesiastical tyranny, made a prayer' and, in a widely published address, reminded his flock of the role of divine providence in the victory.[4] All victories were ascribed to the Lord, the God of armies; although the results of war often confound human wisdom, it was 'certain that virtuous princes and governors have a special title to his protection'. King George had experienced this protection and Troy, praying that Ireland would be spared the 'din and clashing of arms', urged his flock to 'lead a quiet and peaceable life in all piety and chastity'.[5]

Edmund French, half of whose diocese of Elphin had been proclaimed as early as May 1797, echoed these sentiments in his Lenten pastoral which contained a most florid denunciation of the French, their politics and their agents.[6] No earlier pastoral of Bishop French survives and this represents a spirited entry into the anti-republican polemic, with his condemnation of the 'anti-Christian foe' who had waged war against 'nature, God, kings and society'. The revolution he described as an 'all-destroying, unnatural monster which had wrecked everything in its path, denied the existence of God, substituted a tenth day for the Sabbath, shed the blood of King, Queen and clergy, trampled everything sacred and brought devastation and horror into many parts of Europe'.

This 'hell born foe' had visited our coast but God, in his providence, had enabled our 'clement, experienced and brave viceroy' to impress the 'French Tyger [sic] with an idea of its temerity'. Turning his attention to the condition of Ireland, the bishop lamented the presence of 'men of desperate fortunes and still more desperate principles' who had lost no opportunity in spreading disaffection amongst the unthinking and unwary, the consequence of which was the sorry state to which many counties had been reduced. French concluded with a call to loyalty and a reminder that it was in gratitude to the King that 'the shrieks of your widows and the cries of your half-famished orphans do not rend the air'.

The disturbed state of the west was again singled out for attention by Bishop Edward Dillon of Kilmacduagh and Kilfenora, in a sermon at the chapel of Kilcornan on 6 April 1798.[7] There had been reports of United Irish activity in Galway and the bishop became alarmed at the level of nocturnal incursions from neighbouring Killaloe. Several houses had been robbed of arms and burned, and emissaries had been active in the different parishes of the diocese.[8] Dillon's description of the state of the diocese bears out the constant theme in episcopal pastorals that by the spring of 1798 the country was, in effect, in a state of rebellion:

There is not one amongst you, even in the most remote and obscure hamlet, who hath not heard of the oaths and associations which have entailed so many misfortunes on various districts of this kingdom. How many poor exiles from northern counties, have you seen arrive among you, sent adrift without pity or remorse by a barbarous association? How many atrocities have you heard committed by persons belonging to societies of, if possible, a still more dangerous tendency? How many villages destroyed, and districts laid waste in consequence of illegal oaths and conspiracies?

The bishop instructed his flock that obedience to the laws was a sacred precept. In an apologia for the existing social order he reminded his listeners of the benefits they enjoyed– 'while the thunder of anarchy growled at a distance, [they were] allowed quietly to partake of [their] ... frugal fare, and compose [themselves] ... to rest without dread of assassin or the midnight robber'. Dillon condemned the current tendency towards independent judgement amongst those whose education consisted of a 'few scraps taken from immoral or impious writers', yet decided and philosophised on every subject and looked forward to the arrival 'of their brother in impiety'.

The bishop outlined the destruction brought by the French throughout Europe and, in what was to become a constant theme in future pastorals, described how Pius VI had been reviled, calumniated and stripped of his property. He called his people to loyalty; to reject all clandestine oaths and associations. The sermon ended with a call to the congregation present to take an oath of allegiance but, in a reflection both of the disturbed state of the county and of diminished episcopal influence, his appeal was greeted with adamant refusal and the people poured out of the chapel.[9] Despite this reaction, the Grand Jury of Galway voted thanks to Dr Dillon for his pastoral exertions and 'excellent and truly Christian exhortation' which they were certain would have beneficial effects. Dillon replied with gratitude. However, alarmed at his reception at Kilcornan, he declared that but for the dangerous state of the region he would have toured the diocese in person preaching loyalty.[10]

Some of the western bishops questioned the wisdom of his pastoral, on account of its veiled reference to the Orange Order and terror in the north. More than one prelate from the Province of Tuam had, according to French himself, described it as 'an alarm bell, calculated to raise ferment rather than to allay it'. The bishop, however, failed to name his critics and, by the spring of 1798 it was impossible to attribute the rising temperature of the country to any one cause.[11] Much of Munster, too, had become disturbed and Cork was particularly troubled, with reports of atrocities reaching Dublin daily. Against this background, Francis Moylan issued a blistering pastoral in Cork on 26 April 1798.[12] Just as his pastoral on the occasion of the failure of the French invasion in 1796 had been widely acclaimed in loyalist circles, his effort in 1798 received equal praise. The Duke of Portland suggested to Camden that it be translated into Irish and widely circulated.[13]

Moylan's pastoral had a strong theological base; he described the address not as 'a political discussion, but a religious reflection'. Quoting heavily from scripture, he illustrated the 'evils' of illegal oaths which were not only a direct affront to God, but were guaranteed to 'draw down the vengeance of heaven'. The bishop condemned associations of 'atheistical incendiaries' and, in an exasperated reference to the widescale politicisation of the country, called on his people to return to their proper labours rather than vainly 'bewildering your minds in speculation about government, which you cannot comprehend'.

The bishop proceeded to refute levelling principles, reminding his listeners that life is a state of trial in which no rank of society is exempt from suffering. He called on his flock to gladly bear the crosses sent, adding that by loyally 'discharging the duties of our respective states', rather than engaging in 'useless murmurings' or seeking unlawful means of softening their lot, they would be amply rewarded when their fugitive life was over. Speaking of the life's difficulties, he stressed the favours enjoyed by Catholics and their improved position now that the penal laws were almost totally removed and a college had been established for the education of their future priests. Urging gratitude to the King and government and due obedience and respect for the laws, Moylan broadened the scope of his address to discuss the disturbed state of the country which had been under martial law since the end of March.

The bishop condemned the 'incendiaries and their schemes', those who approached the people in 'sheep's clothing, exaggerating, and then pretending to feel your grievances; but they are inwardly ravening wolves' who promised nothing but 'ruin and destruction'. He referred to the strict measures adopted by the military in pacifying the country, but singled out the 'known humanity' of the commander-in-chief (Sir Ralph Abercromby) and the district commander (General Sir James Stewart). Moylan praised their 'benevolent and liberal' hearts and expressed gratitude that they employed no 'unnecessary rigour' in their duty, but he did warn that the commanders might in the future be moved to use the formidable powers at their disposal. He called on people to comply with the printed notices of the military commanders, adding that by so doing their areas would be spared great misery.

Fig. 16 Francis Moylan, Bishop of Cork 1787-1815 (N.G.I.)

Bishop Moylan concluded his pastoral with a statement of his personal integrity. He claimed that he had, in the past, been threatened with violence in an effort to censure his statements, but now he found his name discredited; it was asserted that he acted under the influence of and as a pensioner of the government. Despite the absence of explicit radical condemnations of Moylan, the loyalist fanfare which greeted his 1796 pastoral, particularly the widely publicised praise it received from Camden and Robert Day, exposed him to such suggestions and MacNeven later referred to his bias in favour of the administration. The bishops were aware of these rumblings which Moylan totally rejected, adding that were it not for the impressions they had made, he would have passed them over. In the event, however, he took the opportunity to declare on behalf of the entire episcopacy that they had never sought, nor been offered, a government pension but were motivated purely with regard to their duty to their flock and attachment to King and country.[14]

Moylan refused to allow such accusations to dictate his actions and his published response to his nomination to the Committee for receiving Voluntary Contributions for the Defense of the Kingdom in February 1798 reflects his determination to defend the *status quo* :

I beg leave to request you will be so good as to assure the gentlemen of the Committee ... that I deem myself highly honoured in being named one of its members. The effectual defense of this kingdom at this perilous junction against the foreign foe is a measure truly patriotic and, therefore, must have my warm and best wishes for its success and as far as the small mite I can afford may contribute thereto, I shall most readily and cheerfully offer it, for I feel as sincere an interest in the peace and happiness of the kingdom as any other of H.M's loyal subjects. Circumstanced, however, as I am, on account of a large absence from home, and the variety of avocations, which at this present season press on me, and call for all my time and attention, I trust my attendance at the Board will be dispensed with, as it would be very inconvenient for the moment and could be in no degree necessary, to promote the laudable purpose of the meeting.[15]

II

By the spring of 1798, very considerable external influences were exerting pressure upon the Irish bishops. The position of the papal states had become critical and, on 15 February 1798, French troops under General Louis Berthier entered Rome, declared a republic and forced Pius VI to flee to Tuscany. Troy received regular correspondence from his Roman agent, and these letters recounted the horrors inflicted by the liberators on the city; Pius VI had been banished, the cardinals expelled, many friars had been exiled and the Irish colleges were closed.[16] With Rome occupied, Monsignor Charles Erskine now assumed a pivotal role in the government of the Church and, together with Cardinal Borgia, directed the affairs of Propaganda Fide.[17]

In this crisis, the Holy See became especially dependent on the British, as their war effort offered the only possible chance of salvation. The 1790s brought about a curious turn in relations between Britain and the Holy See; links were forged between the two courts, Prince Augustus visited Rome, the Cardinal Duke of York received a royal pension, and the Catholic Church and Britain became unlikely bedfellows in their common battle against French republicanism.[18] Throughout the decade, *Propaganda* had written to the Irish bishops urging complete loyalty and obedience but now, in the moment of dire crisis, Erskine delivered the most explicit instructions to date to Archbishop Troy.[19] He painted a sorry picture of the state of the Church; the Supreme Pastor had been driven from Rome and the French now intended to disperse his flock. In this situation, it was intolerable that Irish Catholics, 'so commended always for their loyalty', should league with the French. He instructed Troy to recall them to a sense of duty:

> For God's sake, my Lord, do not cease and may your Reverend Brethren never cease (and I am sure they will never forsake so essential a part of their pastoral duties) to make use of all means that your situation affords you, to open the eyes of that deluded people; sermons, exhortations, confession, prayers, nothing should be left untried to recall them from their miserable infatuation!

This letter initiated an interesting sequence of events. While administering the affairs of Propaganda Fide, Erskine conducted his correspondence through the Neapolitan minister in London and, on occasion, through George Canning, under secretary of State.[20] His letter of 6 April, however, was relayed to Troy in a dispatch from the Duke of Portland and was opened and copied in London. Camden inquired from the duke whether Troy and his colleagues might be encouraged to exert greater influence on behalf of the government. He was certain some good would come from Troy's preaching in that it might stem the growth of conspiracy. However, he believed the archbishop to be 'very timid', and feared he would not relay the political content of Erskine's letter to the Catholics.[21]

Monsignor Erskine approached William Wickham, a secretary at Whitehall, and gave him a copy of his letter to Troy, promising a copy of the archbishop's reply. Wickham informed Erskine of fears in Dublin that Troy 'did not make use of the advantages which his situation afforded him of influencing the conduct of the Catholics'. The monsignor, whom Wickham described as a 'very honourable, right minded man', gave assurances that his future correspondence would be directed with that in mind and that 'he would leave nothing unsaid that could influence his [Troy's] conduct without giving suspicion'.[22]

The full extent of Erskine's co-operation with the English government is unknown. Amongst the Erskine papers in the English College in Rome, there is little material of Irish interest. Most of his papers relate to the affairs of the Scots College in the city of which he was protector.[23] While Troy was unaware of the extent of the monsignor's contacts with Whitehall, it is evident that the Irish prelates regarded him with suspicion from his first arrival as papal representative in 1793. At that time, Luke Concanen believed that his presence would supply their enemies with 'sharp and satirical material'.[24] It is surprising that the Castle did not approach Troy directly, given the contacts which had been established, but in the paranoia sweeping through the Irish administration, the archbishop was himself suspect.[25]

The Castle, however, lost no time in making use of Erskine's information. Both Giffard's *Dublin Journal* and *Finn's Leinster Journal*–which was bought off by the government in 1797–carried news that the Pope's nuncio had called on Troy to 'exercise his sacerdotal authority in reclaiming the misguided Roman Catholics of this kingdom'.[26] The tactical value of such reports was questionable; they may have served only to undermine further the credibility and integrity of the Irish bishops in the eyes of an increasingly disaffected flock. Perhaps conscious that they were giving the United Irishmen a stick with which to beat the bishops, the *Dublin Journal* followed the report with a long defence of the independence of the Catholic hierarchy:

> Amongst the various artifices used by agitators in this kingdom, there is one peculiarly insidious and meriting special notice. To destroy as far as in their power the influence and authority of the Roman Catholic hierarchy over the clergy and the people of that communion it has been industrially reported that the Roman Catholic bishops are pensioned and bribed by the government. It is a fact that too many are, thereby, deluded into a persuasion that these prelates are enemies to the country and that they recommend subordination, and respect towards lawful superiors from selfish and mercenary considerations. Every dispassionate and reflecting person must perceive the falsehood and evil tendency of this vile imputation, which, nevertheless, is credited by thousands of the ignorant and unthinking multitude who, unsuspicious and unacquainted with the real designs of artful advisers, are by ill-placed credulity estranged from their pastors, whose peaceful principles and paternal instructions they are taught to despise. [27]

The paper traced the origins of these rumours amongst the committees of the United Irishmen in the north and saw them as part of the Jacobinical conspiracy to degrade the clergy and destroy the influence of religion, as had happened in France.

In many places the hierarchy appeared to be fighting a losing battle in their efforts to combat the spread of rebellion. Bishop James Lanigan complained that priests in parts of Ossory were afraid to speak against the United Irishmen for fear of assassination.[28] Thomas Hussey delivered a sermon on the theme of the contemporary prodigal who 'seeks the company of the libertine and unbeliever where piety is a subject for mockery and scorn'.[29] By contrast, Thomas Bray had little to complain about in Thurles, and Bishop John Young of Limerick praised the efforts of the army which had been dispersed through the county.

The countryside had, according to Young, been intimidated by the military presence and, while there were agitators in the city, these were too few in number to cause concern and the 'lower orders were not disposed to favour them'. Fr Lynch, a Limerick city priest who had campaigned actively against the conspiracy, narrowly escaped with his life when two shots were fired in his window. 'From this', Young declared, 'we may augur what we are to expect should the enemy effect a landing amongst us'. The Limerick Grand Jury attempted to call Catholics to loyalty in a printed address informing them of the sufferings of the Pope at the hands of the French.[30] Patrick Plunket toured Meath and, while constantly condemning 'the complexion of the times', it is noticeable that in April and May he devoted particular attention to 'profane swearing' and to the theme of revolution in Rome and the fate of the Pope.[31]

Episcopal anxiety was further reflected in the instructions of the Maynooth trustees given to the president, Peter Flood, on 12 May. These referred to the 'unhappy spirit of political delerium' which had swept through Ireland. Flood was directed to conduct a vigilant inspection of the student body and was empowered to punish by expulsion any student who 'may by their actions or discourse support or abet any doctrines tending to subvert a due regard to the established orders'. The president was instructed to admonish the students and to exhort them to conduct appropriate to their 'gratitude, their attested allegiance and their sacred professional destination'.[32] The determination of the prelates also reflected their extreme sensitivity to criticism. Hussey's pastoral of the previous year had tarnished the reputation of the college and the bishops hoped to restore some of its credit. The seminary owed its existence to the good will of Parliament and, no doubt anxious to protect it from loyalist aggression, the trustees voted unanimously that Troy, Moylan and Lord Fingall should meet with Thomas Pelham and offer him their 'unfeigned expressions of gratitude for his constant protection and decided support of the institution ... particularly through the House of Commons'.[33]

III

By the spring of 1798 the condition of County Wexford had seriously deteriorated. Lord Mountnorris, a local magnate, decided to call again upon the clergy to organise a display of Catholic loyalty as he had done the previous November. At various chapel meetings throughout the north-eastern part of the county, Catholics were called to loyalty, and loyal oaths were presented for their signature. These oaths contained an explicit renunciation of the United Irishmen.[34] It was during this campaign that James Caulfield issued his pastoral which (uniquely amongst the surviving pastorals of the 1790s) specifically refers to the United Irishmen. Direct references to the United Irishmen were extremely rare, even in the private episcopal correspondence of the period and, as late as the winter of 1797-8, the bishops continued to describe the incendiaries as 'Defenders'.

Caulfield's pastoral was addressed to his clergy and it reflected the critical state of the county. The address is brief and direct, containing little of the elaborate rhetorical denunciations which had characterised his colleagues' addresses. There is no mention of French libertinism, no references to the plight of the Pope or to decadent Europe basking in false liberty, nor to the horrors of hypothetical invasions. Caulfield's address was directed quite specifically to the disaffected of his diocese and cautioned against 'the most imminent and most dreadful dangers' to which Wexford Catholics were exposed. He devoted considerable attention to the horrors of free quarters and military justice and he warned of:

> a military force to be sent on them, on free quarters, who will be warranted to commit the greatest excess; to burn their houses, to destroy or consume their stock, their corn and hay, and every article of their substance except what they may chuse [sic] or reserve for their own use, subsistence, or convenience; they will be authorised to apprehend their persons, to imprison and flog them, if suspected, and if guilty, they will be doomed to die by the sentence of court martial.[35]

Caulfield's pastoral was written to combat the rapid advances of the United Irishmen in County Wexford in the spring of 1798, and he called on his priests to join the magistrates in touring their various parishes. They were to call the people to loyalty, to surrender their weapons and to abjure their oaths 'of combining or conspiring with United Irishmen' which he described as bonds of iniquity. In this way, Caulfield declared, the people could 'avert the avenging arm of the offended laws'. The pastoral reflects the level of trust placed by the bishop in the magistracy and he can only have been pleased at the response to his appeal from amongst his clergy, with fourteen of his priests joining Mountnorris's effort in north-east Wexford.[36] Ironically, however, the alarmist tone of Caulfield's pastoral and the associated oath taking, may have served to intensify tension in the county.

The Archbishop of Dublin's silence throughout the spring of 1798 is curious. Since the revolution and the first signs of the French malady had appeared in Ireland, Troy led the vanguard for the defense of the status quo. In the heated transactions of the Catholic Committee he had not shirked from the radicals' challenge, in the discussions on Maynooth he assumed a primacy amongst the bishops; faced with the rising levels of disaffection in 1795 he had taken the bold step of excommunicating the Defenders and associated combinations. Yet, in the spring of 1798, with the country on the brink of disaster and in virtual open rebellion, little was heard from Troy by way of condemnation of the United Irishmen. It is against this background that Camden began to criticise Troy's lack of activity and timidity, a description hardly applicable to him under normal circumstances.[37]

We can assume that Troy must have regarded with horror the pace and direction of events, the apparent headlong rush towards rebellion. Certainly, his hatred for the United Irishmen was growing and he can only have looked on their writings with alarm. Troy possessed a copy of Arthur O'Connor's *State of Ireland,* published in February 1798, and his annotations written on the cover in the wake of the rebellion represent a rare episcopal commentary on a specific publication which leaves no doubt as to his opinion. O'Connor's address was in essence an apologia for the forthcoming rebellion which set out a full explanation for its necessity. Troy would have had little sympathy for O'Connor's description of the Irish as a 'people cursed with a foreign government and a venal legislature'. He believed 'Citizen O'Connor' had styled himself on Mirabeau and borrowed from his Rights of Man; the two were at most Deists and like Mirabeau O'Connor perverted good principles for the purpose of revolution. The whole tendency of O'Connor's statements, he believed, were seditious and revolutionary, and he condemned his misrepresentation of fact and his description of the French Revolution as 'Catholic'. He declared:

> a bad cause cannot be supported except by falsehood and calumny, with which his State of Ireland and addresses are replete. The truths contained in them are disfigured and tortured to promote the cause and system of the United Irishmen.[38]

Conscious of United Irish attacks on the integrity of the hierarchy, and their use of pastorals for propaganda purposes, Troy only broke his silence on the very eve of the rebellion when he issued instructions to the rural vicars.[39] The archbishop painted a bleak picture of the state of his diocese, where, as a result of threats and personal danger, many priests had been unable to oppose the 'torrent of disloyalty and disaffection'. Once again, the archbishop failed to mention the United Irishmen but continued to condemn disaffection generally without reference to a broader conspiracy. There is in the letter, however, a suggestion that Troy believed the tide had turned; he referred to the deluded returning to their duty in many places. In this situation, when all the powers of the state were being exerted to end the 'mad revolutionary spirit', and when many innocent people had suffered as a result of the 'summary measures of government', the silence and indifference of the clergy was inexcusable. Troy called on them to preach against oaths and associations and to imitate the people of Arklow who had surrendered their arms and made declarations of loyalty to the magistrates. In this way, he believed, the Catholics could be saved from criticism and their persons and property protected.

I V

Two days after Troy addressed his instructions to the rural vicars, the country finally rose in the 'burst' the bishops had long feared. The sword was now drawn and, welcoming the opportunity, Camden vowed not to return it to its scabbard until the conspiracy was finally put down.[40] Ireland was plunged into open rebellion and through the summer months the bishops saw the realisation of their worst nightmare, from which they had unsuccessfully tried to save their flock. In the confusion of battle, communication between the prelates became impossible, yet they continued their efforts and often in great personal danger recalled their people to order.

Bishop William Coppinger of Cloyne and Ross swiftly penned a pastoral deploring the disturbances.[41] Coppinger had experienced sectarian tensions at first hand in the east Cork town of Youghal; for some time the town had been prey to rumours of a planned Orange rising. The bishop himself had been the target of criticism: it was reported in the town—which he described as famed for the most illiberal animosity towards Catholicism—that he had United Irish connections, in spite of the efforts he had taken to stem the spread of conspiracy.[42] The bishop referred to the sorry state of Cork, the devastation brought to the county, the desolated cottages, the cries of the fatherless, the carnage of the sword, famine and all the misery guaranteed to continue as long as the rebellion lasted. Coppinger condemned the folly of the 'French evangelists' and their extravagant notions of equality, and espoused an elaborate social theory in which he outlined the inevitability of social inequality:

> how can there be cultivation, where there are no tillers? and where shall you find tillers, if all become gentlemen? Rank and property must go hand in hand, and the inequality of both in every civilised country must be as various as the talents of men. Were every individual in the land possessed at this day of an equal share of property, a lapse of twelve months would exhibit innumerable gradations. The industrious, the thrifty, the honest, the temperate, would soon surpass the idle, the profligate, the squanderers and the licentious.

He concluded his discourse against the levelling principles of the time with a reminder that 'the poor will still be poor, under every form of government'. The bishop's condemnation of the United Irish oath was novel, although he did not refer to the society by name. The oath, he declared, had promised the protection of secrecy to the timid, the oath had been 'your shelter and your shield', but that very promise had led to their destruction. Coppinger concluded by calling on his listeners to come forward, to surrender their arms and to rely on the mercy of the government.

Bishop Young of Limerick issued a pastoral in the first week of June which was to be read from the altar each Sunday until the country was free from danger. He reminded his people of the Pauline injunction to obey the civil laws and called on them to surrender any arms they may have concealed and not to hesitate in taking the loyal oath. In this they were to follow the example of their priests; reminding them of the ill-fated French landing the previous year, he urged them to show the same determined resistance to 'the domestic disturbers of your peace and welfare'. Young condemned the fraud and force by which the French had spread their ills and, from the strongest ties of gratitude to the King, he repeated his instructions of the previous year, not only to refrain from assisting his enemies, but to actively resist them. Failure to conform to the ordinances of the government, he warned, would endanger man's eternal salvation.[43]

Young was pleased with the response to his address; he informed Thomas Bray that none of his priests had been implicated in the rebellion and that the swearing business had been confined to three parishes. This he attributed to the work of emissaries but, thankfully, no concealed pikes or arms had been found in the diocese.[44] The aged Dominican Bishop of Killaloe also issued a pastoral in 1798. Michael Peter MacMahon had strong aristocratic connections in

Fig. 17 William Coppinger, Bishop of Cloyne & Ross 1787-1831 (N.G.I.)

France where his family had suffered at the hands of the revolutionaries. Although no copy of the address survives, it is not difficult to imagine the tenor the bishop would have adopted.[45]

On 11 June, Charles Sughrue was consecrated Bishop of Kerry, and in a reflection of the tranquility of the region, most of the prelates of the province were able to attend his consecration at Killarney. The bishops chose the opportunity to hold a conference and afterwards issued a collective condemnation of the rebellion, signed by all the province's prelates except Thomas Hussey.[46] The address repeated the Church's teaching on illegal oaths and instructed priests to preach against sedition, regardless of the personal danger. The people were called on to surrender their arms: those persisting in their folly were to be refused admission to the sacraments. The absence of Hussey's name from the pastoral appeared to confirm many of the suspicions of the previous year; yet, his failure to sign the address was due to his unfortunate choice of 1798 as the year to make his *ad limina* visit to Rome. Hussey, however, wrote to Thomas Hearn in July and this letter reflects his strong opposition to the rebellion.[47]

Expressing his consolation that the spirit of rebellion had made no impressions on 'the loyal, industrious and religious Catholics' of his diocese, Hussey was concerned, however, that some had been misled into dangerous associations. He warned that these were forbidden by both the law of God and the land and he urged his priests to impress on the people the evil of these oaths. Justifying such acts on the grounds of religion, he warned, would merely provide their enemies with a pretext to blacken the Church. The good of the Church could never excuse one act of injustice; though the establishment of the Catholic Church might follow such an act, 'evil is not to be done that good might follow'. Whatever grievances the Catholics had to complain of, they could never be corrected by unlawful associations. On the contrary, their 'grievances by such means, will only become more irritated and festered'.

Hussey's pastoral was greeted with cynicism and disregard by loyalists. The bishop's delay in condemning the rebellion led to a questioning of his sincerity. The strongest attack on Hussey appeared in a letter in the *Dublin Journal*.[48] Why, the writer asked, with the country in frenzy, had the bishop waited until 3 July, when the rebel cause was almost at an end, to issue his address? The writer also noted similarities between this letter and the infamous pastoral of the previous year. There was, he noted, 'too much of the same spirit' in this letter, and he drew particular attention to the bishop's reference to past ills and injustice. 'I am sorry', he declared, 'to find that you seem to entertain the same idea of your own people, which Mr John Sheares entertained of their own brethren, that they were most likely to be persuaded into an opinion that they were aggrieved'. An earlier letter to the same paper criticised the bishop's pretended ignorance of the state of Waterford and pointed to the 'shocking spirit of assassination and plunder' which had begun soon after the 'pious Doctor' had published his pastoral in 1797.[49]

In Ulster and in Connaught, where the Catholic revival was not as advanced as elsewhere, the bishops maintained a lower profile. In Ulster, the bishops had traditionally remained aloof from political involvement and during the rebellion they continued this stance. No individual pastorals appear to surivive, but the northern bishops published a collective address in July 1798 in which they excommunicated the rebels and called upon their curates to urge loyalty.[50] Little archival material for the Armagh provinces survives, but Richard O'Reilly, who had issued a pastoral against the Defenders in 1788, expressed his satisfaction privately in January 1799 that the 'fascinating delusion which involved so many of our countrymen during the latter half of last year in misery and wretchedness is so happily removed'. The archbishop was convinced that experience had taught them that 'a peaceable and orderly conduct is truly the best policy because it is the most conducive to happiness, even in this world'.[51]

Of all O'Reilly's suffragans, Patrick Plunket's behaviour during the rebellion is best documented. The Diocese of Meath had been greatly disturbed during the summer months, but the bishop was not deterred from completing his visitation. Plunket considered writing a pastoral, but thought better of it, believing it would only heighten discord. Troy's pastoral, however, was reprinted and distributed in Mullingar, in the west of Meath diocese, at the expense of Captain Rochfort, a local magistrate.[52] The bishop preached against the insurrection in every parish he visited in the spring and early summer of 1798, and noted that the congregations were more attentive than they had been for three years. This he attributed to 'the lessons received in the school of adversity, which had prepared the sufferers for reflection'.[53] On 29 May, a diocesan conference was forced to adjourn because of the disturbances, but not before the bishop had instructed his priests to urge their people to loyalty.[54]

Little was heard from the Connaught bishops during the rebellion, but this lack of combined effort may be attributed to the death of the Archbishop of Tuam earlier in the year. With the exception of Dominic Bellew, Bishop of Killala, all the bishops of the province were above suspicion. Bellew's loyalty was, however, suspect on a number of counts; the bishop's fiery character and the many conflicts he had had with the merchants of Dundalk during his time as parish priest there, did little to help his case, nor did his contempt for Troy, which dated back to his removal from Dundalk during the scalding controversy surrounding Anthony Blake's last years as Archbishop of Armagh.[55]

After the French landing, Bellew allegedly became president of the Ballina Committee of Public Safety, while his brother Matthew, who had been an officer in the Austrian army, was amongst the first to join the invading French.[56] The principal suspicion, however, was based on accusations made against the bishop by one of his priests, Fr Bernard Dease, arrested in 1798. Dease claimed that the bishop had long entertained pro-French sentiments, even though he had instructed that prayers of thanksgiving be read in the various chapels after the failure of their landing in 1796. Indeed, Dease reported that at that time he had approached the bishop about necessary repairs for his chapel, but Bellew had told him not to bother, since 'the French would soon be back and the [Protestant] churches converted to chapels'. According to his information, Bellew had instructed his priests to have no dealings with the Protestants, whom he called 'blacks', on pain of suspension.[57] The bishop responded quickly to Dease's lurid accusations, and lost no time in stating his innocence.[58]

In Leinster, the position of the bishops became critical, and nowhere more so than in Wexford. James Caulfield epitomised the conservative element within the hierarchy and had long been a staunch opponent of progressive Catholic politics. His detestation of radicals such as Edward Hay and James

Edward Devereux was renowned and he greatly resented the influence they exerted in the community.[59] Caulfield had vigorously opposed the spread of radicalism and had been only too willing to join with the magistrates in their attempts to stem the United Irish conspiracy. On 26 May 1798, he stopped at McAuley's inn at Oulart on his return from Dublin and urged the large gathering there to surrender arms and to obtain protections. The bishop called on the assembly to 'relinquish their wild notions of insurrection, to live in peace and charity with each other', and he threatened the disobedient with the heaviest of God's chastisement'.[60] Four days later Wexford town was captured and a republic declared but, while streets buzzed with rejoicing throngs, Dr Caulfield remained insulated in his High Street house for fear of vengeance from the United Irishmen he had so long opposed. The presence of priests amongst the rebel army can only have been a source of extreme anger to him, and there is no tradition of any meeting between the bishop and Father John Murphy after the capture of the town.[61]

Throughout the rebel occupation of the town, the bishop's position was critical. Contrary to the claims of Musgrave, the timid Caulfield, far from feeling safe, was prepared for immediate death.[62] Yet, amongst the Protestant loyalists of Wexford, there was a belief that Caulfield had sway over the rebels; he later claimed to have been busy from morning till night pleading with the leaders for their safety. However, as the tide began to turn in the government's favour, he noted a change in the rebel temper and 'it became treason to plead for protection'. In what must have seemed a realisation of his worst prophesies of 1792, the bishop recalled for Troy the reaction to his intervention on behalf of Lord Kingsborough, the hated commander of the notorious North Cork Militia:

> I declared, if any of them had killed my friend, my brother or my father, that I would protect and save him, if he threw himself on my mercy; for it was by shewing mercy that I could expect mercy myself. This conduct and language graduated me equal to an Orangeman; my house must be pulled down or burnt, and my head knocked off; this last sentence was boldly pronounced to my face, surrounded as I was in the public square, by 4 or 5 thousand pikes, spears or muskets, when I was striving to save Lord Kingsboro's life.[63]

Whatever little influence the clergy may have had over the rebels was declining and, despite their continued efforts to restrain the 'Banditti dispatched from Hell', they became powerless to prevent many atrocities, especially the massacre at the town bridge.[64] When the rebel cause collapsed and the King's army prepared to enter Wexford, Caulfield pleaded with the remaining insurgents to quit the town before the arrival of Lake's troops; Miles Byrne later recalled the bishop at his window 'haranguing the multitude'.[65]

Caulfield's month-long captivity had greatly alarmed his episcopal confrères; in Kilkenny it was reported that he was a prisoner of the rebels, and James Lanigan wrote to Troy requesting news of 'poor Doctor Caulfield'; the archbishop himself believed that Caulfield had fled to Wales.[66] By that stage he was under the protection of General Lake, and he lost no time in informing Troy of his liberation and of his being 'tolerably well after a month of the most terrific confusion and tumult'.[67] Lanigan, who had issued what the *Dublin Journal* called a 'spirited' pastoral against the rebels, was pleased that the country was returning to its senses and he welcomed Cornwallis' arrival 'as the aurora that will soon usher in happy days'.[68] Lanigan's pastoral, published 9 July, reminded his flock of the horrors of France, and the United Irishmen, whom he excommunicated, were described as 'cruel and unnatural children' of King George, 'a tender and merciful parent'.[69] Bishop Daniel Delaney of Kildare and Leighlin was based at Tullow, and visited Lanigan in Kilkenny in the first week in June. While he was there, he took the opportunity of calling on General Asgill who received him well. Delaney reported to Troy the defeat and 'prodigious slaughter' of the rebels at New Ross and Newtownbarry. By that time there were four thousand troops in Tullow, but even prior to their arrival the town had remained quiet, despite being defended by only the local yeomanry corps, consisting of 23 Catholic and 17 Protestant privates. Delaney believed the rebels were 'absolutely possessed by the Devil himself', but he was confident that the 'unhappy miscreants' would be suppressed in a few days.[70]

In Dublin, Troy had anxiously tried to salvage the situation and went to great lengths to recall the people to loyalty and absolve the Church from responsibility for the rebellion.[71] Throughout the crisis he tried to orchestrate the hierarchy's campaign, co-ordinating the publication of pastorals and presenting loyal addresses to the Lord Lieutenant. On 28 May an address was published on behalf of the hierarchy condemning the rebellion and recalling the deluded to a sense of duty. Two days later, an address of loyalty was presented to the Lord Lieutenant signed by the four archbishops, the majority of the prelates and the principal laity.[72] The presence of Boetius Egan, Archbishop of Tuam, amongst the signatories of the address indicates that it may have been written before the outbreak of the rebellion. It is significant that in the wake of Emmet's rebellion in 1803 Hardwicke claimed that Troy's own pastoral on that occasion had been written before the outbreak.[73]

Troy's address created the greatest stir of all. The archbishop published short instructions on 27 May, but he developed the same theme in a full pastoral published some days later.[74] In the short address Troy had condemned the 'wicked endeavours of irreligious and rebellious agitators, to overthrow and destroy the constitution'. He repeated his instructions concerning the evils of oaths and delivered a sharp rebuke to the philosophy of the time:

> let no one deceive you by wretched impracticable speculations on the rights of man, and the majesty of the people, on the dignity and independence of the human mind, on abstract duties of superiors, and exaggerated abuses of authority; fatal speculations! disastrous theories! not more subversive of social order and happiness, than destructive to every principle of the Christian religion.

Troy urged his flock to loyalty, reminding them that submission to the laws was a Christian duty. He called on them to abjure their oaths, unite with their fellow subjects, deliver up their arms and put down the spirit of insurrection. By so doing they would preserve their persons and property; if they refused, they would be cut off from the Church and refused access to the sacraments. The archbishop failed to mention the United Irishmen by name, but he was uncompromising in his excommunication of the rebels.

In the full pastoral, Troy traversed much of the same ground covered in his various addresses throughout the 1790s. He condemned the evils of the French Revolution, the destruction of Europe, the irreligious assault upon the Church and the person of the Pope. Again, he spoke of the illegality of oaths and the necessity of obedience to the laws and reiterated his constant theme of gratitude to the King for his goodness to Irish Catholics. There was, however, a sense in which this pastoral reflected movement in the archbishop's stance. Despite the reminders of the conditions suffered by the Catholics twenty years previously, despite the call for gratitude to the King for his benevolence, Troy now publicly acknowledged the very real obstacles which still excluded 'the most loyal and peaceable Roman Catholics from a seat or vote in parliament, from the privy council, from the higher and confidential civil and military departments of state'. In this the archbishop recognised the demands of the reformers to whom he had consistently refused to lend his support, but he still strongly rejected their methods.

The pastoral also contained an implicit acknowledgement of the changed temper of Irish Catholics and recognition of the heightened levels of anti-clericalism in Ireland. Troy was only too aware of the attacks made by the radical press on the integrity of the clergy; Arthur O'Connor's Dublin-based *Press*, in one example alone, published a 'New English Vocabulary' in late 1797 and along with definitions of 'Liberty' as 'Life' and 'Equality' as 'Emancipation' the list included 'An Archbishop = An Absorbent,' 'A Bishop = A Bacchanalian', and 'A Priest = A Parasite'.[75] At Christmas 1797, the *Press* carried a seasonal reflection with striking parallels between Judea and Ireland:

> The PRIESTHOOD and the Government of the province where he [Jesus] had his birth, found his doctrines incompatible with the foreign yoke which their tyranny imposed.[76]

In the face of these endeavours, and in recognition of their success, Troy was forced to make a rare condescension in an effort to justify his actions. As Francis Moylan had done the previous April, Troy went to great lengths to stress the independence of the hierarchy against allegations that the prelates were like 'so many mercenaries prostituting their venal pens and exhortations for pensions and bribes'. Yet, despite the alteration in Troy's tone, the archbishop's excommunication of the rebels aroused an immediate response. Troy had frequently resorted to excommunications in the past and the sanction remained a favoured weapon in his armoury, but in 1798 the sentence appears to have had little effect in discouraging the rebels. Leonard McNally was amongst the first to report the general response to the pastoral:

> the recent excommunication by the Holy Catholic Church is received by her sons not merely with indifference, but with contempt. It is a measure which in my opinion will nearly go to annihilate all priestly influence, increase deism and draw down upon the priests themselves very severe resentments. In bulk it is laughed at and ridiculed, not only by men, but by women. The [fulminations] of the Pope or his delegates no longer terrify and their anathemas pale like so many *bruta fulmina* upon modern Catholics, or as Mr Shanky [Royal Dublin Militia?] says, it is but firing sparrow shot against a bastion.[77]

Francis Higgins reported that amongst the lower clergy in Dublin there was a good degree of resentment at the excommunication and that they criticised the manner in which the sentence had been passed without warning. The same priests believed more harm than good would ensue, as the excommunications were generally perceived to have been imposed on government instructions.[78] Similarly, Bishop Plunket of Meath informed Troy that he had been 'startled' by the excommunications. Writing in the wake of the rebellion, he acknowledged that such a sentence was perhaps the appropriate remedy for the situation, adding that he had been unable to take similar steps in Meath due to the dangers he faced there.[79] The Bishop of Kilfenora believed that the sentence of excommunication should have been pronounced for the whole kingdom, with varying forms to suit local circumstances.[80]

There was unusually strong reaction to the excommunications from the United Irishmen, who normally reacted to episcopal statements with indifference. In early July 1798, the priests of Lazer's Hill chapel received a notice from the secretary of the 'Star Division' of the United Irishmen, dated the 'first year of the Irish Republic'. The letter is addressed to Frs Morris, P.P., Smyth and Divine and 'the very obliging gentleman who excommunicated first last Sunday', presumably referring to the archbishop.[81] The letter began with a lengthy rendition of the miseries inflicted upon Irish Catholics for centuries, and the cruelties of the Orange men and army in more recent times. The day of reckoning was, however, close at hand and, within a few days Dublin would be free and the city's lamp posts would be decorated with dangling tyrants. The address then turned to consider the excommunications and issued a salutary warning to the priests on account of their preference for the 'murdering government':

> we never before thought any of our clergy false or ill hearted, we thought they were men of piety, men of love, men of God, until last Sunday. We often heard their admonitions which we apprehended was to keep themselves from the censure of government, but how great was our astonishment last Sunday when we could hear ourselves censured and excommunicated alike by the ministers of that very Church we are suffering for—we are sure ye heard the effects of such conduct in France, a place that now overflows with milk and honey as God promised.

The same antipathy was repeated in a political skit found amongst the papers of Dublin radical, Richard Passmore. The skit contained a supposed list of new books and amongst the titles was 'The New Table of Sins', originally published in *The Press*. This was a story of the Catholic laity consigned to the devil for shaking hands with their Protestant or Presbyterian brethren, and the volume contained 'notes on pacific obedience by Most Rev Doctor Troy, respectfully dedicated to Secretary Cooke'.[82] Watty Cox, the militant Dublin United Irishman and polemicist, writing almost twenty years after the rebellion, looked back on the excommunications and condemned that 'terrible anathema, which sent a man to the devil for loving his country'. Yet, the people had chosen to join the rebellion without Troy's leave and, despite defeat 'their glory was not diminished, only in the view of their archbishop and his friends in Britain'.[83]

The level of negative reaction to Troy's pastoral and what Cox called his 'pious alliance' with the government, aroused concerns for his safety. Luke Concanen feared that the archbishop's zeal would expose him to 'the fury of the deluded fanatics' and Charles Erskine referred to the great displeasure with which his pastoral had been greeted in radical circles. The Dublin diocesan historian, John Dalton, records the archbishop narrowly escaping a plot on his life, but he does not substantiate his claim. In any event, Castlereagh felt it necessary to place him under protection in early July.[84]

The bishops, however, were not to be deterred by fear of reprisals. Throughout the summer Troy acted on behalf of the hierarchy and made great efforts to have their various addresses and excommunications printed in the Dublin newspapers in an effort to counter the bitter loyalist backlash in the aftermath of the rebellion. The *Dublin Evening Post*, but particularly the *Dublin Journal* on account of its rabidly anti-Catholic stance, were the archbishop's first choice for these publications, but Dillon of Kilfenora complained that the *Dublin Journal* had made exorbitant charges for carrying the reports.[85] Troy, in turn, sent bundles of the addresses to Charles Erskine for inclusion in the London papers, where the monsignor reported they were received with with just praise and satisfaction.[86]

When the French invasion was finally put down in September, the bishops breathed a sigh of relief, taking consolation in the opposition they had offered to what James Caulfield called the 'Dogs of Hell'.[87] Throughout clerical circles, praise resounded for the loyal exertions of the Irish bishops and even Pius VI, prisoner of the French at Florence, echoed the plaudits.[88] Yet, despite the efforts of the hierarchy throughout 1798, and their steady and uniform loyalty through the decade, the bishops soon found themselves once more under siege, this time from the black propagandists seeking to dub the rebellion a popish plot.

CHAPTER EIGHT

The Mighty Wave

E piscopal reaction to the events of 1798 reflected the level of unity which the turbulence of the 1790s brought to the Irish hierarchy. Little more than twenty years earlier, the prelates had been bitterly divided on the prudence, and content, of the 'Herveyan test'; yet, throughout 1798 they displayed public unity and constancy in rallying to the defence of the Irish establishment. Such a response might indeed have been expected, given the critical circumstances of the continental Church and the hierarchy's anxiety to preserve the achievements of their loyal endeavours at home. The reactions of the lower clergy in the face of open rebellion were not, however, so easily predicted. Their numbers alone made uniform loyalty more difficult to maintain, while their close ties and dependence on the people made them far more susceptible to popular pressure. Even so, despite the frightening predictions of the Castle runners prior to the rebellion and the representations of loyalist historians in its aftermath, the seventy priests actively involved in the rebellion represent less than four per cent of their total number.

Nevertheless, the significance of clerical involvement in the rebellion is reflected in the level of attention devoted to the 'rebel priest' in the historiography of the period. Accounts of 1798 were written from an understandably partisan perspective; the integrity of the priest is often sacrificed to suit the greater purpose of the author. At one extreme, Musgrave strove to portray the rebellion as a popish plot; in this scenario the rebels were depicted as foolish dupes, goaded into insurrection by their priests who were 'the chief abettors of this nefarious conspiracy'.[1] Liberal Protestant and Catholic historians sought to play down the levels of clerical involvement in the rebellion. For Edward Hay and many others implicated in United Irish activities, however, the presence of the clergy amongst the rebels provided a welcome scapegoat. Party accounts could exploit the sensationalist, even baroque, tales of the rebel priest at the head of his infuriated followers. Carefully woven into a broader context, such stories served to confirm the author's desired interpretation of the events of 1798.

The debate was reopened in 1863 with the publication in Paris of Miles Byrne's *Memoirs*. Byrne consciously singled out the rebel priests for attention, condemning earlier accounts of the rebellion and the misrepresentations of Catholic historians who had tarnished the reputation 'of those priests who fought so bravely at the head of the people, in their effort to expel the common enemy'.[2] The timing of the publication of Byrne's memoirs was a source of particular embarrassment to the Church, then preoccupied with the challenge of the Fenians, but the old United Irishman's assessment of clerical involvement as 'three or four priests' driven from their neutral position 'by the blood thirsty Orangemen' understated the reality.

In the wake of the failed Fenian rising of 1867, the Wexford Franciscan, Patrick Kavanagh attempted to reconcile the activity of the rebel priests with the Church's condemnation of oath-bound societies. The result was a history of 1798 which portrayed the priests as involuntary rebels, reluctantly leading the defence of their flocks against tyranny and oppression.[3] This image has survived in popular lore, and Kavanagh was almost single-handedly responsible for the measure of acclaim accorded in the popular memory to 'Brave Father Murphy', the curate of Boolavogue. While the rabidly anti-Catholic Patrick Duigenan had described Murphy as a 'drunken ruffian', Kavanagh singled him out as a hero, casting the curate in the messianic mould of a selfless leader taking up arms in the face of intolerable persecution. Patrick McCall's stirring anthem 'Boolavogue', written in the 1890s, copperfastened this image, while the priest's recent biographer has accepted this heroic role.[4] The mid-nineteenth-century reassessment of the role of Murphy in 1798 complicated the general appraisal of clerical involvement in that *all* priests were set in the image of John Murphy's 'mighty wave'.

In recent studies of the rebellion, which emphasise the broader political context, a great deal of attention has centred on the religious factor in the politicisation of the 1790s. Cullen and Whelan have focused on the role of the priests in 1798; their efforts point to the more complex nature of clerical involvement than had previously been considered.[5] The great difficulty in separating reality from myth stems from an absence of impartial evidence upon which to construct an authoritative study. With the notable exception of James O'Coigley, none of the clerics involved in the radical proceedings of the 1790s left any memoir and explanations of their activities have been drawn from indirect sources. Recent research has focused on the extensive Caulfield-Troy correspondence in the Dublin Diocesan Archives, but this evidence must be placed against the background of the post rebellion polemic and Caulfield's attempt at damage limitation.

Many of the seventy or so priests implicated in the rebellion had very tenuous links with sedition and convictions were often secured on the word of informers or under severe threats. The Wexford clergy suffered greatly as a result of 'evidence' of the notorious paid informer Richard Grandy, while a full 'confession' was extracted from the Drogheda United Irish priest, John Martin, at the mouth of a cannon.[6] What has survived, then, are sketchy party accounts which have perpetuated the myth of the 'patriot priest' on one hand, or overstated the loyalty of the clergy on the other.

I

Apart from defending the rebel clergy in his *Memoirs*, Miles Byrne voiced a strong criticism of the priests in general, condemning their 'pious assiduity and earnest endeavours' to keep the people in thralldom which he believed had 'saved the infamous English government in Ireland from destruction'.[7] Yet, as the myth of the 'rebel priest' has been re-examined, this image of unswerving clerical loyalty requires equal deconstruction. Just as clerical disaffection had taken many forms, the loyalty of the clergy was also reflected in different ways.

On one level, a loyalist tag could certainly be attached to the endeavours of the Cork Franciscan Arthur O'Leary, but it is more difficult to categorise the pamphlets of the Dublin Augustinian, William Gahan. While provincial of his order in the 1780s, Gahan became a prolific writer of devotional texts, the best known of which was the *Manual of Catholic Piety*.[8] Gahan was typical of the leading clergy of the late eighteenth century, eagerly exploiting the opportunities presented by Catholic relief measures. In 1777 he founded John's Lane school; education was to remain his greatest priority and, in this task, he worked alongside the famous Dublin Jesuit, Dr Thomas Betagh.[9] Gahan established strong links with Troy and many of the crucial episcopal gatherings prior to the foundation of Maynooth, and the early trustees' meetings took place at his John's Lane priory. He had also connections with John Butler (Lord Dunboyne), the former bishop of Cork, and these ties placed him at the centre of an unquestionably loyal circle.

On the eve of the rebellion in 1798, Gahan published a pamphlet entitled *Youth Instructed* which contained a blunt rejection of Tom Paine and his 'idle speculations, wild ideas and conjectures'.[10] The Augustinian's pamphlet condemned the *Age of Reason* which he declared was:

Fig. 18 Fr William Gahan O.S.A.

no more than a confused medley of captious sophisms, groundless assertions, unsupported dogmas, heterogeneous ribaldry, sarcasms, and ridicule calculated not to instruct and edify, but to pervert and puzzle his uninformed readers, by scattering dust in their eyes, and attempting to make them insensibly swallow the poison of infidelity, disguised under the dress and appearance of solid reason and truth.[11]

Youth Instructed was published by subscription and the list of contributors reflects the range of his influence. Amongst those named were Troy, who received twenty copies, Bishops O'Donnell of Derry and Egan of Tuam, many students of Maynooth, and numerous priests including Father Andrew O'Toole, parish priest of Wicklow.[12] Gahan's pamphlet represents a rare example of published comment from the lower clergy on the radical literature of the period. The assault on *Age of Reason* may simply have been a preemptive strike against Paine's theology, but it may also reflect the level to which these ideas had filtered through to the Catholic community and, therefore, warranted explicit rebuttal in catechetical texts. Yet, despite their conservative content and tone, Gahan's writings cannot be as easily categorised as Father O'Leary's. Certainly, his pamphlets contained valuable material for the loyal preacher, but their purpose was essentially pedagogical. Their author had no consciously loyalist or political agenda, nor were these texts directed towards a popular audience.[13]

While unsolicited intellectual defences of the establishment were welcomed by the government, the threat of imminent rebellion in the spring of 1798 demanded more immediate measures. The prominent clerical role in the local activities of the Catholic Committee throughout the 1790s gave loyalists an unfounded perception of their power. Despite the apparent bond between priests and people, the relationship was often very strained; in many cases the clergy co-operated with the radicals reluctantly. This reality was lost on the Castle administration which continued to assume that prelates and priests commanded the unquestioning loyalty of a compliant people. While the existence of independent minded radical Catholics was acknowledged, there was a conservative consensus that the great body of the Catholic Church would fall in behind their natural leaders in the moment of crisis.

For outsiders, the chapel meetings and petitioning of the 1790s presented a powerful image of Catholic unity; thus, prior to the rebellion, many magistrates had attempted to harness the great potential of the Church in an effort to instill loyalty. Just as the radicals raised petitions, the magistrates orchestrated loyal resolutions, often choosing the chapel in which to administer oaths of allegiance. Andrew Newton of Coagh, County Tyrone, claimed to have been the first magistrate to encourage Catholics to enter into these resolutions. Alarmed at the extent to which the Orange Order had instilled fear into the Catholic community, Newton embarked on a campaign to allay their anxieties and to stem the growth of the United Irishmen.

In June 1797, at his local chapel at Arboe in County Tyrone, his resolutions received the signature of the parish priest, Bernard O'Neill, and 678 parishioners. These resolutions affirmed that many had been induced to take the United oath by 'the arguments of designing men who buzzed into our ears Catholic emancipation, and the danger of being massacred by Orangemen'. Newton repeated this exercise throughout much of mid-Ulster and was satisfied with the result of 'making a split between them [Catholics] and the Presbyterians'.[14] Newton's example was adopted elsewhere; published resolutions provide an interesting barometer of regional tension in late 1797 and early 1798. The earliest addresses are mainly from Antrim, Down and other parts of the north but, from early 1798 they appear in the south, with the Catholics of Musgrave's parish of Cappoquin, County Waterford, being amongst the first to publish a declaration.[15] Petitioning reached a peak in March 1798, generally forming part of a wider campaign. Some were occasioned by specific incidents, such as the address signed by Father Joseph Power and the Catholics of Tuosist, County Kerry, following an attack on a local tithe proctor.[16] The level of petitioning depended on several factors, most significantly, the initiative of an active local magnate or magistrate. In consequence, many of the published resolutions were inspired by magistrates such as Andrew Newton, Caesar Colclough, Lord Mountnorris and Richard Musgrave.

Resolutions were viewed with scepticism in some loyal quarters; the Marquis of Downshire had little faith in them, but believed that they 'did no harm' and might at least be useful in separating 'some of these poor deluded fools' from the general conspiracy.[17] It was common for proclamations to be read in chapels. The governor of Queen's County, William Pole, had extracts from the Insurrection Act read in the chapels while Charles Tottenham of New Ross instructed that a letter from Venice, giving a negative account of the impact of the French armies there, should be read in the churches and chapels of his district in an effort to detach the people from French sympathies.[18] The authorities also involved the clergy in the disarming of the country. In Templekenny, County Tipperary, Sir James Foulis praised the 'zealous exertions and pathetic eloquence' of the curate Fr O'Meagher who assisted him in returning the area to order. In Drumcree, County Armagh, the tranquility of the area and the 'remarkable change' in the minds of the 'lower orders' was attributed to the sermons of the clergy.[19]

Nicholas Phepoe, parish priest of Kilcullen, County Kildare, co-operated with General Dundas in persuading his people to surrender arms before the outbreak of the rebellion. So successful was he in this task that the general intervened with the archbishop in early June to stop his proposed transfer to another parish. Dundas believed that such a move would be imprudent, as the priest was 'labouring to restore and confirm his deluded flock ... to a just sense of their duty to their King and country'.[20] Similarly, Roger Miley, parish priest of Blessington, County Wicklow, won the praise of Dundas and Lord Gosford for the manner in which he remained in his war-torn village throughout the rebellion in an effort to restore peace.[21]

Patrick Ryan, parish priest of Coolock, County Dublin, achieved great distinction among the conservatives as a result of his co-operation in disarming the district. Francis Higgins had spent some days collecting rents in St Margaret's area of the parish in May 1798, and he informed Edward Cooke of the pastor's exertions:

At the time of the rebellion raging, and many of his parishioners declaring that their servants, gardeners etc. were quitting their service to join the rebels, this Fr Ryan sought after them and publicly as well as privately admonished them. He made his terms with Rt. Hon Mr Beresford and the Gent. of the Coolock Association not to molest the people on account of giving up firearms, pikes etc. The consequence was that in the course of five days he caused to be piled up and delivered to the Coolock Cavalry nine cars filled with pikes, old scythes on poles, swords, fire arms etc and as truly observed by him, 'take from them the implements of destruction and you deprive them of the means of doing mischief.[22]

Leonard McNally described Coolock as 'extremely refractory', and referred to the danger to which Ryan was exposed.[23] The newspapers carried reports of Ryan's co-operation with Captain Annesley and Captain Vernon of the South Fingal Yeomanry Corps and, from these accounts it may be inferred that the people were addressed at chapel meetings. In the aftermath of the rebellion, Father Ryan published an acknowledgement of the 'vigilant exertions' of the Fingal Corps, co-ordinated by the Beresfords, on behalf of himself, his curate Eugene McKenna and the Catholics of the Barony of Coolock.[24]

Yet, suspicions about Father Ryan's motivation came back to haunt him, particularly after his appointment as coadjutor to James Caulfield of Ferns in 1804. Ryan's fiercest critic was Watty Cox, former United Irishman and editor of the *Union Star* who was, by then, producing the *Irish Magazine*. Cox was highly critical of the hierarchy and their role in the rebellion, and during the veto controversy he published a piece in which both Troy and Ryan were portrayed as pawns of the Castle. The article took the form of a dialogue across a fence between 'Jack Farrell' and 'Billy Dowling', supposedly two farmers from the Barony of Forth in County Wexford. After a long discussion of the character of both bishops, Jack concludes that 'since Dr Troy makes such bishops, they might as well be appointed by the King'.[25]

Ryan succeeded Caulfield as bishop in 1814 and Cox, once again, revived memories of his loyal exertions in 1798. Above all, the former rebel rounded upon Ryan for his conspicuous loyalty and haughtiness, which the priest had made great efforts to cultivate. According to Cox, Ryan remained totally aloof from his parishioners, with the exception of that 'eloquent and opulent, ignorant man' Randal McDonnell, a prominent merchant and former member of the Catholic Committee. Ryan moved amongst the local Protestant gentry and enjoyed the greatest intimacy with Lord Annesley of the Revenue Commission and Captain Swan, the deputy town major. Apart from his loyal display in 1798, Ryan had assisted Annesley in an inheritance dispute.

Cox claimed that Annesley and McDonnell had both used their influence with Troy in his favour on the 'understanding that one good turn deserves another', a reference to the promotion of Troy's nephew in the revenue service. Troy, in turn, recommended Ryan as coadjutor to James Caulfield, and his appointment, in preference to Fr William Chapman of New Ross, led to resentment in the diocese. All in all, Patrick Ryan was to be exposed as a sycophant, in stark contrast to Francis Higgin's contemporary if suspect image of a timid pastor interceding on behalf of his flock.[26]

The persistence of such debates after 1798 illustrates the difficulties in assigning motives for clerical loyalty. James McCary, curate of Carrickfergus, provides further example of this. A native of Culfeightrim, County Antrim, McCary joined the Dominicans at Coleraine and was educated in Lisbon. He was ordained in 1781 and appointed to Carrickfergus, where he built a chapel six years later.[27] McCary first came to the attention of the authorities in May 1796 when a Father Cassidy informed his landlord of the level of oath swearing in the district and of the great harm done by McCary who, he claimed, had been busy preaching to large numbers in the fields near Ballymena.

'Astonishing numbers' had gathered to hear the sermon, which was announced by public notice, on the theme of 'A new commandment I give you, that you love one another'.[28] Captain Andrew McNevin realised McCary's potential and decided to exploit his position, confident that he would prove an 'essential instrument to government ... he being at the head of every infamous and rebellious transaction'. McNevin was certain that 'no man in either the county of Down or Antrim can give such real information, nor can be of such material service as himself'.[29] Compromised by Cassidy's information, McCary chose to co-operate with the authorities and regularly impressed on them the value of his services and the dangers to which he was exposed.

In January 1796 the body of Michael Phillips, a Franciscan informer, was taken from the Lagan. Possibly fearing a similar fate, McCary published a notice in the Northern Star, denying that a recent visit to Dublin had been for the purpose of informing. In the same month he requested government protection from assassins, declaring that 'prolonging my life might save thousands by all I could do'.[30] McCary maintained regular contact with Captain McNevin over a period of two years, during which time he provided information about the United Irish organisation in Carrickfergus, links with France, and rebel plans.[31] In 1797 he published a collection of devotional material, entitled The Sure Way to Heaven, and the inclusion of Luke and Charles Teeling and the Dublin United Irishman Hugh MacVeagh in the subscription list suggests Defender links.[32]

McCary revived the White Scapular Confraternity in the Diocese of Down and Conor; this would have provided him with a useful cover under which to carry out Defender/United Irish activity. Like so many of the politically active priests, he presented a loyal address in January 1798, illustrating the ambiguity of such declarations.[33] From the onset of his contact with the authorities there were signs of his unreliability as an informer. In one of his first communications, he requested £300 in return for information and similar appeals were a constant feature of his correspondence.[34] The diocesean historian refers to McCary's fall into 'intemperate habits', for which he was suspended in 1802, but the priest continued to 'disgrace the Church and outrage society' until his death in 1833.[35] Rather than reflecting principled loyalty, McCary's career as an informer was, at most, a successful attempt to salvage himself from a potentially dangerous situation.

There are further examples of priests receiving financial rewards for their efforts, but most of these date from the post rebellion period. Charles Doran, parish priest of Monasterevin, County Kildare, was paid £20 by Lord Tyrawly in acknowledgement of his role in preventing people from joining the rebels.[36] Thomas Flannery of Cappoquin, County Waterford, whose name was attached to one of the earliest loyal resolutions in the south, received £50.[37] Thomas Hearn, Hussey's dean in Waterford received £70, while Fr James Jennings of Ballinrobe, County Galway, received £50 for his part in the rebellion and his later assistance in the arrest of 'Captain Hough', a well known Defender leader.[38]

In Mallow, County Cork, Fr Thomas Barry, was rewarded £100 for informing on a conspiracy in the Meath Militia.[39] Fr Michael Barry, parish priest of Midleton in the same county, had been shunned by his people for preaching loyalty during the rebellion and defending a Castlemartyr tithe proctor against threats in 1799. In consequence, his living was destroyed and he petitioned the Castle for support, suggesting that he be recommended Dr Troy for the mitre of the first diocese which became available.[40] In 1801 Francis Higgins made an appeal on behalf of Peter Moran, a Franciscan of Adam and Eve's, Dublin, requesting that Troy provide him with some income. Moran had supplied 'most interesting intelligence' in 1798 about planned attacks on the city's prisons and the intentions of the Rathfarnham yeomanry corps to shoot their officers.[41]

The vast majority of the clergy who openly declared their loyalty to King and government in 1798 did so in the context of published resolutions, discussed above. But in these too, many pressures were brought to bear upon priests to attach their names to addresses. Arthur O'Connor's *Press* mounted a sustained assault against the process, delivering its fiercest attack in December 1797:

> Of all the wretched attempts of the wretchedest tools of the most abandoned administration that ever cursed the most miserable country on the earth, that practice which is now going forward, is the most thoroughly abominable.[42]

These addresses, 'so humiliating, so sickening to the human soul', had been collected it was claimed under 'terror of fire and sword', while the resolution from Rathlin Island was misrepresented to the people there as a petition to bring the Armagh magistrates to justice for their treatment of Catholics.[43]

The editorial line of the *Press* stopped short of an all-out condemnation of the priests involved and acknowledged unknown reasons which might have compelled them 'to compliment the Castle'.[44] The paper's patience was, however, beginning to wear thin by February 1798. Readers were reminded that 'servile priests have in all ages pressed their surplices into the service of despotism', while 'in France, Christianity would never have lost its respect if the ecclesiastics had not on every occasion supported the princes and the Bible justified the Bastille'.[45]

Considerable pressure was brought to bear on priests to co-operate with magistrates and the army. Immediately prior to the rebellion, the *Dublin Journal* carried an account of the efforts of Captain Swayne of the City of Cork Militia in County Kildare. Swayne, whose men were lodged in free quarters, addressed the congregation of Fr John Lynch of Ballysax, near Kilcullen. So successful was his exhortation that five hundred pikes and vast quantities of arms were 'voluntarily surrendered' over the next two days.[46] While the *Dublin Journal* carried the official account of the proceedings, William Farrell, a Carlow United Irishman, recalled a more brutal, though certainly embellished, memory of Swayne's visit to the chapel of Fr Higgins at Prosperous, County Kildare. According to this account, the captain interrupted Mass and ordered the people to bring in their arms. Then turning to the old priest, who later became a target of the United Irishmen, Swayne warned, 'if you don't have it done, I'll pour boiling lead down your throat'. Farrell recalled that the congregation dispersed 'in sullen and silent indignation, whispering their wrongs and insults and breathing vengeance at any hazard'.[47]

The *Irish Magazine* later carried many similar stylised accounts, which illustrate the popular perception of the conditions under which the clergy were forced to function. One account tells of the measures taken by a Meath

magistrate to intimidate Catholics in Kilmainham Wood. Smyth, 'who exercised his pro-consular powers with singular firmness', erected a gallows at the
chapel door and forced the congregation to take their hats off to the gibbet;
refusal to do so meant death, while hesitation resulted in pitchcapping or
flogging. Smyth seized the priest, John O'Reilly, and would have hanged him
but for the intervention of Captain Hedon of the Morgallian Cavalry.[48]

Cox printed another account of the brutal torture of Fr Reeney, a Carmelite
at Kilcullen. This description, couched in Christian imagery, tells how the
priest was flogged by an 'Ethiopian' soldier of the Londonderry Militia.[49]
Accounts such as these, while certainly exaggerated, reflect some of the
pressures inducing priests to openly declare their 'loyalty'. Sworn declarations
were, therefore, of dubious value and may have been made merely to appease
the local magnates. In Wexford, for instance, the presence of John Murphy,
Michael Murphy and Nicholas Stafford amongst the signatories of Mountnorris's
resolutions in the spring of 1798 illustrates the folly of the process, since these
men were later prominent amongst the rebels.[50]

While the oath swearing campaign of the magistrates may have hampered
the spread of the United Irishmen in some areas, in others it merely provided
a smoke screen behind which to organise. In the wake of the rebellion, Irvin
Johnson informed Castlereagh that every one of the Cavan signatories 'were
less or more concerned in Defenderism and United business', and that they had
continued their meetings in spite of their loyal professions. Musgrave believed
that most of the priests in Mayo and Sligo had orchestrated loyal resolutions
in order to 'disarm the suspicion, and lull the vigilance of the government and
magistrates'.[51] he would say that — 1801

Just as a variety of circumstances led priests to 'declare' their support for the
government, so too a spectrum of motives led the clergy to embrace the rebel
cause in 1798. By far the largest group among the clergy, however, were those
who merely laid low and avoided taking any part, either for or against, the
rebellion. Their inactivity, interpreted in the light of the declarations of the
hierarchy, has supported the image of a loyal clergy in '98. But equally, their
silence has been interpreted as providing tacit support for the rebel cause.

II

Since 1945, Hayes' analysis of the role of the clergy during the rebellion has
provided the starting point for most research on this subject.[52] He flatly
rejected the notion that the Catholic clergy had opposed the 'national move-

ment' of the time, and sought to illustrate beyond doubt their crucial role in the events of 1798. In pursuit of this aim, he assembled information on the activities of 58 priests implicated in sedition and provided a potted biography of each. Of this number, three were killed in the fighting, eight were executed, eleven became fugitives after the rebellion, twenty-six were arrested and another ten had no action taken against them.[53] Out of a total of almost 1,800 priests in the country, Hayes's figure represents but a tiny fraction–even amongst these 58 priests many had only tenuous links with sedition–but he argued that silence and hostility to the cause were not synonymous.[54]

Clergy became involved in the rebellion for many reasons. These remain difficult to discern, due to the nature of the sources and, thus, clerical motivation has become entangled in a complex historiographical web, which allows for little analysis of the relationship between actions and possible motives. There are instances of clerical involvement in the United Irishmen but, just as pressure had been used to elicit loyal responses, so too the 'rebel priests' often found themselves in invidious circumstances. There are many accounts of priests being intimidated by radicals. On the eve of the rebellion, Troy identified these fears in a letter to his rural vicars. James Lanigan had earlier referred to the fear of assassination which prevented the priests of Ossory denouncing the United Irishmen.[55] After preaching against disaffection in March 1798, the parish priest of Cashel, Fr Mackey, received an anonymous note warning 'death before dishonour'. The note included a salutary reminder of the use to which the guillotine had been put amongst the French clergy.[56]

In Dublin, Francis Higgins informed the Castle of information he had learned from Fr Sherlock, the parish priest of Meath Street. According to Higgins, the Dublin priests had followed Troy's instructions and counselled loyalty, but the various chapels were then visited by some of the well-known leaders (John Keogh, Hugh Hamill, Richard McCormick and Edward Byrne) and they had issued the priests with stern warnings:

> if they should, in any manner whatsoever, presume to interfere or to advise, or to admonish the people on political subjects, or against the means of their obtaining their rights–the different committees who collect for the support of their chapels and for the maintenance of their priests had so settled that they should not get so much as a single sixpence to support them, and let those who cannot be silent go to the government for support.[57]

Such threats cannot have been easily ignored by the clergy and undoubtedly count for a good deal of the clerical silence during the rebellion.

The clergy of the city of Dublin came under the closest scrutiny by the Castle runners in the years preceeding the rebellion, and their reports to government pointed to their unreliability. Corbett's accounts reflected a large group of 'democrats' in their midst while, in May 1797, Francis Higgins warned that 'there is not, out of the vast number of priests in this city, twenty loyal Roman Catholic clergymen'.[58] While the city failed to rise in '98, many Dublin priests were taken up; yet none of these were called to answer any charges more substantial than 'seditious practices'.

Ceasar Colclough urged that a strict eye be kept on John Connolly, a Franciscan from Booterstown, County Dublin who, he was convinced, had done great damage by his preaching.[59] Corbett's celebrated report of 1796 described the friar as a 'democrat' but, during the rebellion Connolly informed John Lees, a noted hardline loyalist, of rebel activity above Dublin. This information, which may very well have been a ploy to disguise his own activity, described in detail the rebel plans for an assault on the city and told of the numbers of people missing from their homes, whom he presumed had joined the rebels.[60] In any event, despite this loyal display, Connolly was imprisoned for some time and although he remained parish priest of Booterstown until his death in 1811, there is little doubt of the Franciscan's radical links.

He constantly visited the state prisoners at Kilmainham and, in later years developed a close friendship with Miles Byrne, who was at the centre of a circle of former radicals in Dublin. Byrne recalled in his *Memoirs* spending many evenings with Connolly discussing the state of the country after the Act of Union. He described him as 'very well informed and enlightened' and, as Byrne listened to him 'with delight', he was flattered at the confidence the priest placed in him.[61] Miles Byrne had a similar friendship with Fr John Barrett. Imprisoned at the end of June 1798, Barrett was lodged at Newgate and although his name appeared on the Banishment Act, there is no record of the charges brought against him.[62] On his release later in the year, Barrett opened a school in Lucan, but later returned as a curate to Francis Street.[63] In July 1798, Miles Byrne left Dublin and sought refuge for some days with Barrett in Lucan; in later years he frequently visited the 'patriotic priest' in Francis Street.[64]

Barrett was assisted in his Lucan academy by Father Long, formerly prior of the Carmelite priory in Stephen's Street, another of the Dublin priests implicated in United Irish activity. Like so many of the 'patriot priests', Long was caricatured in reports to the Castle as a drinker, and deemed an orator 'among the vulgar of his sect'. He wore his hair in the 'croppy cut', and was reported frequently drinking in the Widow Reilly's in Johnson's Court. With his fondness for feasting, he dined every Friday in Hearn's Hotel, 'it being a fish day'. Long was active swearing members of the United Irishmen and, in the aftermath of the rebellion he was reported in uniform with Humbert and the French officers at Litchfield in England. Banished from Dublin in 1798, Long subsequently lived in the friary at Loughrea, County Galway. [65]

Perhaps the most celebrated of the Dublin priests exiled in 1798 was James Harold, parish priest of Saggart. Educated in Antwerp, Harold served as parish priest of Kilcullen before being transferred to Saggart in 1794.[66] In the course of 1798 he was variously reported to have been actively preaching peace in his parish, while on other occasions he rebuked the yeomanry and militia for their barbarous conduct.[67] Harold was arrested on the word of John Clinch, a United Irish captain who confessed to have been sworn by him; elsewhere, it was reported that pikes had been found in his thatch.[68] Harold was apprehended in August by the Rathcoole Cavalry while returning from a visit to his friend, Father John Leonard, the parish priest of Ardcath in the Diocese of Meath. According to the *Dublin Journal*, Harold produced a protection from the military commander at Drogheda but, in spite of this he was taken prisoner to Dublin Castle.[69]

Troy wrote to Edward Cooke three times seeking information about the captured priest, but his efforts came to nothing.[70] Harold was transported to Australia along with Joseph Holt on the prison ship *Minerva*. In the 1850s, Madden collected information on Harold for his intended history of the persecution of the Catholic clergy in 1798. Included in this was material relating to his time in Australia where Harold quickly established himself as a popular figure in the colony, having entertained the crowds on the quay in Sydney with a rendition of, 'The Exile of Erin', the famous United Irish song attributed to Rev. James Porter. Some months later he was removed to Norfolk Island following accusations that he had incited a revolt amongst the convicts.[71]

Significantly, Watty Cox published an account of Fr Harold in 1812, which reported that the priest was in good health and enjoying the company of Peter Ivers, the United Irish leader from Carlow arrested in Oliver Bond's house.[72] Again, this connection suggests a sympathy for the rebel cause, if not a direct link with the conspiracy, despite the priest's claim to have known 'no more of the rebellion or the United Irishmen than the child unborn'.[73] Harold returned to Dublin and was reinstated as parish priest of Kilcullen by Troy in 1815. Nicholas Kearns, a curate in Meath Street was arrested in June 1798, but shortly afterwards was 'honourably liberated'.[74] Kearns had been labelled a

Fig. 19 Fr John Murphy (Courtesy of Nicholas Furlong)

'democrat' by Corbett in 1796, and was reported to be continually visiting the
state prisoners at Kilmainham. On another occasion, the informer Samuel
Sproule reported that 'Father Kearns of Meath Street chapel had attended Lord
Edward Fitzgerald in his last moments'.[75] James Bush of Denmark Street friary
was banished, and most probably went to New York, as did his fellow
Dominican, Batholomew Augustine MacMahon, of the same friary. MacMahon
too had been described by Corbett as a 'democrat'; Leonard McNally believed
he had been 'both active and successful' in the conspiracy. MacMahon's name
appeared in the confession of a United Irishman who claimed to have been
sworn by the priest, who was assisted in the swearing by Fr Luby of Liffey
Street chapel. MacMahon made his way, via Philadelphia, to New York where
he died of yellow fever in 1800. In 1801, Francis Higgins predicted an
imminent French invasion of Ireland. He based his report on information
received from Fitzimmons of Capel Street, 'a violent United Irishman' who
had received three letters from Paris in relation to his attempts to recover a
legacy left to his wife by Fr MacMahon.[76]
   Two Augustinians of John's Lane, Kelly–also a 'Democrat'–and Kearns,
were reported to have been actively swearing United Irishmen in the Thomas
Street district, the very heart of United Irish activity in the south side of the city.
They had previously assisted John Sweetman in this but, since his arrest in

March 1798, they had worked along with James Moore, the ironmonger of Thomas Street.[77] By then, Moore's Work House Division of the United Irishmen had assumed the role of the Directory in the national structures of the organisation. It is significant that another Augustinian, John Martin of Drogheda, was commissioned by Moore to meet up with the Wicklow rebels in 1798, and it is likely that Augustinian channels were used to carry communications between Thomas Street and Drogheda. No measures appear to have been taken against the friars. Similarly, James Moran of Adam and Eve's was arrested in 1798 and held for over a year; no charges were brought against him and he appears to have been held solely because he had been personated during the rebellion.[78]

In all, eleven Dublin priests were implicated in United Irish activities; the small total illustrates the exaggerated nature of the Castle's intelligence prior to the rebellion. But, despite the lack of evidence brought against these eleven priests and their shadowy role in the conspiracy, the close connections between them suggests they formed part of a radical network in the city. It is also of interest that two of their number, Connolly and Harold, were parish priests while Long was the prior of his religious community. This is in contrast to the generally accepted picture of the 'patriot priests' as curates, often isolated or maginalised within Church structures. It is also significant that both Connolly and Harold were reappointed by Troy to their parishes once they had served their sentences. Within Dublin diocese, there were also conspicuous displays of loyalty. Father Christopher Low of Glendalough, County Wicklow, went on his knees before the rebels and prevented the destruction of the homes of several loyalists. As the battle raged in Arklow, Daniel Murray, later Archbishop of Dublin, made his way to the local magistrate and declared his fidelity to the crown.[79] While Troy deplored 'the perversity or insanity' of some of his clergy, he was comforted by the loyal conduct of the others. He was convinced that had it not been for his own prompt action the chapels of the city would certainly have been closed.[80]

Troy's neighbouring diocese, Kildare and Leighlin, witnessed a great deal of fighting in 1798, but only two priests there were associated with the rebel cause. Lord Tyrawley had no doubts about the others in the area, all of whom had refused absolution to the United Irishmen. By the middle of June he was confident that the people were 'heartily sick of rebellion'.[81] In Monasterevin which was levelled in '98, however, the curate, Edward Prendergast, was taken up by the yeomanry and tried by courtmartial under Lord Tyrawley. Protections had been given to the rebels who surrendered, but there was sufficient evidence against the priest to warrant his execution.

Prendergast had been reported at the rebel camp, encouraging the men with a pistol in his hand and giving absolution to United Irishmen. Following his execution, the local people tried to claim the priest's body, but Sir James Duff had it buried beneath the tree on which he was hanged. Local tradition maintained that Prendergast had gone to the camp to baptise a child, and the priest's memory lived long after his death. The local member of the Catholic Board became known as 'Prendergast' Cassidy, as he lived opposite the tree on which the priest died and, in 1815, Watty Cox mockingly announced that the tree was to be placed on the Ecclesiastical Establishment List. On such a tree, he declared, 'only shall such popish priests be hanged as may be convicted on the drum head of aiding and comforting foreign or domestic enemies'.[82]

A second priest of the diocese, Fr Travers, pastor of Baltinglass, was imprisoned shortly after the outbreak of the rebellion. Travers made himself obnoxious to the local magistrates in the early months of 1798, and they were particularly angered at his failure to collect arms. In early May it was reported that he rode up and down his parish, feigning to be collecting arms and took great delight in presenting the odd pike when he knew there were hundreds concealed in the area.[83] Similar charges were frequently made against him; in mid-May, a local correspondent to the Castle enquired if an 'honest and loyal popish priest' would have any better effect, but he doubted that one existed since 'it is inconsistent with the very object and principles of their religion'.[84]

At the outbreak of the rebellion, Travers approached a local magistrate and offered his assistance in recovering arms, but his offer came to nothing. Captain O'Neal-Stratford decided to arrest the 'drunken' priest and Travers was courtmartialed and sentenced to death. Evidence was given against him by one of Rochfort's Cavalry, and by Lord Aldborough who alleged that he had joined the rebels.[85] At the trial, a paid informer swore that Travers was a United Irishman and that he had travelled as a delegate from Dublin to Belfast and on to France. On hearing this, the priest exclaimed from the dock: 'It was far enough to send me to Dublin', he cried, 'or even to Belfast, but to send me all the way to France goes beyond all the bounds of probability'.[86] The sentence on Travers was never carried out and he was eventually released. A letter from 'a Carlow Friend' in the *Irish Magazine* attributed his release to the intervention of Troy at the Castle, but this is unlikely. It is more probable that execution was suspended, as the same letter suggests, due to the levels of perjury at the trial, or possibly as a consequence of Cornwallis's policy of reviewing all courtmartial convictions.[87]

Much of the blame for the sectarian tension in County Carlow from the early months of 1798 was laid at the door of the local clergy. The prison inspector

Rev. Foster Archer reported that the priests had been 'extensively at work, promoting and cherishing those vile rumours' of an imminent Orange massacre.[88] Yet, despite of these suggestions, other indications point to widespread clerical opposition to the United Irishmen. Peter Ivers claimed that, apart from 'two or three', the priests were 'universally against them', while William Farrell recalled the unsuccessful attempts made by Henry Staunton and William Fitzgerald–clergymen who had narrowly escaped France during the revolution–to dissuade Ivers from joining the United Irishmen.[89] During the fighting, John O'Neill, parish priest of Tinryland, went on his knees and begged Michael Heydon and his party of rebels to return to their homes. Heydon, who had assumed command in Carlow following Ivers's arrest, ignored the priest's appeal and his men continued their march on the town.[90]

Francis Hearn, a former student of Carlow College, was executed in Waterford in November 1799 on charges of United Irish membership, swearing, and organising rebellion as late as the previous September.[91] Hearn was a nephew of Thomas Hussey's vicar general and this, together with the fact that he had formerly been a student at Maynooth, was seized upon as further ammunition for the black propagandists. Hearn's execution in Waterford became a public spectacle; on the scaffold he was interrogated by William Power, the parish priest of Ballybricken, in an effort to demonstrate the loyalty of the Church and of Maynooth College. In the course of this examination Hearn condemned Henry Jackson and Dr Drennan who had sworn him, declared them unfit persons to live in society, and 'lamented his ever having seen them'.[92]

Troy was particularly incensed by allegations in the Dublin Journal that he had made 'great exertions' at the Castle in an effort to secure a pardon for Hearn, who was incorrectly described as a student of Maynooth.[93] In a hard hitting letter to Alexander Marsden at the Castle, Troy railed against the partisan bias of the Journal and urged him to exert the editor to withdraw the account, which had intended to discredit both the hierarchy and the college. Troy denied having made any appeals on Hearn's behalf, in spite of requests to do so, and outlined for Marsden Hearn's record, including his expulsion from Maynooth for United Irish activity in May 1798. Hearn had been just three months in Carlow College, but Troy was adamant he had not imbibed seditious principles there, as 'the superior and masters of it were to my own knowledge as loyal as myself or any other person in the kingdom'.[94] The Dublin Journal published a feeble correction, but Hearn's behaviour had greatly damaged the reputation of Maynooth and added fuel to the bitter polemic then raging.[95]

III

Much of the post-rebellion war of words focused on the role of the clergy in the diocese of Ferns where, of a total of 85 priests, eleven became actively involved in the rebellion. The rebellion in Wexford was labelled a sectarian war, and a myriad of loyalist writers developed the early impressions of the Lord Lieutenant who described a:

> religious frenzy which agitates the rebels in Wexford; that they are headed by their priests and that they halt every half mile to pray, that the deluded multitude are taught to consider themselves as fighting for their religion, that their enthusiasm is most alarming.[96]

While the exaggerations of the violently anti-Catholic accounts of Duigenan and Musgrave are apparent, the basis of their allegations is well founded.[97] The Bishop of Ferns, James Caulfield, was acutely embarrassed by the scale of clerical involvement in the rebellion in his diocese and he engaged the assistance of Archbishop Troy and J. B. Clinch, professor of rhetoric at Maynooth, in an attempt to vindicate the reputation of the clergy of County Wexford. A great deal of the surviving Caulfield/Troy correspondence from this period consists of information supplied by Caulfield which was to form the basis for the essay published under the pseudonym *Veritas*, and for the *Reply* of the Bishop of Ferns to the allegations of Musgrave.[98]

Caulfield consciously played down the role of the clergy amongst the rebels and made great efforts to stress the loyalty of the majority of his priests. The rebel clerics were presented as unreliable individuals, with only three of them, John Murphy, Nicholas Stafford and Philip Roche, being offically accredited priests of the mission. The remainder he dismissed as 'giddy' men, drinkers, or 'notorious agitators'. Caulfield's anxiety to refute loyalist allegations against his clergy, and the ease with which he dismissed the 'rebel priests', played into the hands of Edward Hay, Thomas Cloney and other former United Irishmen anxiously striving to play down the existence of any conspiracy in 1798. The priests were now cast in the role of the 'reluctant rebel' discussed above.

Whelan's examination of the role of the Catholic clergy has questioned the conventional wisdom of the 'patriot priest'. In place of the all-embracing 'mighty wave', he describes the complex motives and circumstances which led the priests to take up the rebel cause, and their subsequent careers, shorn of the hagiography, have been mapped in detail.[99] Whelan points to the close social and family connections between the 'rebel priests' and particular United Irishmen–thus Edward Synnott was a distant relative of the Cloneys, the Dorans of Oulart, and the Rices of Tinnacross, all committed United Irishmen; Fr Thomas Dixon's family had marriage links with the Roches of Garrylough, to whom Fr Michael Murphy was also related; Fr John Murphy had been a regular visitor to the Fitzgeralds of Newpark. Such links were bound to bring the clergy within United Irish circles; the distances travelled by priests to join the rebels, and their recognition within rebel command structures–in preference to known United Irish members–reflects more than involuntary participation.

Whelan's studies have placed the rebel priests in a broader perspective, showing very real connections between the clergy and the United Irishmen, but his reliance on the Caulfield/Troy correspondence fails to establish whether or not they were actually United Irish members. This latter possibility has occupied a good deal of Cullen's attention; he hints at significant clerical membership of the United Irishmen in Wexford.[100] Rescued from Caulfield's bias, the United Irish priests in Wexford are emerging with greater clarity as men immersed in communities that were gradually being penetrated by United Irish principles, with they themselves being inexorably drawn in.

IV

Neighbouring Munster remained relatively quiet in 1798 and, perhaps in consequence, few priests of the Province of Cashel were arrested for sedition or involvement in United Irish activities. In the Diocese of Cashel, three priests were arrested for alleged involvement in the rebellion, but in all three cases, the charges brought against them were unsubstantiated. John O'Brien, parish priest of Doon, County Limerick, was taken before three justices of the peace in Tipperary and sentenced to transportation for treason. O'Brien spent six weeks at Duncannon but was released by General Fawcett on taking an oath of allegiance. He was rearrested the following March, but was again freed following petitions to the Castle on his behalf from Lord Donoughmore and Archbishop Bray, who described the priest as 'undesigning and inoffensive'.

Fr O'Brien made a personal appeal to Cornwallis in which he outlined the history of his case. He explained how, in early June 1798, he had met with a very large party of men on the road late at night. Without recognising any of the group, he admonished them and urged them to return to their homes.

Shortly afterwards he was arrested, but was unable to give satisfactory information as to the mens' identities and was imprisoned as a result. Released after a short time, he was not restored to his parish, because Dr Bray was certain that such a hasty move would give offence.[101]

The parish priest of Nenagh, William O'Meara, was arrested on 22 May 1798 following claims that a United Irish committee had met in his house.[102] O'Meara was never brought to trial, but remained confined on board the prison ship *Princess* at Cove, County Cork, despite the ruling of a court of enquiry which denounced his irregular situation. In evidence to the court, it was said that O'Meara deserved 'the greatest indulgence', since he had alerted the authorities to a planned mutiny and capture of the ship by the prisoners on the voyage from Waterford to Cove. Local tradition, however, held that O'Meara died on board the ship as a result of harsh treatment. Fr Talbot, parish priest of Duhara, County Tipperary, supposedly met a similar fate.[103]

In the Diocese of Cloyne, two priests were banished for United Irish activity. Anthony Kelly of Mallow was forced to flee the town in mid-May having been charged with United Irish membership. In September, he appealed to Cornwallis for permission to return, declaring his greatest detestation of recent acts of outrage and his willingness to take the loyal oath.[104] The parish priest of Ballymacoda near Youghal was transported to Van Diemen's Land for his part in the rebellion. Peter O'Neill, had been a professor at the Irish College Paris, but his appointment to Ballymacoda was marked by controversy; disappointed that the existing curate had been passed over, locals initially refused him entry to his church.

In 1798, much of east Cork was marked by bitter sectarian tension and in the town of Youghal a great deal of animosity was directed towards the Catholic clergy.[105] Following the outbreak of rebellion, forty-year-old O'Neill was charged with treason and aiding in the murder of a deserter from the army, a former United Irishman turned informer. Thomas Neill of Cork was hanged for his part in the murder; in a confession on the gallows, he denied any knowledge of O'Neill's part in the crime; nevertheless the priest was taken to Youghal and given a severe flogging.[106] In the course of his torture before Lord Loftus and the magistrate Rev. Mr Rogers, he confessed to an involvement in planning the murders and of giving the killers absolution afterwards.[107]

O'Neill was confined for a year on board the prison ship *Anne* before being transported to Australia.[108] He had been sentenced solely on the basis of his own uncorroborated confession, extracted during a severe flogging. Following various representations, Lord Cornwallis ordered a re-examination of the conviction under General Graham. This enquiry ordered O'Neill's release, but

Colonel Littlehale's instructions arrived after the *Anne* had departed for Sydney.[109] Further appeals were made on O'Neill's behalf, by Troy amongst others, and his case was reopened by Lord Hardwicke. O'Neill finally returned to Ireland in mid-1802 and was reinstated in his parish by Bishop Coppinger, returning as Lord Redesdale declared 'a martyr in triumph, with insult to the offended justice of the laws'.[110]

On his return O'Neill published a controversial account of his sufferings, which initiated a bitter polemic, illustrating the sectarian tensions in Youghal. The official response to O'Neill's *Remonstrance* maintained that Coppinger had reinstated him in Ballymacoda in an effort 'to kindle fanaticism in the popish multitude, who approached him with enthusiastic zeal, and revered him as a martyr, persecuted by heretics on account of his holy religion'.[111] O'Neill remained in Ballymacoda until his death in 1846 at the age of 88.

Similar uncertainty surrounded the sentence imposed on John Brookes, parish priest of Shinrone, King's County in the Diocese of Killaloe. Shinrone had a long history of sectarianism. As early as 1778, Brookes was embroiled in local disputes which singled him out as a target in 1798.[112] He was charged with treason and sentenced to the unusual punishment of transportation to Connaught for seven years. Bishop Michael Peter MacMahon, convinced of his innocence, made representations on his behalf to Cornwallis; his account of the courtmartial is a stark reflection of both the weakness of the charges against him and the levels to which the clergy were exposed to the political upheavals of the time;

Q: Did you apply to General Dunn through Sir Lawrence Parsons for a trial?

A: I did.

Q: Are you now prepared for your trial?

A: Feeling myself perfectly innocent of the crime with which I stand charged, I am always ready for trial.

Q: Did you not say a first Mass in Shinrone with a view to prevent the people from taking the loyal oath?

A: No, for in the year 1796 I took the oath in the court house at Birr myself. Since that period, I took it at the head of my flock and the flock also took it at the same time.

Q: Did you not receive a letter of mine [Capt. Rollestone] to read at your altar which you did not read?

A: I proved that I read it.

Q: Had you not a United Irish oath concealed in your house?

A: I have been in common with many others of the surrounding neighbourhood a subscriber to the Roscrea newspaper called the *Southern Star*. This paper I received, as did many others at the office at Shinrone, in one of which was inserted the form of the Orangeman's and the United Irishman's oath. The paper was received by many others on the same day containing the same copies and I presume my receiving that paper is [not more] notorious criminal, in me than in them.

Q: Had you in your possession a seditious paper called *The Press*?

A: I had a paper of that description but once, and the gentleman of whom I borrowed it for mere curiosity to read, is here present. The gentleman came forward and avowed having lent it to him.[113]

Brookes was driven out of the town to Connaught and his chapel was burned to the ground by a party lead by Jackson Rea, a justice of the peace. He was as unwelcome across the Shannon where the people, seeing his banishment as a slight on their loyalty, forced him back to Shinrone.[114] MacMahon made further appeals on Brookes's behalf, emphasising the shortage of priests in his diocese. In a compromise, the authorities settled on his leaving Leinster and Brookes moved to Ballingarry in County Tipperary.[115] According to local tradition he later returned to Shinrone and assisted the pastor, Francis Kennedy, who had been charged with United Irish membership in 1798. At his trial, it was stated that Kennedy had been sworn by Fr O'Meara of Nenagh, but a sentence against him was dropped and he received a pardon.[116]

There were further outbreaks in the Diocese of Killaloe in early January 1799 as a series of disturbances in Clare threatened to develop into a full-scale agrarian revolt. Despite the history of Whiteboy activity in the county, the violence of 1799 formed more of a postscript to the rebellion than agrarian disorder. The *Clare Journal* reported that the insurgents were 'led on and instigated by strangers who have got among them, supposed to be some of those who escaped the late rebellion'.[117] From Ennistymon, it was reported in late January that 'the priests from the country were at the bottom of all this business', but that no information could be found to convict them.[118] It is in this context that Coleman Hynes and Charles Carrig were arrested, rather than in connection with the rebellion as has generally been assumed.[119]

Fr Coleman Hynes of Corofin had been educated in France and joined the French army, from which he deserted and returned to Ireland in 1798. In January 1799, he was arrested by the Romney Fencibles and lodged in Ennis, but was released without trial.[120] Fr Charles Carrig of Kilfenora was taken to

Ennis gaol in March and courtmartialed on charges of treason. Following an appeal to the Lord Lieutenant, he was brought to trial in September 1799. He produced supporting witnesses, but remained in jail following the evidence of a 'notoriously infamous' horse thief.[121] Archbishop Troy made appeals on his behalf and, despite initial refusals, he was eventually released and returned to his parish.[122]

V

In spite of the rumbling discontent in Connaught from the middle of the decade, the west of Ireland remained quiet throughout the summer of 1798. This silence was abruptly shattered in late August as a French expeditionary force of one thousand men under General Humbert landed at Killala and began the last campaign of the rebellion. The French were greeted with unrestrained enthusiasm by the locals, but the events of the summer had taken their toll upon the United Irishmen, who were unable to mount a significant response to the news of the long awaited landing.

Humbert was not deterred and vainly began a march towards the midlands which was to end in ignominious defeat at Ballinamuck. The presence of the French gave the rebellion quite a different character in the west and a significant number of the clergy, many of whom had been educated in France, lent their assistance to the campaign. The clergy became involved in varied capacities; some acted as translators, others as guides, some took responsibility for securing provisions, while others, including Dominic Bellew, the Bishop of Killala, were alleged to have served on the municipal councils established by the French.

The standard history of the rebellion in the west remains Richard Hayes' *Last Invasion of Ireland*, first published in 1937.[123] Despite its shortcomings, in particular its total lack of reference to the broader United Irish context, this contributes a great deal of our knowledge of the role of the clergy in the west. Appropriately, the first French officer to land was the Mayo priest, Henry O'Kane. Educated in the Irish college at Paris, O'Kane served as parish priest of Saint Hermand near Nantes. He was a member of *Les Irlandais du soleil levant*, an Irish Masonic lodge in Paris in the 1780s, and joined the French army at the outbreak of the revolutionary wars.

As he was the only Irish speaker in the invading army, Captain O'Kane was appointed translator and aide-de-camp to General Humbert.[124] Musgrave, who wished to present the campaign as a popish crusade, records O'Kane on a platform in Ballina addressing a vast crowd and inciting them with stories of apparitions he received from the Virgin Mary, instructing him to lead an army to Ireland. In the liberal Bishop Stock's account, the French officers were hailed by the crowd as heroes in arms 'for France and the Blessed Virgin', while James Little recalled the use of the scapulars by the crowd. In the following year Edward Dillon, the Archbishop of Tuam, felt it necessary to issue pastoral instructions regulating the use of scapulars which he declared had become 'badges of sedition'.[125] O'Kane distinguished himself in the attacks on Killala and Castlebar, and his exertions on behalf of the local Protestants were praised by Stock in his *Narrative*. Surprisingly, Musgrave included a barbed acknowledgment of O'Kane's humanity, referring to his efforts on all occasions to curb 'the bloodthirsty disposition of the popish multitude'.[126]

O'Kane was courtmartialled in November and faced execution for treason. However, on account of his undisputed rank in the French army, he was banished for life. Returning to France, he resumed his military career and was awarded the Legion of Honour for his services in the republican armies in Germany, Spain and Portugal. Miles Byrne recalled meeting him regularly in Paris, where he frequently entertained the Irish officers. O'Kane apparently wrote an account of Humbert's campaign which he passed to Dr MacNeven for publication, but this appears to have been lost.[127]

Also prominent amongst the French was Fr Michael Gannon of Louisburgh, County Mayo, educated in France and former chaplain to the Duke of Crillon. He returned to Ireland after the revolution, but rushed to join the French at Killala, serving as 'fournisseur general' and as a translator to the army. Musgrave records him haranguing the crowd from the window of Humbert's apartment, calling on them to join the rebel ranks. It was claimed that he had shown the crowd holy oils which he promised would cure their wounds.[128] After the collapse of the rebellion, Gannon hid in Connemara, resisting all attempts at capture, despite a reward of £100 offered for him.[129] Escaping from Ireland, he made his way to Spain and from there to Paris with the assistance of Lucien Bonaparte, French ambassador in Madrid. As parish priest of St Germain en Laye, Gannon developed friendships with Miles Byrne and Thomas Addis Emmet.[130]

A similar reward was offered for the capture of Manus Sweeny of Newport. Sweeny had studied at Paris and quickly joined the French at Killala, bringing many of his parishioners with him. He was captured in September 1798 but escaped, only to be betrayed by Michael Conmee, parish priest of Ardagh, who received £50 for his information.[131] Sweeny was subsequently executed for

Fig. 20 Leonard McNally
(N.L.I.)

treason. Myles Prendergast, the Augustinian prior of Murrisk, had a more successful escape and remained at liberty in Connemara until his death more than thirty years later. Prendergast had joined the rebels and made a considerable contribution to the campaign on account of his popularity.[132] He was captured after the Battle of Ballinamuck and lodged in Castlebar, but managed to escape, killing a prison guard in the process. While in hiding in Connemara, Prendergast joined with other former rebels, including the notorious smuggler Johnny 'the outlaw' Gibbons and they successfully avoided capture.

Musgrave, who described Prendergast in particularly jaundiced terms, incorrectly recorded his death in 1801. Prendergast, however, lived on for almost another thirty years, and was maintained by the provincial of the Augustinians, with whom he maintained a correspondence. John Rice, assistant general of the order–whose brother Edmund founded the Irish Christian Brothers–applied to Propaganda on Predergast's behalf, for a dispensation for killing the prison guard. This was granted on the understanding that the dead man was a Protestant, but once it emerged that he had killed a Catholic the decision was reversed and the case referred to the Holy Office.[133] A great deal of folklore has survived about Prendergast, who was celebrated in the poetry of Antoine Ó Raifteirí.[134]

A second Augustinian, Owen Killeen of Ballyovey in County Galway, also joined the rebels. It was reported that he had done a great deal of United Irish organising in Sligo, before going to Mayo where he had 'sworn half the county'. Killeen surrendered under the terms of the proclamation in September 1799 and was banished overseas.[135] Fr. Bernard Dease of Kilglass, County Galway, was arrested outside Ballina on 4 September and fired at the yeoman trying to apprehend him. Once captured, Dease made a full confession incriminating several clerics, including Bishop Bellew.

The bishop, who allegedly served as president of the Ballina Committee of Public Safety and whose brother, Matthew, was one of the leading military commanders, lost no time in trying to clear his name.[136] In spite of his protests, suspicion continued to surround Bellew and almost a year later he was aware that many still believed him 'unfit to act in ... [his episcopal] capacity any longer'.[137] Bellew's application for compensation from the Commission for Suffering Loyalists was rejected in September 1799, but he continued to stress his loyalty, giving his active support to the advancement of the Act of Union and acting, on occasion, as agent to the local magnate, Lord Tyrawley.[138]

The four priests mentioned by Dease were less fortunate. Owen Crowley, of Castleconner, County Sligo, had been educated in France and served as translator to Truc, the commander at Ballina. Musgrave accused him of intending to massacre 120 Protestants in the jail of Ballina, and only the rebel defeat at Ballinamuck prevented the slaughter.[139] Similar accusations were made against him by General Trench, who described Crowley as a 'very principal leader of the rebellion'. The priest avoided capture, in spite of a reward of £300 offered for him, but continued to agitate the county, remaining a thorn in the side of the authorities until his death. Musgrave's allegations of Crowley's sectarianism, repeated in *Veridicus,* were a source of acute embarrassment to Bishops Troy and Caulfield, then actively attempting to suppress such accusations against the clergy of Wexford.[140]

Fr James Conroy of Adragool, County Roscommon, was active in swearing United Irish members in 1798. He assisted the French and is credited with planning Humbert's route across the mountains by Crossmolina to Castlebar, which allowed them to surprise the garrison. The discovery of various proclamations, along with guns and ammunition in his house, sealed his fate and he was subsequently executed.[141] Of the remaining priests inplicated in the rebellion, little but passing references survive. Fr Boetius Egan, vicar general and parish priest of Castlebar, served on Humbert's municipal council of that town.[142] Fr. McGowan of Crossmolina had been 'very active' in the rebellion, but there was insufficient evidence to convict him.

Musgrave depicted McGowan as a notorious drunkard who had narrowly
escaped the gallows, only to die in a fall from a horse as a result of excessive
indulgence 'in the joys of Bacchus'.[143] Fr Thomas Monelly, administrator of
the Backs, led many of his parishioners to Ballina where he served under
Captain Truc. He was one of those informed on by Bernard Dease, and was
imprisoned in New Geneva in November 1799, but escaped from there to the
United States where he became pastor of a parish in Maryland.[144] David Kelly,
of Ballysakerry, County Mayo, joined Humbert together with a large number
of his parishioners. He too avoided capture as did Fr Browne of Foxford, Fr
Pheilim McDonnell of Easkey and Fr O'Donnell of Kilmeckshalgan.[145]

In all sixteen priests, including the Bishop of Killala, or just over five per
cent of a total of 314 priests in the province, were implicated in the French
campaign to varying degrees. The scant nature of the sources, however, makes
a thorough analysis of clerical involvement difficult. Most accounts of the
rebellion in the west have relied on Bishop Stock's *Narrative* which plays
down the political conspiracy in the region. The presence of the French
removed a United Irish focus from the rebellion and consequently it is difficult
to place the priests in a broader political perspective.

In his recent study of Protestant Ireland in the eighteenth century, Connolly
appears to accept the narrow partisan interpretation of the western rebellion,
believing that Humbert and his men were welcomed, 'not as bearers of liberty,
equality and brotherhood, but in the name of confessional and dynastic
loyalties of the ancien régime'. They were, in Stock's words (which Connolly
attributes to Elliott), saviours 'come to take arms for France and the Blessed
Virgin'.[146] At its very simplest, clerical participation may be explained by
arguing that the priests' continental connections made them natural allies of
the French, yet the commitment they showed to the cause indicates otherwise.
The substantial evidence of priests swearing and marshalling their flocks
behind the French and the distances some travelled to join with Humbert's
army indicates principled motivation. Miles Byrne's account of the close ties
between the former rebels and clerical exiles in Paris is further testimony of
their sympathies for the United Irish cause.

VI

The ecclesiastical Province of Armagh was arguably the most highly politicised of the four in Ireland. It included not only Ulster, but much of the northern
parts of Connaught and Leinster, and covered the heartland of both the

Defenders and the United Irishmen. The unceasing flux of the 1790s had released enormous political energy which the United Irishmen had successfully harnessed. Yet, General Lake's 'dragooning' of Ulster and the draconian measures adopted by the military inflicted severe damage on the United Irish organisation in the province in 1796-7. When the eventual 'burst' came in 1798 the rebels were a poor match for the forces of the crown.[147]

While the United Irish organisation and rebellion in Ulster have traditionally been characterised as a predominantly Protestant affair, recent scholarship has increasingly pointed to the crucial nexus between Presbyterian radicals and Catholic Defenders.[148] From their foundation in 1791, the United Irishmen recognised the potential of such an alliance and invested considerable energy in forging a union with the Defenders. Although Bartlett dates an effective alliance to the post Fitzwilliam period, it is in this context that we should see the various missions of Tone, Teeling, Tandy, Russell and Keogh throughout Ulster earlier in the decade.[149]

From the outset, a crucial part in this 'uniting business' was played by James O'Coigley, a priest of the Armagh diocese. O'Coigley was unique among the 'patriot priests' of the 1790s in that he left a memoir of his life and from this and other sources, particularly the reports of his trial, it is possible to place him firmly within a United Irish context.[150] This memoir was edited by his close friend and relative Valentine Derry, a leader of the Louth Defenders, and it was drawn from a series of autobiographical letters written by O'Coigley during his imprisonment. To these letters, Derry added a preface and O'Coigley's 'Address to the People of Ireland'; the *Life* was originally published in the *Courier* newspaper. It was subsequently printed in London and, according to Benjamin Binns, forty thousand copies were circulated, reflecting again the extensive use of the printed word.[151]

The memoir, described by O'Coigley on the scaffold as 'a sketch of my unfortunate and afflicted life', was an appeal for clemency, and many implicating details of his career were suppressed by Derry.[152] Madden later claimed that 'declarations of innocence were given in that published statement, which were never made by the Armagh priest.[153] O'Coigley is also set apart from the 'rebel priests' in that a full record of his trial survives which throws light on his activities throughout the 1790s. In this also, O'Coigley's case is unique, and the flimsy courtmartial reports of Father John Martin of Drogheda and John Redmond of Wexford are the only comparable accounts.[154]

O'Coigley was born in 1761. As a student in the Lombard College, Paris, he witnessed the French Revolution at first hand. There, like so many other clerics, he ran many risks and narrowly escaped being lanternised by the mob.

O'Coigley's political involvement spanned the 1790s and his life reflects many of the changes which overtook the Catholic community in Ireland during that decade. On his return to Ireland, he was immediately struck by the 'persecution' facing Ulster Catholics. With sectarian tensions running high, he found Armagh 'engaged in civil war and religion made the pretext'.[155] These divisions were, he believed, of great utility to the government and in 1791, 1792 and 1793 he busily engaged in the 'uniting business' travelling to Randalstown, Maghera, Dungiven, Newtown and Magilligan. These journeys closely mirror the missionary efforts of Wolfe Tone and John Keogh in the elections to the Catholic Committee and Convention and Thomas Russell's visits throughout Ulster.[156]

O'Coigley became a key player in the early attempts to form a nexus between the Catholic Defenders and the predominantly Presbyterian Belfast United Irishmen. It is in this context, too, that Cullen has attributed authorship of the famous 'Byrne pamphlet' of 1792 to O'Coigley.[157] The recall of Fitzwilliam in 1795 and the foundation of the Orange Order in the same year, led to escalating violence in Ulster. O'Coigley's family home was attacked and burned by what was in essence a 'King and Church' mob. His library was lost in the blaze and amongst his 'choice collection of books', the priest's notes for a history of seventeenth-century Ireland were destroyed. W. J. Fitzpatrick believed O'Coigley was working on a history of the 1641 rebellion. This gives O'Coigley's political activities an added dimension and reflects the ever present eighteenth-century consciousness of what Bartlett has called 'the comet of 1641', manipulated memories of which blighted attempts to solve the Catholic question.[158] Perhaps O'Coigley was attempting to interpret the events of that year, as 'Byrne' had done for 1792, in an effort to remove the 'occult force' of Sir John Temple's *Irish Rebellion* which was used to hinder the growth of the 'union of affection'.[159]

Based in Dundalk, O'Coigley remained, as the ever watchful Speaker Foster described him, 'busy and meddling'.[160] McEvoy has suggested that O'Coigley was never a Defender, a view which is difficult to sustain given his close connections with them.[161] He had certainly been active amongst them in the years 1791-3; his close friend and relative Valentine Derry was the leader of the Louth Defenders–Madden believed O'Coigley had introduced Napper Tandy to the Defenders in that county–and the 'Switcher Donnelly', a Tyrone Defender, was his first cousin.[162] His membership of the United Irishmen is beyond doubt; he was sworn by Valentine Lawless and, together with Samuel Neilson, Henry Joy McCracken, Thomas Russell and the Teelings, actively helped to forge an alliance between the Defenders and the United Irishmen.[163]

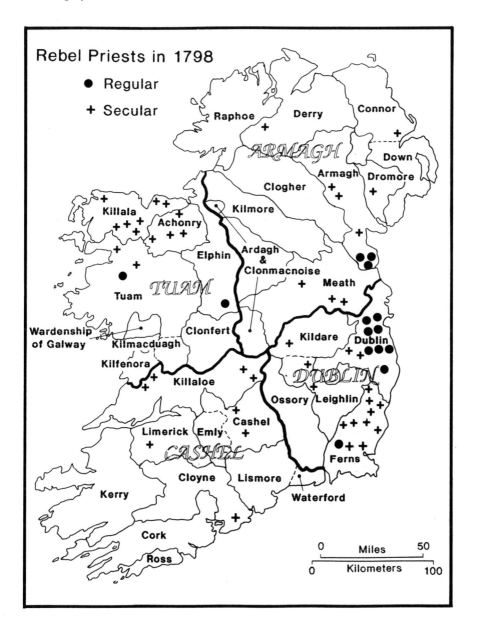

Fig. 21 National distribution of 'rebel' Catholic clergy

In April 1797, when the Armagh freeholders decided to petition the throne for peace, O'Coigley made himself 'as active on that occasion as possible', riding through the county, distributing notices and persuading the freeholders to 'do their duty'.[164] It was also at this time that an anonymous pamphlet appeared, entitled *A View of the Present State of Ireland with an account of the Origin and Progress of the Disturbances in that Country.* This pamphlet outlined the bitter history of sectarian divisions in Ireland and the draconian measures employed by the military. Pointing to the efforts of the United Irishmen towards the creation of an 'union of affection', it called for freedom and an end to repression.[165]

The pamphlet, which James Hope believed 'contained more truth than all the volumes I have seen written on the events of 1797 and 1798', was attributed implausibly by Francis Plowden to Arthur O'Connor, but Reamonn Ó Muirí has convincingly argued that the anonymous 'Observer' was in fact James O'Coigley. He bases this theory on the style and local concern of the pamphlet, but its appeal to a British audience and its publication in England also point towards the authorship of the Armagh priest.[166] Given the level of opposition to his 'task masters, commonly called His Majesty's ministers', it is little wonder that, from that time O'Coigley believed he had been singled out for vengeance by Castlereagh, Beresford and Annesley.[167]

O'Coigley fled to Manchester and there busied himself in the promotion of the United Britons. By the end of 1797 he had spread the system to Bolton, Stockport, Warrington, Nottingham, Liverpool and Birmingham.[168] There is also evidence that while in Britain he worked to unite the republicans of Ireland, England and Scotland.[169] In August of the same year, he journeyed with Rev. Arthur McMahon, via Hamburg, to Paris and there fell in with the Tandy faction of the United Irishmen.[170] O'Coigley returned to Ireland several months later, but prepared to sail again to France in February 1798, this time in the company of Arthur O'Connor and John Binns who went with a view to securing French assistance for an invasion. Since his return from France, however, O'Coigley had been trailed by Bow Street runners and, on 28 February the entire party was arrested at the King's Head, Margate.[171]

O'Coigley's low key defence was in stark contrast to that of Arthur O'Connor who was acquitted. No witnesses were called by his counsel, despite the fact that Valentine Derry and Bernard Coyle had been subpoenaed, and the priest was convicted on very thin evidence.[172] Nor is there any indication that O'Coigley received any assistance from the clergy; on the contrary, Bishop Douglas of London willingly countenanced Wickham's attempts to use O'Coigley's confessor, Fr Griffiths, as a source of information.[173] Unlike

O'Connor, whose close Whig connections undoubtedly saved him, John Pollock confessed after O'Coigley's execution at Pennington Heath, that 'it was plain [he] must be hanged–no one cared about him'.[174]

O'Coigley's role in Ulster radicalism in the 1790s had been crucial. He had been central to the 'uniting business' and had played a prominent role in bringing about the crucial junction between the Defenders and the United Irishmen. In 1797 and 1798, his actions reflected the growing dissatisfaction of the more militant United Irishmen. However, despite Benjamin Binn's eulogy for O'Coigley, 'a man than whom no greater or better ever lived', the priest has been curiously neglected in the recent historiography of the period.[175] Both Madden and Fitzpatrick devoted considerable attention to him, and two accounts of his life have been published within the last fifty years, but more recent writers have paid him merely cursory attention.[176] Elliott has devoted the greatest attention to O'Coigley, particularly in her study of Irish republicanism in England, and Cullen has discussed at length his supposed authorship of the 'Byrne pamphlet'.[177] By and large, however, the current unprecedented levels of research into the 1790s have ignored O'Coigley, and few of the period's radicals cry out so loudly for thorough re-examination.

In a similar way, Fr John Martin, an Augustinian from Drogheda, took the United Irish oath in 1797 and, from that time busied himself in the promotion of the 'union of affection', exploiting all the opportunities his priesthood afforded him. The radical missionary pattern which characterised clerical involvement in the United Irishmen in Ulster is also reflected Martin's work; yet, he too has been neglected by historians.[178]

Little is known of Martin's early life, except that he was born in Muckerstaff, County Longford and was professed in Salamanca in January 1781.[179] On his return to Ireland, he was appointed to the order's priory at Drogheda where he began work on his translation of the *Meditations of Saint Augustine*, published in Dublin in 1798.[180] The friar dedicated his work to the Archbishop of Armagh, Richard O'Reilly. Ironically, considering his subsequent actions, Martin referred in the dedication to his own 'feeble efforts in the propagation of piety and Christian devotion in a period when I behold with sorrow the poisoned arrows of libertinism directed against the sacred flock of the Heavenly Shepherd'.[181]

Bishop Patrick Plunket granted Martin faculties for the Diocese of Meath in March 1789, but the friar's pastoral efforts took him farther afield into the neighbouring Dioceses of Armagh and Dublin and there are reports of him preaching as far away as Kilbride, County Wicklow.[182] Martin's travels, celebrating Mass, preaching and questing brought him throughout south Ulster and north Leinster, the heartland of Defenderism. As tensions in the country-side spilled over into Drogheda, the town became increasingly receptive to the radical ideas brought by the travellers on the road from Dublin to Belfast, the two main centres of United Irish activity.[183]

Drogheda in the 1790s was thriving and, with a population of about 15,000, it was the sixth largest town in Ireland. It was also industrialised, the main industry being the manufacture of linen. Apart from its geographical location, the presence of the linen industry in Drogheda placed the town firmly within the Ulster sphere of influence and many of the political tensions of Armagh, Antrim and Down spilled over into Louth and Meath. Smyth's recent work on popular politicisation in the 1790s discussed these tensions in Louth, which surfaced regularly at fairs as northern Protestant weavers were attacked by local Defenders. In the town itself, these tensions were heightened by the show trials orchestrated by the hardline Speaker John Foster.[184]

Against this background Martin was sworn into the Drogheda society of United Irishmen at Easter 1797 by two Franciscan friars, Patrick Duffy and James MacCarten.[185] Much of our information concerning this crucial phase in the priest's life is drawn from his confession made subsequent to his arrest in June 1798 and must be viewed in the light of the intense pressure placed on him by the courtmartial. Nevertheless, at that stage he attributed his motives in joining the United Irishmen to a belief that they intended to 'put all units on a level' and to 'dissolve all establishments'.[186] He declared that he had 'entered into engagement with the United Irishmen to obtain their rights, thinking themselves an injured people'. Curiously, he was emphatic that he did 'not take the engagement as an oath, but as an affirmation', since such an oath would have run contrary to the oath of allegiance to the King.[187]

This late conversion to the United Irishmen is not as surprising as it may first appear; the failure of the United men to gain numbers in Counties Meath and Louth has been attributed to the effective, if harsh, measures taken by Foster against the Defenders. John Pollock observed that 'papists here who were first among the Defenders were the last among the rebels, because they had been so roughly handled by the Speaker and all the Protestant gentlemen of property'.[188] In the face of this opposition, Martin busied himself with Augustinian enthusiasm to promoting the principles of the United Irishmen. Drogheda soon became well organised, several of Lord Gormanston's yeomanry corps were sworn and General Lombard warned that 'every day the public mind here about is becoming more ripe for action'.[189]

The defeat of the insurgent army at the Battle of Tara on 26 May 1798 cast the rebel plans in north Leinster into disarray. The United Irishmen were

Fig. 22 Surrender of General Humbert (N.L.I.)

quickly dispersed by Captain Blanche's Scotch Fencibles; the road to the north was reopened and the immediate threat to the capital lifted. A similar defeat was suffered by the Kildare men at the Curragh and within a week the rebels were on the defensive. The exception to this was Wexford, where insurgent numbers were higher than elsewhere, but even they had failed to break out into the surrounding counties.[190] Indecision amongst the rebel leadership led to the loss of precious time and by failing to capture the strategic town of New Ross the chances of success quickly faded.[191] It was against this background that Father John Martin found himself with an extraordinary commission from the Dublin United Irish Committee, based in Thomas Street.

In the first week of June, Martin met with the Committee members in Thomas Street. He was commissioned to go to Dunboyne and Kilbride, where the rebellion had collapsed, and to encourage the rebels there 'to co-operate at a fixed time–and to excite the people to act'.[192] He returned to Drogheda after this meeting and informed his own committee of his mission. The friar visited Dunboyne and Kilbride twice and preached to the people, encouraging them to continue with the rebellion; 'if you are men that have sworn to be faithful to one another, now that you see your houses burned is the time you are called upon to keep your oath'.[193] Martin then travelled on to Greenogue in County Kildare, where the rebels had been particularly active and, rode from there to Dublin to report on his progress.

The rebels in Wexford and Wicklow still maintained a good deal of their original momentum and Martin was instructed to ride south to hasten the march on Dublin and to co-ordinate their efforts. Hopes of assistance from the south seemed well founded and the timing of the friar's mission was crucial. Martin set off for Arklow, but stopped at Rathfarnham where he met with William Ledwich, the local parish priest; he in turn gave him a letter of introduction to Christopher Lowe, parish priest of Glendalough.[194] Above Rathfarnham, Martin met with Joseph Holt, the United Irish general, and the two men spent three quarters of an hour together discussing plans. The General had given assurances to the Dublin Committee that he would not act without instructions from the executive, a fact which reflects the importance of the friar's mission.[195] From Martin's courtmartial, it appears that the two were already well acquainted; the general informed Martin of rebel strength in the area and their eagerness to attack Dublin which, despite government victories, was still potentially vulnerable.

Martin's plan was straightforward. It was presumed that the rebels could knock out the poorly defended garrison at Rathdrum. Once this crucial Wicklow town had been taken, Arklow would be defenceless. It was hoped that by then the rebels of Wexford and Wicklow would have obtained the long awaited French assistance; as soon as Arklow was captured, the march on Dublin could begin in earnest. The attack on the city was to be a four-pronged manoeuvre, with detachments converging from Rathcoole, Glenasmole, Rathfarnham and Templeogue. The purpose of this plan was to draw the government forces out of Dublin, leaving the city defenceless and an easy target for United Irishmen advancing simultaneously from Meath and Kildare. Leaving Holt behind, Martin set off for Arklow where he was assured by the Dublin Committee that he would find friends and support.

By this stage, however, the rebels had been defeated at Arklow and the main plank of the plan had been removed. To exacerbate an already situation, the friar was captured by the yeomanry before he could make contact with the remnant of the rebel army.[196] The rabid Orangeman, Captain John Giffard of the Dublin city militia warned the friar that unless a full confession was made he would be put to death. If he complied, however, he would be left at the disposal of the 'merciful' Viceroy. If he hesitated, he would be instantaneously 'blown away at the mouth of a cannon'.[197] The friar dropped to his knees and begged to be taken to a private room where he would make a full and candid confession.

Much of what has been said earlier about the friar's initiation into the United Irishmen, the organisation in Drogheda, his preaching and mission, together with the rebel plans, has been drawn from this confession; in it he added a denunciation of the United Irish system;

> He now hates the United Irishmen because they have not stood together and that he considers them as a cowardly rabble, he conceived that they would all have fought and died in the cause. That he did not intend to take arms himself, but he intended to have instigated the people with a fine death in the cause. That he had read Machiavel [sic] and that Machiavel taught that they should spare no time whatever to effect the object they had depended on.[198]

The authorities lost no time in making use of their prisoner and it was hoped his confession would provide much useful information. On 14 June he was sent to Dublin and in an accompanying letter Captain Giffard described the friar as 'the greatest villain in society'. Giffard continued, 'his confession you will see ... [is] not very honourable to Mr Grattan. The lesser traitors should be easily taken up'.[199] Martin was lodged in Kilmainham Gaol. In March 1800 he made an appeal to Richard Annesley at the Custom House to intervene on his behalf, but to no avail.[200] Finally on 5 August 1801 he escaped from the prison by ladder. A reward of fifty guineas was offered for the capture of the friar but he was never apprehended.[201]

The subsequent career of John Martin remains shrouded in mystery. It is unlikely that he returned to an Augustinian friary to be harboured there. The absence of the pages covering 1797 to 1799 in the House Book of the Drogheda Augustinians might suggest some attempt to protect the renegade, but there are no further references to him in the Augustinian Provincial Archives after his escape. Possibly, like Frs McMahon, Monelly and Campbell, three other 'rebel priests', he escaped to America and fitted easily into a new life there.

John Martin has been curiously neglected in the historiography of the 1798 rebellion. This may be accounted for by the attempts in the aftermath of the rebellion to play down the United Irish aspect of the events of that year and to present the impression that clerical involvement was involuntary. In this version of events it is difficult to see how Father John Martin, a self-confessed United Irishman and organiser, could be accommodated. Martin's 'confession' must also have contributed to his exclusion from the pantheon of rebel priests. The image which has survived is of a disillusioned informer. The evidence, however, suggests that his information was of little use to the authorities and may, in fact, have been intended to protect more influential leaders of the rebellion.

Martin's memory suffered at the hands of loyalist historians in the wake of the rebellion, especially in Musgrave's *Memoirs*. It is clear from this account of the friar's activities, that John Giffard had given Musgrave access to the report of the courtmartial and that Martin's 'confession' forms the basis of his narrative of events. Giffard's seventeen-year-old son, Lt. William Giffard had been killed in the rebel attack on Kildare, and the Captain can only have welcomed the capture of the friar as confirmation of the loyalist view of the rebellion as a papist plot.

Like O'Coigley, Martin's position among the rebel priests of 1798 is rare; his United Irish background is beyond question and a clear record of his political philosophy and conscious role in the rebellion survives. Martin was not a solitary priest, forced unwillingly to take up the cause of his flock, but had assisted in the organisation of Drogheda and had preached the United Irish gospel throughout much of north Leinster. His connections with the Dublin United Irish committee place him firmly within a national context.

Musgrave interpreted the missions of Fr James McCary, in Antrim, in a similar missionary fashion, recording him preaching and recommending 'union and fraternity' to the Catholics and Presbyterians of the Ards Peninsula in the summer of 1797.[202] Further evidence of clerical involvement amongst the United Irishmen of Antrim and Down is reflected in the case of Bernard Maginnis, a priest of the Diocese of Dromore, arrested in 1798 and lodged in Carrickfergus. Maginnis' family connections place him squarely within the Defender tradition. His close ties with Fr. Edmund Derry, who assisted Tone at Rathfriland in 1792 and who was a brother of O'Coigley's close friend Valentine Derry, point to his role in a far wider network.[203] Indeed, there are many striking similarities between the lives of O'Coigley and Magennis.

In 1800 Edmund Derry, parish priest of Clonduff, and later Bishop of Dromore (1801-1819), appealed to Castlereagh on Magennis's behalf and this correspondence provides us with the fullest account of his career.[204] Like the Armagh priest, Magennis studied at the Irish College, Paris, where he received a bursary. It is tempting to surmise that it was actually Magennis' receipt of the burse which led O'Coigley to initiate a civil law suit against the rector of the college, which began his controversial career.[205] Again, as in the case of O'Coigley, Magennis was forced to leave Paris at the outbreak of the rebellion, and Derry declared that 'after his return I often heard him with detestation detail the cruelties of the French'. On account of his poor circumstances, Magennis was ordained by Bishop Matthew Lennan of Dromore (1780-1801) in the hope that by serving in the diocese he could finance his future studies. Derry does not date the ordination but it can only have been after 1795, since the bishop intended him for Maynooth. Amongst the highly politicised people of County Down, Magennis realised the wisdom of the old Irish saying, *ni bhfaigheann an sagart balbh beatha* (the dumb/silent priest doesn't get a living), and before long he fell in with the radicals. Derry attributed this to 'youth, a want of firmness and a desire of raising the necessary contributions' but, in a telling comment, admitted to Castlereagh that 'this was the ready way of obtaining such charities from the greater part of the strangely intoxicated multitude at that time'.[206]

Derry severely reprimanded the young priest on his return to Clonduff and brought him, under threat of suspension, to take the loyal oath. From that time Magennis lived with him at Clonduff, but was taken up on the instructions of Major Porter by the Rathfriland Yeomanry after the battle of Ballinahinch. In spite of Derry's declaration that he had not 'deviated from the paths of loyalty', Porter suspected otherwise and he was charged with 'acting, aiding and assisting in the rebellion'.[207] Derry's appeal met with an unfavourable response and Magennis remained at Carrickfergus Castle for over two years without trial. He repeatedly refused to accept the banishment offered under the terms of General Nugent's proclamation. Tone's former friend, Sir George Hill visited Magennis in Carrickfergus in December 1801, with the intention of encouraging him to go into exile.[208] Magennis, however, died as parish priest of Newry in March 1814.[209] Given the nature of Magennis' missionary involvement in the United Irishmen and the striking parallels with the life of James O'Coigley, he too has been neglected in the history of the rebellion, failing even to merit inclusion even in Richard Hayes's celebrated list.

There are passing references to other priests implicated in the rebellion in the northern dioceses. Two 'notorious' Armagh clerics, Cullen and McKain, were reportedly engaged in seditious conversations. Cullen first came to the attention of the authorities in 1791 when reports implicated him in the Defender attack on the family of Alexander Barkley in Forkhill. Following a period of suspension, he moved to Killevy, County Armagh, where he was joined by the equally 'infamous' Fr. McKain. It was suggested that the two be apprehended, but there is no record of their subsequent careers.[210] Thomas Campbell, parish priest of Dromore in County Tyrone, travelled to Longford in 1798–supposedly to visit his uncle–but was arrested and imprisoned for two months. Suspected of travelling to join the French, Campbell ended his days at Baltimore in the United States.[211]

Meath had been greatly disturbed by Defender violence, but the vigilance and regular visitations of Bishop Patrick Plunket may account for the surprisingly low level of disaffection amongst the priests there.[212] There were no priests involved in the fighting in the diocese and the loyalty of only two priests was called into question. On 6 June Plunket visited Dunboyne where the chapel and almost all the houses in the town, including the priest's, had been burned by the loyalists in retaliation for what the bishop called, 'the treasonable practices of the people'. James Connell, the parish priest, fled and although he later returned, his politics were still under suspicion in 1803 when Alexander Marsden complained of him to Troy. The archbishop relayed this complaint to Plunket who vowed to 'leave nothing undone to enlighten the minds of the Catholic inhabitants with respect to the enormity of seditious practices and to compel the pastor to renounce the madness of countenancing such unnatural guilt'.[213]

Similarly, Patrick Farrell, parish priest of Donaghmore and Kilbride fled during the rebellion, but Plunket later invited him to return, 'if unconscious of being concerned in the late political commotions'.[214] After the Battle of Tara, which cut off the western portion of the diocese, rumours of Orange reprisals abounded. Unable to communicate with Plunket, Thomas Ganley, the parish priest of Mullingar, sought instructions from Troy. Captain Rochfort had the archbishop's pastoral printed and distributed gratis in the town in an effort to calm tension.[215]

VII

In all 70 priests, or almost four per cent of the country's 1,800 Catholic clergy were called on to account for their conduct in 1798. Some of these played a prominent part in the rebellion, many had slight connections with the rebels and others were implicated on the basis of the vaguest passing references. Nevertheless, the significant role of the clergy in the events of 1798 cannot be screened behind images of the 'reluctant rebel', or the 'drunken ruffian', (a stereotype to which both Musgrave and Caulfield contributed). Far from being a motley crew, a disparate collection of suspended priests or frustrated curates anxious to settle old scores, the rebel clerics were predominantly parish priests, and the patterns of clerical involvement reflect the complex nature of the radicalised society from which they emerged.

CHAPTER NINE

Rally and Consolidate

The suppression of the rebellion in Leinster removed the kingdom from immediate danger. While the fate of the Ascendancy appeared secure, the future of the Catholic Church in Ireland was far less certain. Throughout the 1790s the Catholic hierarchy had opposed every manifestation of 'the French disease'. No effort was spared to impress on priests and people the folly and destructive tendency of their flirtation with radicalism. Yet, in spite of the overwhelmingly loyal display of the bishops and priests during the rebellion, the well publicised clerical activity amongst the insurgents was sufficient to feed interpretations of the rising as a mere 'popish plot'. Memories of 1641 were revived; once more, loyalists rallied to the call for revenge, giving rise to a polemical conflict no less bitter than the rebellion itself. The experience of the previous decade, however, had transformed the Catholic hierarchy. Now faced with their most critical challenge to date, they mounted a formidable, and ultimately successful, defence of their achievement.

I

With the collapse of the United Irish cause in Leinster, the bishops breathed a sigh of relief and drew consolation from their part in the defeat of the rebellion. In the spring of 1798 Charles Erskine, under pressure from Whitehall, urged the Irish bishops to a greater public show of loyalty.[1] In the wake of the rebellion, however, the monsignor had no doubts concerning the episcopal response and echoed the praise then resounding in London of the hierarchy's loyal exertions in critical circumstances.[2] While James Caulfield's conduct in Wexford had brought tears of sympathy to Erskine's eyes, Troy's efforts stood out, confirming his position at the head of the Irish hierarchy. Edward Dillon, Bishop of Kilmacduagh, expressed the general sentiments of the prelates when he wrote in July:

> Had providence permitted that a prelate of an indolent unfeeling disposition should preside in the capital in the present circumstances how deplorable would be our situation.[3]

More than this, the failure of the rebellion had established Troy at the head of the Catholic body as a whole.

The ignominious United Irish defeat had brought the reform cause in Ireland to an abrupt end. The Catholic Committee was already dissolved, but now the leading Catholic radicals, tainted by their association with the United Irishmen, were forced to vacate the political arena. In their absence Troy became the acknowledged voice of Irish Catholics, a development which placed him in a critical position as the events of the following years unfurled. There were no regrets amongst the bishops at the departure of John Keogh and his coterie. James Caulfield, whose detestation of the radical elements of the Catholic Committee was well known, expressed caustic satisfaction at their demise. Following the execution of John Hay, he declared his hope that ' they will now see the differences between their principles and mine'.

In September 1798, reflecting on the destruction of the rebellion and the rejection of the bishops' counsel, he confessed to Troy that 'many will believe us now, especially those who have any property, but no security and are smarting sorely by the result of their crazy union, that has caused more disunion through this country, than it ever perhaps experienced before'.[4] If the experience of the previous ten years had taught Troy any lessons, he now appreciated that praise counted for little. While acknowledging the garlands from wherever they came, he was also aware of a growing tendency in loyalist circles to depict the rebellion as a 'popish plot'.

By the end of May the country abounded in tales of widespread sectarian massacre. As June progressed, accounts became more grotesque and events at Scullabogue and Wexford Bridge rekindled folk memories of similar atrocities at the bridge of Portadown in 1641. Loyalist correspondence was replete with such details, and Troy greeted the newspaper reports with increasing alarm. The *Dublin Journal* was particularly vicious in its attack on the Catholic body, no doubt due to the influence of its editor, John Giffard. He was adamant that the death of his 'hero'–his seventeen-year-old son, Lieutenant William Giffard, killed in the rebel attack on Kildare–would not go unavenged.[5] In the first week of June Giffard's paper carried many accounts of alleged rebel excesses and, while praising the loyal efforts of the militia, declared its inability to 'palliate the conduct of the many thousand Roman Catholics who, led by some of their priests, are in open rebellion'. Even where the *Journal* conceded the existence of a loyal effort by some Catholics, a barbed rejoinder was added declaring that 'the superior clergy know that the same renegade priest who would urge his blind and miserable flock to the murder of heretics would not scruple to bathe his impious hand in the blood of his bishop.'[6]

Troy took immediate steps to stem press misinformation and complained to Edward Cooke of what he called 'false and impolite paragraphs attaching guilt to the body of Catholics'. Cooke apparently acknowledged the justice of Troy's complaint, and the archbishop noticed a lull in the paper's discussion of a 'general plot', which he attributed to the Secretary's intervention.[7] Troy had initially opposed Charles Erskine's appointment to London in 1793, but he now decided to exploit his presence. Erskine acted on Troy's behalf, orchestrating the publication of the bishops' pastorals there and making representations to Lord Camden and Thomas Pelham, with whom the archbishop had successfully negotiated the establishment of the Royal College. Towards the end of June, Erskine optimistically reported that 'everybody is fully convinced that the word religion has only been an instrument' to seduce the ignorant multitude during the rebellion.[8] In Dublin, however, the *Journal* resumed its assault on the 'rebel' priests and the flamboyant fall of Michael Murphy at the Battle of Arklow was quickly seized upon as further proof of the popish mania, which could not go unchecked.[9]

As the war of words intensified, so too did the loyalist backlash. Shortly after his arrival, Cornwallis (perhaps influenced by Erskine's efforts) informed the Duke of Portland of 'the folly which has been too prevalent in this quarter of substituting the word Catholicism instead of Jacobinism as the foundation of the present rebellion'.[10] While the Lord Lieutenant declared his intention of opposing such notions, he was virtually powerless in his attempt to curb the power of the Orange faction which began to wreak a heavy revenge on the Catholic community. Chapels proved an obvious target for such reprisals, and the burning of the thatched chapel at Ramsgrange, County Wexford, on 19 June 1798 was the first of almost sixty such attacks over the next two years.[11] Yet, just as the Orange bogey had been used to such effect by the United Irishmen prior to the rebellion, so too rumours soon circulated that the chapels had been burned by the rebels in an attempt to discredit the yeomanry and rekindle the rebellion.[12]

The levels of recrimination were such that Troy believed that had it not been for his own exertions the chapels in the city would have been closed.[13] Francis Higgins's report of an incident in Francis Street chapel in late June reflects the feverish tension in the city:

A disagreeable event took place at Francis Street chapel today. The common people have got impressed on their minds that the government wishes to suppress those Roman Catholic places of worship, which has much irritated and inflamed their minds. A party of yeomen passing the chapel yard, some wicked incendiary called out, 'they have come to kill and set fire to the chapel'. This alarm given to an immense concourse of people within, occasioned in the struggle to get into the street, many accidents, the breaking of several legs arms etc.[14]

Similar rumours of planned attacks on both the chapels and churches were circulated in Athlone on 12 June, as a result of which religious services in the town were largely unattended. So great was the fear that General Barnett published a notice guaranteeing protection of places of worship.[15]

Loyalist attacks on priests became a common occurence. Many innocent Wexford priests suffered in the aftermath of the rebellion. John Redmond, the curate of Camolin, was tried peremptorily before a courtmartial and hanged on Gorey Hill on 22 June 1799. Redmond had been incriminated by his presence at the sack of Camolin Park, but his loyalty was beyond doubt; Miles Byrne described his death as poor reward for 'his great zeal and devotion to the enemies of his country'.[16] A number of other priests were court martialed and later freed except for James Dixon, described by Caulfield as 'an honest, innocent priest,' who was sentenced to transportation.[17] In June 1799 the home of Fr Frank Kavanagh at Ballyoughter was raided by a party of the Gorey Yeomanry and his curate John Barry badly beaten.[18]

In the following October Pat Cogly, parish priest of Monageer– described by his bishop as 'a truly loyal subject and good pastor'–was attacked by two men while on a sick call. Earlier in the day, one of his attackers had boasted that 'there would not be a priest alive in the County Wexford in twelve months time'.[19] In this poisoned atmosphere, it was little wonder that Caulfield was unable to get a priest to venture to the Macamores or the neighbourhood of Camolin or Gorey for fear of the yeomanry.[20] In Dublin diocese, there were two fatal attacks on priests. In December 1798 William Ryan, parish priest of Arklow, was shot dead in his home by a party of Orangemen and the parish priest of Wicklow, Andrew O'Toole, was killed on the road in the following August. James Caulfield believed that O'Toole's death had been accidental, but circumstances point to a factional killing.[21]

II

Initial loyalist reaction to the rebellion led to reflection. The tales of wanton sectarian attacks were stitched together to illustrate the existence of a comprehensive 'popish plot' conducted under the watchwords of 'reform' and 'emancipation'. This process of reflection reached a climax with the publication of Sir Richard Musgrave's *Memoirs of the Different Rebellions in Ireland* in 1801, where the lessons found in Sir John Temple's history of 1641 and William King's *State of the Protestants of Ireland* (1691) were graphically repeated.[22]

In June 1798 Patrick Duigenan, dubbed 'the black doctor' by the radical press, published a reply to Henry Grattan's address to the citizens of Dublin.[23] Duigenan launched a bitter anti-Catholic attack; describing the rebellion as a 'popish plot', he illustrated what he believed was the 'necessary connection between popish supremacy in spirituals, with its tyranny in temporals'. Duigenan's publication placed the polemical struggle on a new plane and the hierarchy initially intended to refute his representation of the rebellion. Erskine was particularly incensed and urged Troy to challenge the connection between popery and rebellion. The prominence of so many Protestants amongst the executed rebel leaders, however, removed attention temporarily from the Catholics and Erskine came to believe that the pamphlet, if unanswered, would drop off by itself.[24] Significantly, Samuel Sproule had informed the Castle that 'the Catholics exult at the present executions–it takes the odium off them–[and they] say the idea can remain no longer of it being a popish plot or massacre'.[25]

This reprieve was short lived. Thomas Rennell, fellow of King's College and Master of the Temple, preached a sermon before the University of Cambridge couched in classical anti-Catholic rhetoric. Rennell pointed to the 1641 massacre–'still fresh in memory'–and declared that 'whenever the public has been distressed by internal commotions, the strength of popery in Ireland has been fatally experienced'.[26] Rennell traced a pattern of Catholic bigotry from the Lateran Council, through to the 'discreet, evasive' pastoral instructions of Dr Troy in 1793 and on to the 'inflammatory menaces' contained in Hussey's 1797 address;

> The history of all ages demonstrates what it has actually been. The tenor of events is uniform. The rebellion and massacre in Ireland in 1641, and that of St Bartholomew in France, and the present commotion in Ireland, all exhibit the same features.[27]

Such generalities were avoided in a letter signed 'Verax', published in the *Dublin Journal* on 16 August 1798. Writing in reply to an account in the *Birmingham Chronicle*, Verax [Richard Musgrave?] challenged the view that the clergy of Wexford were prisoners of the rebels. On the contrary, Verax claimed that the priests were the only ones possessed of any influence and questioned the timing of their intervention on behalf of the Protestants in the town, arguing that the priests failed to take action until the rebel cause was lost.

Verax proved a far more serious and well informed threat to the Catholic establishment in Ireland than the earlier general tracts. The specific accusations against Caulfield and his clergy could not go unchallenged. Indeed, Caulfield was convinced that the letter had been written with the express purpose of drawing the bishop into the sectarian debate, since copies were sent by the author to himself and Fr Corrin.[28] In spite of his original reservations, Caulfield rose to the challenge and entrusted Troy with publication of his defence, under the pen name *Veritas,* in the following month.[29] This marked the beginning of the polemical war in earnest.

Veritas aimed at a vindication of the clergy of Wexford, but its scope was broadened to demonstrate that the rebellion was a political conflict, not a 'popish plot'. The rebels, *Veritas* argued, 'who possessed a semblance of Catholicity, were, for the greater part, of Tom Paine's school, Catholics in profession, but Deists in religion, the leaders for the most part Protestants'.[30] Ultimately, despite the affidavits included, Caulfield was unable to convincingly refute the charges made by Verax against the Catholic clergy. The great dilemma remained; if the priests had any influence over the rebels, they were implicated in the 'plot'; if they failed to exert influence, they were passive accomplices.[31] Similarly, the bishop could not deny the active part taken by many of his own priests and, in the only defence possible, he rejected these as 'excommunicated priests, drunken and profligate couple beggars, the very faeces of the Church'.[32]

Musgrave had already written anti-Catholic tracts in the *Dublin Journal* under the pen name 'Camillus' but, following the publication of Veritas he published a pamphlet in March 1799 under the name Veridicus, in which the rebellion of 1798 was inserted into a broad historical and theological study of popery.[33] Musgrave was vicious in his attack on the Wexford clergy and he published endless accounts of their role in the rebellion. Once more Caulfield was criticised for the indiscipline of his clergy and his failure to prevent the massacre of Protestants on Wexford Bridge. Charles Jackson's defence of Fr Corrin was summarily rejected on the grounds that he was married to a Catholic.[34] Caulfield was greatly alarmed by the escalating polemic, believing

Fig. 23 Book label of Hugh Fitzpatrick, printer to Maynooth College

that Veridicus intended 'the general extermination of bishops and priests, nay all Roman Catholics because their religious principles necessarily make them rebels'.[35] As before, Caulfield appealed to Troy who, in turn, engaged James Clinch, professor of classics at Maynooth to write a reply to Veridicus. Caulfield collected voluminous details on the priests implicated by Musgrave and these materials were passed to Clinch.

Caulfield was unsure as to the prudence of a reply, given the 'shocking number' of priests 'who had most wickedly volunteered in the damned rebellion'.[36] It was impossible to refute all of Musgrave's charges, and he believed it was not enough to expose Veridicus as a 'slanderous villian' if the good name of the clergy could not be established. Without that, he believed, it was 'better to say nothing for public view'.[37] In any event, the reply to Veridicus appeared towards the end of 1799 and it represents an elaborate attempt at damage limitation on behalf of the hierarchy. Musgrave's arguments were meticulously refuted. The embarrassing existence of rebel priests was treated with great care, and these were dismissed with an economy of truth as unemployed, under censure, or suspended; one, Fr John Keane was described as a 'notorious idiot'.[38]

Clinch's voluntary efforts greatly satisfied Troy. He had it reprinted in London and circulated widely amongst the Lords and Commons in Dublin.[39]

Caulfield was equally pleased. He congratulated Clinch, declaring that 'without hurting your modesty, you can at this day boast and rejoice with me, that you [answered Veridicus] ... with ability and effect, for that monster with all his inhumanity and infernal malice, and consummate effrontery, never dared to reply'.[40] However, in the wake of the publication of Musgrave's *Memoirs* in 1801, Caulfield was forced once more to defend his behaviour in 1798, but little ground could be gained from a renewed debate.[41]

The clergy had been too conspicuous amongst the rebels to be ignored, and it was futile to dismiss them as unreliable marginal figures. Enormous damage had been done to the Catholic cause; not even the liberal Protestant accounts of the rebellion could remove religion from the debate.[42] George Taylor, while allowing for the exertions of the clergy on behalf of the prisoners, includes accounts of the rebels calling on him to be baptised and 'to join them in arms, to fight for the cause of Liberty and the Roman Catholic Church and faith'. James Alexander's history reflects similar contradictions, moving immediately from a discussion of the zeal of the priests to prevent the rebellion into an account of the merciless slaughter of the 'poor Protestants of Scullabogue, Wexford Bridge and Vinegar Hill'.[43] Neither could the Catholic historians avoid controversy.

Edward Hay's evasive *History* followed Caulfield's line of presenting the rebel priests as renegades. 'Although they were not all, at the time, under suspension or ecclesiastical censure, [they were] under one so nearly allied to it as to prevent any of them from having arrived to the situation of parish priest'.[44] Hay's apologetic work, however, carried little weight with either party. Caulfield believed his intention had been to 'build a loyal reputation on the ruins of the friars and clergy', while the Chancellor Lord Redesdale dismissed the *History* as an 'abominable traitorous libel'.[45]

Redesdale had been the author of the English Catholic relief legislation of 1791 but his experience in Ireland transformed his liberalism into violent opposition to Irish Catholic designs. He attacked Troy, condemning his pastorals which he believed were 'full of violent invective in effect, though often covered in language against everything positive, and not scrupling any lie for this purpose'.[46] Ironically, the apostate Franciscan, Denis Taaffe, who had taken an active role in 1798, defended Troy from such loyalist attacks, when writing his vindication of the Catholics in 1802, no doubt grateful of the archbishop's example behind which to shield his former comrades :

> I should be glad to know what religion Messrs Troy and Moylan profess, or Lord Fingall, with other Catholic gentlemen and priests, who lent

their active services to put down Irish rebels. Are they to be ranked with
the disaffected, notwithstanding the zeal with which they supported the
government merely because they are Catholics? In vain has Fingall
fought and Troy cursed, unless they can purchase a certificate of civism
from this Orange Robespierre [Richard Musgrave].[47]

III

The rebellion of 1798 reawakened Irish loyalists' fear. Once again, the
precarious security of their situation was illustrated only too vividly. Preoccu-
pation with the sectarian complexion of the rebellion blighted any real
reflection on the causes of discontent in Ireland, while the obsession with the
existence of a rebel plan to establish Catholicism reflected the pathological
insecurity of the Ascendancy.[48] Yet the perceived instability of the establishment had serious repercussions for the Catholic community, and there were
genuine fears that many of the gains of the previous decade might now be lost.
This tension was reflected graphically in a tract entitled *A Fair Representation
of the Present Political State of Ireland*, published by the anti-Catholic Patrick
Duigenan in 1799.[49] Describing the rebellion as a 'popish plot', Duigenan
pointed to the unreliability of Catholics, claiming that the rebels were not only
sanctioned, but commanded, to revolt by their faith. In an obvious inference
from Troy's controversial *Pastoral Instructions* of 1793, he declared that the
decrees of the Lateran Council had made Catholics natural Jacobins. Duigenan
sought to illustrate the innate threat posed by Catholics to the establishment
and this he demonstrated both from the argument of numbers and the tenets of
their faith.

Not only was Duigenan opposed to further concessions to Catholics, but he
railed against the ills which had resulted from those already conceded. In the
case of the concessions made in 1793, he pointed to the 'woeful experience'
of the rebellion and the folly of the landlords who had supposed that the votes
of their tenants would be at their disposal. On the contrary, he claimed, 'these
half savages are mostly under the direction and influence of their priests, who
would generally sway county elections'.[51] Yet, in spite of the fears generated
by the radicals prior to the rebellion that the government intended a renewal
of the penal laws, the political reality in the early months of 1799 was that the
proposed Union held out hopes of full emancipation for the Catholics. In this
sense, Duigenan's rantings represent a prophetic warning rather than a realistic
attempt to turn back the clock, no matter how appealing that might have

appeared.[52] Nevertheless Duigenan was deeply resentful at the inroads made by Catholics on the Protestant establishment and regarded Maynooth College, that 'noxious and unconstitutional weed', as the manifestation of this corruption, a glaring monument to 'the spirit of Burkism'.[53]

Duigenan was not alone in his opposition to Maynooth and the debate on the annual grant to the college in the House of Lords quickly developed into an anti-Catholic tirade. When a grant of £6,000 was proposed to the house, the Orange peer, Lord Farnham moved that the grant be made by bill and not by vote. In the ensuing debate the ultras vented a great deal of anti-Catholic rhetoric and the continued presence of Thomas Hussey as president of the college was taken as confirmation of the nefarious principles of the establishment. Since the publication of his celebrated pastoral in 1797, Hussey had provided a constant hate figure and was still regarded in loyalist circles 'as the viper in the fable who bit the bosom that fostered it'.[54] In the course of the debate, Lord Clare rounded on Hussey and characterised the Catholic clergy as republican instigators of rebellion. Using an expression from Duigenan's *State*, he described Maynooth as an asylum for the children of paupers. The Catholic body was unwilling to contribute towards the college, yet they had been very generous in their support of Tone and his fellow radicals.[55] To the great surprise of the administration, the Lords rejected the grant, but the implications for the Catholic hierarchy were far more significant.

I V

The level of clerical involvement in the rebellion and the tenor of the subsequent polemic had deeply embarrassed the Catholic hierarchy. Edward Dillon, the recently appointed archbishop of Tuam, expressed disappointment to Thomas Bray at the rejection of the grant which he attributed 'in a great measure to the misconduct of the Dublin clergy'. The timing of the Lord's decision, however, was crucial and the rejection of the grant set in process a marked shift in episcopal attitudes towards the proposed government veto and provision for the clergy. In spite of his initial regret, Dillon remarked to Bray, that this 'should be a warning to us not to give up our present subsistence for any precarious grant that can be offered'.[56]

Throughout the 1790s, the question of the establishment of a government veto on episcopal appointments and a provision for the support of the Catholic clergy had never been far from the political agenda. This policy had been mooted as far back as 1782 by Thomas Lewis O'Beirne, then secretary to the

Viceroy Portland, but the bishops had successfully resisted successive attempts at its introduction. In the spring of 1795, however, signs of a softening of the hierarchy's opposition began to appear; with Emancipation in the offing, it became increasingly obvious that some concession of independence would have to be offered. The collapse of the Fitzwilliam administration made the urgency of such concessions unnecessary; the bishops meanwhile achieved the great object of their desires, a national seminary, without any sacrifice of independence.

Yet, the government continued to contemplate the desirability of a provision for the clergy. In May 1797 at Troy's difficult meeting with Pelham in the wake of Hussey's pastoral, the Chief Secretary had again raised the issue of a veto. Troy swiftly replied that 'it was absurd to bribe our prelates to enforce loyalty, as they had always done it from principle, and that the bribe should rather come from the United Irishmen to estrange our bishops from their uniform conduct'.[57] Yet the events of the rebellion illustrated too clearly the influence of a seditious priest and, as before, the frailty of the priest's allegiance was attributed to his overdependence on the people. In the winter of 1798, the Castle made discreet soundings of Troy and the Catholic gentry. Compromised by the behaviour of his clergy, Troy responded favourably to the proposal and Cornwallis reported that Fingall and Kenmare were both anxious 'to see the Catholic clergy rendered less dependent on the lower orders, by having a reasonable provision under the State'.[58] Castlereagh apparently outlined to Troy a comprehensive package which he intended for the Irish Church. The proposal allowed for a broad scale of payment for the Catholic bishops and priests, the recognition of a role for the government in the appointment of bishops, and the establishment of a system of clerical registration.[59]

Troy presented these proposals to a meeting of the Maynooth trustees in mid-January 1799 and they were accepted with certain qualifications.[60] The resolutions were passed on to Castlereagh, in the understanding that they should remain confidential until all outstanding differences were settled, while Bishops Troy, O'Reilly and Plunket were instructed to carry out any necessary negotiations with the administration.[61] Clerical reaction to the apparent willingness of the trustees to accept the administration's proposals was mixed. Since the foundation of the college, the trustees had held quarterly meetings which assumed the role normally filled by a national bishops' conference. Ever since the Catholic Convention, there had been a reluctance amongst the bishops to meet as a conference, lest their gathering be misinterpreted as an upper house of the Back Lane Parliament. The establishment of the board of trustees had removed this anxiety and their regular meetings provided a perfect channel through which the Church could be governed. With the exception of Thomas Hussey, the absent bishops had been canvassed before the January meeting, and all except John Young of Limerick agreed to the proposals, with Michael MacMahon of Killaloe offering no opinion.[62]

Troy was perturbed at the Bishop of Limerick's opposition to the scheme, which had resulted from the government's suspicion of 'the loyalty of many of our clergy since the late rebellion'.[63] Young, however, was to remain a formidable opponent of any measure of state intervention in the government of the Church which, he believed, would have dangerous consequences for the cause of religion.[64] Besides, he believed that the provision was merely intended as 'a douceur' for the proposed Union; expressing satisfaction 'with the constitution of our country in its present form', he declared his intention to refuse any 'bribe to acquiesce in the annihilation of its independence'.[65]

Thomas Hussey had returned to London shortly after the publication of his pastoral in 1797, but from there he mounted an effective opposition to the proposed veto. Traditionally, it has been accepted that Hussey carried little weight within the hierarchy, but it is apparent that during the spring of 1799 he exerted considerable pressure upon Charles Erskine to alert the Holy See to the inherent dangers of the government proposals.[66] Hussey had been a close disciple of Edmund Burke and in the spring of 1799 he echoed many of his late mentor's arguments against any diminution of the independence of the hierarchy. His letter to Clinch in early 1799 is entirely Burkean in its inspiration:

> Another project upon which I have been consulted is to grant salaries or pensions to the Catholic clergy, of the higher and lower order. The condition upon which they are to be granted, as first proposed to me, are directly hostile to the interests of religion and taken in the most favourable point of view, must be detrimental to the Catholics, by cutting asunder the slender remaining ties between the pastor and his flock, by turning the discipline and laws of the Church into a mercantile, political speculation and must end in making the people unbelievers and consequently Jacobins upon the French scale.[67]

Hussey believed himself to be a victim of the ungrateful administration, but there is little doubt that his manoeuvres in London greatly affected the course of negotiations on the veto question. As in the case of his acceptance of the oath in 1793, Troy had conducted his negotiations with the government without consultation with the Holy See or with Charles Erskine in London. Perhaps his reluctance to involve outside parties was a reflection of his own belief that a provision for the clergy would never materialise, given the opposition of the ultras in Dublin to any measure resembling an establishment of Catholicism. Troy failed to inform Erskine of the agreed resolutions until 12 March 1799 and his first communication with Propaganda came in June, after he had received an angry rebuff from the Pro-Prefect, Cardinal Borgia, who had learned of the proposals from Erskine.[68]

In a complex exchange of letters, Troy sought to defend his actions in relation to the veto against Erskine's argument about the destructive potential of such a concession to government and from Borgia reprimanding him for an infringement of the prerogative of the Holy See. Given his initial enthusiasm for the proposal and his own role in the negotiation of a similar grant to the Scottish clergy, Erskine's opposition to the proposed provision is curious.[69] It is likely that Hussey, whom Hobart believed 'had wormed himself into Erskine's good books', had informed him of the government's proposals and it was his warnings which alerted the monsignor to the likely consequences of the scheme.[70] Nevertheless, Erskine did appreciate Troy's dilemma and the pressure upon the hierarchy to 'disarm the insinuations which malicious persons have been making about them'.[71]

In any event, the Union debate overtook all other issues in priority, allowing the veto question and the proposed provision for the clergy to slide quietly down the agenda. Behind their apparent willingness to co-operate with such proposals, the bishops jealously guarded their independence. Throughout 1799 there was marked hardening of opposition to the government's plan. The unreliability of such schemes had been illustrated by the Lords' rejection of the Maynooth grant, and the opposition of the Holy See to any veto, in spite of their own dependence upon the British, was a cause of concern. Nevertheless, the offer of some concession to the government remained the bishops' trump card; in 1795 they had offered it as the price of promised emancipation and the establishment of a national seminary; now it was offered once more as a token of loyalty and reparation. On neither occasion was the spirit of the offer put to the test.

Troy's relief was reflected in letter on the subject to his Dominican confrère, Luke Concanen, with whom he conducted a frank and honest correspondence:

> The proposal has not been renewed by government since January 1799 ... We all wish to remain as we are, and we would so, were it not that too many of the clergy were active in the wicked rebellion or did not oppose it ... If we had rejected the proposals in toto, we would be considered here

as rebels. This is a fact. If we agreed to it without reference to Rome, we would be branded as schismatics. We were between Scylla and Charybdis.[72]

The aftermath of the Act of Union, however, saw a revival of the veto controversy, creating bitter divisions within the Catholic body and blighting all attempts at a solution of the Catholic question for almost twenty years.[73]

V

Protestant security in Ireland depended upon the preservation of their own unity and the good will of England. From the 1750s, serious strains had begun to show; the Dissenters proved a menacing threat to Protestant unity, while the money bill dispute and the decline of the undertakers led to rising Protestant nationalism and subsequent tensions in Anglo-Irish relationships. While the vaunted constitution of 1782 offered apparent security, the impact of the French Revolution and London's willingness to 'play the Catholic game', illustrated clearly the vulnerability of the Protestant establishment. Increasingly an union of the two kingdoms appeared to offer a solution to the complex problem of the Anglo-Irish relationship, and in the wake of the rebellion it emerged as the best hope of halting the march of the popish phalanx. Yet, ironically, the Act of Union passed with the support of the Catholic prelates whose quiescent role in the debates on the issue stands out in stark contrast to the vigour with which they battled to secure the establishment of Maynooth College.[74]

Troy, in particular, has been widely castigated for his part in the management of the negotiations on the proposed measure. With the reform cause in disgrace, he had become the sole effective voice of the Catholic community and his willingness to co-operate with the government has, therefore, been interpreted as a betrayal of Catholic aspirations. But while Cornwallis believed Troy was 'perfectly well inclined' towards an Union, provided that such an arrangement placed no bar on future Catholic hopes, the archbishop continued to have serious reservations about the act. Writing to Lord Castlereagh in December 1798, just a few days after Cornwallis's assessment of his position, Troy boldly declared that 'no arrangement to tranquilize' Ireland could have any hope so long as the Catholics remained 'excluded from the benefit of the constitution, and remained subject to their present disqualifications'.[75] Yet, in spite of vague hopes and Pitt's sympathy for the Catholic cause, the King's known oppposition to Catholic emancipation ruled out any further concessions.

The Catholic bishops were in a quandary. While one anti-union pamphleteer believed that the fruit of emancipation was 'ready to drop into your hands, unless the tree be cut up by the roots', it made little sense, as Edward Cooke pointed out, 'to oppose a measure that was opposed by their enemies the Orangemen'.[76] In April 1795 the famous meeting of the 'Francis Street orators', reeling from news of Fitzwilliam's recall, had declared any future emancipation unacceptable if linked to an Union. Bishop Patrick Plunket was less enthused about Irish independence. Writing to Troy in December 1798, he confessed that 'as a separate kingdom, I cannot recollect at what period of our existence we were a contented happy people'.[77] Thomas Hussey put it more bluntly, stating his preference for 'a union with the Beys and Mamelukes of Egypt to that of being under the iron rod of the Mamelukes of Ireland'.[78] The sole dissenter amongst the hierarchy was John Young of Limerick who opposed what he believed was an 'annihilation' of Irish independence. Nevertheless, such opposition to the proposed Act of Union would never amount to more than a pious gesture, given the scale of the Orange backlash to the rebellion.[79]

In any event, the government, concerned to avoid a confusion of issues, was determined that the union would be unaccompanied by further Catholic relief.[80] The remnant of the old Catholic Committee met at Fingall's Dublin home on 15 December 1798 to consider an appropriate policy on the legislation. The Committee had been shorn of its radical members and the forty attending were described by Troy as 'respectable persons, gentry and the principal merchants of the city'.[81] William Bellew expressed his anger at the failure of the union package to address the Catholic question and he rejected the belief that emancipation would have an easier passage through a united parliament.[82] The meeting failed to reach a conclusive decision and was adjourned until 20 December, in order that the subject could be 'discussed finally in a meeting of a more general description of the Roman Catholic body'.[83]

The subsequent meeting was equally indecisive and, with Bellew withdrawing his objections following private discussions with Cornwallis, the assembly dispersed without agreement. Ironically, the anti-union faction led by George Ponsonby was anxious to involve the Catholics in the debate and they too held out offers to the Catholic body in return for their support for a petition opposing the measure. Incredibly, John Foster, the pillar of the Ascendancy, promised Catholics 'everything on condition of their joining to defeat the project of union'.[84] Yet, despite the initial defeat of the union proposals in the Irish House of Commons on 23 January 1799, the government were not prepared to enter into a renewed race for the Catholic. A meeting of Dublin Catholics in February 1799 resolved to take no part in the union debate.[85]

In spite of these resolutions the Catholic hierarchy, prompted by the administration, threw themselves behind the measure and actively canvassed the support of their flock. Much of this effort was, no doubt, due to their anxiety to demonstrate loyalty to the government; Troy was conducting negotiations on the question of compensation for the many burned chapels, and there was also the belief that a union of the two kingdoms afforded the best safeguard to the tyranny of the Orange faction. There was, however, a more substantial issue involved in that the union provisions, in failing to bar future Catholic advances, contained implicit encouragement of their aspirations. Bishop Caulfield's letter to Troy on the issue in July 1799 reflected the mixed motives prompting episcopal support for the measure:

> I consider the case, the time and the circumstances exceedingly delicate and tender. Union is looked for; in order to obtain it the Ascendancy is not to be irritated, but rather to be kept in tolerable good humour, but that point gained, I am persuaded in my own mind, we shall be better off than ever. For the ruling powers are convinced, that the late unfortunate and wicked rising was not on the part of Catholics, a rebellion against the King, but against the Protestant Ascendancy and Orangemen. Persuaded as I am of the good and honest intentions of government on both sides of the channel, I would not press or urge any measure that can tend to defeat or obstruct government in the way to the main point.[86]

Troy busied himself behind the scenes promoting the proposal. In February 1799 he enlisted the support of Bishop Matthew Lennan of Dromore to secure the election of the liberal, pro-union candidate, Isaac Corry, in the Newry by-election.[87] James Lannigan signed a petition in Ossory and Troy encouraged Caulfield to present an address on behalf of the Catholics of Wexford in favour of the measure. Caulfield dutifully obliged and an address, appropriately repentant for the folly of the rebellion and couched in loyal rhetoric was presented in the following November.[88] Similar resolutions were signed by Bishops Bray (Cashel), Dillon (Tuam), Sughrue (Kerry), Cruise (Ardagh), Coyle (Raphoe), French (Elphin), MacMahon (Killaloe) and Bellew (Killala), while Thomas Hearn signed the Waterford address in Hussey's absence.

The tenor of the Raphoe address was particularly penitential; referring to 'the baneful seeds of the French rebellion', it lamented the late rising and 'especially such of our own religion as have ungratefully and in direct opposition to the principles of our holy religion enlisted under the laborum or standard of the most unnatural and ever to be reprobated rebellion'.[89] In many dioceses the bishops sent priests from parish to parish promoting similar resolutions which were published widely in the press.

Yet, the bishops' campaign had not gone unopposed. The renegade Franciscan Dennis Taaffe was arrested in March 1799 and charged with the publication of a seditious paper, the *Shamrock*, which the *Dublin Journal* believed was designed to produce mischievous and disloyal results 'under the convenient mask of anti-unionism.[90] Catholic opposition to the union was ambiguous, since it implied either a desire for more than emancipation or a belief that it would be offered from another quarter.[91]

Dublin Catholics, many of whom had been in favour of accepting the offers of the Ponsonby faction, opposed the union. There was similar sentiment in the neighbouring Diocese of Meath, where Bishop Plunket, despite his support for the measure, was unwilling to raise a petition believing that, 'in political questions it becomes us rather to follow than to lead'.[92] The Archbishop of Cashel reiterated these sentiments to Pelham, claiming that 'if we act in any ostensible capacity in the business of union, either by a personal signature to an address in favour of it, or otherwise, in my humble opinion, instead of serving the cause we may injure it'.[93]

This seemingly unqualified episcopal support for the administration aroused considerable resentment amongst the laity. Thomas Hussey believed 'a great part' of the Catholic community regarded the higher clergy as 'willing slaves under Government and instruments ever disposed to keep their people under the harrow'. This conviction had made the clergy 'hateful and contemptible in their eyes'.[94] In Wexford, James Caulfield met with considerable opposition from James Edward Devereux and Philip Hay who, he claimed, was 'leading the wise men of Ross' in the presentation of an independent petition.[95] The opposition to Caulfield's deferential address in New Ross reflected the levels of political awareness amongst the people there; one objection was that 'we should not criminate anyone', while others protested that 'the Quakers have greater privilege in England than the Catholics'.[96] In Galway, Bishop Dillon was initially reluctant to sign a pro-union address, for fear the crowd would brand him 'an Orange bishop, the tool of government, well paid for my services etc'.[97] It was not by chance, then, that Castlereagh defended the integrity of the clergy during the union debate:

> I shall notice the insinuation that the Roman Catholic clergy have been bribed to the support of this measure; it is an illiberal imputation thrown out for the dangerous purpose of weakening their authority, by lowering them in the opinion of their flocks.

If, he continued, the measure of the union was a measure of bribery, 'if bribery and public advantage are synonymous, I must readily admit that it is a measure of the most comprehensive bribery that was ever produced'.[98]

There was no cynicism involved in the hierarchy's support for the Act of Union, nor did they regard the measure as a panacea for all Ireland's ills. The rebellion had exposed Irish Catholics to the charge of disloyalty and, against the background of a sustained loyalist backlash, an union was perceived to offer the best security for Catholic interests. During the House of Lords debate on the issue, Fitzgibbon rounded on the Catholic clergy, declaring that 'conscientious popish ecclesiastics will never become well attached subjects to the Protestant State'.[99] Equally, the Protestant State had never shown great attachment to Catholic interests and, in the terror of the post rebellion period, it appeared as if the Orange faction was intent not merely on exacting revenge, but on the destruction of the Church itself. The politicisation and turbulence of the 1790s made the Union inevitable; the only alternative to its enactment was complete separation. However, in the absence of Catholic emancipation the Act of Union contained a fatal flaw which eventually transformed the Catholic question into the Irish question.[100]

CHAPTER TEN

Epilogue

The events of the 1790s had massively altered the fortunes of the Catholic community in Ireland. The impact of the French revolution had brought the country to an unprecedented level of political awareness. The Catholic Committee, the vehicle of Catholic political expression, was transformed and was eventually surpassed by the United Irishmen as its radicalised members sought reform and relief, not as an indulgence to be requested with deference, but as a right to be pursued with vigour. The social and political transformation and the threat posed by impending war with France had serious implications for the security of the kingdom. Once more the question of management dominated the political agenda; London opted to 'play the Catholic game' and the constitutional revolution of 1793 saw Catholics admitted to the forty shilling franchise. Yet, concession of the vote made little sense without conceding the right to sit in parliament, and Catholics admitted to part of the constitution increasingly demanded the whole.

For the hierarchy, too, the progress of the 'French disease' had serious implications. In France, the Catholic Church had been abolished under the terms of the Civil Constitution and throughout Europe the spread of the revolution had made serious inroads into religion. The Irish bishops were particularly conscious of European events. The restrictions of the penal laws had given the continental colleges a crucial role in the Irish Church, while their educational experience gave the clergy a heightened sensitivity and insight into the plight of the Church in Europe. It was with increasing alarm, then, that the bishops watched the headway made by French principles amongst Irish Catholics. This transformation was illustrated only too clearly in the events surrounding the acrimonious Kenmare secession from the Catholic Committee, during which Caulfield bitterly complained of the 'puppies, the rabble' dictating to the prelates.[1] More ominously, however, the bishops watched with increasing anxiety the active role taken by so many of their priests amongst the

*Fig. 24   John Thomas Troy,
Archbishop of Dublin 1786-
1823 (N.G.I.)*

radicals, culminating in the implication of as many as seventy clerics in the rebellion of 1798.

In a curious twist of fate, however, the crisis of the 1790s resulted in Catholic emergence from the penal era and the transformation of the Irish mission into a Church with the appropriate institutions. The continental crisis brought a novel convergence of interests between the British government and the Catholic Church and their mutual concern created a new atmosphere of trust and dialogue. The Catholic Church became the perceived bulwark against the advance of Jacobinism in Ireland, while British arms offered the only hope of salvation for the continental Church. Shared sentiments were transformed into action under the influence of Edmund Burke and Charles Erskine, and the foundation of Maynooth College represented the end of the restrictions that the penal laws had placed on the practice of religion in Ireland. More significantly, however, the complex process which had led to the foundation of the College witnessed both the emergence of a national episcopal conference and the establishment of a *modus operandi* between the Catholic Church and the Protestant State.

The turbulence of the latter half of the decade, particularly the perceived sectarian complexion of the rebellion of 1798, placed this relationship in jeopardy. The bishops, however, successfully salvaged their reputation. Troy enjoyed unrestricted access to the Castle where he had the confidence of Cornwallis, while Francis Moylan was rewarded for his loyal exertions, spending a week as the guest of the Duke of Portland at Bulstrode, a sojourn James Caulfield regarded as 'a strong prognostic of very great benefits to this country, which I have strong hopes of being realised ere long'.[2]

The great achievements of the decade had resulted largely from the leadership of Troy. The archbishop had shown courage and determination in the face of successive crises which threatened the survival of the Catholic Church in Ireland. The revolution in France, its associated radicalism and the loyalist reaction in Ireland all combined to present an apparently insurmountable challenge. John Troy, however, through a combination of tenacity and shrewd but stern diplomacy, skillfully transformed crisis to opportunity, creating the modern Irish Church in the process. Hated by the radicals, hailed by the hierarchy, the archbishop's greatest admirer, James Caulfield, declared that 'St Peter's Chair would not be an extravagant reward for ... [Troy's] great, judicious and zealous efforts'.[3]

Notes

CHAPTER ONE: WINTER'S END

1 See James Kelly's study of Ardagh in R. Gillespie and G. Moran (ed.), *Longford* (Dublin, 1991). Fearghus Ó Fearghail has examined Ossory in *Kilkenny: history and society* while Kevin Whelan has studied Tipperary and Patrick Corish Wexford in the same series. The first two volumes of Ignatius Murphy's *Diocese of Killaloe* have also appeared. P. Corish, *The Catholic community in the seventeenth and eighteenth centuries* (Dublin, 1981); *The Irish Catholic experience* (Dublin, 1985); H. Fenning, *The Irish Dominican province, 1698-1797* (Dublin, 1990).

2 T. P. Power and K. Whelan (ed.), *Endurance and emergence* (Dublin, 1990); Daniel Corkery, *The hidden Ireland: a study of Gaelic Munster in the eighteenth century* (Dublin, 1925).

3 Cullen, 'Catholics under the penal laws' in *Eighteenth-Century Ireland* (1986), pp 23-36; 'Catholic social classes under the penal laws' in Power and Whelan (ed.) *Endurance and emergence*, pp 57-84; Thomas Bartlett, *Fall and rise of the Irish nation* (Dublin, 1992), pp 17-29; S. J. Connolly, 'Religion and history' in *Irish Economic and Social History* (1983), pp 66-80.

4 S. J. Connolly, *Religion, law and power: the making of Protestant Ireland, 1660-1760* (Oxford 1992), p.263.

5 William King, *The state of the Protestants of Ireland under the late King James' government* (Dublin, 1691), p.292.

6 Bartlett, *Fall and rise*, p.18.

7 Mant, *History of the Church of Ireland* (London, 1840), ii, pp 75-7; Murray, 'The Church in the revolution' in W. A. Phillips (ed.), *History of the Church of Ireland from the earliest times to the present day* (Oxford, 1933), p.157; Renehan, *Collections in Irish history*, i, (Dublin, 1861), p.88; Burke, *Irish priests in penal times* (Shannon, 1969), pp 164-5.

8 Burke, *Irish priests*, p.112; Lecky, *England in the eighteenth century*, i, p.288.

9 Connolly, *Religion, law and power*, p.273.

10 L. M. Cullen, 'Catholics under the penal laws', pp 29-31.

11 Connolly, *Religion, law and power*, p.311; idem, *Priests and people*, p.27. D. Dickson, 'Catholics and trade in eighteenth-century Ireland' in Power and Whelan (ed.), *Endurance and emergence*, pp 85-100; Cullen, 'Catholic social classes' in Power and Whelan (ed.), *Endurance and emergence*, pp 57-84.

12 R. E. Burns, 'Irish popery laws: a study of eighteenth-century legislation and behaviour', *Review of Politics* (1962); Maureen Wall, 'Penal laws', in G. O'Brien (ed.) *Catholic Ireland*, p.8; Bartlett, *Fall and rise*, p.19.

13 M. Wall, 'The penal laws', pp 11-12, J. G. Simms, 'The bishops' Banishment Act of 1697' in *I.H.S.*, xvii (Sept. 1970), pp 185-99.

14 P. J. Flanagan (ed.), 'The Diocese of Clogher in 1714' in *Clogher Record*, 1, No. 2 (1954), p.42.

15 1731 Report on the state of popery, *Arch. Hib.* (1913), pp 146-51.
16 Rogers, *The Volunteers and Catholic emancipation*, p.18.
17 Rogers, *The Volunteers and Catholic emancipation*, p.2; K. Whelan, 'Regional impact of Irish Catholicism', p.254.
18 Young, *Tour in Ireland* (1892); Thomas Campbell, *Philosophical survey of the south of Ireland* (Dublin, 1778).
19 *Castlereagh Correspondence*, IV, pp 97-103.
20 Flanagan, 'Clogher in 1714', p.14.
21 H. Fenning, 'John Kent's report on the state of the Irish mission, 1742' in *Arch. Hib.* (1966), pp 59-102.
22 Connolly, *Priests and people*, pp 32-3.
23 *'Memoire pour son eminence monseigneur le Cardinal Corsini, protecteur d'Irlande, touchant l'état présent de la religion dans ce pays-ci'*, A.P.F., C.P. 110, ff 171-74. This memoir was considered by the congregation of 28 and 31 July 1750, Fenning, *Undoing of the friars*, p.193.
24 Cashel statutes in Renehan *Collections*, i, App C, p.477; P. MacDavatt to Antonelli, 22 July 1791, A.P.F., S.O.C.G., 892, f 251 in P. O'Donoghue, 'The Catholic Church in the age of revolution and rebellion, 1782-1815' (Ph.D., U.C.D., 1975), p.40.
25 Cullen, 'Catholic social classes', p.77.
26 Connolly, *Priests and people*, p.65.
27 Sweetman, Visitation diary 1753, in W. H. Grattan Flood, 'Diocesan manuscripts of Ferns during the reign of Bishop Sweetman', *Arch. Hib.*, II (1913), II (1914); P. Plunket, Visitation July 1780, Cogan, *Diocese of Meath*, iii, p.28.
28 P. Plunket, 1780 Visitation, Cogan, *Diocese of Meath*, iii, p.38.
29 Cogan, *Diocese of Meath*, iii, p.30.
30 M. Brennan, 'The confraternity of Christian doctrine in Ireland' in *I.E.R.* (1934), pp 560-77.
31 O'Donoghue, 'Catholic Church', p.22.
32 *Missale Romanum ... Et novorum festorum missis hujusque concessia auctum. His accedunt festa, quae ex indulto apostolico in regno Hiberniae celebrantur ... ex officina Morrisiana MDCCLXXVII*; T. Wall, 'Archbishop Carpenter and the Catholic Revival, 1770-1786' *Rep. Novum (1955)*, pp 178-9.
33 J. Troy, *Schema for diocesan clerical conference for 1790*, 9 December 1789, D.D.A.
34 Statement of the bishops of Munster, 1786, contained in James Butler, *A justification of the tenets of the Roman Catholic religion* (London, 1787), in J. A. Murphy, 'The support of the Catholic clergy of Ireland, 1750-1850' in *Historical Studies* (London, 1966), p.115.
35 See F. Ó Fearghail, 'The Catholic Church in Kilkenny, 1600-1800' in W. Nolan and K. Whelan (ed.), *Kilkenny: history and society* (Dublin, 1990), p.243.
36 Ó Fearghail, 'Catholic Church in Kilkenny', p.243.
37 *Castlereagh Corr.*, iv, pp 97-173.
38 T. McKenna, *Thoughts on the civil condition ... of the Roman Catholic clergy* (Dublin, 1805), pp 79-80 cited in Murphy, 'Clerical income', p.112.
39 Cullen, 'Catholic social classes', p.76.
40 *Castlereagh Corr.*, iv, p.154.
41 Whelan, 'The regional impact of Irish Catholicism', p.7.

42 K. Whelan, 'The Catholic parish, the Catholic chapel and village development in Ireland', *Irish Geography* (1983), pp 1-16.

43 A. MacAuley, *Septennial parliaments vindicated* (Dublin, 1766), cited in Rogers, *Irish Volunteers and Catholic emancipation*, p.5.

44 C. O'Dwyer (ed.), 'Butler visitations' in *Arch. Hib.* (1975), pp 1-90; (1976), pp 1-49.

45 K. Whelan, 'Catholic Church, 1700-1900' in W. Nolan and T. McGrath (ed.), *Tipperary: history and society* (Dublin, 1985), pp 225-7.

46 Whelan, 'The Catholic parish', p.7.

47 MacKenna to Antonelli, 20 March 1785, A.P.F., S.C. Irlanda, vol. 16, f.28; James Butler to Antonelli, 13 September 1784, A.P.F., S.C. Irlanda, vol. 16, f. 132; F. Moylan to S.C. of the Council, 18 June 1785, A.P.F., SOCG, vol. 871, f. 12 in O'Donoghue, 'Catholic Church', pp 24-7; P. Corish, The *Irish Catholic experience* (Dublin, 1985), p.160.

48 The Troy-Concanen correspondence is contained in the Dublin Diocesan Archives.

49 C. Giblin, 'The Stuart nomination of Irish bishops, 1687-1765' in *I.E.R.* (1966), pp 35-47.

50 *Castlereagh Corr.*, iv, pp 97-173.

51 D. Dickson, *New foundations*, p.145; J. R. Walsh, *Frederick Augustus Hervey, 1730-1803* (Maynooth, 1972).

52 Hervey to J. L. Foster, 29 November 1779, in J. Kelly, 'The parliamentary reform movement of the 1780s and the Catholic question' in *Arch. Hib.* (1988), p.99.

53 Dower to Hervey, 9 March 1767, PRONI, D1514/1/5/1, Kenmare to Hervey, 12 March 1768, PRONI, D1514/1/5/3 in Bartlett, *Fall and rise*, p.79.

54 See E. O'Flaherty, 'The Catholic question in Ireland, 1774-1793' (M.A., U.C.D., 1981), pp 2-8.

55 T. R. Power, 'The Most Rev. James Butler, Archbishop of Cashel, 1774-91', in *I.E.R.* (1892), p.310; p.Wallace, 'Archbishop James Butler II', p.49.

56 M. Wall, 'Catholic loyalty to King and Pope' in G. O'Brien (ed.), *Catholic Ireland*, p.113.

57 Wall, 'Catholic loyalty', p.114.

58 J. Butler to Castelli, September 1776, in Power, 'James Butler', p.314.

59 Fenning, *Irish Dominican province*, p.439.

60 J. Butler to Propaganda, 26 February 1777, Irish College Archives, Rome, Liber xix f. 107, in H. Peel, 'The appointment of Dr Troy to Dublin' in *Rep. Novum (1965)*, pp 10-11.

61 J. Troy to T. Fallon, 15 May 1778, Troy Letter Book, D.D.A.

62 V. Bodkin to J. Butler, 24 June 1789, C.D.A.

63 P. Whelan, 'Anthony Blake, Archbishop of Armagh 1758-1787' in *Seanchas Ard Mhacha* (1970), pp 289-323.

64 Armagh Chapter to Borgia, 16 July 1778. A.P.F., Scritture riff., vol. 13, f. 286; B. Hoban, 'Dominic Bellew 1745-1812' in *Seanchas Ard Mhacha* (1972), pp 333-69.

65 J. M. Flood, 'Dr Plunket, Bishop of Meath, 1779-1827' in *I.E.R.* (1949), pp 234-43.

66 J. Butler to P. Plunket, 11 January 1781, Cogan, *Diocese of Meath*, iii, pp 54-5.

67 J. Carpenter to Busca, 13 June 1781, A.P.F., S.C., Irlanda , vol. 15, f. 65; J. Troy to Antonelli, 18 June 1781 and 14 January 1782, D.D.A. in O'Donoghue, 'Catholic Church', p.14.

68 Butler to P. Plunket, 23 October 1781, Cogan, *Diocese of Meath*, iii, p.61.

69 Cogan, *Diocese of Meath*, iii, p.61.
70 Antonelli to Clogher, Derry, Down and Conor, Dromore and Meath, 18 December 1781, A.P.F., Lettere, 238; 962-32 in V. McNally, 'John Thomas Troy and the Catholic Church in Ireland' (Ph.D., Dublin University, 1977).
71 J. Butler to P. Plunket, 2 December 1786, Cogan, *Diocese of Meath*, iii, p.115.
72 J. Hill, 'Religious toleration and the relaxation of the penal laws: an imperial perspective, 1763-1780' in *Arch. Hib.* (1988), pp 98-109; T. Bartlett, 'The origins and progress of the Catholic question in Ireland, 1690-1800', in Power and Whelan (ed), *Endurance and emergence*, pp 7-8.
73 E. Burke to G. Nagle, 25 August 1778, *Burke Corr.*, iii, pp 18-20.
74 T. Wyse, *Historical sketch of the late Catholic Association of Ireland*, i (Dublin, 1829), p.101.
75 O'Flaherty, 'Catholic question', p.12; Troy to Bishop Fallon, 15 March 1778, D.D.A.
76 J. Troy to J. Carpenter, 18 February 1778, D.D.A.
77 John Carpenter pastoral, 19 August 1778, D.D.A.; J. Troy to Dr Fallon, 14 September 1778, D.D.A.
78 O'Flaherty, 'The Catholic question', pp 45-70; Bartlett, *Fall and rise*, pp 98-102.
79 J. Troy to J. Butler, 2 October 1779, D.D.A.
80 J. Butler to J. Troy, 11 October 1779, Troy to Butler, 27 October 1779, D.D.A.
81 Troy to M. MacMahon, 27 November 1779, D.D.A. The five bishops present were John Carpenter (Dublin), James Butler (Cashel), John Troy (Ossory), Denis Maguire (Kilmore) and Patrick Plunket (Meath).
82 Troy to Butler, 12 January 1780, D.D.A.
83 Bartlett, 'Origins and progress of the Catholic question', pp 10-11.
84 *Parliamentary Register, 1781-2* (Dublin, 1782), p.196
85 Kenmare to Burke, 4 Feb 1782, *Burke Corr.*, iv, p.401; Burke to Kenmare, 21 February 1782, *Burke Corr.*, pp 410-14.
86 J. Kelly, 'The context and course of Thomas Orde's plan of education of 1787' in *Irish Journal of Education*, xx (1987), pp 236-63.
87 M. MacMahon to Troy, 15 March 1782, D.D.A.
88 Troy to MacMahon, 19 March 1782, D.D.A.
89 Troy to MacMahon, 19 March 1782, Busca to Carpenter, 9 April 1782, Busca to Carpenter, 19 April 1782, D.D.A.; See O'Flaherty, 'The Catholic question', pp 66-8.
90 J. S. Donnelly. 'The Whiteboy movement, 1761-5', *I.H.S.* (1978), pp. 20-54; 'The Rightboy movement', *Studia Hibernica*, nos 17 and 18 (1977-8), pp 120-202.
91 P. Wallace, 'Irish cathesis', p.44.
92 Pastoral of Sweetman of Ferns, 15 July 1775 in M. Bric, 'The Whiteboy movement, 1760-80' in W. Nolan (ed.), *Tipperary: history and society* , pp 148-184.
93 J. Troy, Pastoral and excommunication, Kilkenny, October 1779, cited in V. McNally, 'John Troy', p.22.
94 Conway to J. Butler, July 1786, C.D.A., cited in I. Murphy, *Diocese of Killaloe in the eighteenth century* (Dublin, 1991), pp 129-30.
95 Thomas Orde to J. Troy, November 1784, D.D.A.; Lutteral to J. Troy, 27 September 1786.
96 E. Burke to John Corry, 14 August 1779, *Burke Corr.*, iv, p.119.
97 Troy to Dillon, 18 September 1783, D.D.A. see J. Kelly, 'The parliamentary reform

movement of the 1780s and the Catholic question' in *Arch. Hib.* (1988), pp 95-116.
98 R. Dudley-Edwards (ed.), 'The minute books of the Catholic Committee, 1773-92', *Arch. Hib.* (1942), pp 87-8.
99 Dudley-Edwards, 'Minute book', pp 111-13.

CHAPTER TWO: 'THE FRENCH DISEASE'

1 Thomas Hussey to Richard Burke, 28 August 1790, *Burke Corr.*, iv, p.134.
2 See Patrick Kelly, 'Irish writers and the French Revolution' in *La storia della storiografia Europea sulla rivoluzione Francese* (Rome, 1990), pp 329-49.
3 For a succinct account of events see R. Gibson, *A social history of French Catholicism 1789-1914* (London, 1989), pp 30-55; J. McManners, *The French Revolution and the Church* (London, 1969).
4 Gibson, *French Catholicism*, p.33.
5 Gibson, *French Catholicism*, p.37.
6 See Claude Lefort, 'La révolution comme religion nouvelle' in F. Furet and M. Ozouf, *The French Revolution and the creation of modern political culture* (Pergamon, 1987), iii, pp 391-99.
7 McManners, *French Revolution*, p.38.
8 Claude Langlois, 'La rupture entre l'Eglise Catholique et la révolution' in Furet and Ozouf, *French Revolution*, iii, p.383; Timothy Tackett, *Religion, revolution and regional culture in eighteenth-century France; the ecclesiastical oath of 1791* (Princeton, 1986), p.xv.
9 Farquharson, Douai to Mr Thompson, 1 April 1791, cited in C. Johnson, *Developments in the Roman Catholic Church in Scotland 1789-1829* (Edinburgh, 1983), p.92
10 Philippe Loupés, 'The Irish clergy in the Diocese of Bordeaux during the French Revolution', in D. Dickson and H. Gough (ed.), *The French Revolution and Ireland* (Dublin, 1990), pp 28-39.
11 Cullen, 'Late eighteenth-century politicisation in Ireland: problems in its study and French links' in P. Bergeron and L. M. Cullen (ed.), *Cultures et pratiques*, pp 136-57.
12 *Cork Gaz.*, 25 June 1791.
13 *Cork Gaz.*, 29 June 1791.
14 T. Blanning, 'The role of religion in the European counter-revolution 1789-1815' in D. Beales and G. Best (ed.), *History, society and the Churches: essays in honour of Owen Chadwick* (Cambridge, 1985), p.200.
15 C. Kearney, Paris, to P. Plunket, 14 July 1791, Cogan, *Diocese of Meath*, iii, p.194.
16 J.W. to —— 6 June 1798, Nat. Arch. Reb. Papers, 620/10/121/111. For recent studies on Irish links with France in the late eighteenth century, see L. M. Cullen 'Late eighteenth-century politicisation'; 'The political structure of the Defenders' in Dickson and Gough (ed.), *French Revolution*, pp 117-39; Kevin Whelan, 'Politicisation in County Wexford and the origins of the 1798 Rebellion' in Dickson and Gough (ed.), *French Revolution*, pp 156-79.
17 Valentine Derry's preface to *The life of the Rev. James Coigley: an address to the people of Ireland, as written by himself during his confinement in Maidstone Gaol.*(London,1798), Cf. p.27.
18 John Jones, *An impartial narrative of the most important engagements which took place*

between His Majesty's forces and the rebels during the Irish Rebellion 1798 (Dublin, 1799), p.31.

19 Musgrave, *Memoirs*, p.339.

20 John T. Troy, *The excommunication of the Rev Robert M'Evoy, priest of the Dublin Archdiocese for promulgating and upholding principles established by the French Revolution* (London,1798).

21 Troy, *Excommunication*, p.9

22 Gibson, *French Catholicism*, p.44.

23 O'Donoghue, 'Catholic Church', p.313. See P. Scholfield, 'British politicians and French arms: the ideological war of 1793-5' in *History* (June, 1992), pp 183-202.

24 Abbé Paul MacPherson, Bruge, to Bishop Geddes, 26 August 1793 in Johnson, *Church in Scotland*, p.87; *Lim.Chron.*, 3 October 1792.

25 See *Letter of the French bishops residing in England to the late Pope Pius VI and the answer of His Holiness* (Dublin, 1800), in which the Pope expresses his gratitude to King George for his many kindnesses.

26 T. Hussey, *Sermon preached at the Spanish chapel, London, 14 May 1798* (London, 1798).

27 *F.D.J.*, 3 January 1792.

28 M. Buschkühl, *Great Britain and the Holy See 1746-1870* (Dublin, 1982), p.30.

29 Troy to T. Bray, 26 April 1794, D.D.A.

30 *F.D.J.*, 25 September 1798.

31 L. Concanen to J. Troy, 4 September 1793, D.D.A.

32 L. Nihell, Bishop of Kilkmacduagh and Kilfenora to J. Troy, 20 February 1794, D.D.A. Nihell noted that this was in spite of the persecutions they had suffered in France.

33 Cardinal Livizzani to J. Troy, 3 March 1795; L. Concanen to J. Troy, 30 June 1795, D.D.A.

34 T. Hussey to E. Burke, 30 November 1796, *Burke Corr.* viii, pp 140-3

35 J. Carroll, Baltimore, to J. Troy, 19 July 1794, D.D.A.

36 J. Troy to T. Bray, 26 April 1794, D.D.A.; *F.D.J.*, 8 May 1794 contained a laudatory review of the work, taken from the *Reviewers and Anthologiae Magazine* of March 1794. 'Since the formation of human society, so odious and detestable a picture of man's depravity was never more exhibited as in the massacre and persecution of 138 archbishops and bishops and 64,000 *curés* in France. The shocking detail is authenticated by an appeal to 600 French clergy now in Winchester, and by numerous well known facts. The history commences with May 1789 and is brought down to the present times–there is more to be learned from this book than from all the publications written since the revolution'. Many such anti-revolutionary pamphlets were reprinted in Dublin. *Declaration and retractions of Francis Teresa Panisset, Constitutional Bishop of Mont-Blanc in Savoy* (Dublin, 1797). The printer, Fitzpatrick, Dublin, is described as 'printer to the Royal College Maynooth'.

37 Cardinal Antonelli, Propaganda Fide to the Irish Bishops, 7 February 1795, D.D.A.

38 Pius VI, *Pastoralis sollicitudo*, 5 July 1796, in *F.D.J.*, 15 September 1796.

39 L. Concanen to J. Troy, 2 July 1796, D.D.A.

40 L. Concanen to J. Troy, 16 July 1796. The Bishop of Edinburgh had also informed Troy of these apparitions witnessed by Mons Latille, chaplain to the Count d'Artois, Dr Hay to John Troy, 26 August 1796.

41 Cited in Blanning, 'Role of religion in European counter-revolution', p.209.

42 *F.D.J.*, 1 November 1796. See John Troy, *Pastoral address on the defeat of the Bantry Bay invasion, February 1797* (Dublin, 1797).

43 *Morn. Post.* 18 August 1796.

44 For the Bantry expedition see Marianne Elliott, *Partners in revolution: the United Irishmen and France* (Yale, 1982), pp 77-124 and 'The role of Ireland in French war strategy, 1796-1798' in Dickson and Gough (ed.), *French Revolution*, pp 202-20.

45 *F.D.J.*, 3 January 1797.

46 *An address delivered to the Grand Jury of the County of Dublin, on Tuesday the 10th of January 1797, by Robert Day M.P.* (Dublin, 1797). See *Letters from a gentleman in Ireland to his friend at Bath* (Cork, 1797), p.30.

47 Examination of W. J. MacNeven before the Secret Committee of the House Of Lords, 7 August 1798 in, W. J. MacNeven, *Pieces of Irish History*, p.254.

48 *Morn. Post.* 18 February 1797.

49 O'Donoghue, 'Catholic Church', p.303

50 Troy, Pastoral address, February 1797 in Moran, *Spicil. Ossor.*, iii, pp 490-504.

51 *ibid*, p.494.

52 *Ennis. Chron.*, 27 February 1797.

53 *A sermon preached at St Patrick's chapel, Sutton Street, Soho Square, on Wednesday March the 8th 1797, on the day of solemn fast, by the Rev Arthur O'Leary* (Dublin and London, 1797).

54 *Public characters of 1798* (Dublin, 1799).

55 *Ennis. Chron.*, 16 March 1797; L. Concanen to J. Troy, 8 April 1797, D.D.A.; *Morn. Post.*, 28 February 1797.

56 *Morn. Post.*, 18 March 1797,

57 *Press*, 1 October 1797.

58 *Press*, 30 January 1798.

59 *Press*, 10 October 1797.

60 L. Concanen, Rome, to Troy, 24 February 1798, 17 March 1798, and 5 May 1798. D.D.A. See Fenning, *The undoing of the friars*, pp 354-79

61 Address of Mr Grady, chairman of Limerick, at the close of the Limerick quarter sessions, *F.D.J.*, 1 May 1798.

62 C. Erskine to Troy, 6 April 1798, D.D.A.

63 *An address to the Irish Roman Catholics on the necessity of arming the government and constitution with the whole energies of Ireland at the present crisis by a true born Irishman* (Dublin 1797), p.28.

64 Musgrave, *Memoirs* , p.122

65 *Life of James Coigley* (London, 1798), preface.

66 W. J. MacNeven to the French Directory, 1796, cited in R. Hayes, 'Priests and the independence movement of 1798' in *I.E.R.* lxvi (Dublin, 1945), p.259.

CHAPTER THREE: THE RADICAL CHALLENGE

1 Tone, *Autobiography*, i, p.50; S. McSkimmin [E.J.McCrum, ed.], *Annals of Ulster, 1790-1800* (Belfast, 1906), p.31. See J. Smyth, *The men of no property* (London, 1992); K. Whelan, 'Catholics, politicisation and the 1798 Rebellion' in R. Ó Muirí (ed.), *Irish Church history today* (Armagh, 1991), pp. 63-84; idem, 'Politicisation in County

Wexford' in *French Revolution*, pp 156-78.

2 Dudley Edwards (ed.), 'Minute Book', p.116; O'Flaherty, 'The Catholic question'.

3 T. Hussey to R.Burke, 28 August 1790, *Burke Corr.*, iv, p.134.

4 O'Donoghue, 'Catholic Church', pp 126-129; O'Flaherty, 'The Catholic Convention and Anglo-Irish Politics, 1791-93' in *Arch. Hib.*, xl (1985), p.16.

5 J. Butler to J. Troy, 1 March 1790, D.D.A.

6 J. Troy to a member of the Catholic Committee, 13 Feb. 1790.

7 For a discussion of the 'uniting business', see Smyth, *Men of no property*, pp 52-78.

8 Samuel Barber, *Synodal sermon* (1791), cited in K.Whelan, 'Catholics, politicisation and the 1798 Rebellion', p.65.

9 Peter Burrowes, *Plain arguments in defence of the people's absolute dominion over the constitution in which the question of Roman Catholic emancipation is fully considered*, cited in M. Elliott, *Wolfe Tone, prophet of Irish independence* (New Haven, 1989), p.114.

10 Cullen, 'Late eighteenth-century politicisation', pp 137-159.

11 J. O'Coigley, *Life of the Rev. James Quigley* (London, 1798), pp 12-13.

12 MacNeven, *Pieces*, p.119.

13 Grenville to Westmorland, 20 October 1791, Dropmore Ms., ii, 213-214. cited in J. Smyth, *Men of no property*, p.55.

14 J. O'Coigley, *Life*, pp 12-13.

15 W. Steel Dickson, *Narrative of the confinement and exile of William Steel Dickson* (Dublin, 1812) in B. Clifford (ed.), *Scripture politics: selections from the writings of William Steel Dickson* (Belfast, 1991), p.23.

16 Antonelli to Troy, 24 Dec. 1791; Antonelli to Charles O'Conor, 24 Dec. 1791, D.D.A.

17 Westmorland to ——, 21 Nov. 1791, H.O. 100/33/1/116. O'Donoghue, 'Catholic Church', p.151.

18 William Knox to Thomas Jefferson, 17 Jan. 1792, U.S. Nat. Archives., T. 199/3 cited in Elliott, *Tone*, p.151.

19 *F.D.J.*, 17 Dec. 1791.

20 'Minute Book', pp 137-140.

21 I am grateful to Conor Cruise O'Brien for this suggestion. See C. Cruise O'Brien, *The great melody* (London, 1992).

22 Troy to Hobart, 29 Nov. 1791, P.R.O., H.O., 100/34/33

23 'Minute Book', p.141.

24 The events of the split have been dealt with in great detail by O'Flaherty, 'The Catholic question'; O'Donoghue, 'Catholic Church'; M. Wall, 'John Keogh and the Catholic Committee' in G. O'Brien (ed.) *Catholic Ireland in the eighteenth century: collected essays of Maureen Wall*. (Dublin, 1989), pp 163-70.

25 Declaration of loyalty of the Catholics of Ireland, *F.D.J.*, 27 Dec. 1791.

26 Smyth, *Men of no property*, p.54.

27 'Minute Book', p.144.

28 D. Keogh, 'Archbishop Troy, The Catholic Church and radicalism, 1791-93' in D. Dickson, D. Keogh and K. Whelan (ed.), *The United Irishmen* (Dublin, 1993), pp 124-34.

29 Troy to Moylan, 23 Dec. 1791, D.D.A.

30 *F.D.J.*, 15 Dec. 1791.

31 Caulfield to Troy, 22 April 1792, D.D.A.; *Hib. Jn.* 4 Jan. 1792; K. Whelan, 'The role

of the Catholic priest in the 1798 Rebellion in Wexford' in K. Whelan and W. Nolan (ed.), *Wexford: history and society* (Dublin, 1987), p.297.

32 Caulfield to Troy, 28 Nov. 1791, D.D.A.

33 Caulfield to Troy, 27 Jan. 1792.

34 P. Plunket to Thos. Betagh, 29 Jan. 1792 in Cogan, *Diocese of Meath*, iii, pp 167-72; Elliott, *Tone*, p.153.

35 'Minute Book', pp 146-47.

36 E. Burke to R. Burke, 3 January 1791, *Burke Corr.*, vii, pp 11-12.

37 See T. Bartlett, '"A weapon of war yet untried": Irish Catholics and the armed forces of the crown, 1760–1830' in T. G. Fraser and K. Jeffry (ed.), *Men, women and war* (Dublin, 1993), pp 66-85.

38 Bartlett, 'Origins and progress of the Catholic question', p.13.

39 Westmorland to Pitt, 1 Jan. 1792, S.P.O.I., Westmorland Corr., 1789-1808, carton i, f. 35.

40 Westmorland to Pitt, 18 Jan. 1792, S.P.O.I., Westmorland Corr., 1789-1808, carton i, f. 45.

41 Froude, *The English in Ireland*, iii, p.59; Elliott, *Tone*, p.154.

42 32 Geo.III, c.21.

43 Dickson, *New foundations* , p.176.

44 R. Burke to E. Burke, 23 Feb. 1792, *Burke Corr.* viii, pp 68-74; MacNeven, *Pieces*, p.23.

45 *History of Belfast,* 19 April 1792, cited in Froude, *English in Ireland,* iii, p.61.

46 P. Duigenan, *An answer to the address of Rt. Hon. Henry Grattan to his fellow citizens* (Dublin, 1798), p.24; *F.D.J.*, 14 Feb. 1792.

47 W. T. Tone (ed.), *Life*, i, p.60.

48 'Minute Book', pp 151-52.

49 'Minute Book', p.157.

50 'Minute Book', pp 157-60.

51 'Minute Book',.p. 156.

52 D'Alton, *Archbishops*, p.484.

53 Troy to Brancadoro, Liege, 18 May 1792, D.D.A.

54 E. Burke to J. Cox Hippisley, 3 October 1793, *Burke Corr.*, vii, pp 439-44.

55 D. Delaney to Troy, 30 Mar. 1792, D.D.A.. See Wall, 'Catholic loyalty to King and Pope in eighteenth-century Ireland' in G. O'Brien (ed.), *Catholic Ireland*, pp 107-115.

56 Smyth, *Men of no property*, p.63.

57 Caulfield to Troy, 31 Mar. 1792, D.D.A.; Keogh to Hussey, 29 Mar. 1792, P.R.O., H.O. 100/38/243.

58 ''Minute Book', p.160. Caulfield to Troy, 31 Mar. 1792, D.D.A.

59 ''Minute Book', p.167.

60 Plan for the Convention, contained in *Vindication of the cause of the Catholics of Ireland adopted by the General Committee at a meeting December 7, 1792*. (Dublin, 1793), p.35.

61 Tone, *Life*, i, pp 170-72.

62 Tone, *Life*, i, p.184.

63 Hobart to Nepean, 8 Oct. 1792, S.P.O.I., Private Official Corr., 1789-93, p.231, cited in O'Donoghue, 'Catholic Church', p.177; Murphy, 'The support of the Catholic clergy', pp 103-121.

64 Keogh to Bray, 4 Aug. 1792, C.D.A.

65 Tone, *Life*, i, p.168.

66 Keogh to Bray, 4 August 1792, C.D.A.

67 B. McEvoy, 'Fr James Quigley,' in *Seanchas Ard Mhacha* (1970), p.254; R. R. Madden, *Lives of United Irishmen*, ii, p.2; L. M. Cullen, 'Political structure of the Defenders', in Dickson and Gough (ed.), *French Revolution*, p.127. It is perhaps within this context that Fr James O'Coigley's missionary activity amongst the Presbyterians of Antrim and Down may be interpreted. O'Coigley's role in the 'uniting business' was crucial, and his Defender links and family connections placed him firmly within a highly radicalised circle. Tone and Keogh were accompanied to Rathfriland by Fr Edmund Derry, subsequently Bishop of Dromore (1801-19), a close friend and relative of O'Coigley.

68 T. Bartlett, 'Religious rivalries in France and Ireland in the age of the French Revolution' in *Eighteenth-Century Ireland* (1991), p.68.

69 ..... Loughgilly to Ed. Cooke, 29 May 1798 Nat. Arch. Reb. Papers. 620/37/212; Camillus, *To the magistrates, the militia and the yeomanry of Ireland* (Dublin, 1798), p.4; Bartlett, 'Defenders and Defenderism', p.376.

70 Patterson MSS T. 1722. The pamphlet in printed in D. Miller, *Peep o' Day Boys and Defenders. Selected documents on the County Armagh disturbances 1784-6* (Belfast, 1990). Extracts from the pamphlet are printed in W. H. Crawford and B. Trainor (ed.) *Aspects of Irish social history* (Belfast, 1969), pp 171-75

71 Louis Cullen has attributed this pamphlet to James O'Coigley, regarding it as part of the overall politicisation of County Armagh and, more specifically, as a preparation for missions similar to those of Keogh and Tone in Down. Cullen's thesis is not altogether convincing. He identifies a number of features in the text pointing to O'Coigley; hints of a classical and scriptural education, familiarity with the situation in France, and a keen knowledge of the events of 1641. The latter point is significant since O'Coigley had begun a history of the seventeenth century, but his library and notes were lost when his house was destroyed. The author's use of language also places the pamphlet in a context beyond County Armagh and Cullen singles out 'Byrne's use of the word 'junto'. There are, however two further possibilities. The pamphlet may have been the work of John Byrne-son of Edward Byrne, a Dublin merchant and prominent member of the Catholic Committee-who was elected to represent Armagh City at the Convention. It could also be argued, as Musgrave has suggested, that the author was one of the Byrne family of County Louth. See Cullen, 'Late eighteenth-century politicisation in Ireland', pp 137-43.

72 *Lim.Chron.*, 3 October 1792.

73 Musgrave, *Memoirs*, p.63.

74 Donegal Grand Jury in *Vindication of the cause of the Catholics*, p.8.

75 E. Burke to Moylan, 18 November 1792, *Burke Corr.*, vii, p.293.

76 *Cork.Gaz.*, 13 October 1792.

77 L. Nihell to T. Bray, 18 October 1792, C.D.A.

78 W. Egan to T. Hearn, 2 Oct. 1792, W.D.A.

79 *The excommunication of the Rev. Robert M' Evoy, priest of the Archdiocese of Dublin for promulgating and upholding the principles established by the French Revolution; Published 29 September 1792 by John Thomas Troy* (London, 1798).

80 G. Teahan to Troy, 5 Oct. 1792, D.D.A.

81 Tone, *Life*, i, pp 183, 198; Froude, *English in Ireland*, iii, p.67.

82 Keogh to ———, 2 Oct. 1792. P.R.O. H.O. 100/38/275-8.

83 B. Egan to Troy, 3 Nov. 1792, D.D.A.; Bray to Troy, 22 Oct. 1792, D.D.A.

84 Troy to Bray, 8 Dec. 1792, C.D.A.

85 *ibid.*

86 Troy to Bray, 8 December 1792, C.D.A.

87 *F.D.J.,* 31 January 1793.

88 *Pastoral of the four metropolitans,* 25 Jan. 1793. C.D.A.

89 *Lim.Chron.,* 6 April 1793.

90 J. Troy, *Pastoral instructions on the duties of Christian citizens* (Dublin, 1793).

91 P. Duigenan, *A fair representation of the present political state of Ireland* (London, 1799), p.18; J. Troy to T. Bray, 16 March 1793, C.D.A.; O'Donoghue, 'Catholic Church', p.206.

92 A. Thompson to T. Bray, 5 Mar. 1793., C.D.A.

93 J. Troy, *Pastoral instructions,* pp 124-34; J. Troy to T. Bray, 26 Mar. 1793, C.D.A.

94 J. Troy to T. Bray, 9 April 1793, C.D.A; V. Bodkin to T. Bray, 11 Jan. 1794, C.D.A.

95 A. Thompson to T. Bray, 5 Mar. 1793, C.D.A. See Musgrave *Memoirs,* p.5.

96 A. Thompson to T. Bray, 28 Feb 1793, C.D.A.; J. Troy to T. Bray, 7 May 1793, C.D.A.

97 R. Hobart to E. Nepean, 6 Mar. 1793, S.P.O.I., Private Official Correspondence, 1789-93, pp 294-5 in O'Donoghue, 'Catholic Church', p.210; A. Thompson to T. Bray, 2 Mar. 1793, C.D.A.

98 J. Troy to T. Bray, 16 Mar. 1793, C.D.A.; J. Troy to T. Bray, 7 May 1793, C.D.A.

99 A.P.F., Atti, vol. 164, f 495, meeting of Congregation 16 June 1794; Antonelli to J. Troy, 13 December 1794, D.D.A.; For a full discussion of Roman reaction to the oath of 1793, see O'Donoghue, 'Catholic Church', pp 210-19.

100 V. Bodkin to T. Bray, 30 Aug. 1794, C.D.A.; Troy to Antonelli, 28 February 1795, D.D.A.

101 A. Thompson to T. Bray, 9 April 1793, C.D.A.

102 *Report of the debates ... of 1793,* pp 310-11 in T. Bartlett, *Fall and rise,* p.168.

103 Tone, *Life,* i, p.101; *A candid appeal to the nation upon the present crisis and recent change of ministers* (London, 1801), p.45; Bartlett, 'Origins and progress of the Catholic question', p.14.

104 E. Burke to H. Grattan, 8 Mar. 1793, *Burke Corr.* vii, p.361; Musgrave, *Memoirs,* p.122; J. Troy to T. Bray, 19 Feb. 1793, C.D.A.

105 Antonelli to J. Troy, 17 Aug., 28 Aug, 4 Sept. 1793, D.D.A.

CHAPTER 4: THE ROYAL COLLEGE

1 For a full discussion of the background to the foundation of Maynooth College see Maurice R. O'Connell,'The political background to the establishment of Maynooth College' in *I.E.R.,* LXXXV(May 1956), pp 325-34; *ibid,* LXXXVI (June, 1956), pp 406-15; *ibid,* LXXXVI (July 1956), pp 1-16.Vincent J. McNally later took up this question but, unlike O'Connell, he had access to the Dublin Diocesan Archives; 'John Thomas Troy, Archbishop of Dublin, and the establishment of Saint Patrick's College Maynooth, 1791-95' in *Catholic Historical Review,* LXVII, 1981, pp 565-88. O'Donoghue also discusses the foundation of the college at great length in 'Catholic Church', pp 205-44.

2 E. A. Smith, *Whig principles and party politics; Earl Fitzwilliam and the Whig Party*

(Manchester, 1975), p.188.

3 T. L. O'Beirne to Castlereagh, Nov. 1800, *Castlereagh Corr.*, iii, p.400.

4 Duke of Portland to Earl Fitzwilliam, 17 October 1792, Fitzwilliam Mss., Sheffield, F. 31(a), cited in O'Donoghue, 'Catholic Church', p.228.

5 Ed. Burke to R. Burke, [Post, 21 November, 1792], *Burke. Corr.*, vii, 298.

6 Troy to Bray, 9 April 1793, C.D.A.

7 Troy to Bray, 27 April 1793, C.D.A.

8 P. Plunket to J. Troy, 14 April 1793, D.D.A.; F. Moylan to T. Bray, 7 May 1793, C.D.A.

9 F. Moylan to T. Bray, 7 May. 1793

10 J. Troy to T. Bray, 7 May 1793, C.D.A.

11 J. Troy to T. Bray, 9 April 1793, C.D.A.

12 E. Burke to F. Moylan, 6 December 1793, *Burke Corr.*, vii, pp 499-500; L. Nihell to J. Troy, 20 Feb. 1794, D.D.A.

13 R. O'Reilly to J. Troy, 10 March 1793, D.D.A.

14 D. Conway, to T. Bray, 20 April 1793, C.D.A.

15 J. Troy to T. Bray, 9 April 1793, C.D.A.

16 The remaining members of the sub-committee were Hugh Hamill, Thomas Braughall, Edward Byrne and Denis T. O'Brien.

17 J. Caulfield to J. Troy, 14 May 1793, D.D.A.; J. Troy to T. Bray, 7 May 1793, C.D.A.

18 B. Egan to J. Troy, 3 Nov. 1792, J. Troy to A. Wolfe, 9 Dec. 1793, (copy), D.D.A.

19 E. Burke, to Kenmare 21 February 1782 in *Burke Corr.*, iv, p.405-418. This letter was printed with some omissions in 1783 under the title *A letter from a distinguished English gentleman to a peer in Ireland* (Dublin, 1783); Lecky, *Ireland*, iii, p.349. See E. O'Flaherty, 'Ecclesiastical politics and the dismantling of the penal laws in Ireland, 1774-82' in *I.H.S.*, xxvi, no. 101, (1988), pp 33- 50.

20 E. Burke to Kenmare, 21 February 1782, *Burke Corr.*, iv, p.414.

21 B. Egan, to J. Troy, 19 February 1788, *Spicil. Ossor*, iii, p.410, see J. Kelly, 'The context and course of Thomas Orde's plan of education', pp 3-26.

22 E. Burke to F. Moylan, 6 Dec. 1793 in O'Connell, The political background', *I.E.R.* (May, 1956), p.334.

23 J. Caulfield to J. Troy, 4 May 1793, D.D.A.

24 T. A. Emmet, 'Part of an essay towards a history of Ireland' in MacNeven, *Pieces*, pp 61-63.

25 T. Bray to F. Moylan, 2 May 1793, Kerry Diocesan Archives, cited in McNally, 'John Troy', p.146; Tone, *Life*, i, p.197.

26 Tone, *Life*, i, p.173.

27 J. Troy to T. Bray, 16 Mar. 1793, C.D.A.

28 J. Caulfield to J. Troy, 23 Mar. 1793, D.D.A.

29 J. Troy to T. Bray, 26 Mar. 1793, C.D.A.

30 J. Troy to T. Bray, 27 April 1793, C.D.A.

31 J. Troy to Major Hobart, 29 Nov. 1793, D.D.A.

32 Educational plans, 20 Nov. 1793, D.D.A.

33 Bishops to Arthur Wolfe, Attorney General, 20 Nov. 1793, D.D.A.

34 E. Burke to F. Moylan, 6 Dec. 1793, *Burke Corr.*, vii, pp 499-500. For a discussion of the role of Thomas Hussey in the foundation of St Patrick's College see William G. Murphy, 'The Life of Dr Thomas Hussey (1746-1803), Bishop of Waterford and

Lismore' (Unpublished M.A. thesis, U.C.C., 1968), pp 99-135.

35 A. Wolfe to J. Troy, 16 Dec. 1793, D.D.A.

36 J. Troy to T. Bray, 21 Dec. 1793, C.D.A.

37 J. Troy to T. Bray, 21 Dec. 1793, C. D.A.

38 J. Troy to L. Concanen, 24 Dec. 1793, A.P.F., S. O.C.G., Vol. 899, f. 289.

39 J. Troy to T. Bray, 21 Dec. 1793, C.D.A.

40 J. Troy to J. Sweetman, 19 Dec. 1793, D.D.A.; J. Troy to T. Bray, 21 Dec. 1793, C.D.A.

41 E. Burke to R. Burke, [Post 21 November 1792] *Burke Corr.*, vii, p.301.

42 J. Troy to L. Concanen, 24 Dec. 1793, A.P.F. S.O.C.G. Vol. 899, f.289.

43 Sackville Hamilton to J. Troy, 13 Jan. 1794, O'Connell, 'Political background' in *I.E.R.* (May, 1956), p.330.

44 J. Troy to Major Hobart, 29 Nov. 1793, D.D.A.; Draft copy of memorial of Bishops to Lord Lieutenant Westmorland on seminaries, 14 Jan. 1794, D.D.A.

45 J. Troy to Sackville Hamilton, 10 Jan. 1794, D.D.A. ; S. Hamilton to Sergeant General and Solicitor General, 11 Oct. 1794, D.D.A.

46 J. Troy to Lanigan, 27 Jan. 1794, D.D.A.

47 O'Connell, 'Political background', p.330.

48 J. Troy to T. Bray, 27 Nov. 1794, C.D.A.

49 *Morn. Post*, 1 Jan. 1795.

50 P. Plunket to T. Braughall, Jan 1795, S.P.O. 620/34/50

51 *Hib. Jn.*, 2 Jan. 1795. A selection of the petitions include those from the Barony of Shillelagh, County Wicklow, 13 Jan. '95, *F.D.J.* [includes signatures of James Brennan P.P. and John Fitzgerald P.P.]; Rathdrum, 19 Jan. '95, *F.D.J.*, [John Meagher P.P. in the chair]; Kildare Catholics, 27 Jan. '95, *D.E.P.*; Wexford, 27 Jan.'95, *D.E.P.*; Kings County, 29 Jan. '95, *D.E.P.* ; Kilkenny, 29 Jan. '95, *D.E.P.* ; Kerry, 3 Feb. '95, *F.D.J.*; Meath, 7 Feb. '95, *D.E.P.*; Galway, Dr Bellew and Dr Egan, 7 Feb. '95, *D.E.P.*; Tipperary Catholics, 10 Feb. '95, *D.E.P.*; Longford [Rev. Dr Flood, Rev. Peter Daly], 17 Feb. '95, *D.E.P.*; *Burke Corr.*, viii, 150.

52 *D.E.P.*, 15 Jan. 1795.

53 The bishops present were Troy (Dublin), Bray (Cashel), O'Reilly (Armagh), Egan (Tuam), Moylan (Cork), Teahan (Kerry), Coppinger (Cloyne), Caulfield (Ferns), Delaney (Kildare and Leighlin), Bellew (Killala), French (Elphin), Plunkett (Meath), Lennan (Dromore), O'Reilly (Clogher), Cruise (Ardagh), McMullen (Down and Connor), O'Reilly (Coadjutor of Kilmore), Dillon (Coadjutor of Kilmacduagh), O'Donoghue, 'Catholic Church', p.263.

54 *Morn. Post.*, 29 Jan. 1795.

55 E. Burke to H. Grattan, 3 Sept. 1794, *Burke Corr*, iv ; E. Burke to T. Hussey, Dec, 1796, *Burke Corr.*, iv, p.389.

56 T. Hussey to——6 Dec. 1794, Fitzwilliam MSS, Sheffield, F 29, (a) in O'Donoghue, 'Catholic Church', p.234.

57 J. Troy to L. Concanen, 25 Sept. 1794, A.P.F., Fondo di Vienna, 28/187 in McNally, 'John Thomas Troy', p.157.

58 J. Troy to Antonelli, 10 Jan. 1795, A.P.F., S.O.C.G., 900, f. 217

59 Antonelli to Irish bishops, 7 Feb. 1795, D.D.A.

60 Smith, *Whig principles*, p.188.

61 T. Hussey to E. Burke, 29 Jan. 1795, *Burke Corr.*, vii, 125.

62 Moran, *Spicil. Ossor.*, iii, pp 470-2.

63 *Spicil. Ossor*, iii, pp 470-2.

64 T. Bray to Wm. Egan, 31 Jan. 1795, C.D.A.

65 H. Grattan to J. Troy, N.D., 1795, D.D.A. Eighteen bishops to H. Grattan, 2 Feb. 1795, D.D.A.

66 T. Bray to Wm. Egan, 31 January 1795, C.D.A.

67 A. Aspinal and E.A. Smith (ed.), *English historical documents 1783 -1832,* (London, 1969), p.158.

68 Portland to Fitzwilliam, 16 February 1795, H.O. 100/56/261-4, 265-70.

69 T Hussey to E. Burke, 27 Feb. 1795, *Burke Corr.*, vii, p.162.

70 T. Hussey to E. Burke, 3 March 1795, *Burke Corr.*, iv, p.288.

71 Fitzwilliam to E. Burke, 4 Mar. 1795, *Burke Corr.*, vii, pp 169-172.

72 *F.D.J.*, 12 Mar. 1795.

73 Cruise O'Brien, *The great melody*, p.512.

74 *Morn. Post*, 17 March 1795.

75 J. Troy to L. Concanen, March 1795, A.P.F., Fondo di Vienna, Vol. 28, f. 207.

76 T. Hussey to E. Burke, 14 Mar. 1795, *Burke Corr.*, vii, p.198.

77 Instructions to Camden, 16 Mar. 1795, H.O. 100/45 ff. 301-8. See Bartlett, *Fall and rise,* pp 207-209.

78 E. Burke to T. Hussey [ante 10 February 1795], *Burke Corr.*, vii, pp 199-205.

79 35 Geo. 111, c.21. An Act for the better education of persons professing the popish or Roman Catholic religion.

80 E. Burke to T. Hussey, 17 Mar. 1795, *Burke Corr.*, viii, 199-205.

81 Camden's Letter Books, i, pp 11-14 in O'Connell, 'Political background', p.3.

82 Camden to Portland, 14 April 1795, H.O. 100/57 /123-5.

83 E. Burke to T. Hussey, *Burke Corr.*, viii, p.263 in O'Brien, *The great melody*, p.521.

84 J. Troy to T. Bray, 25 April 1795, C.D.A.

85 P. Duigenan, *A fair representation*, pp 216-17.

86 Lecky, Ireland, iii, p.361.

87 J. Troy to T. Bray, 14 May 1795, C.D.A., T. Hussey to Fitzwilliam, undated, Fitzwilliam MSS, Sheffield, f. 30. in O'Donoghue, 'Catholic Church', p.276.

88 H. Grattan to Fitzwilliam, 28 Mar. 1795, cited in Smith, *Whig principles.*, p.207.

89 Lecky, *Ireland*, iii, p348.

90 *F. D.J.*, 2 May 1795.

91 E. Burke to T. Hussey, 18 May 1795, *Burke Corr.*, vii, pp 245-250.

92 *Irish. Parl. Deb.*, xv. 201-303.

93 Lecky, *Ireland*, iii, p.363. He continues, 'if its recommendations had been carried out, the Irish priesthood might have been a very different body from what it has become'.

94 O'Connell, 'Political background', p.5.

95 Froude, *English in Ireland*, iii, pp 150-51.

96 Memorandum in Troy's hand, 30 June 1795, D.D.A.; J. Troy to Gerdil, 23 July 1795, A.P.F., Fondo di Vienna, Vol. 28, f 233-4.

97 Minutes of Maynooth trustees meeting, 24 June 1795, Maynooth Archives, B2/1/1/1. The Protestant trustees attended a meeting of trustees on 28 July 1795; ibid, B2/1/1/7; Fingall to Plunket, 25 July 1795, Cogan, *Diocese of Meath*, iii, pp 203-4.

98 T. A. Emmet, 'Part of an essay towards a history of Ireland' in MacNeven, *Pieces* , pp 61-3.

99 J. Troy to P. Plunket, 7 May 1795, cited in Cogan, *Diocese of Meath*, iii, pp 199-200.

100 Minutes of a conversation between Lord Hardwicke and Lord Clare, 20 Dec. 1801, transcript of state paper 788/2, D.D.A. in O'Donoghue, 'Catholic Church', pp 272-3.

101 J. Troy to T. Pelham, 2 Sept., 1801, B.M, Add. MSS 30107, f.405.; F. Moylan to T. Pelham, 1 Jan. 1802, B.M., Add. MSS, 33109, ff. 4-5.

102 E. Burke to T. Hussey, 10 February 1795, *Burke Corr.*, vii, p.143; *F.D.J.*, 14 Feb. 1795; Michael Daly, Lisbon, to T. Bray, 27 June '95, C.D.A.

103 J. Troy to T. Bray, 14 Aug. 1794, C.D.A.

104 C. Erskine to J. Troy, 13 Aug. 1795, D.D.A.

105 E. Burke to R. Burke [Post 21 November 1792], *Burke Corr.*, vii, pp 298-301.

106 *A report of the debate in the House of Commons of Ireland on the bill presented by Henry Grattan for further relief of His Majesty's popish or Roman Catholic subjects* (Dublin, 1795), p.107.

CHAPTER FIVE: GATHERING PACE

1 Pelham to Portland, 30 March 1795, in Froude, *English in Ireland*, iii, p.140.

2 T. Hussey to E. Burke, 19 February 1795, *Burke Corr.*, iv, p.278.

3 See Smyth, *Men of no property*, pp 100-20; Bartlett, 'Defenders and Defenderism', pp 373-94; idem, *Fall and rise*, pp 211-27.

4 *F.D.J.*, 3 February 1795.

5 *N.Star*. 18-21 May 1795, cited in Smyth, *Men of no property*, p.109.

6 Camden to Portland, 16 May 1795, H.O. 100/46/324 cited in Bartlett, *Fall and rise*, p.211

7 *F.D.J.* 3 February 1795

8 J. Troy to P. Plunket, 7 May 1795, Cogan, *Diocese of Meath*, iii, p.199.

9 J. Troy to P. Plunkett, 7 May 1795, Cogan, *Diocese of Meath*, iii, p.199; *Orations delivered at a ... meeting of the Roman Catholics of the City of Dublin, held at Francis Street Chapel on ... ninth April 1795 on the grand question of emancipation* (Cork, 1795); *D.E.P.*, 9 April 1795.

10 See D. Lindsay, 'The Fitzwilliam episode revisited' in Dickson, Keogh and Whelan (ed.), *United Irishmen*, pp 197-208.

11 M. Beresford to J. Beresford, 5 May 1795, *Beresford Corr.*, ii, p.108.

12 Smyth, *Men of no property*, pp 115-16; J. Brady, 'Lawrence O'Connor–a Meath schoolmaster' in *I.E.R.*, 5th series, xlix (1937), pp 281-7.

13 J. Troy to P. Plunket, 21 July 1795, Cogan, *Diocese of Meath*, iii, p.202.

14 Fingall to P. Plunket, 25 July 1795, Cogan, *Diocese of Meath*, iii, p.203.

15 Fingall to P. Plunket, 25 July 1795, Cogan, *Diocese of Meath*, iii, p.203.

16 Bartlett, 'Defenders and Defenderism', p.377; S. Hamilton to T. Pelham, 8 September 1795 in Lecky, *Ireland*, iii, p.392 and Froude, iii, p.169; *The martyr of liberty, a poem on the heroic death of Lawerence O'Connor, executed at Naas in Ireland on a charge of high treason, September 7 1796. Addressed to all Irishmen by an English brother* (Dublin, 1798). Printed for the use of United Irishmen).

17 Antonelli to Irish bishops, 7 February 1795, D.D.A.

18 J.Troy. Pastoral against Defenders, cited in Moran, *Spicil. Ossor.*, iii, pp 476-9; *Ennis Chron.* 17 August 1795.

19 *Ossory Dioc. Reg.*, i, pp 162-5. See Ó Fearghail, 'The Catholic Church in County Kilkenny 1600-1800', p.243.

20 J. Troy to P. Plunket, 7 May 1795, Cogan, *Diocese of Meath*, iii, p.199.

21 J. Troy to R. Marshall, n.d.[early Aug. 1795] Nat. Arch. Reb. Papers, 620/22/29

22 T. Pelham to J. Troy, 13 August 1795, Nat. Arch. Reb. Papers, 620/22/29 see McNally, 'John Troy', p.170.

23 J. Troy to T. Pelham, 14 August 1795, Nat. Arch. Reb. Papers, 620/22/29.

24 C. Erskine to J. Troy, 13 August 1795, D.D.A.

25 J Carroll to J. Troy, 14 December 1795, D.D.A.

26 *Morn. Post*, 3 September 1795.

27 J.W. to ———, 12 September 1795, Nat. Arch. Reb. Papers, 620/10/121/27.

28 Smyth, *Men of no property*, p.104; *Parl. Reg.*, xv (1795), 289.

29 P. Plunket, 1795 Visitation, cited in Cogan, *Diocese of Meath*, iii, pp 267-275.

30 E. Burke to R. Burke, 21 November 1792, *Burke Corr.*, vii, p.297.

31 J. Troy to T. Bray, 8 December 1795, C.D.A.; 'A notice to be read in all Dublin churches 13 December 1795', D.D.A.

32 *F.D.J.*, 23 April 1796.

33   *Hib.Jn.*, 21 April 1796, J. Gunn, 'The foundation of Maynooth College 1795' in I.*E.R.* (1883), pp 316-26.

34 Plunket's diary, 20 April 1796, Cogan, *Diocese of Meath*, iii, p.277.

35 J. Connolly to P. Plunket, 10 November 1796, Cogan, *Diocese of Meath*, iii, p.207.

36 J. Troy, Pastoral against Defenders, August 1795, D.D.A.

37 Bartlett, 'Defenders and Defenderism', p.377.

38 Bartlett, *Fall and rise*, pp 213-23.

39 Camden to Portland, 30 May 1795, H.O. 100/69/345-50 in Bartlett, *Fall and rise*, p.213.

40 Bartlett, *Fall and rise*, p.214.

41 Lake to Pelham, 17 March 1797, in Lecky, *Ireland*, iv, p.41.

42 J. Troy, Lenten pastoral, 14 February 1796, D.D.A.

43 J. Troy to J. Carroll, 13 August 1796, Baltimore Diocesan Archives, cited in O'Donoghue, 'Catholic Church', p.299.

44 J. Troy to J. Carroll, 15 August 1796, O'Donoghue, 'Catholic Church', p.299.

45 Smyth, *Men of no property*, p.111.

46 Lord Gosford's address to magistrates of Armagh, 28 December 1795, in *F.D.J.*, 5 January 1796.

47 *F.D.J.*, 24 September 1796.

48 *F.D.J.*, 24 September 1796.

49 *F.D.J.*, 8 November 1796; O'Coigley, *Life*, p.23.

50 J. Troy to E. Cooke, 8 August 1796, Nat. Arch. Reb. Papers, 620/24/95.

51 P. Plunket to J. Troy, August 1796 enclosed in J. Troy to E. Cooke, 8 August 1796, Nat. Arch. Reb. Papers, 620/24/95.

52 T. Hussey to T. Bray, 26 September 1796, C.D.A.

53 E. Burke to Fitzwilliam, 13 March 1795, *Burke Corr.*, viii, 188-96.

54 E. Burke to French Laurence, 23 November 1796, *Burke Corr.*, ix, 124-25

55 E. Burke to French Laurence, 11 November 1796, *Burke Corr.*, ix, 116.

56 E. Burke to French Laurence, 18 November 1796, *Burke Corr.*, ix, 117
57 E. Burke to T. Hussey, 18 January 1796, *Burke Corr*, viii, 387, 9 Dec. 1796, *Burke Corr.*, ix, 171. See Cruise O'Brien, *The great melody*, pp 572-77; Conniff, 'Edmund Burke's Reflections on the coming revolution in Ireland', pp 37-59.
58 For the Bantry expedition see Elliott, *Partners in revolution*, pp 77-124 and 'The role of Ireland in French war strategy, 1796-1798' in Dickson and Gough (ed.), *French Revolution*, pp 202-20.
59 *F.D.J.*, 3 January 1797
60 *F.D.J.*, 3 January 1797; Anon, *'Letters from a gentleman in Ireland to his friend at Bath* (Cork, 1797), p.30.
61 *F.L.J.*, 7 January 1797; *An address delivered to the Grand Jury of the County of Dublin ...*
62 *Morn. Post.*, 28 January 1797.
63 Examination of MacNeven before the Secret Committee of the House of Lords, 7 August 1798 in W.J. MacNeven, *Pieces*, p.254.
64 *D.E.P.*, *M.P.*, 28 January 1797.
65 J. Young to T. Bray, 28, 30 December 1798, C.D.A.,
66 *Morn. Post*, 18 February 1797.
67 J. Troy, Sermon of thanksgiving for delivery of kingdom, 16 February 1797, D.D.A. See Moran, *Spicil Ossor.*, iii, pp 490-504; O'Donoghue, 'Catholic Church', p.303.
68 C. Erskine to J. Troy, 25 March 1797, D.D.A.
69 T. Graham, 'The organisation of the Dublin United Irishmen' (Ph.D. forthcoming, University of Dublin).
70 J. W. to Mr Pollock, 10 February 1797, Nat Arch. Reb. Papers, 620/36/227.
71 *Morn. Post*, 28 February and 18 March 1797.
72 *Truth unmasked or food for the liberty*, containing 'The appeal of the people of Ulster to their countrymen and to the empire at large', 'A friend of civil and religious liberties advice to the people'. Also 'An advice to the United men of Ireland by an Irishman'. (Dublin, 1797).
73 Lake to Pelham, 16 April 1797, Lecky, *Ireland*, iv, p.50.
74 *Parl. Reg.* xvii(1796-8) 131-40. Lecky, *Ireland*, iv, p.61; Smyth, *Men of no property*, p.173.
75 Dickson, *New foundations*, p.189.
76 *Press*, 14 November 1797.
77 E. Burke to T. Hussey [9], December 1796, *Burke Corr.*, ix, 161-2.
78 T. England, *Life of Rev Arthur O'Leary* (London, 1822), p.192; J. Healy, *Centenary history of Maynooth* (Dublin, 1895), p.163.
79 C. Butler, *Historical memoirs of the English, Irish and Scottish Catholics since the Reformation* (London, 1822), iv, p.39.
80 E. Burke cited in Healy, *Maynooth, p.*169.
81 D. Chart (ed.), *The Drennan letters* (Belfast ,1931), p 228. For Drennan's anti-Catholic prejudice see L. M. Cullen, 'The internal politics of the United Irishmen' in Dickson, Keogh and Whelan (ed.), *United Irishmen* , pp 176-96.
82 R. Cumberland, *Memoirs* (London, 1806), p 139 . For an account of Hussey's part in the Cumberland mission see S. Flagg Bemis, *The Hussey-Cumberland mission and American independence* (Princeton, 1931).
83 Hippisley to Hobart, 12 Jan 1799, *Castlereagh Corr.*, iii, p.86.

84 As early as 1790 Hussey had been requested to represent the committee of English Catholics in Rome to lay before the Pope their views on the Protestation. No reason for Hussey's failure to go to Rome is given, but it is generally believed that the Spanish Ambassador would not give permission. Cf Butler, *Memoirs*, iv, p 43.

85 F.H. to —— 27 September 1796, Reb. Papers, 620/18/14; *Cork Gaz.*, 5 Nov. 1791.

86 E. Burke to T Hussey, 4 Feb 1795, *Burke Corr.*, viii, p.136

87 T. Hussey to R Burke, 28 August 1790, *Burke Corr.*, vi, p.134

88 T. Hussey to E. Burke, 19 February 1795, *Burke Corr.*, viii, p.152

89 T Hussey to E Burke, 3 March 1795, *Burke Corr.*, viii, p.169.

90 T. Hussey to E. Burke, 3 March 1795, *Burke Corr.*, viii, p.169.

91 E. Burke to Moylan, 6 December 1793, *Burke Corr.*, vii, p.499

92 F. Moylan to Ed. Burke, December 1793, cited in Healy, *Maynooth*, p 169.

93 J. Troy to T. Bray, 23 December 1794, D.D.A.

94 T. Hussey to Edmund Burke, 30 November 1796, *Burke Corr.*, ix, p.141

95 Bishop Douglas's diary for August 1796, quoted in *Burke Corr.*, ix p 82;*Freeman's Jn.*, 11 Aug. 1796

96 Portland to Pelham, 1 November 1796, Fitzpatrick, *Secret Service*, p 285.

97 Hussey to E Burke, 29 January 1795, *Burke Corr.*, viii, p.125

98 E. Burke to Fitzwilliam, 10 Feb. 1795, *Burke Corr.*, viii, p.145. Eighteen bishops to Earl Fitzwilliam, 11 February 1796 in McNally, 'John Troy', p.179.

99 Hussey to E Burke, 30 November 1796, *Burke Corr.*, ix, p.141

100 Hussey to E. Burke, 30 November 1796, *Burke Corr.*, ix, p.141.

101 Hussey to E. Burke, 30 November 1796, *Burke Corr.*, ix, p.141.

102 Hussey to E. Burke, 30 November 1796, *Burke Corr.*, ix, p.141.

103 Pelham to Portland, 26 October 1796, H.O. 100/62/298

104 Portland to Pelham, 1 November 1796, H.O. 100/62/310-311

105 E. Burke to T. Hussey, Post 9 December 1796, *Burke Corr.*, ix, pp 161-72; Cruise O'Brien, *The great melody*, p.572.

106 Bray to Moylan, September 1796, cited in Healy, *Maynooth*, p.174.

107 Concanen to Troy, 10 December 1796, D.D.A.

108 O'Donnell to Troy, 17 January 1797, D.D.A.

109 Resolutions of the bishops of Ireland on the veto question, 1799, in the Troy Papers, D.D.A.; Fitzpatrick, *Secret service*, p.282.

110 J. Fitzpatrick, *Edmund Rice*, (Dublin 1945), p.87.

111 J.W. to ——, 1 February 1797, Nat. Arch. Reb. Papers, 620/36/227.

112 T. Hussey to Burke, 2 April 1797, *Burke Corr.*, x, p.304.

113 T. Hussey, *A pastoral letter to the Catholics of the united Dioceses of Waterford and Lismore* (Waterford,1797).

114 *Pastoral*, p.3

115 *Pastoral*, p.3.

116 *Pastoral*, p.4.

117 *Pastoral*, p.9.

118 *Pastoral*, p.5.

119 *Pastoral*, p.6.

120 *Pastoral*, p.9.

121 *Pastoral*, p.10.

122 *Pastoral*, p.10.

123 *Pastoral*, p.12.

124 Rev. Brittle, *Strictures and remarks on Dr Hussey's late pastoral address to the clergy of Lismore and Waterford* (Dublin 1797); T. Tickle, *A letter to the Rev. Dr Hussey* (Dublin, 1797); Anon., *Remarks on the Rev Dr Hussey's pastoral letter by one of the people* (Dublin, 1797); Anon., *Letter to the Roman Catholic laity occasioned by Dr Hussey's pastoral letter* (Dublin, 1797) and R. McKee, *Remarks on a pastoral letter lately written by the Rev. Dr Hussey* (Waterford, 1797).

125 *Remarks*, p.1

126 *Remarks*, p.6-8

127 *Strictures*, p 3

128 *A letter*, p.1

129 *Strictures*, p.4.

130 *Remarks*, p.1.

131 *Remarks*, p.6

132 *Remarks*, p.5.

133 *Strictures*, p.6.

134 *Remarks*, p.1

135 *Remarks*, p.7.

136 *F.D.J.*, 6 May 1797; *D.E.P.*, 6 May 1797.

137 P. Duigenan, *A fair representation*, p.20

138 F.D.J., 27/2/1798.

139 O'Beirne to Castlereagh, 27 April 1799 in *Castlereagh Corr.*, ii, p.283.

140 F. Moylan to Cardinal Gerdil, 6 January 1798, cited in O'Donoghue, 'Catholic Church', p.302

141 Troy to Bray, 15 April 1797, C.D.A.

142 Troy to Carroll, 13 April 1798, cited in O'Donoghue, 'Catholic Church', p.301.

143 Troy to T. Bray, 15 April 1797, C.D.A.

144 L. Concanen to J. Troy, 10 June 1797, D.D.A.

145 Bray to Moylan, 22 February 1802, E. Bolster (ed.), 'The Moylan correspondence' in *Collect. Hib.*, ix, 1971, p.121.

146 Troy to Plunket, 23 May 1797, Cogan, *Diocese of Meath*, ii, p.212.

147 Burke to Hussey, 16 May 1797, *Burke Corr.*, ix , p 342-45.

148 Hussey to Plowden cited in England, *O'Leary*, p.204.

149 Hussey to Moylan, 22 April 1797, in England, *O'Leary* p.202.

150 F.H. to ———. 24 April 1797, Nat. Arch. Reb. Papers, 620/18/14

151 C. Colclough to Pelham, 1 May 1797, Nat. Arch. Reb. Papers, 620/30/3

152 R Musgrave to ——— 28 October 1797, Nat. Arch. Reb. Papers, 620/32/188.

153 Musgrave to Pelham, 15 November 1797, Nat. Arch. Reb. Papers, 620/33/63; P. Power, *Waterford and Lismore* (Cork, 1937), p.275.

154 Troy to Bray, 17 December 1797, cited in McNally, 'John Troy', p.180.

155 Duigenan in the Irish House of Commons, 26 Feb. 1798, *F.D.J.*, 27 February 1798.

156 L. Concanen to Troy, 12 January 1799, D.D.A.

157 Camden to Portland, 15 April 1797, HO 100/69/201.

158 P. Boyle, 'Documents relative to the appointment of an Archbishop of Cashel, 1791, and a co-adjutor of Waterford, 1801' in *Arch. Hib.*, VII (1918), p.15.

159 England, *O'Leary*, p 206; John Healy doubts any such involvement, *Maynooth*, p 182;

James L. O'Donnell, Newfoundland to J. Plessis, Quebec, 10 May 1801, in C. J. Byrne (ed.) *Gentlemen bishops and faction fighters: the letters of Bishops O'Donnell, Lambert, Scallan and other Irish missionaries,* (St. John's, 1984), p.188.

160   For Hussey's involvement of Waterford and Lismore see D. Keogh, 'Thomas Hussey, Bishop of Waterford and Lismore 1797-1803, and the rebellion of 1798' in Power (ed.), *Waterford: history and* society (Dublin, 1992), pp 403-26.

161   T. Hussey to J.B. Clinch, 10 January (1799?), Madden MSS, T.C.D., 873/197.

162   T. Hussey to J. Carroll, Baltimore, 29 September 1799, Baltimore Diocesan Archives. I am grateful to Fr Hugh Fenning for bringing this letter to my attention.

163   T. Hussey to J.B. Clinch, 10 January (1799?), Madden MSS, T.C.D., 873/197.

164   *Gentleman's magazine* (Dublin 1803) p.881.

165   Hearn to Donoughmore, 16 July 1803, P.R.O.N.I., T3459/D34/1

166   Normoyle,p. 49; *The Morning Register,* 18 January 1825; Nat. Arch. Reb. Papers, 620/65/142.

167   O' Donoghue, 'Catholic Church', p.295.

168   J. Carroll, Baltimore, to J. Troy, 12 November 1798, D.D.A.

169   E. Burke to T. Hussey, 16 May 1797; Camden to Portland, 6 May 1798, H.O. 100/69/275-8.

170   J. Troy to R. Marshall, *Castlereagh Corr.,* i, pp 176-77.

171   F.H. to E. Cooke, 18 May 1797, Nat. Arch. Reb. Papers, 620/18/14.

CHAPTER FIVE: Priests, People and Popular Politicisation

1   *Morn Post,* 21 Mar. 1795.

2   Tone, *Life of Wolfe Tone* (Washington, 1826), i, p.278.

3   K. Whelan, 'The United Irishmen, the enlightenment and popular culture' in Dickson, Keogh and Whelan (ed.), *United Irishmen,* pp 269-96.

4   J. W. to —— Sept. 1795, Nat. Arch. Reb. Papers, 620/10/121/27

5   Maurice Tracy to T. Pelham, 26 May 1797, Nat. Arch. Reb. Papers, 620/ 30/198.

6   *F.D.J.,* 2, 9 Jan. 1798.

7   C. Moore, *Reflections on the present state of our country* (Dublin, 1798).

8   R. Day, *A charge delivered to the Grand Jury of the County of Dublin, 9 January 1798* (Dublin, 1798).

9   Report of the Committee of Secrecy, *F.D.J.,* 1 Sept. 1798.

10   C. Moore, *Reflections on the present state of our country,* p.13; Anon., *Letters from a gentleman in Ireland to his friend at Bath* (Cork, 1798), p.9.

11   J. R. R. Adams, *The printed word and the common man: popular culture in Ulster 1700-1900* (Belfast, 1987), p.39

12   Capt. McNevin, cited in Whelan, 'United Irishmen, the enlightenment and popular culture', p.280; *F.D.J.,* 8 Mar. 1796.

13   Lord Ely to Camden, 29 May 1797, Nat. Arch. Reb. Papers, 620/30/ 226

14   Nat. Arch. Reb. Papers, 620/51/255 [late 1797?].

15   J. Smyth, 'Dublin's political underground in the 1790's' in G. O'Brien (ed.), *Parliament, politics and people,* pp 134-135; T. Graham, 'Organisation of the Dublin United Irishmen.' in Dickson, Keogh and. Whelan (ed.), *United Irishmen.,* pp 244-55.

16   C. Mazauric, 'Political clubs and practices of sociability in revolutionary France', in

Dickson, Keogh and Whelan (ed.), *United Irishmen,* pp 16-32.

17 R. Day, *Address to the Grand Jury of the County of Dublin, January 1797* (Dublin, 1797), p.32.

18 K. Whelan, 'The Catholic parish, the Catholic chapel', pp. 1-16.

19 J. W. to ——— 24 July 1796, Nat. Arch. Reb. Papers, 620/36/227

20 F. H. to ——— 1 February 1797. Nat. Arch Reb. Papers, 620/18/14.

21 F. H. to Cooke, 15 July 1797, Nat. Arch. Reb. Papers, 620/18/14.

22 F. H. to ——— 26 February 1798, Nat. Arch. Reb. Papers, 620/18/14

23 Wm. Godfrey to ———, 22 January 1797, Nat. Arch. Reb. Papers, 620/28/130; E. Newenham to ———, 1 November 1797, Nat. Arch. Reb. Papers, 620/33/104.

24 *F.D.J.*, 1 March 1798. This verse is very likely a fabrication of Giffard's.

25 I am grateful to Niall Coghlan for this reference; F. H. to E. Cooke, 24 April 1797, Nat. Arch. Reb. Papers, 620/18/14.

26 T. Roche to E. Cooke, 12 May 1798, Nat. Arch. Reb. Papers, 620/37/61.

27 Mrs Brownrigg to E. Cooke, 27 Aug. 1797, Nat. Arch. Reb. Papers, 620/32/77

28 J. Little, Diary, in *Anal. Hib.*, ll, p.67.

29 June 1797, Nat. Arch. Reb. Papers, 620/31/180. Another undated letter from the same time refers to assassins plotting in Ash Street chapel, 620/5/246.

30 7 January n.d.[1797], Nat. Arch. Reb. Papers, 620/36/225.

31 1 January 1795, D.D.A, Troy Papers, 43.

32 Colclough, Kilkenny to——— 18 January 1799, Nat. Arch. Reb. Papers, 620/56/62; See K. Whelan, 'The Catholic community in eighteenth century Wexford' in Power and Whelan (ed.) *Endurance and emergence*, p.149; Little, 'Diary', pp 64-5; Circular letter of Dr Dillon of Tuam, 27 March 1799, D.D.A.

33 *Morn. Post*, 8 December 1796

34 *The Times*, 12 April 1797, cited in Smyth. 'Dublin political underground', p.143; F. H. 9 April 1797 Nat. Arch. Reb. Papers, 620/18/14.

35 Henry Echlin to ———, 17 May 1798, Nat. Arch. Reb. Papers, 620/37/95.

36 *The trial of Richard Dry* (Cork ,1797), p.42.

37 *Morn. Post,* 27 May 1797.

38 *N. Star*, reported in *Morn.Post*, 8 Dec. 1796.

39 F. H. to E.Cooke, 27 June 1797, Nat. Arch. Reb. Papers, 620/18/14; In Tullow, a publican called Mourne handed over to the magistrates the papers of the United committee who had met in his pub, 23 May 1798, Nat. Arch. Reb. Papers, 620/37/130

40 Information of William Walter, T.C.D. Sirr Papers, MS 869/5 ff 5-6 in Smyth, 'Popular politicisation', p.158.

41 Wakefield, ii, p.554.

42 Stock cited in Maxwell, *History of the Irish Rebellion*, p.318.

43 N. Furlong, *Father John Murphy*, p.17.

44 de la Tocnaye, *A Frenchman's walk through Ireland* (Belfast, 1917), p.135; *Castlereagh Corr.*, iv, p.99; Murphy, 'The support of the Catholic clergy in Ireland, 1750-1850', pp 103-121; Duigenan, *A fair representation.*, p.213.

45 *Reform or ruin, take your choice!* (Dublin, 1798), pp 17-18.

46 W. MacNeven, Secret Committee of the House of Lords, 3 August 1798. *F.D.J.*, 13 September 1798.

47 J.W. to J. Pollock, July 1796, Nat. Arch. Reb. Papers, 620/36/227.

48 Nihell to J. Troy, 20 February 1794, D.D.A.
49 J. W. to ——— 6 June 1798, Nat. Arch. Reb. Papers, 620/10/121/111
50 E. Newenham to Mrs Montgomery, 12 February 1794. Newenham Papers, Princeton University. I am grateful to Eugene Coyle for this reference.
51 R. Doyle, Ballymore Eustace, 4 August 1796, D.D.A.
52 J. W. to ——— 22 May 1797, Nat. Arch. Reb. Papers, 620/10/121/58; F. H. to E. Cooke, 25 May 1797, Nat. Arch. Reb. Papers, 620/14/18; E. Newenham, 31 May 1797, Nat. Arch. Reb. Papers, 620/30/257.
53 J. Troy to P. Plunket, 23 May 1797, Cogan, *Diocese of Meath* , iii, p.211
54 W. M. O'Riordan, 'The succession of parish priests in the Archdiocese of Dublin, 1771-1851' in Re*p. Novum*, i, no. 2 (1956), pp 406-33.
55 W. M. Corbet to E. Cooke, 15 October 1796, Nat. Arch. Reb. Papers, 620/25/170.
56 J. W. to ——— 2 January 1797, Nat. Arch. Reb. Papers, 620/10/121/44 [Spring 1797]; Nat. Arch. Reb. Papers, 620/51/209.
57 M. Ronan, 'Priests in the independence movement of 1796-8' in *I.E.R.*, lxviii (1946), p.96.
58 Information [1797] Nat. Arch. Reb. Papers, 620/51/214, 620/51/120, 620/51/119, 620/54/30; J. W. to ——— 1 January 1797, Nat. Arch. Reb. Papers, 620/36/227.
59 Secret Committee Report, May 1797.
60 F. H. To E. Cooke, 25 May 1797, Nat. Arch. Reb. Papers, 620/14/18.
61 Corbet to ——— [late 1796] Nat. Arch. Reb. Papers, 620/27/1
62 In July 1797 a priest from the north, Father Mayne, threw himself out of the window of the White Cross Inn and was killed. *F.Jn.*, 1 July 1797.
63 J. W. May 1797, Nat. Arch. Reb. Papers, 620/10/121/58; J. Verner to E. Cooke, 29 May [1798], Nat. Arch. Reb. Papers, 620/51/43.
64 [1797], Nat. Arch. Reb. Papers, 620/5/253.
65 J. W. ——— [late 1797], Nat. Arch. Reb. Papers, 620/10/121/143; *Press,* 14 November 1797.
66 J. W, 27 May 1797, Nat. Arch. Reb. Papers, 620/10/121/61 in Smyth, 'Dublin's political underground', p.144.
67 B. T. to ———, 12 May 1797, Nat. Arch. Reb. Papers, 620/30/60.
68 J. Caulfield, *The reply of the Rt. Rev. Dr. Caulfield Roman Catholic bishop and of the Roman Catholic clergy of Wexford to the misrepresentations of Sir Richard Musgrave, bart.* (Dublin, 1801), p.20.
69 B.T. 12 May 1797, Nat. Arch. Reb. Papers, 620/30/60.

CHAPTER SIX: Rebellion

1 E. Cooke to Wickham, 26 May 1798, H.O. 100/76/289-90; Bartlett, *Fall and rise*, p.321.
2 G. Holdcroft, Kells, to John Lees, 6 February 1798, Nat. Arch. Reb. Papers, 620/35/119.
3 Cogan, *Diocese of Meath*, iii, pp. 293-5. The January meeting was attended by O'Reilly (Armagh), Troy (Dublin), Bray (Cashel), Egan (Tuam), Plunket (Meath), Moylan (Cork), Delaney (Kildare), French (Elphin) and Cruise (Ardagh). The meeting from 9-12 May was attended by O'Reilly (Armagh), Troy (Dublin), Plunket (Meath), Moylan (Cork), Cruise (Ardagh) and French(Elphin). It is not certain that Caulfield attended this meeting despite Plunket's claim to the contrary.

4 *Press*, 16 January 1798; *F.L.J.*, 13 January 1798.

5 *D.E.P.* 16 January 1798.

6 E. French, Lenten pastoral, 1798, C.D.A.

7 E. Dillon, Pastoral address, 6 April 1798, *Spicil. Ossor.*, iii, pp 579-82; Printed in *F.L.J.*, 1 May 1798; B. O'Cuiv, 'Treid litir O' 1798', *Eigse*, 1964-6, vol. xli, pp. 57-63.

8 E. Dillon to J. Troy, 9 July 1798, D.D.A.

9 ———, Galway, 10 April 1798, Nat. Arch. Reb. Papers, 620/36/159.

10 *F.D.J.*, 21 April 1798.

11 E. Dillon to J. Troy, 9 July 1798, D.D.A.

12 F. Moylan, *Pastoral instructions* (Dublin, May 1798), *Spicil. Ossor.*, iii, pp 582-88.

13 Portland to Camden, 11 May 1798, H.O. 100/80/279.

14 J. Young to T. Bray, 28 December 1798, C.D.A.; F.D.J., 3 January 1797; *Grand Jury address by Robert Day* (1797); Morn. Post., 28 January 1797; Examination of MacNeven before the Secret Committee of the House of Lords, 7 August 1798, in MacNeven, *Pieces*, p.254.

15 F. Moylan to John Anderson, chairman of the committee for receiving voluntary contributions for the defence of the kingdom, 27 February 1798, cited in *F.L.J.*, 7 March 1798.

16 L. Concanen to J. Troy, 24 February 1798, 17 March 1798, and 5 May 1798, D.D.A. see Fenning, *Undoing of the friars*, pp 354-79.

17 M. Büschkuhl, *Great Britain and the Holy See, 1746-1870* (Dublin, 1982) p.38. See O'Donoghue, 'The Holy See and Ireland, 1780-1803', pp 99-108.

18 See T. Hussey, *Sermon preached at the Spanish chapel London, 14 May 1798*, (London, 1798).

19 C. Erskine to J. Troy, 6 April 1798, D.D.A.

20 Buschkühl, *Great Britain and the Holy See*, p.38.

21 Camden to Portland, April 1798, H.O. 100/76/91-4

22 W. Wickham to E. Cooke, 21 April 1798, Nat. Arch. Reb. Papers, 620/36/192; Portland to Camden, 20 April 1798, H.O. 100/76/95-6.

23 Erskine Papers, English College, Rome, ERS, 1-11, 52.7, ERS 52.8, ERS 29-32.

24 L. Concanen to J. Troy, 4 September 1793, D.D.A.

25 Camden to Portland, 6 May 1798, H.O. 100/69/275-8.

26 *F.D.J.*, 1 May 1798; *F.L.J.*, 5 May 1798.

27 *F.D.J.* 8 May 1798.

28 J. Lanigan to J. Troy, March 1798, *Castlereagh Corr.*, 1, pp 160-62.

29 T. Hussey, *Spanish chapel sermon.*

30 J. Young to T. Bray, 10 May 1798, C.D.A.; Address of Mr Grady at the close of the Limerick quarter sessions, *F.D.J.* 1 May 1798.

31 Cogan, *Diocese of Meath*, iii, pp 297-299.

32 Maynooth trustees minutes, 11 May 1798, Maynooth Archives, B2/1/1/14; Patrick Plunket recorded the attendance at the meeting of O'Reilly (Armagh), Troy (Dublin), Plunket (Meath), Moylan (Cork), Caulfield (Ferns), Cruise (Ardagh), French (Elphin) and Fingall, Gormanston and Kenmare, Cogan, *Diocese of Meath*, iii, p.297. However, Caulfield's name does not appear in the minutes of the meeting.

33 Maynooth trustees minutes, 12 May 1798, Maynooth Archives, B2/1/1/15.

34 Whelan, 'The Catholic priest in the 1798 Rebellion', p.301..

35 J. Caulfield, Pastoral instructions, n.d. [April 1798], D.D.A., *Spicil. Ossor.*, iii, pp 561-2.

36 The priests were, Nicholas Redmond, Nicholas Stafford (Ballygarrett), Nicholas Murphy (Oulart), Frank Kavanagh, John Redmond (Ballyoughter), John Murphy (Boolavogue), Michael Lacy (Kilmuckridge), David Cullen (Blackwater), Michael Murphy (Ballycanew), Edward Redmond (Ferns), Michael Redmond (Castlebridge), Redmond Roche (Crossabeg), John Synott (Gorey) and Edan Murphy (Kilrush), Whelan, 'The Catholic priest in the 1798 Rebellion', p.301.

37 Camden to Portland, April 1798, H.O. 100/76/91-4.

38 A. O'Connor, *State of Ireland* (Dublin, 1798). A hand-written note, dated 9 November 1798, by 'J.T.T.', R.I.A. Haliday Pamphlets, vol. 757.

39 *John Troy to the rural vicars of the Archdiocese of Dublin, 22 May 1798*, D.D.A.

40 Camden to Portland, 24 May 1798, H.O. 100/76/256 in Bartlett, *Fall and rise*, p.233.

41 W. Coppinger, Pastoral instructions, May/June 1798, *Spicil Ossor*, iii, pp 588-94.

42 Statement of facts relating to Youghal in the year 1798, by the Rev. Dr Coppinger, Bishop of Cloyne, 19 February 1803 in Moran, *Spicil. Ossor*, iii, pp 605- 13.

43 J. Young, Pastoral instructions, 9 June 1798, in J. Begley, *The Diocese of Limerick from 1691 to the present time* (Dublin, 1938) pp 270-1; *Hib. Jn.*, 27 June 1798.

44 J. Young to T. Bray, 4 July 1798, C.D.A.

45 *The State of His Majesty's subjects in Ireland professing the Roman Catholic religion* (Dublin, 1800), p.53. See Murphy, *Killaloe* , pp 112-39.

46 *Hib. Jn.* 27 June 1798.

47 T. Hussey to T. Hearn, 3 July 1798, *Hib. Jn.* 23 July 1798

48 'Letter to the Rev. Dr H——y, R.C.B. of W—— and L——, occasioned by his letter to Rev. Dr. H—n, R.C.V.G. of the D—— of W— and L— 3 July 1798, *F.D.J.* 4 Aug. 1798.

49 *F.D.J.*, 21 July 1798.

50 *F.D.J.* 12 July 1798, the address was signed by Richard O'Reilly (Armagh), Hugh O'Reilly (Clogher), Charles O'Reilly (Kilmore), Anthony Coyle (Raphoe) John Cruise (Ardagh), Denis Maguire (Kilmore), Charles O'Donnell (Derry), Patrick McMullan (Down and Conor), Matthew Lennan (Dromore) and Patrick Plunket (Meath).

51 R. O'Reilly to H. Conwell, 9 January 1799, A.D.A.

52 P. Plunket to J. Troy, 13 December 1798, D.D.A. T. Ganley to J. Troy, 3 June 1798, D.D.A.

53 P. Plunket to J. Troy, 13 December 1798, D.D.A.

54 Cogan, *Diocese of Meath*, iii, p.298.

55 B. Hoban, 'Dominic Bellew, 1745-1812' in *Seanchas Ard Mhacha* (1972), pp 333-69; P. Walsh, 'Anthony Blake, Archbishop of Armagh, 1758-1787' in *Seanchas Ard Mhacha,* pp 288-323. See K. Harvey, 'The Bellews of Mount Bellew; a Catholic gentry family in the age of the penal laws', (Unpublished Ph. D. thesis, Pennsylvania State University, 1984), 'The Family Experience: The Bellews of Mount Bellew', in Power and Whelan (ed.), *Endurance and emergence*, pp 171-98.

56 R. Hayes, *Last invasion of Ireland* (Dublin, 1937), p.79.

57 Testimony of Rev B. Dease, 15 September 1798, Nat. Arch. Reb. Papers. 620/40/58.

58 Nat. Arch. Reb. Papers, 620/56/200; H.O. 100/78/418-21.

59 J. Caulfield to J. Troy, 31 March 1792, D.D.A.

60 Luke Cullen MS f. 12.

61 Furlong, *Father John Murphy*, p.86.

62 J. Caulfield to J. Troy, 4 September 1798, D.D.A.

63 J. Caulfield to J. Troy, 31 July 1798, D.D.A.
64 J. Caulfield to J. Troy, 31 July 1798, D.D.A.
65 Byrne, *Memoirs*, i, p.181.
66 J. Troy to T. Bray, 12 June 1798, D.D.A; J. Lanigan to J. Troy, 22 June 1798, D.D.A.
67 J. Caulfield to J. Troy, 25 June 1798, D.D.A.
68 'Letter from Scullabogue' in *F.D.J.* 4 August 1798; J. Lanigan to J. Troy, 22 June 1798, D.D.A.
69 Pastoral address of James Lanigan, 9 July 1798, in *F.L.J.*, 11 July 1798.
70 D. Delaney to J. Troy, 8 June 1798.
71 There is confusion surrounding the exact date of his death: the *Dublin Evening Post* announced it on 10 July, but does not indicate when it occurred, but Burke, the Tuam diocesan historian, believed that he died as early as 28 January. Since Egan was attending the bishops' meeting in Dublin in late January, Burke's date is obviously incorrect, yet the absence of any comment from him during the rebellion may indicate that the addresses were prepared in advance, reflecting the bishops' acknowledgement of a state of rebellion long before the 'burst' in late May.
72 *Hib. Jn.* 28 May 1798, 4 June 1798; *D.E.P.* 31 May 1798.
73 Hardwicke to York, 24 August 1803, in Bartlett, *Fall and rise*, p.276.
74 John Troy, Pastoral instructions, 27 May 1798, D.D.A.; idem., *Pastoral Instructions to the Roman Catholics of the Archdiocese of Dublin* (Dublin, 1798).
75 *Press*, 10 October 1797.
76 *Press*, 26 December 1797.
77 J. W. 26 June 1798, Nat. Arch. Reb. Papers, 620/10/121/116
78 F. H. 22 August 1798, Nat. Arch. Reb. Papers, 620/18/14
79 P. Plunket to J. Troy, 13 December 1798, D.D.A.
80 Dillon to J. Troy, 9 July 1798, D.D.A.
81 Dr Nephen to Priests of Lazer's Hill, n.d.[July 1798] Nat. Arch. Reb. Papers, 620/51/224.
82 R. Passmore, n.d. Nat. Arch. Reb. Papers, 620/53/73.
83 W. Cox, *Irish Magazine*, March 1815
84 L. Concanen to J. Troy, 9 July 1798; C. Erskine to J. Troy, 6 July 1798, D.D.A.; J. Troy to T. Bray, 10 June 1798, C.D.A.; J. Dalton, *The memoirs of the Archbishops of Dublin* (Dublin, 1838), p.486; Castlereagh, 2 July 1798, D.D.A.
85 J. Dillon to J. Troy, 9 July 1798, D.D.A.
86 C. Erskine to J. Troy, 23 June 1798, 6 July 1798, D.D.A.
87 J. Caulfield to J. Troy, 15 September 1798, D.D.A.
88 Pius VI to C. Erskine, 28 July 1798, in Brady, *Anglo-Roman papers*, p.143.

CHAPTER EIGHT: THE MIGHTY WAVE

1 Camillus to the Roman Catholics, *F.D.J.*, 25 Sept. 1798.
2 M. Byrne, *Memoirs*, i, pp 54-7.
3 P. F. Kavanagh, *A popular history of the insurrection of 1798* (Dublin, 1916); A. Kinsella, 'Father Patrick Kavanagh' (M.Litt. thesis, University of Dublin. 1992); L. M. Cullen, 'Late eighteenth-century politicisation', p.150.
4 Duigenan *A fair representation*, p.11 and N. Furlong, *Father John Murphy, 1753-1798* (Dublin, 1991).
5 L. M. Cullen, 'The 1798 Rebellion in its eighteenth-century context' in p.Corish (ed.),

Radicals, rebels and establishments (Belfast, 1985), pp 91-113; 'The 1798 rebellion in County Wexford. United Irishman organisation, membership and leadership' in K. Whelan, *Wexford*, pp 248-95; K. Whelan, 'The religious factor in the 1798 Rebellion in County Wexford' in O'Flanagan, Ferguson and Whelan (ed.), *Rural Ireland*, pp 62-85; 'The role of the Catholic priest in the 1798 Rebellion in County Wexford' in Whelan (ed.), *Wexford*, pp. 296-315; Bartlett, *Fall and rise*, pp 228-68.

6   Evidence of Richard Grandy, *F.D.J.* 3 July 1798, Musgrave, *Memoirs*, pp 390-91.

7   Byrne, *Memoirs*, 1, p.54.

8   W. Gahan, *Manual of Catholic piety* (Dublin, 1788). See F. X. Martin, 'Guillaume Gahan, 1732-1804' in *Dictionnaire de Spiritualite*, vi (1965), col. 69-70; P. A. Doyle, 'Father William Gahan, Augustinian of the penal days' in *Good Counsel* (Dublin, 1957), pp 119-31.

9   *D.E.P.*, 17 Dec. 1791.

10 W. Gahan, *Youth instructed in the grounds of Christian religion, with remarks on the writings of Voltaire, Rousseau, T. Paine etc.* (Dublin, 1798), p.149.

11 Gahan, *Youth instructed*, p.148.

12 *F.D.J.*, 29 Aug. 1799. O'Toole's house was destroyed by loyalists in July 1799 but, following his mysterious death a month later, the *Dublin Journal* described him as a 'man of steady loyalty'.

13 D. Dickson, 'Paine and Ireland' in Dickson, Keogh and Whelan (ed.), *United Irishmen*, p.145.

14 Resolutions of the Catholics of Arboe, County Tyrone, *D.E.P.*, 24 Jun. 1797; Andrew Newton, Coagh, to —— 1 Feb. 1798, Nat. Arch. Reb. Papers, 620/35/102.

15 Address of the Catholics of Cappoquin, Co. Waterford, *D.E.P.*, 25 Jan. 1798,

16 Address of the Catholics of Tuosist, Co. Kerry, *D.E.P.*, 17 Mar. 1798,

17 Downshire to ——,14 Jan. 1798, Nat. Arch. Reb. Papers, 620/35/34

18 *F.D.J.,* 13 Jan. 1798; Charles Tottenham, Ross to ——, 3 Feb. 1798, Nat. Arch. Reb. Papers, 620/35/109.

19 James Foulis to Castlereagh, 23 May 1798, Nat. Arch. Reb. Papers, 620/37/134, W. Smyth, Drumcree to E. Cooke, 15 May 1798, Nat. Arch. Reb. Papers 620/37/72.

20 Dundas to J. Troy, 7 Jun. 1798, D.D.A. Nicholas Phepoe to J. Troy, 8 Jun. 1798, D.D.A.

21 R. Miley to J. Troy, 4 Jun. 1798, D.D.A.

22 F. H. to E. Cooke, 22 Aug. 1798, Nat. Arch. Reb. Papers, 620/18/14.

23 J. W. n.d. [30 May 1798], Nat. Arch. Reb. Papers, 620/10/121/158.

24 *S.N.L.*, 31 May 1798; *F.D.J.*, 8 Dec. 1798.

25 *Irish Magazine*, 1808.

26 *Irish Magazine*, 1815; F. H. 22 Aug. 1798, Nat. Arch. Reb. Papers, 620/18/14.

27 O'Laverty, *Down and Conor*, iii, p.110.

28 J. Corry, Newry, to ——, 10 May 1796, Nat. Arch. Reb. Papers, 620/23/102.

29 A. McNevin, to E. Cooke, 7 July 1796, Nat. Arch. Reb. Papers, 620/24/31.

30 Bartlett, 'Defenders and Defenderism', p.379; *N. Star*, 20 July 1796; J. McCary to W. Williams, Post Office Dublin, 19 July 1796, Nat. Arch. Reb. Papers, 620/24/43.

31 McCary 29 Mar. 1797, Nat. Arch. Reb. Papers, 620/29/129, 29 Mar 1798, 620/29/130, McCary to E. Cooke, 28 May 1798, 620/37/195, 8 Oct. 1798, 620/40/140.

32 J. McCary, *The sure way to Heaven; being a new volume, much as never published before in English, on the truths of salvation; compiled and published by Rev. James Matthew MacCary, Catholic rector of Carrickfergus and Larne, S.O.P. Hy-br—norm,*

prior of Coleraine, restorator and director of the Confraternities of the White Scapular and Rosaries in the Diocese of Down and Conor (Belfast, 1797).

33 O'Laverty, *Down and Conor*, iii, p.111.
34 McCary to W. Williams, Post Office Dublin, 23 July 1796, Nat. Arch. Reb. Papers, 620/24/45.
35 O'Laverty, *Down and Conor*, iii, p.112.
36 Nat. Arch. Reb. Papers, 620/52/9
37 Gilbert, *Documents*, p.73 12 June 1798, *D.E.P.*
38 Altamont to ———, 17 May 1799, Nat. Arch. Reb. Papers, 620/47/28; James Jennings, receipt for £50, 27 Jun. 1799, Nat. Arch. Reb. Papers, 620/47/28; G. Miller to Marsden, 1801, Nat. Arch. Reb. Papers, 620/60/32.
39 Lord Shannon to ———, 8 May 1801, Nat. Arch. Reb. Papers, 620/60/76; Gilbert, *Documents*, p.75.
40 *F.D.J.* 24 Aug. 1799; Petition of Rev. M. Barry, 15 Nov. 1799, Nat. Arch. Reb. Papers, 620/56/49.
41 F. H., 18 Mar. 1801, Nat. Arch. Reb. Papers, 620/10/118/10.
42 *Press*, 21 Dec. 1797.
43 *Press*, 13 Jan. 1798, Resolution of the Roman Catholics of Rathlin Island, signed Ed. McMullan P.P. and 180 inhabitants, *F.D.J.* 13 Jan. 1798.
44 *Press*, 21 Dec. 1797.
45 *Press*, 8 Feb. 1798.
46 *F.D.J.*, 22 May 1798.
47 W. Farrell, *Carlow in '98*, p.224. Kevin Whelan suggests that Farrell may have been an informer and that his memoirs should be approached with some caution.
48 *Irish Magazine*, 1814, p.127.
49 *Irish Magazine*, 1815, p.248.
50 Whelan, 'The Catholic priest in the 1798 Rebellion', p.301.
51 I. Johnson, Cavan, to Castlereagh, 17 Jun. 1798, Nat. Arch. Reb. Papers, 620/38/169; Musgrave, *Memoirs*, p.567.
52 R. Hayes, 'Priests in the independence movement, pp 258-70.
53 Connolly, *Priests and people in pre-Famine Ireland*, p.227.
54 Some twelve more priests could be added to this list.
55 J. Troy, *Letter to the rural vicars of the Archdiocese of Dublin*, 22 May 1798, D.D.A.; J. Lanigan to J. Troy, Mar. 1798, *Castlereagh Corr.*, l, pp 160-62,
56 Fr Mackey to T. Bray, 6 Mar. 1798, C.D.A.
57 F. H., 22 Aug. 1798, Nat. Arch. Reb. Papers, 620/18/14.
58 F. H. 25 May. 1797, Nat. Arch. Reb. Papers, 620/18/14; W. Corbett, 25 Oct. 1796, Nat. Arch. Reb. Papers, 620/25/170.
59 Colclough to ———, 29 May 1797, Nat. Arch. Reb. Papers, 620/30/232.
60 J. Connolly to J. Lees, Post Office, n.d.[10 June 1798], Nat. Arch. Reb. Papers, 620/53/66.
61 F. H. 28 Aug. 1798, Nat. Arch. Reb. Papers, 620/18/14; Byrne, *Memoirs*, i, p.121; Riordan, 'The succession of parish priests in the Archdiocese of Dublin, 1771-1851', p.422.
62 Byrne, *Memoirs*, i, p.118; *S.N.L.*, 20 Jun. 1798; *F.D.J.*, 25 Oct. 1798; Prisoners expense list, 11 Sept. 1798, Nat. Arch. Reb. Papers, 620/40/39.
63 Hayes, 'Priests in the independence movement', p.261.

64 Byrne, *Memoirs*, i, pp 118-21.

65 Information of Alderman William James, 20 Oct. 1798, Nat. Arch. Reb. Papers, 620/3/32/17; Anon information, Galway, 25 Jan. 1799, Nat. Arch. Reb. Papers, 620/46/18.

66 Riordan, 'Succession lists', p.413.

67 P. F. Moran, 'The Irish convict priests of 1798' in *Irish Rosary*, Apr. 1898, p.189.

68 Madden MSS, 873/291.

69 *F.D.J.*, 14 Aug. 1798.

70 J. Troy to E. Cooke, 8 Aug. 1798. D.D.A.

71 Madden MSS, 873/291.

72 *Irish Magazine*, 1812, p.59.

73 Madden MSS, 873/291.

74 *F.D.J.*, 7 June 1798.

75 F. H., 28 Aug. 1798, Nat. Arch. Reb. Papers, 620/18/14., Sproule, Nat. Arch. Reb. Papers, 620/51/22. See J. Meagher, 'Father Nicholas Kearns and the state prisoners' in *Rep.Novum*, i, no. i (1955), pp 197-212.

76 J. W. May 1797, Nat. Arch. Reb. Papers, 620/10/121/58, Confession of Finnucane, 28 May[1798], Nat. Arch. Reb. Papers, 620/52/153; F. H., 5 Jan. 1801, Nat. Arch. Reb. Papers, 620/10/118/3; V. F. O'Daniel, *The Dominican province of St Joseph* (New York, 1942), pp 128-29. I am grateful to Fr Hugh Fenning for this information.

77 J. Verner to E. Cooke, 29 May [1798], Nat. Arch. Reb. Papers, 620/51/43.

78 Prisoners list, n.d.[1799], Nat. Arch. Reb. Papers, 620/51/135; Petition on behalf of Rev. Jas. Moran, 28 March 1799, Nat. Arch. Reb. Papers, 620/8/82/11.

79 *Freeman's Jn.*, 19 June 1798; Rev. Ed. Bayly, Certificate of Rev. Dan. Murray, P.P. Arklow, 19 June 1798, Nat. Arch. Reb. Papers, 620/38/181.

80 J. Troy to T. Bray, 12 June 1798, D.D.A.

81 Tyrawley to E. Cooke, 13 June 1798, Nat. Arch. Reb. Papers, 620/56/192.

82 P. MacSuibhne, *Carlow in '98* (Carlow, 1974), p.27; *Irish Magazine*, 1815, p.280.

83 Anon., Baltinglass, 7 May 1798, Nat Arch. Reb. Papers, 620/37/35.

84 Anon., Baltinglass to E. Cooke, 19 May 1798, Nat. Arch. Reb. Papers, 620/37/109.

85 B. O'Neal-Stratford, 23 May 1798, Nat. Arch. Reb. Papers, 620/37/133; F.D.J., 28 July 1798; Lord Aldborough to W. Elliott, 5 June 1798, Nat. Arch. Reb. Papers, 620/38/51.

86 Farrell, *Carlow in '98* , p.215.

87 *Irish Magazine*, 1811, p.307.

88 Foster Archer, Carlow, to ———, 3 Jan. 1798, Nat. Arch. Reb. Papers, 620/35/11; *F.D.J.*, 13 Jan. 1798; *F.L.J.*, 13 Jan. 1798.

89 Peter Ivers, Aug. 1798, Nat. Arch. Reb. Papers, 620/3/32/12; Farrell, *Carlow in '98*, pp 39-40.

90 Farrell, *Carlow in '98*, p.88.

91 *F.D.J.*, 5 Nov. 1799.

92 W. Power to J. Troy, 6 Jan. 1800, D.D.A.

93 *F.D.J.*, 9 Nov. 1799; J. Caulfield to J. Troy, 27 Oct. 1799, D.D.A.; T. Hearn to T. Hussey, 8 Oct. 1799, W.D.A.

94 J. Troy to A. Marsden, 10 Nov. 1799, Nat. Arch. Reb. Papers, 620/18A/10/5.

95 *F.D.J.*, 12 Nov. 1799, Duigenan, *A fair representation*, pp 220-22; P. Flood, A *Letter from the Rev. Peter Flood, D.D., President of the R. C. Col. Maynooth* (Dublin, 1800).

96 Camden to T. Pelham, 11 June 1798, in Lecky, *Ireland*, iv, p.433.

97 Duigenan, *A fair representation.*; [R. Musgrave], *A concise account of the material events and atrocities which occurred in the present rebellion, by Veridicus* (Dublin, 1799).

98 Veritas, *The State of His Majesty's subjects in Ireland professing the Catholic religion* (Dublin, 1799); J. Caulfield, *The reply of Rt. Rev. Dr. Caulfield, Roman Catholic bishop and of the Roman Catholic clergy of Wexford to the misrepresentations of Sir Richard Musgrave, bart.* (Dublin, 1801).

99 Whelan, 'The role of the Catholic priest in the 1798 rebellion in County Wexford', pp 296-315, 'The religious factor in the 1798 rebellion in County Wexford', pp 62-85, 'The Catholic community in eighteenth-century County Wexford', pp 129-70.'Catholics, politicisation and the 1798 Rebellion', pp 63-84.

100 Cullen, 'The 1798 Rebellion in Wexford; United Irishman organisation, membership, leadership', pp 248-295.

101 Donoughmore to E. Littlehales, 24 March 1799. Petition of J. O'Brien, 24 March 1799. Recommendation of T. Bray on behalf of J. O'Brien, 20 Dec. 1799, Nat. Arch. Reb. Papers, 620/58/42.

102 Tobias Bourke, 22 May 1798, Nat. Arch. Reb. Papers, 620/37/126.

103 R. Dowell, Cobh.———, 2 July 1798, Nat. Arch. Reb. Papers, 620/39/2, see R. Hayes, 'Priests in the independence movement', p.268.

104 Petition of Rev. Anthony Kelly, Mallow, 1 September 1798, Nat. Arch. Reb. Papers, 620/40/1.

105 Statement of facts relating to Youghal in the year 1798, by Rev. Dr Coppinger, Bishop of Cloyne, 19 February 1803, in Moran, *Spicil. Ossor*, iii, pp 605-613.

106 *F.D.J.*, 21 June 1798. Neill possessed land worth £500 p.a. and personal property of £5,000.

107 Sir J. Stewart, Youghal, to Capt. Taylor, 7 August 1798, Nat. Arch. Reb. Papers, 620/39/152. Lord Shannon, 4 October 1798, enclosing letter of W.A. Hayman, Mayor of Youghal, Nat. Arch. Reb. Papers, 620/40/128.

108 List of Prisoners at Cobh, 5 May 1799, Nat. Arch. Reb. Papers, 620/7/79/15(25).

109 E. Littlehales to ———, 30 June 1800, in Moran, 'The convict priests of '98', p.285.

110 Lord Redesdale to Lord Fingall, 6 Sept. 1803. in *Correspondence between Rt Hon. Ld. Redsdale and Rt. Hon. the Earl of Fingall, also a letter from R.C. Bishop of Cloyne and Ross to Rt. Hon. Ld. Redsdale with his lordship's answer. To which is added the narrative of the Rev. Peter O'Neill* (London, 1804). Reply to the narrative of Rev. P. O'Neill, n.d. [1804] Nat. Arch. Reb. Papers, 620/52/143.

111 *The humble remonstrance of the Fr Peter O'Neill to the nobility and gentry of the County of Cork, 23 October 1803,* and *observations on the remonstrance of the Rev. Peter O'Neil, P.P. Ballymacoda in the County of Cork.* (Dublin, 1804). Moran, 'Convict priests', p.287.

112 *Hibernian Magazine*, Aug. 1778, cited in Murphy, *Killaloe*, p.235.

113 M. P. MacMahon to Cornwallis, 4 Dec. 1798, Nat. Arch. Reb. Papers, 620/41/66.

114 Murphy, *Killaloe, p.236.*

115 M. P. MacMahon to E. Cooke, 24 Nov. 1800, Nat. Arch. Reb Papers, 620/48/68; M. P. MacMahon to ———, 3 Dec. 1800, Nat. Arch. Reb. Papers, 620/9/99/2.

116 Murphy, *Killaloe*, p.236; Hayes, 'Priests in the independence movement', p.265.

117 *Clare Jn.*, 11 Jan. 1799.

118 Kenny, Ennistymon to ——— 26 January [1799], Nat. Arch. Reb. Papers, 620/46/19

119 Hayes, 'Priests and the independence movement', pp 258-70; O'Donoghue, 'Catholic Church', p.362.
120 Murphy, *Killaloe*, p.242.
121 Petition of Rev. J. Carrig, 19 Feb. 1800.
122 Col. Littlehales to J. Troy, 15 May 1800, D.D.A.
123 R. Hayes, *The last invasion* ; J. Stock, *A narrative of what passed at Killala, in the County of Mayo and parts adjacent, during the French invasion of Ireland in 1798* (Dublin, 1800); See Elliott, *Partners in revolution*; J. P. Bertaud,'Forgotten soldiers; the expedition of General Humbert to Ireland in 1798' in Dickson and Gough (ed.), *French Revolution*, pp 220-29.
124 I am grateful to Liam Swords for this information.; Bertaud, 'Forgotton Soldiers' in Dickson and Gough (ed.). *French Revolution*, p.225. Bertaud mistakenly refers to the priest as 'MacKeon', *F.D.J.*, 1 Sept. 1798.
125 Musgrave, *Memoirs*, p.583; Stock, *Narrative,* p.59; Little, Diary in *Anal. Hib.*, II, pp 64-5; Circular letter of Dr Dillon of Tuam, 27 Mar. 1799, D.D.A.
126 Stock, *Narrative*, p.59; Musgrave, *Memoirs*, p.583.
127 Byrne, *Memoirs*, iii, pp 63-66; Hayes, *Last invasion*, pp 205-7.
128 Musgrave, *Memoirs*, p.601; Evidence of Michael Burke, Nat. Arch. Reb. Papers, 620/ 52/123-125.
129 *F.D.J.*, 29 Nov. 1798.
130 Byrne, *Memoirs*, iii, p.62; Hayes, *Last invasion*, p.195; N. Costelloe, 'Jobit's journal of the French expedition 1798' in An*al. Hib.*, II (1941), pp 40-1.
131 Altamont to ——, 17 May 1799, Nat. Arch. Reb. Papers, 620/47/28.
132 Capt Taylor to E. Littlehales, 22 Mar. 1799, Nat. Arch. Reb. Papers, 620/46/83; R. Aylmer (Lisburn) to Castlereagh, 5 Oct. 1799, Nat. Arch. Reb. Papers, 620/54/12; Musgrave, *Memoirs*, p.584; H. McManus, *Sketches of the Irish highlands* (London, 1863) p.78.
133 Myles Prendergast Papers, Augustinian Provincial Archives, Dublin. A.P.F., Udienza, 6 June 1819, 57. f. 483. 5., 23 Apr. 1820, A.P.F. Udienza, 58 f. 298.3.(304).
134 This lore is included in an appendix to the 2nd edition of Hayes's *Last invasion* (Dublin, 1939), but is not printed in subsequent editions; J. Gibbons, 'Fr Myles Prendergast' in *An Coinneal*, Dec. 1980, pp 79-82; Leon O'Broin, *Slán le Muirish* (Dublin, 1944).
135 Denis Browne to —— 19 Oct. 1799, Nat. Arch. Reb. Papers, 620/56/48; Trial and protection of Owen Killeen, 7 Oct. 1799, Nat. Arch. Reb. Papers, 620/56/220.
136 C. Verner to ——, 4 Sept. 1798, Nat. Arch. Reb. Papers, 620/10/117/6; Testimony of Bernard Dease, 15 Sept. 1798, Nat. Arch. Reb. Papers, 620/40/58; B. Dease to E. Cooke, n.d. [March 1799] Nat. Arch. Reb. Papers, 620/10/117/6; Nat. Arch. Reb. Papers, 620/56/200, H.O. 100/78/418-21; B. Hoban, 'Dominic Bellew, 1745-1812' in *Seanchas Ard Mhacha* (1972), pp 333-69.
137 D. Bellew to Lord Tyrawley, 19 September 1799, Nat. Arch. Reb. Papers, 620/56/ 200.
138 R. Carter to Bellew, 11 September 1799, Nat. Arch. Reb. Papers, 620/56/222. See P. Hogan, 'Some observations on contemporary allegations as to Bishop Dominic Bellew's (1745-1813) sympathies during the 1798 rebellion in Connaught' in *Seanchas Ard Mhacha* (1982), pp 417-25.
139 Musgrave, *Memoirs*, pp 607-8.

140 Caulfield to J. Troy, 7, 19 Oct. 1799, D.D.A.; Poer Trench to A. Marsden, 13 March 1799, Nat. Arch. Reb. Papers, 620/46/74.
141 Hayes, *Last invasion*, pp 22, 210-11.
142 Hayes, *Last invasion*, p.59.
143 Musgrave, *Memoirs*, p.590.
144 Information of Bernard Dease, Sept. 1798, Nat. Arch. Reb. Papers, 620/40/58; Hayes, *Last invasion*, p.195.
145 Hayes, *Last invasion*, p.197.
146 Connolly, *Religion, law and power*, p.249; Cullen, 'Late eighteenth-century politicisation', p.146.
147 N. J. Curtin, 'The United Irish organisation in Ulster, 1795-8' in Dickson, Keogh and Whelan (ed.), *United Irishmen*, pp 209-21.
148 R. B. MacDowell, 'The age of the United Irishmen: revolution and the union, 1794-1800' in *New History of Ireland*, v, pp 339-73; Smyth, *Men of no property*.
149 Whelan, 'Catholics, politicisation and the 1798 Rebellion', p.68; Bartlett, *Rise and fall*, p.212.
150 O' Coigley, *Life* ; Howell, *State trials*, vol. 26-27.
151 B. McEvoy, 'Father James Quigley', p.266; Ben Binns to R.R. Madden, Jan. 1843, Madden Mss, T.C.D., 873/448.
152 *Lim. Chron.*, 16 June 1798.
153 O'Coigley, *Life* ;.R. R. Madden, *United Irishmen*,.third series, vol. 2, p.43.
154 Howell, *State trials*,.vols 26-27; D. Keogh, 'Father John Martin; an Augustinian friar and the rebellion of 1798' in *Analecta Augustiniana*, li, (1988); 'The most dangerous villain in society': John Martin's mission to the United Irishmen of Wicklow in 1798' in *Eighteenth-Century Ireland* (1992), pp 115-35.
155 O'Coigley, *Life*,.p. 12.
156 C. J. Woods (ed.), *Journals and Memoirs of Thomas Russell* (Dublin, 1992), p.71 ff.
157 Cullen, 'Late eighteenth-century politicisation', *pp 138-44*; J. Byrne,.*Impartial account of the late disturbances in the County of Armagh, containing all the principle meetings, battles, executions, whippings, etc. of the Break of Day men and Defenders, since the year 1784 down to the year 1791 with a full and true account of the rising of both parties, by an inhabitant of the town of Armagh* (Dublin, 1792) in D. Miller, *Peep O' Day Boys and Defenders* (Belfast, 1990).
158 W. J. Fitzpatrick, *Life, times and contemporaries of Lord Cloncurry* (Dublin, 1855), p.153; Bartlett, *Rise and fall*, pp 1-16.
159 A.T.Q Stewart, *The narrow ground: aspects of Ulster, 1609-1969* (London, 1977), p.49.
160 J. Foster to ———, [n.d.] Nat. Arch. Reb. Papers, 620/52/192.
161 McEvoy, 'Fr James Quigley', p.254.
162 Madden, *United Irishmen*, ii,.p. 42;. Musgrave, *Memoirs*, p.58; Cullen, 'The political structures of the Defenders',.pp 117-138.
163 Smyth, *Men of no property*, p.117-19.
164 O'Coigley, *Life*, p.20.
165 *A view of the present state of Ireland with an account of the origin and progress of the disturbances in that country; and a narrative of facts addressed to the people of England by an observer,* (London, 1797).
166 R. Ó Muirí, 'The Killing of Thomas Birch, United Irishman, March 1797 & the

meeting of the Armagh freeholders, 19 April 1797, *Seanchas Ard Mhacha* (1982), pp 267-320; J. Hope in Madden, *United Irishmen*, Third Series, ii, App. 6. p.392; Plowden, *Historical review of Ireland*, vol. 2, p.537. I am grateful to R. Ó Muirí for his generous help.

167 O'Coigley, *Life*, p.21.

168 See M. Elliott, 'Irish republicanism in England' in T. Bartlett and D. Hayton (ed.), *Penal age*, pp 208-215.

169 A. A. E., Corr. Pol. Ang 592, fo. 43, the Revs. Coigley and MacMahon to Talleyrand, 4 Oct. 1797, in Elliott, 'Irish republicanism in England', p.211.

170 J. Nugent, London, to E. Cooke, 7 Aug. 1797, Nat. Arch. Reb. Papers,620/1/4/2.

171 *F.D.J.*, 8 Mar. 1798.

172 J. White, Lincoln Inn to Wickham, 3 May 1798, Nat. Arch. Reb. Papers, 620/37/14

173 O'Coigley, *Life*, p.43; Wickham to E. Cooke, 21 Apr. 1798, Nat. Arch. Reb. Papers, 620/36/192.

174 J. Pollock to ――――, 26 May 1798, Nat. Arch. Reb. Papers, 620/37/175. See R. J. Kelly, 'The trial and execution of Father Quigley' in *I.E.R.* (1906), pp 528-536.

175 Ben. Binns to R. R. Madden, Jan. 1843, Madden Mss. T.C.D. 873/448

176 S. Simms, *Rev. James Quigley* (Belfast, 1937); McEvoy, 'Fr James Quigley'.

177 Elliott, 'Irish republicanism in England', pp 208-215; *Partners in revolution; the United Irishmen in France* (Yale, 1982); Cullen, 'Late eighteenth-century politicisation', pp 138-44.

178 For a full discussion of Martin see D. Keogh, 'The most dangerous villain in society': Fr John Martin's mission to the United Irishmen of Wicklow in 1798' in *Eighteenth-Century Ireland* (1992), pp 115-135; 'Fr John Martin, an Augustinian friar and the Irish Rebellion of 1798' in *Analecta Augustiniana* (Rome, 1988), pp 227-46; Ronan, 'Priests in the independence movement of 1798', *I.E.R.*, LXVI (1945), 'An episode of 1798' in *Essays in commemoration* (Dublin, 1958).

179 Augustinian profession book, Salamanca, 1771-1806, F. 31R, Valladolid Archives, 540 bis. Previously, there had been some confusion between this John Martin and his near contemporary of the same name. The second John Martin studied in Seville and was granted viaticum in November 1751 and in 1759 was.appointed prior of the Irish Augustinian community of San Mattheo in Merulana Rome; Simancas Archives, l, 966, Augustinian General Archives, Rome, Dd 201, f. 55r.

180 The Latin text may be found in Migne, *Patrologia Latina*, vol. 40, col. 901-42; Myles Ronan wrongly attributes an edition of the *Confessions of Saint Augustine* to Martin; 'Priests and the independence movement of 1798', p.99.

181 When a second edition of the friar's translation appeared.in 1879, the translator was listed as 'A Catholic priest'. *The meditations of Saint Augustine* (Dublin, 1879).

182 Cogan, *Diocese of Meath*, ii,.p. 210; Nat. Arch. Reb. Papers 620/38/160.

183 D. Dickson, 'Centres of motion; Irish cities and the origin of popular politics' in P. Bergeron and L. M. Cullen, *Culture et Pratiques*, pp 101-122.

184 Smyth, *Men of no property*, p.51; Bartlett, 'Defenders and Defenderism', pp 373-94; C. J. Woods (ed.), *Journals and memoirs of Thomas Russell* (Dublin, 1992), p.141. A. P. W. Malcomson, *John Foster: the politics of the Anglo-Irish Ascendency* (Oxford, 1978), pp 162-63; J. Fitzgerald, 'The organisation of the Drogheda economy, 1780-1820' (U.C.D., M.A. thesis, 1974).

185 Rev Brabazon Smith, Newry to ――――, 1 June 1797, Nat. Arch. Reb. Papers, 620/31/6.

186 Nat. Arch. Reb. Papers, 620/38/126
187 Nat. Arch. Reb. Papers, 620/38/160
188 J. Pollock, Navan, to Marsden, 25 Sept. 1800, Nat. Arch. Reb. Papers, 620/49/55 in Whelan, 'Catholics, politicisation and the 1798 Rebellion', p.75.
189 Nat. Arch. Reb.Papers, 620/38/60, Lombard to ———, 4 May 1798, Nat. Arch. Reb. Papers, 620/38/20.
190 Dickson, *New foundations*, p.191.
191 Furlong, *Father John Murphy*, pp 103-17.
192 Nat. Arch. Reb. Papers, 620/38/126
193 Nat. Arch. Reb. Papers, 620/28/126
194 In 1804 Fr Ledwich was attacked by members of the Roscommon Militia; Meagher, 'Nicholas Kearns, State Prisoner' in *Rep. Novum.*, 1, 1 (1955)
195 B. Senior to E. Cooke, n.d. [June 1798], Nat. Arch. Reb. Papers, 620/18/1 in R. O'Donnell, 'General Joseph Holt and the Rebellion of 1798 in County Wicklow' (Unpublished M.A. thesis, U.C.D., 1991), p.151.
196 Musgrave, *Memoirs*, pp 390-1; *F.D.J.*, 14 June 1798.
197 Nat. Arch. Reb. Papers, 620/38/!60
198 Nat. Arch. Reb. Papers 620/38/160.
199 Gilbert, *Documents relating to Ireland, 1795-1804*, p.17; Nat Arch. Reb. Papers, 620/38/160.
200 Nat. Arch. Reb. Papers, Prisoners petitions, 490.
201 F. Falkiner, Abbotstown to ———, 10 August 1801, Nat. Arch. Reb. Papers, 620/49/115.
202 Musgrave, *Memoirs*, p.183.
203 McEvoy, 'Fr James Quigley', p.254.
204 E. Derry to Castlereagh, 6 June 1800, Nat. Arch. Reb. Papers 620/9/100/6.
205 O'Coigley, *Life*, p.11.
206 Nat. Arch. Reb. Papers, 620/9/100/6.
207 Belfast, 24 August 1798, Nat. Arch. Reb. Papers, 620/39/203.
208 Belfast, 24 August 1798, Nat. Arch. Reb. Papers 620/39/203; Jas. Drummond to E. Cooke, 25 Jan. 1801, Nat. Arch. Reb. Papers, 620/10/116/3; Carrickfergus, 13 July 1801, Nat. Arch. Reb. Papers, 620/10/116/13; Sir G. Hill (Derry), to A. Marsden, 5 December 1801, Nat. Arch. Reb. Papers, 620/59/91.
209 *Freeman's Jn.,* 10 March 1814.
210 ———, Loughgilly to E. Cooke, 29 May 1798, Nat. Arch. Reb. Papers, 620/37/212; see Bartlett, 'Defenders and Defenderism', p.367.
211 Madden MSS, T.C.D., 873/290.
212 Cogan, *Diocese of Meath*, iii, pp 293-300.
213 Cogan, *Diocese of Meath*, i, pp 196-7, iii, p.299; J. Brady, 'Documents concerning the Diocese of Meath' in *Arch. Hib.*, viii (1941), pp 228-9.
214 Cogan, *Diocese of Meath*, i, p.414, iii, p.299.
215 T. Ganly to J. Troy, 3 June 1798, D.D.A.

CHAPTER NINE: RALLY & CONSOLIDATE
1 C. Erskine to J. Troy, 6 April 1798, D.D.A.
2 C. Erskine to J. Troy, 23 June 1798, D.D.A.
3 C. Erskine to J. Troy, 29 July 1798, D.D.A., L. Concanen to J. Troy, 29 September 1798,

D.D.A., E. Dillon, to J. Troy, 9 July 1798, D.D.A.

4 J. Caulfield to J. Troy, 3 July 1798, 6 October 1798, D.D.A.

5 Bartlett, *Fall and rise*, p.236.

6 *F.D.J.*, 5, 7 June 1798.

7 J. Troy to T. Bray, 12 June 1798, D.D.A.

8 C. Erskine to J. Troy, 23 June, 6 July 1798, D.D.A.

9 *F.D.J.*, 12, 14, 16, 19 June 1798.

10 Cornwallis to Portland, 28 June 1798, H.O. 100/77/200-1.

11 J. Caulfield to J. Troy, 1 June 1799, See L. M Cullen, *Emergence of modern Ireland 1600-1900* (London, 1983), p.217. Between August 1798 and October 1800, 27 Chapels were burned in Ferns, 15 in Wicklow, 4 in Kilkenny, 4 in Carlow and 4 in the remainder of the country. *Irish Magazine*, Jan. 1808, pp 214-25, Luke Cullen MSS, T.C.D., 1472/3-6

12 J. Caulfield to J. Troy, 3 November 1798, D.D.A. T.C.D. MSS, 871 p.22. Affidavit of Sullivan of County Kildare, offered £400 to swear against yeoman burning chapel, 9 April 1800.

13 J. Troy to T. Bray, 12 June 1798, D.D.A.

14 F. H., 24 June 1798, Nat. Arch. Reb. Papers. 620/18/14.

15 *F.D.J.*, 23 June 1798.

16 Byrne, *Memoirs*, i, p.12. Hay, *History*, p.267, Account of the courtmartial of J. Redmond, 30 June 1798, S.P.O. 620/3/26/4, J. Caulfield to J. Troy, 2 September, 15 October 1798, D.D.A.

17 J. Caulfield to J. Troy, 6 September 1798, D.D.A. See Whelan, 'The Catholic priest in the 1798 Rebellion', pp 311-312.,

18 J. Caulfield to J. Troy, 27 June 1799, 12 July 1799, 28 July 1799, D.D.A.

19 J. Caulfield to J. Troy, 10 October, 10 November, 17 December 1799, D.D.A.

20 J. Caulfield to J. Troy, 1 June 1799, D.D.A.

21 *D.E.P.*, 18 December 1798, *F.D.J.*, 20 December 1798, Madden MSS 873/292. *F.D.J.*, 29 August 1799, J. Troy to Dublin Castle, 29 August 1799, Nat. Arch. Reb. Papers, 620/58/100, J. Caulfield to J. Troy, 29 August, 3 September 1799, D.D.A., Luke Cullen MSS, T.C.D., 1472/5.

22 See Bartlett, *Fall and rise*, pp 6-9; John Temple, *The Irish Rebellion* (Dublin, 1746), (ed.) William King, *The State of the Protestants of Ireland under the late King James' Government* (Dublin, 1691).

23 *Press*, 14 December 1798; P. Duigenan, *An answer to Grattan*.

24 C. Erskine to J. Troy, 29 June, 6 July, 7 August 1798, D.D.A.

25 Sproule, 21 July 1798, Nat. Arch. Reb. Papers. 620/39/02.

26 T. Rennell, *Ignorance productive of atheism, faction and superstition; a sermon preached before the University of Cambridge, Commencement Sunday, 1 July 1798* (Dublin, 1799); *F.D.J.*, 18 December 1798.

27 Rennell, p.38

28 J. Caulfield to J. Troy, 15 September 1798, D.D.A.

29 Veritas, *A vindication of the Roman Catholic clergy of the town of Wexford, during the late unhappy rebellion, from the groundless charges and illiberal insinuations of an anonymous writer, signed Verax* (Dublin, 1799).

30 *Veritas*, pp 16-17.

31 *Veritas*, p.15.

32 *Veritas*, p.18.

33 [R. Musgrave] *A concise account of the material events and atrocities which occurred in the present rebellion, by Veridicus* (Dublin, 1799).

34 *Veridicus*, p.17. C. Jackson, A *narrative of the sufferings and the escape of Charles Jackson* (Dublin, 1798).

35 J. Caulfield to J. Troy, 26 April 1799, D.D.A.

36 J. Caulfield to J. Troy, 9 June 1799, D.D.A.

37 J. Caulfield to J. Troy, 26 April, 3 June 1799, D.D.A.

38 *The State of His Majesty's subjects in Ireland professing the Roman Catholic Religion, containing an account of the conduct of the Roman Catholic clergy in Wexford during the Rebellion of 1798, and the refutation of a pamphlet signed Veridicus* (Dublin, 1799), p.48. Curiously, McNally believed that no copy of Clinch's work has been found, but he was 'certain it did appear bearing the same name Veritas'; 'John Troy', p.230.

39 J. Troy to J. Clinch, 7 January 1800, D.D.A.

40 J. Caulfield to J. Clinch n.d. [1800] , Madden MSS, 873/194-5. This correspondence relates to a misunderstanding between the two over an unwanted payment made to Clinch for his effort, which he returned to the bishop.

41 Caulfield, *The reply of the Rt. Rev. Dr Caulfield, Roman Catholic bishop and of the clergy of Wexford to the misrepresentations of Sir Richard Musgrave Bt.* (Dublin, 1801); [R. Musgrave] *Observations on the reply of the Rt Rev Dr Caulfield, Catholic bishop and of the Roman Catholic clergy of Wexford to the misrepresentations of Sir Richard Musgrave B.T.* (Dublin, 1802).

42 For a recent discussion of the historiography of 1798, see L. M. Cullen, 'Late eighteenth-century politicisation', pp 141-151.

43 J. Alexander, *Some account of the first symptoms of the late rebellion in the county of Kildare and the adjoining part of the King's County* (Dublin, 1800); G. Taylor, *An history of the rise, progress and suppression of the rebellion of Wexford* (Dublin, 1800), p.8.

44 E. Hay, *History of the insurrection of the county of Wexford* (Dublin, 1803), p.183.

45 J. Caulfield to J. Troy, 10 September 1799, D.D.A., Redesdale to Perceval, 23 October 1803, P.R.O.N.I., T. 3030/7/10. See M. Whelan, 'Edward Hay "Styled Mr Secretary Hay"; Catholic Politics 1792-1822' (Unpublished M.A. thesis, U.C.G. 1991), pp 62-98.

46 Redesdale to Percival, 23 October 1803, P.R.O.N.I. T. 3030/7/10. See A. p.W. Malcomson, *John Foster*, pp 438-40.

47 Julius Vindex[Dennis Taaffe], *Vindication of the Irish Nation and particularly its Catholic inhabitants from the calumnies of Libellers* (Dublin, 1802), p.63.

48 Proceedings of the Secret Committee of the House of Commons, 14 August 1798. *F.D.J.*, 16 March 1799, Jackson, *Narrative*, p.44. MacNeven, *Pieces*, p.273.

49 Duigenan, *A fair representation*. See Peter Lattin, *Observations on Dr Duigenan's fair representation of the present political state of Ireland, particularly with respect to his strictures on a pamphlet entitled the case of Ireland reconsidered* (London, 1800).

50 Duigenan, *A fair representation*, p.18.

51 Duigenan, *A fair representation*, p.35.

52 F. H. ———, 15 May 1798, Nat. Arch. Reb. Papers. 620/18/14.

53 See Flood, *A letter from the Rev Peter Flood D.D., President of Maynooth College to the Hon... ... M.P., relative to a pamphlet entitled 'A fair representation of the present political state of Ireland* (Dublin, 1800).

54 *F.D.J.*, 16 June 1798.

55 Duigenan, *A fair representation*, p.223. J. Troy to T. Bray, 18 April 1799, C.D.A.

56 E. Dillon to T. Bray, 17 April 1799, C.D.A.

57 J. Troy to P. Plunket, 23 May 1797, Cogan, D*iocese of Meath*, iii, p.211.

58 Castlereagh to Wickham, 23 November 1798, H.O. 100/79/150-2, Cornwallis to Portland, 5 December 1798, H.O. 100/79/233-5.

59 Castlereagh to Portland, 16 January 1799, H.O. 100/85/73-6, H.O. 100/85/81-2, H.O. 100/85/82-84. See O'Donoghue, 'Catholic Church', pp 378-420.

60 The attendance at these meetings from 17-19 January was O'Reilly, Bray, Dillon, Troy, Plunket, Delaney, Caulfield, Moylan, French and Cruise.

61 Resolutions 28 January 1799, D.D.A.

62 J. Troy to J. Young, 23 February 1799, D.D.A.

63 J. Troy to J. Young, 23 February 1799, D.D.A.

64 Note in Young's hand on Troy's letter of 23 February 1799, D.D.A.

65 J. Young to T. Bray, 30 December 1798, C.D.A.

66 O'Donoghue claims that his influence amongst the hierarchy was 'non-existent', 'Catholic Church', p.386.

67 T. Hussey to J. B. Clinch, n.d. [January 1799], Madden MSS, 873/197. See E. Burke to T. Hussey, 10 February 1795, *Burke Corr.*, viii, pp 142-3, E. Burke to T. Hussey, 17 March 1795, *Burke Corr.*, viii, pp 199-205.

68 C. Erskine to Borgia, 3 April 1799, A.P.F., S.C. Irlanda, vol. 17, f. 538, Borgia to J. Troy, 15 June 1799, D.D.A.

69 C. Erskine to J. Troy, 24 February 1799, D.D.A. see Johnson, *Developments in the Roman Catholic Church in Scotland*, pp 119-29.

70 J. C. Hippisley to Lord Hobart, 12 January 1799, *Castlereagh Corr.*, iii, p.86.

71 C. Erskine to Borgia, 3 April 1799, D.D.A.

72 J. Troy to L. Concanen, n.d. [Spring 1800], D.D.A.

73 Bartlett, *Fall and rise*, pp 268-304.

74 For a discussion of the Union and the Catholic question, see Bartlett, *Fall and rise*, pp 240-45.

75 Cornwallis to Portland, 5 December 1798, *Castlereagh Corr.*, ii, pp 35-6; Troy to Castlereagh, 15 December 1798, P.R.O.N.I., D 3030/412.

76 Anon, *An address to the Roman Catholics of Ireland on the conduct they should pursue at the present crisis on the subject of a union. By an old friend* (Dublin, 1799), p.8; E. Cooke to Castlereagh, 17 December 1798, *Castlereagh Corr.*, ii, pp 46-7.

77 P. Plunket to J. Troy, 13 December 1798, D.D.A.

78 Hussey to J.B. Clinch 10 Jan [1799], Madden Mss, 873/197.

79 J. Young to T. Bray, 30 December 1798, C.D.A.

80 Castlereagh to Camden, 22 October 1798, PRO 30/8/327/19-20.

81 J. Troy to Castlereagh, 24 December 1798, *Castlereagh Corr.*, ii, p.61

82 Cooke to Castlereagh, 17, 20 December 1798, *Castlereagh Corr.*, ii, pp 46-7, 49-50.

83 *F.D.J.*, 18 December 1798.

84 Castlereagh to W. Wickham, 18 February 1799, H.O. 100/88/125-6.

85 Bartlett, *Fall and rise*, p.255.

86 J. Caulfield to J. Troy, 15 July 1799, D.D.A.

87 M. Lennan to J. Troy, 7 February 1799, *Castlereagh Corr.*, ii, p.168.

88 *F.D.J.*, 23 July 1799, *F.D.J.*, 9 November 1799,

89 Pro-union address of R.Cs of Raphoe, 3 December 1799, S.P.O. 620/49/6.

90 *F.D.J.*, 16 March 1799.

91 Anon, *Considerations upon the state of public affairs in the year MDCCXCIX*, (Dublin, 1799), p.61.

92 P. Plunket to Castlereagh, 29 October 1799, *Castlereagh Corr.*, iii, pp 226-7.

93 T. Bray to T. Pelham, 1 July 1799, *Castlereagh Corr.*, ii, pp 344-5.

94 T. Hussey to J. Carroll, Baltimore, 29 September 1799, Baltimore Diocesan Archives. I am grateful to Fr Hugh Fenning for this reference.

95 J. Caulfield to J. Troy, 30 October 1799, D.D.A.

96 J. Caulfield to J. Troy, 16 September 1799, D.D.A.

97 E. Dillon to J. Troy, 9 July 1799, *Castlereagh Corr.*, ii, pp 347-8, 386-7.

98 *The speech of the Rt. Hon. Lord Castlereagh upon delivering to the House of Commons of Ireland his Excellency' the Lord Lieutenant's message on the subject of an union, 5 February 1800* (Dublin, 1800).

99 *The speech of the Rt. Hon. John Earl of Clare in the House of Lords, 10 February 1800* (Dublin, 1800), p.69.

100 Bartlett, *Fall and Rise*, pp 264-67.

CHAPTER TEN: Epilogue

1 J. Caulfield to J. Troy, 31 March 1792, D.D.A.

2 J. Caulfield to J. Troy, 12 August 1799, D.D.A.

3 J. Caulfield to J. Troy, 23 June 1799, D.D.A.

Appendix

SAMPLES OF CATHOLIC LOYAL DECLARATIONS

1797

24 June   Declaration of the Catholics of Arboe, County Tyrone, acknowledged by Rev. Bernard O'Neill.

10 Dec.   Declaration of the Catholics of Rathlin, signed by Ed. McMullan PP, Alexander McDonnell and 180 inhabitants.

23 Dec.   Declaration of the Catholics of Loughgeel, Killraughts & Grange of Killogan, County Antrim, signed by Tully McNally PP, James McCormick and 751 inhabitants.

29 Dec.   Declaration of the Catholics of Ballinderry, County Tyrone, signed by Pat Devlin PP.

31 Dec.   Declaration by the Catholics of Clonegall, Moyacomb & Barragh, County Carlow signed by 1,561 inhabitants.

21 Dec.   Declaration of the Catholics of Culfaghtrim & Grange, County Antrim, signed by Pat Brennan PP.

1798

23 Jan.   Declaration of the Catholics of Ramoan, County Antrim, signed by Roger O'Murray, pastor.

23 Jan.   Declaration of the Catholics of Saul, County Down, signed by Rev. McCartan PP.

25 Jan.   Declaration from Catholics of Cappoquin, County Waterford, parish signed by Thomas Flannery PP and 817 inhabitants.

30 Jan.   Declaration of the Catholics of Templeshanbo, County Wexford, signed by Miles O'Connor PP, Silvester Clinch, David Doyle, Thomas Redmond and 564 inhabitants.

3 Feb.   Declaration of the Catholics of Marshallstown, County Wexford, signed by John Doyle PP.

6 Feb.   Declaration of the Catholics of the parishes of Crosses of Kilmatial [Kilmyshall] & Ballindaggan, County Wexford, signed by 100 inhabitants.

6 Feb.	Declaration of the Catholics of Rinagh & Gallen, King's County, signed by Peter Reynolds PP, for 320 parishioners.
6 Feb.	Declaration of the Catholics of Tisaran & Rillegally, King's County signed by Felix McHugh PP, for 690 parishioners.
6 Feb.	Declaration of the Catholics of Seven Churches, County Wicklow, signed by Ed. Reddy for 415 parishioners.
13 Feb.	Similar declaration from parish of Affane and Modeligo, County Waterford, signed by John Hearn PP and 780 parishioners.
13 Feb.	Similar declarations of Catholics of the parishes of Litter, Killincooley and Monamolin, County Wexford, signed by Michael Lacy PP and 500 parishioners.
20 Feb.	Declaration of the Catholics of Lismore, County Waterford, signed by Daniel Lawler PP and 300 residents, assented to by 1,022 Catholics.
1 March	Similar declaration 'from inhabitants of all religious professions resident in the parish of Clonoe, County Tyrone', signed by James Devlin PP, 'at the desire of all the Catholics of Clonoe'.
1 March	Similar declaration of Catholic inhabitants of the parish of Killrush, County Wexford, signed by Edanus Murphy PP, and 514 of its inhabitants.
3 March	Similar declaration of 'Catholic inhabitants of the united parishes of Lissan and Kildress in the counties of Derry and Tyrone', signed by Bernard Muldoon PP and 800 parishioners.
10 March	Similar declarations of the Catholic inhabitants of the parish of Kinawley, commonly called Knockninny, in the county of Fermanagh, signed by Michael Wynne PP, for 557 parishioners.
13 March	Declaration of the Catholics of Killiarvan County Donegal, signed by John McElwea PP and 900 parishioners.
17 March	Declaration of the Catholics of Tuosist, County Kerry, signed by John Power, pastor.
17 March	Declaration of the Catholics of Killillee & Castle Ellis, County Wexford, signed by David Cullen PP, William Talbot and 230 parishioners.
18 April	Address of the magistrates and leading inhabitants of Tipperary, signed by Robert White PP of Moderny, and D. Murphy, pastor of Nenagh.
1 May	Declaration from the Catholics of Castlebridge County Wexford, signed by Michael Redmond PP.

1 May	Declaration from the Catholics of Kilmallock, County Wexford, signed by Raymond Rourke [recté Roche]PP.
1 May	Declaration from the Catholics of Ferns and the union, County Wexford, signed by Edward Redmond PP of Gorey and John Murphy, Curate, Kilcormuck.
1 May	Declaration from the Catholics of Ballynamonaboy, County Wexford, signed by Nicholas Synott PP.
29 May	Declaration of loyalty signed by John O'Callaghan D.D., PP of Inniscarra and Matehy, County Cork; Cornelius O'Mahony, PP of Magourney and Aghabullogue, County Cork; Denis Coakly, PP of Ahimma [sic] County Kerry..
7 June	Declaration of the Catholics of Carrick-on-Suir, County Waterford, with 106 names
12 June	Declaration of the Catholics of Clonmel, County Waterford,signed by Rev. Thomas Flannery.
12 June	Address of principal Catholics of Clones [Clogher], County Monaghan,signed by the priests of Clogher, including Hugh O'Reilly PP; James Murphy, Tedavnet; Pat McGinn, Monaghan; Pat Coyle, Killeevan; Michael McGinn, Clontibret; William McGuire, Drummully; Ed. McArdle, Donagh; Bernard Duffy, Clones; John McAnally, Roslea; Pat Murphy, Ematris; Ed. Malone, Kilmore; Pat Bellew, Curran; Edm. McMahon, Fintona; Jas. McMahon, Aghalurcher; Thos. Raverty, ditto; John McMahon, Dromore; Charles McKenna, Kilskeery; Ter. McKosker, Clogher; Chas. McMahon, Enniskillen; Philip McGruaran, Cleenish; Stephen Keenan, Templecarn; Bernard Raverty, Derryvullan; T. Corrigan, Maheracoolmaine; James McGar, Thuro [Trough]; Edmund Muldoon, Moy; Pat Thally, Devenish. Curates: Pat Hughes, Chas. McPherson, Pat Duffy, Thos. Campbell, Pat McCawell, Philip Kelly, Peter Ingoldsby, James Mee, Pat Henraty.
16 June	Address of Catholics of Desartgreat and Derryloran, County Tyrone, signed by 'upwards of a thousand of the inhabitants and Arthur Tegart PP.
16 June	Address to the Lord Lieutenant from the Catholics of County Longford [72 names].
19 June	Declaration of the Catholics of Longford, signed by T. Cruise, Bishop of Ardagh for himself and the clergy.
19 June	Declaration of the people of Dungarvan, County Waterford,signed by Edmond Prendergast PP.

21 June	Declaration of the people of Dundalk, County Louth.
28 June	Declaration of the Catholics of Omagh, County Tyrone, signed by Rev. P. McLaughlin for himself and 500 inhabitants.
28 June	Declaration of the Catholics of Newry.
30 June	Declaration of the Catholics of Ballinahinch,
1 July	Address of the Catholics of Moat, County Meath, signed by Thos. Reynolds PP, John Jennings PP, Pat McNamee PP, Dan Malledy PP, James Fagan PP.
7 July	Declaration of the Catholics of Seaforde and Tyrella, County Down, signed by Patrick McCartan for himself and 1,200 of his congregation.
7 July	Declaration of the Catholics of Moat.
12 July	Declaration of the Catholics of Ulster.

Bibliography

PRIMARY SOURCES: MANUSCRIPTS

National Archives
Official papers
Rebellion papers, 620/1-67
State of the country papers, 1015/1- 1017/66
State prisoners petitions, 1796-1799

National Library of Ireland
Ms 886   Lord Lieutenant's correspondence 1786-1798
Ms 1,548   List of Irish Catholic priests 1735-1835
Ms 1,562   Documents relating to the Catholic Church in Ireland in the eighteenth and nineteenth centuries.
Ms 8,123   Plunket papers, Letters of the Bishop of Meath, Patrick J. Plunket

Cashel Diocesan Archives
Correspondence and papers of Thomas Bray, Archbishop of Cashel 1792-1820.

Dublin Diocesan Archives
Correspondence and paper of John Thomas Troy, Bishop of Ossory 1776-86 and Archbishop of Dublin 1786-1823.

University of Dublin (TCD)
Ms 868-9   Russell-Sirr papers
Ms 871   Depositions Musgrave papers
Ms 872   Court Martial papers, 1798
Ms 873   Madden papers
Ms 3,360-86   Thomas Prior papers
Ms 3,365   Thomas Prior diaries of 1798 Rebellion
Ms 10,347   Papermaker's diary, 1793-99
Ms 10,354   Dobbin papers

St Patrick's College, Maynooth
B2/1/1   Trustees' Minute Book.

Public Record Office, London
H.O. 100   Home Office papers

Archives of Propaganda Fide, Rome
Atti della Sacra Congregazione, vols 146-73
Scritture riferite nei Congressi, Irlanda, vols 14-18
Scritture riferite nei Congressi, Anglia, vols 5-6
Fondo di Vienna, vol. 28
Lettere della Sacra Congregazione, vols 240-85

Vatican Archives: Archives of the Secretary of State
Nunziatura di Inghilterra, vols 25-30

English College, Rome
Papers of Charles Erskine.

PRIMARY SOURCES: PRINTED

Collections of documents

——*The Correspondence of Edmund Burke*, (ed). Thomas Copeland *et al* (Cambridge, 1958-78), 10 vols.

——*Correspondence of Viscount Castlereagh*, (ed.) Marquis of Londonderry (London, 1848-53), 4 vols.

Bartlett, Thomas. 'Select documents xxxviii: Defenders and Defenderism in 1795', *Irish Historical Studies*, xxiv, no. 95 (1985), pp 373-94.

Beresford, William (ed.), *The correspondence of the Rt. Hon. John Beresford* (London, 1854), 2 vols.

Chart. D. A. (ed.), *The Drennan letters:1776-1819* (Belfast, 1931).

[Cornwallis]: *The correspondence of Charles, First Marquis Cornwallis*, (ed.) Charles Ross (London, 1859), 3 vols.

Edwards, Robin Dudley (ed.), 'The minute book of the Catholic Committee, 1773-92, *Archiv. Hib.*, ix (1942), pp 1-172.

Gilbert, J. T. (ed.), *Documents relating to Ireland, 1795-1804* (Dublin 1893).

Howell, T. B. & T. J. (ed.) *A complete collection of state trials* (London, 1811-26), 34 vols.

Luke, Br. (ed.), *Rev. Conwell 1798-1804: letters from Maynooth* (Dundalk, 1941).

McDermott, Brian (ed.), *The Catholic question in England and Ireland: The papers of Denys Scully* (Dublin, 1988).

Miller, David (ed.), *Peep of Day Boys and Defenders* (Belfast, 1990).

William, Charles (ed.), *Correspondence of Rt. Hon. Edmund Burke between 1744 and the period of his decease in 1797* (London, 1844).

Woods, C. J. (ed.), *Journals & memoirs of Thomas Russell* (Dublin, 1991).

Parliamentary Proceedings and Reports

The Parliamentary register: or history of the proceedings and debates of the House of Commons of Ireland, vi (1786), xii-xvii (1792-98).

Journals of the House of Commons of the kingdom of Ireland, x, part 1 (1779-1782), xv-xvii (1792-1798) (Dublin, 1796-1800).

Report from the Committee of Secrecy of the House of Commons (London, 1798). This pamphlet includes the reports from the Lords' secret committee (1793) and the reports from the Commons and Lord's secret committees (1797). These reports are also reproduced in the *Journal of the House of Commons* (1798).

Report of the Committee of Secrecy of the House of Lords of Ireland (London, 1798).

Newspapers

Belfast Newsletter	1790–1801
Cork Gazette	1790–97
Dublin Evening Post	1790–1802
Ennis Chronicle	1789–1802
Faulkner's Dublin Journal	1789–1802
Freeman's Journal	1789–1803
Hibernian Journal	1790–1801
Limerick Chronicle	1789–1800
Morning Post	1789–97
Northern Star	1792–May 1797
The Press	1797–March 1798
The Rights Of Irishmen	Nov. 1791–92
Saunder's Newsletter	1789–1802

Contemporary accounts, pamphlets, memoirs

A Defense of the Catholic Church against the assaults of certain busy sectaries being a dialogue between an itinerant preacher and Sylvester Lynch (Dublin, 1803).

A full and accurate report of the debates in the parliament of Ireland, in the session 1793 on the bill for the relief of His Majesty's Catholic subjects (Dublin, 1793).

A history of the Irish Rebellion in the Year 1798 (Dublin, 1799).

A letter to His Excellency the most noble Marquis Cornwallis (Belfast, 1798).

A second letter to the Right Honorable Mr. Grattan,by the author of 'A short history of opposition (Dublin, 1797).

A statement and observations on cases that occurred in the counties of Cork, Wexford and Wicklow particularly during the last campaigns (Dublin, 1799).

An impartial narrative of the most important engagement which took place between His Majestys forces and the rebels during the Irish Rebellion of 1798 (Dublin, 1799).

An address to the thinking independent part of the community on the present alarming state of public affairs, by a lover of the constitution (Dublin, 1797).

An address to the people of the Ireland on the present alarming state of the kingdom, by an independent native (Dublin, 1798).

An account of the late insurrection in Ireland, in which is laid open the secret correspondence between the United Irish and the French govt. through Ld. Edward FitzGerald, Mr Arthur O'Connor, James Quigley & others, together with a short history of the principal battles ... with observations on the confessions of the chiefs and on their connections with certain societies in Great Britain (London, 1799).

An account of some of the sufferings of His Holiness Pius VI being forced from Rome (Dublin, Fitzpatrick, 1799).

An address to the Irish Roman Catholics on the necessity of arming the government and constitution with the whole energies of Ireland at the present crisis, by a true born Irishman (Dublin, May 1797).

Ancient Irish prophecies translated from original parchments to which is prefixed a vindication of prophecy in general and of Irish prophecy in particular (Cork, 1800).

Alexander, James. *Some account of the first symptoms of the late rebellion in the county of Kildare and an adjoining part of the King's County* (Dublin, 1800).

Barrington, Jonah. *Personal sketches* (London, 1827-32), 2 vols.

Bolster, E. (ed.), 'The Moylan correspondence' in *Collect. Hib.*, 14 (1971), 15 (1972).

Brittle. *Strictures & remarks on Dr Hussey's late pastoral address* (Dublin, 1797).

Burke, Edmund. *A letter from the Rt. Hon. Edmund Burke to His Grace the Duke of Portland on the conduct of the minority in parliament containing fifty-four articles of impeachment against the Rt. Hon. C. J. Fox* (London, 1797).

—— *A letter from a distinguished English commoner to a peer of Ireland* (Dublin, 1783).

Butler, Charles. *A letter to a nobleman on the proposed repeal of the penal laws which now remain in force against the Irish Roman Catholics* (London, 1801).

Butler, Charles. *Historical memoirs of the English, Irish and Scottish Catholics since the Reformation* (London, 1822), 4 vols.

[Byrne, J.?], *An impartial account of the late disturbances in the county of Armagh* (Dublin, [1792]).

Byrne, Miles. *Memoirs.* (Paris, 1863, Shannon, 1972), 2 vols.

Camillus [Musgrave, R]. *To the Magistrates, the military and the yeomanry of Ireland* (Dublin, 1798).

Castlereagh, Lord Viscount. *The speech of the Rt. Hon. Lord Viscount Castlereagh upon delivering to the House of Commons of Ireland His Excellency the Lord Lieutenant's message on the subject of an union* (Dublin, 1800).

Caulfield, James. *The reply of the Rt. Rev. Dr. Caulfield, Roman Catholic bishop and of the Roman Catholic clergy of Wexford to the misrepresentations of Sir Richard Musgrave Bart* (Dublin, 1801).

Chartres, Mark. *Vinegar Hill, a poem* (Dublin, 1802).

Clifford, B. (ed.), *Scripture politics: selections from the writings of William Steel Dickson* (Belfast, 1991).

Clifford, R. *Application of Barruel's memoirs on Jacobinism to the secret societies of Ireland and Great Britain, by the translator of that work* (London, 1798).

Cloncurry, Valentine. *Personal recollections of the life & times with extracts from the correspondence of Valentine Lord Cloncurry* (Dublin, 1849).

Cloney, Thomas. *A personal narrative of those transactions in the County Wexford in which the author was engaged during the awful period of 1798* (Dublin, 1832).

[Cobbett, W.]. *Democratic principles illustrated by example* (Dublin, 1798).

Considerations on the state of Ireland and on the impolicy and impracticability of separation (Limerick, 1799).

Considerations on the situation to which Ireland is reduced by the government of Lord Camden [Attributed to Lord Carhampton] (Dublin 1798, 6th edition).

[O'Coigley, J?] *A view of the present state of Ireland with an account of the origin & progress of the disturbances in that country, and a narrative of facts addressed to the people of England, by an observer* (London, 1797).

[O'Coigley, James]. *The life of the Rev. James Coigley. An address to the people of Ireland as written by himself during his confinement in Maidstone Gaol* (London, 1798).

Collins, J. *A funeral oration on the late Right Rev. Dr Francis Moylan ... preached 20 April 1815* (Cork, 1815).

Cuffe, Hamilton. *A sermon preached in the church of Kells on Thursday the 16th February 1797, being the day appointed for a national thanksgiving, on account of the providential deliverance of this kingdom from the late threatened invasion* (Dublin, 1797).

Cumberland, Richard. *Memoirs* (London, 1806).

[Day, R.] *An address delivered to the Grand Jury of the County of Dublin on Tuesday the 10th of January 1797, by Robert Day M.P.* (Dublin, 1797).

De La Tocnaye, M. *Rambles through Ireland* (London, 1799), 2 vols.

Devereux, James Edward. *Observations on the factions which have ruled Ireland: on the calumnies thrown upon the people of that country and on the justice, expediency and necessity of restoring to the Catholics their political rights* (London, 1801).

Duigenan, Patrick. *A fair representation of the present political state of Ireland* (London, 1799).

—— *An answer to the address of the Rt. Hon. Henry Grattan to his fellow citizens of Dublin* (Dublin, 1798).

—— *Speech of Dr. Duigenan in House of Commons* (Dublin, 1800).

England, T. *The life of the Rev. Arthur O'Leary* (London, 1822).

Fitzpatrick, W. J. *Secret service under Pitt* (London,1892) 2nd edition.

Fleming, Robert. *A discourse on the rise and fall of anti-Christ wherein the revolution in France and the downfall of monarchy in that kingdom are distinctly pointed out* (Dublin, 1800).

Flood, Peter. *A letter from the Rev. Peter Flood D.D. president of the R.C. College Maynooth to the Hon. —— M.P. relative to a pamphlet entitled "A fair representation of the present political state of Ireland"* (Dublin, 1800).

French alliance! or Jacobinism portrayed in an address to the people of America on the prospect of war with France with extracts of letters from New York, Charlestown, Boston, submitted to the perusal of Irishmen (Dublin 1798).

French fraternity and French protection as promised to Ireland and as experienced by other nations, by a friend of the people (Dublin, 1798).

Gahan, William *Youth instructed in the grounds of the Christian religion with remarks on the writings of Voltaire, Rousseau, T. Paine, intended as an antidote against the contagious doctrines of Atheists, Materialists, Fatalists, Deists, Modern Arians, Socinians* (Dublin, 1798).

Gordon, James. *A history of the rebellion in Ireland in the year 1798* (Dublin, 1801).

Grattan, Henry. *The Rt. Hon. Henry Grattan's celebrated address to his fellow citizens* (Dublin, 1797) 2nd. edition.

—— *Memoirs of the life and times of the Rt. Hon. Henry Grattan*, ed. Henry Grattan (London 1839-46), 5 vols.

History of the origin of the Irish yeomanry with the steps taken to bring forward the measure previous to the final adoption (Dublin, 1801).

Hay, Edward. *History of the insurrection of the county of Wexford* (Dublin, 1803).

Holt, Joseph. *Memoirs* (T. Crofton Croker, ed.) (London, 1838), 2 vols.

Important reflections on the present state of Ireland tending to the restoration of peace, order & happiness addressed to the Quondam opposition party, country gentlemen & people, by their true friend (Dublin, 1798).

Hussey, T. *A pastoral letter to the Catholic clergy of the united Dioceses of Waterford & Lismore* (Waterford, 1797).

—— *A sermon preached by the Rt. Rev. Dr Hussey in the chapel in Spanish Place, on the sixth of May 1798* (London, 1798).

—— *A short account of the public prayers in the Spanish chapel for H.H. Pius VI on the fourteenth of May 1798* (London, 1798).

Jackson, Charles. *A narrative of the sufferings and escape of Charles Jackson late a resident at Wexford in Ireland* (Dublin, 1799), 8th edition.

Kennedy, P. *A short defense of the present men and present measures with occasional strictures on some recent publications of democratic notoriety in a letter to a friend in the country* (London, 1797).

King, William. *The state of the Protestants of Ireland under the late King James's government* (Dublin, 1691).

Kingston, George Earl of. *A narrative of the proceedings of the Commisioners of Suffering Loyalists in the case of Capt. Philip Hay with remarks thereon* (Dublin, 1808).

Larkin, J. (ed.), *The trial of William Drennan* (Dublin, 1991).

Lattin, Patrick. *Observations on Dr. Duigenan's fair representation of the present political state of*

Ireland particularly with respect to his strictures on a pamphlet entitled "The case of Ireland reconsidered" (London, 1800)

Letter of the French bishops residing in England to the Late Pius VI and the answer of His Holiness (Dublin, 1800).

Letters to the Roman Catholic laity occasioned by Doctor Hussey's pastoral letter (Dublin, 1797)

Letters from a gentleman in Ireland to his friend at Bath (Cork, 1798).

McCarthy, D. (ed.), *Collections on Irish Church history from the MSS of the Late V. Rev. Laurence F. Renehan* (Dublin, 1861).

McCary, James. *The sure way to Heaven.* (Belfast, 1797)

McHugh, Roger (ed.), *Carlow in '98. The autobiography of William Farrell of Carlow* (Dublin, 1949).

McLaren, Archibald. *A genuine account of the capture and death of Lord Edward Fitzgerald: an impartial description of the battles* (Bristol, 1799).

MacNeven, W. J. *Pieces of Irish history illustrative of the conditions of the Catholics of Ireland of the origin & progress of the political system of the United Irishmen and of their transactions with the Anglo-Irish government* (New York, 1807).

Martin, John. *The meditations of St Augustine* (Dublin, 1798)

Moore, Charles William. *Reflections on the present state of our country: addressed to the parishioners of Moira by their affectionate friend and Rector Charles William Moore* (Dublin, 1798).

Mowbray, Geoff. *Remarks on the conduct of the opposition during the present parliament* (Dublin, 1798).

Moylan, Francis. *Pastoral instructions to the Roman Catholics of the Diocese of Cork.* (Cork, 1798)

Musgrave, Richard. *Memoirs of the different rebellions in Ireland* (Dublin, 1801).

O'Beirne, Thomas Lewis. *The charge of the Rt. Rev. Thomas Lewis O'Beirne DD to the clergy of the Diocese of Meath at his primary visitation held on the 18th October 1799* (Dublin, 1800).

Observations on the reply of the Rt. Rev. Doctor Caulfield, Roman Catholic bishop and of the Roman Catholic clergy of Wexford to the misrepresentations of Sir Richard Musgrave (Dublin, 1802).

O'Byrne, Eileen (ed.), *The convert rolls* (Dublin, 1981).

O'Leary, Arthur. *A sermon preached at St Patrick's chapel, Sutton Street, Soho Square, on Wednesday March the 8th 1797, on the day of solemn fFast* (London & Dublin, 1797).

—— *Funeral oration of the late sovereign Pontiff Pius the Sixth by the Rev. Arthur O'Leary to which is prefixed an account of the solemn obsequies performed to his memory at St. Patrick's Chapel, Sutton Street Soho Square on Saturday 16 Nov 1799* (Dublin, 1800).

Orange! A political rhapsody (Dublin, 1798)

Paddy's resource: being a select collection of original and modern patriotic songs for the use of the people of Ireland nos. 1&2 (Belfast, 1795, 1796).

Paine, Thomas. *The rights of man* (H. Collins, ed. London, 1976).

Panisset, Francis Teresa *The declaration & retraction of Francis Teresa Panisset, Constitutional Bishop of Mont-Blanc in Savoy* (Dublin, 1797).

Petition of the Whig club to the King, as transmitted by the Earl of Moira & Mr Fox (Dublin, 1798)

Plowden, Francis. *A historical review of the state of Ireland, from the invasion of that country under Henry II to its union with Great Britain* (London, 1803), 2 vols.

Public characters of 1798 (Dublin, 1799).

Reflections on the Irish conspiracy and on the necessity of an armed association in Great Britain to which are added observations on the debates and resolutions of the Whig club on the sixth of June 1797 (London, 1797).

Reform or ruin. Take your choice! (Dublin, 1798).

Remarks on the Rev. Dr. Hussey's pastoral letter, by one of the people (Dublin, 1797).

Rennell, T. *Ignorance productive of atheism, faction and superstition: a sermon preached before the University of Cambridge, Commencement Sunday July 1798* (Dublin, 1799).

Report from the Committee of Secrecy appointed to take into consideration the treasonable papers presented to the House of Commons of Ireland on the twenty ninth of April last. Reported 10th May 1797, by Rt. Hon. Mr Secretary Pelham (London, 1797).

Robison, John. *Proofs of a conspiracy against all the religions and governments of Europe carried on in the secret meetings of free masons, illuminati and reading societies* (London, 1798), 3rd. Edition.

Rowan, A. H. *Autobiography of A. Hamilton Rowan* (Dublin, 1840, Shannon, 1972).

Serious reflections on the late and continued disturbances in Ireland addressed to the people at large, by a citizen of the world (Dublin, 1798).

Snowe, William. *A fair and candid statement of transactions at Enniscorthy on the 28th of May and at Wexford on the 30th of May 1798 in a letter addressed to the Rev. James Gordon author of the "History of the rebellion in Ireland in the year 1798"* (Dublin, 1801).

Strictures & remarks on Dr. Hussey's late pastoral address to the clergy of Lismore & Waterford (Dublin, 1797).

Taylor's narrative. The Monitor [No.1] *giving an account of the sufferings, persecutions, tortures and cruel deaths of near forty persons who were taken prisoners by the rebels.* (Wexford, 1799)

Teeling, Charles Hamilton. *History of the Irish Rebellion of 1798: a personal narrative and sequel to the history of the Irish Rebellion of 1798* (Glasgow, 1876, Shannon, 1972).

Temple, Sir John. *The Irish Rebellion* (Dublin, 1746).

Tempora mutantor or reasons for thinking that it is inconsistent with the welfare of this kingdom to persist in withholding from the Roman Catholics the political power, offices & honours enjoyed exclusively by Protestants (Dublin, 1799).

The monitor or useful miscellany (Dublin, 1800)

The state of His Majesty's subjects in Ireland professing the Roman Catholic religion, Part II (Dublin, 1800).

The union doctrine, or poor man's catechism (Dublin, 1798).

The causes of the rebellion in Ireland discussed in an address to the people of England in which it is proved by incontrovertible facts that the system for some years pursued in that country has driven it into its present dreadful situation! By an Irish emigrant (London, 1798).

Thoughts on the present rebellion; addressed to all thinking and honest Irishmen, by Eumenes (Dublin, 1798).

Tickle, Timothy. *A letter to the Rev. Doctor Hussey* (Dublin, 1797).

Tone, T.W. *Life of Theobald Wolfe Tone,* ed. W.T. Tone (Washington DC, 1826), 2 vols

——— *An argument on behalf of the Catholics of Ireland* (Dublin, 1791))

Trial of James O'Coigley, otherwise called James Quigley, otherwise called John Fivey, Arthur O'Connor Esq., John Binns, John Allen and Jeremiah Leary for high treason at Maidstone, Kent, Mon 21 & Tue 22 and Days in May 1798 (London, 1798).

Troy, J. T. *The excommunication of Rev. Robert McEvoy priest of the Archdiocese of Dublin for promulgating and upholding principles established by the French Revolution: Published 29 September 1792* (London, 1798).

——— *A pastoral address on the duties of Christian citizens.* (Dublin, 1793).

——— *Pastoral address to the Roman Catholics of the Arch diocese of Dublin . . . delivered in the chapel at Francis Street, 16 February 1797.* (Dublin, 1797)

——— *Pastoral instructions to the Roman Catholics of Dublin,* (Dublin, 1798).

Vane, Ch. (ed.), *Memoirs & correspondence of Viscount Castlereagh* (London, 1850).

Vindex, Julius [Dennis Taafe].*Vindication of the Irish nation and particularly its Catholic inhabitants from the calumnies of libellers* (Dublin, 1802).

———— *Succinct views of Catholic affairs in reply to T. McKenna's "Thoughts" which prove that second thoughts are best* (Dublin, 1805).

Wakefield, Edward. *An account of Ireland, statistical and political* (London, 1812), 2 vols.

Young, Arthur. *An enquiry into the state of the public mind amongst the lower classes and on the means of turning it to the welfare of the state in a letter to William Wilberforce Esq. M.P.* (Dublin, 1798).

SECONDARY SOURCES

Adams, J. R. *The printed word and the common man. Popular culture in Ulster, 1700-1900* (Belfast, 1987).

Bartlett, Thomas. 'An end to moral economy: The Irish Militia disturbances of 1793', *Past and Present*, 99 (May 1983), pp 41-64.

———— 'Defenders and Defenderism in 1795', *I.H.S.*, xxiv (May 1985), 373-94.

———— 'Indiscipline and disaffection in the armed forces in Ireland in the 1790s' in P.J. Corish (ed.), *Radicals, rebels and establishments* (Belfast, 1985), pp 115-34.

———— "A people made rather for copies than originals": the Anglo-Irish, 1760-1800', *International History Review*, xii, I (Feb., 1990), pp 11-25.

———— 'The origins and progress of the Catholic question, 1690-1800' in Thomas Power and Kevin Whelan (ed.), *Endurance and emergence: Catholics in eighteenth-century Ireland* (Dublin, 1990), pp 1-19.

———— *The fall & rise of the Irish nation: The Catholic question 1690-1830* (Dublin, 1992).

Begley, John. *The Diocese of Limerick from 1691 to the present time* (Dublin, 1938).

Birch, Peter. *St. Kieran's College Kilkenny* (Dublin, 1951).

Blanning, T. C. W. 'The role of religion in European counter-revolution 1789-1815' in D. Beales and G. Best (ed.), *History, society and the Churches* (Cambridge, 1985), pp 195-214.

Bolster, M. 'Insights into fifty years of episcopal elections (1774-1824)' in *Kerry Arch. Soc. Jn.*, v (1972), pp 60-76.

———— *A history of the Diocese of Cork from the penal era to the Famine* (Cork, 1989).

Bossy, John. *The English Catholic community, 1570-1850* (London, 1975).

Boyne, P. (ed.), *Memoirs of Miles Byrne* (Dublin, 1946).

Brady, J. 'Lawrence O'Connor–a Meath schoolmaster', *Irish Ecclesiastical Record*, 5th ser. xlix (1937), p.281-7.

———— Documents concerning the Diocese of Meath', *Archiv. Hib.*, viii (1941), pp 228-9

Brady, John. *Catholics and Catholicism in the eighteenth-century press* (Maynooth, 1965).

———— and Corish, P. J. *The Church under the penal code* (Dublin, 1971) in (*A history of Irish Catholicism*, ed. Patrick J. Corish, iv. fasc.2.).

Brady, W. Maziere. *Anglo Roman papers Vol. III* (London, 1890).

———— *The episcopal succession in England, Scotland and Ireland, A.D. 1400-1875* (London, 1971).

Brennan, M. 'The Confraternity of Christian Doctrine in Ireland', *I.E.R.* (1934), pp 560-77.

Bric, Maurice. 'The Whiteboy movement in Tipperary, 1760-80' in W. Nolan (ed.), *Tipperary: history and society* (Dublin, 1985), pp 148-84.

Burke, Nuala. 'A hidden Church?: the structure of Catholic Dublin in the mid-eighteenth century' in *Archiv. Hib.*, xxxii (1974), pp 81-92.

Burke, O. J. *The History of the Catholic Archbishop of Tuam* (Dublin, 1882).

Burke, W. P., *The Irish priests in the penal times, 1660-1750* (repr. Shannon, 1969).

Burns, R. E., 'The Irish popery laws: a study in eighteenth-century legislation and behaviour', *Review of Politics*, xxiv (1962), pp 485-508.

Buschkühl, M. *Great Britain & the Holy See 1746-1870* (Dublin, 1982).

Butler, T. C. *John's Lane: A history of the Augustinian friars in Dublin 1280-1980* (Dublin, 1983).

Butterfield, Herbert. *George III, Lord North and the people, 1778-80* (London, 1949).

Callahan, W. J., and Higgs, David (ed.), *Church and society in Catholic Europe of the eighteenth century* (Cambridge, 1979).

Clark, Samuel and Donnelly, J. S. *Irish peasants: violence and political unrest, 1780-1914* (Manchester, 1983).

Clifford, B. (ed.), *Scripture politics: selection from the writings of William Steel Dickson* (Belfast, 1991).

Cogan, A. *The Diocese of Meath ancient & modern* (Dublin, 1870).

Connolly, S. J. 'Religion and history' in *Ir. Ec. and Soc. Hist.*, x (1979), pp 66-80

—— *Priests and people in pre-famine Ireland* (Dublin, 1981).

—— 'Catholicism in Ulster, 1800-1850' in P. Roebuck (ed.), *Plantation to partition* (Belfast, 1981).

—— 'Violence and order in the eighteenth century' in P. O'Flanagan, P. Ferguson and K. Whelan (ed.), *Rural Ireland 1600-1900* (Cork, 1987), pp 42-62

—— 'The penal laws' in W. Maguire (ed.), *Kings in conflict: The revolutionary war in Ireland and its aftermath 1689-1750* (Belfast, 1990), pp. 157-72.

—— *Religion, law and power: the making of Protestant Ireland, 1660-1760,* (Oxford, 1992).

Corish, P. J. *The Catholic community in the seventeenth and eighteenth centuries* (Dublin, 1981).

—— (ed.), *Radicals, rebels and establishments* (Belfast, 1985).

—— *The Irish Catholic experience: a historical survey* (Dublin, 1985).

—— 'Two centuries of Catholicism in County Wexford' in K. Whelan (ed.), *Wexford: history and society* (Dublin, 1987), pp 222-47.

Corkery, Daniel. *The hidden Ireland, a study of gaelic Munster in the eighteenth century* (Dublin, 1925).

Costello, Con. *In quest of an heir: the life and times of John Butler, Catholic Bishop of Cork, Protestant baron of Dunboyne* (Cork, 1978).

Cox, L. 'Westmeath in the 1798 period' in *Irish Sword*, ix (1969-70), pp 1-15.

Cullen, L. M. *An economic history of Ireland since 1660* (London, 1976).

—— 'The Irish merchant communities of Bordeaux, La Rochelle and Cognac in the eighteenth century' in L.M. Cullen and Paul Butel (ed.), *Négoce et industrie en France et en Irlande aux XVIIIe et XIXe Siecles* (Paris, 1980), pp 51-64.

—— *The emergence of modern Ireland, 1600-1900* (London, 1981).

—— 'The 1798 rebellion in its eighteenth-century context' in Corish (ed.), *Radicals, rebels and establishments*, pp 91-113.

—— 'Catholics under the penal laws' in *Eighteenth Century Ireland*, i (1986), pp. 23-36.

—— 'Catholic social classes under the penal laws' in Power and Whelan (ed.), *Endurance and emergence*, pp 57-84.

—— 'The political structures of the Defenders' in H. Gough and D. Dickson (ed.), *Ireland and the French Revolution* (Dublin, 1990), pp 117-38.

—— 'Late eighteenth-century politicisation in Ireland: problems in its study and its French links' in P. Bergeron and L. M. Cullen (ed.), *Culture et pratiques politique en France et en Irlande XVIe-XVIIIe Siècle (*Paris, 1991), pp 137-58.

Curran, M. J. 'Correspondence of Archbishop Carpenter with Bishop Sweetman', *Rep. Novum* (1956), pp 399-405.

—— 'Archbishop Carpenter's epistolae, 1770-1780', *Rep. Novum* (1955), pp 154-72 (1956), pp 381-98.

Curtin, Nancy. 'The transformation of the United Irishmen into a mass-based organisation, 1794-96', *I.H.S.*, xxiv (Nov. 1985), pp 463-92.

Daly, Mary, and Dickson, David (ed.), *The origins of popular literacy in Ireland* (Dublin, 1990).

Dickson, Charles. *The Wexford rising in 1798, its causes and course* (Tralee, 1955).

—— *Revolt in the North: Antrim and Down in 1798* (Dublin, 1960).

Dickson, David. 'Middlemen' in Bartlett and Hayton (ed.), *Penal era and golden age: Essays in Irish history, 1690-1800* (Belfast, 1979), pp 162-85.

—— The Cork merchant community in the eighteenth century: a regional perspective' in Cullen and Butel, *Négoce et Industrie*, pp 45-50

—— 'The place of Dublin in the eighteenth-century Irish economy' in D. Dickson and T. Devine, (ed.) *Ireland and Scotland, 1600-1850* (Edinburgh, 1983), pp 177-92.

—— 'Bibliography' in T. Moody and W. Vaughan (ed.), *A new history of Ireland. Volume IV. Eighteenth-century Ireland 1691-1800* (Oxford, 1986), pp. 713-95.

—— *New foundations: Ireland 1660-1800* (Dublin, 1987).

—— and Gough, Hugh (ed.), *Ireland and the French Revolution* (Dublin, 1990).

—— 'Catholics and trade in eighteenth-century Ireland: an old debate revisited' in Power and Whelan (ed.), *Endurance and emergence*, pp 185-200.

Donnelly, James. 'The Whiteboy movement, 1761-5' in *I.H.S.*, xxi (Mar. 1978), pp 20-54.

—— 'Propagating the cause of the United Irishmen' in *Studies*, lxix, 273 (1981), pp 5-23.

Dowling, Edward. 'Irish seminaries in the eighteenth century' in *I.E.R.*, xcviii (1962), pp 213-21.

Dunne, Tom. *Wolfe Tone, colonial outsider* (Cork, 1982).

Elliott, Marianne. 'The origins and transformation of early Irish republicanism', *International Review of Social History*, xxiii (1978), pp 405-28.

—— *Partners in revolution: The United Irishmen and France* (Yale, 1982).

—— *Watchmen in Sion: the Protestant idea of liberty* (Derry, 1985).

—— 'Ireland' in O. Dann and J. Dinwiddy (ed.), *Nationalism in the age of the French Revolution* (London, 1988), pp 71-86.

—— *Wolfe Tone: prophet of Irish independence* (Yale, 1989).

Fenning, Hugh. *The undoing of the friars of Ireland* (Louvain, 1972).

—— 'Clerical recruitment, 1735-83' in *Archiv. Hib.*, xxx (1972), pp 1-20.

—— *The Irish Dominican province 1698-1797* (Dublin, 1990).

Ferguson, K. P. 'The Volunteer movement and the government, 1778-93' in *Irish Sword*, xiii (1979), pp 208-16.

Fitzpatrick, J. D. *Edmund Rice* (Dublin, 1945).

Fitzpatrick, W. J. *The secret service under Pitt* (London, 1892).

Flagg Bemis, Samuel. *The Hussey-Cumberland mission and American independence* (Princeton, 1931).

Flood, J. M. 'Dr. Plunket, Bishop of Meath, 1779-1827 in *I.E.R.*, lxxii (1949), pp 234-42.

Froude, J. A. *The English in Ireland in the eighteenth century* (London 1874), 3 vols.

Furlong, N. *Fr. John Murphy of Boolavogue 1753 -1798* (Dublin, 1991).

Giblin, Cathaldus. 'The Stuart nomination of Irish bishops, 1687-1765' in *I.E.R.*, cv (1966), pp 35-47.

Gibson, Ralph. *A social history of French Catholicism, 1789-1914* (London, 1989).

Gray, John. 'Millennial vision ... Thomas Russell re-assessed' in *Linen Hall Review* (1989).

Gunn, J. 'The foundation of Maynooth College 1795' in I.E.R. (1883) pp 316-26.

Hayes, R. *The last invasion of Ireland* (Dublin, 1937).

—— *Old Irish links with France: some echoes of exiled Ireland* (Dublin, 1940).

—— 'Priests in the independence movement of '98' in *I.E.R.* (1945), pp 258-70.

Hill, Jacqueline. 'Religious toleration and the relaxation of the penal laws: an imperial perspective, 1763-1780' in *Arch. Hib.* (1989), pp 98-109.

Hoffman, Ross. *Edmund Burke, New York agent* (Philadelphia, 1956).

Hogan, Patrick. 'Some observations on contemporary allegations as to Bishop Dominick Bellew's

(1745-1813) sympathies during the 1798 Rebellion in Connaught' in *Seanchas Ard Mhacha* (1982) pp 417-25.

Inglis, Brian. *The freedom of the press in Ireland, 1784-1841* (London, 1954).

Jacob, Rosamond. *The rise of the United Irishmen* (London, 1937).

Johnson, C. *Developments in the Roman Catholic Church in Scotland 1789-1829* (Edinburgh, 1983).

Johnson, E.M. *Ireland in the eighteenth century* (Dublin, 1974).

Jupp, Peter. 'Irish parliamentary elections and the influence of the Catholic vote' in *Hist. Jn.*, x, 2 (1967), pp 183-96.

Kelly, James. The context and course of Thomas Orde's plan of education of 1787' in *Irish Journal of Education*, xx (1986), pp 20-31.

—— 'The origins of the Act of Union: an examination of Unionist opinion in Britain and Ireland, 1650-1800' in *I.H.S.*, xxv (1987), pp 236-63.

—— 'The parliamentary reform movement of the 1780s and the Catholic question' in *Arch. Hib.* (1988), pp 95-117.

—— 'The genesis of Protestant Ascendancy: The Rightboy disturbances of the 1780s' in Gerard O'Brien (ed.), *Parliament, politics and people: essays in eighteenth-century Irish history* (Dublin, 1989), pp 93-127.

—— (ed.), *Dublin & Dubliners* (Dublin, 1990).

—— 'The Catholic Church in the Diocese of Ardagh 1650-1870' in R. Gillespie and G. Moran (ed.), *Longford: essays in county history* (Dublin, 1991).

—— *Prelude to Union* (Cork, 1992).

Kelly, Patrick. 'Irish writers and the French Revolution' in *La storia della storiografia Europea sulla rivoluzione Francese* (Rome, 1990) pp 327-49.

Kelly, R. J. 'The trial and execution of Father James Quigley' in *I.E.R.* (1906), pp 528-36.

Kenny, Colum. 'The exclusion of Catholics from the legal profession in Ireland, 1537-1829' in *I.H.S.*, xxv (1987), pp 337-57.

Keogh, Dáire. 'Fr John Martin: An Augustinian friar and the rebellion of 1798' in *Analecta Augustiniana* (1988), pp 225-46.

—— 'Thomas Hussey, Bishop of Waterford & Lismore, 1797-1803' in W. Nolan, T. Power and D. Cowman (ed.) *Waterford: history and society* (Dublin, 1992).

—— 'The Catholic Church, Archbishop Troy and radicalism, 1791-93' in D. Dickson, D. Keogh and K. Whelan (ed.), *The United Irishmen: radicalism, revolution & rebellion* (Dublin, 1993).

—— '"The most dangerous villian in society": Fr. John Martin's mission to the United Irishmen of Wicklow in 1798' in *Eighteenth-Century Ireland*, vii (1992), pp 115-35.

Langlois, Claude. 'La rupture entre l'Eglise catholique et la révolution,' in F. Furet and M. Ouzouf (ed.), *The French Revolution and the creation of modern political culture*, (Pergamon, 1987), iii, pp 375-90.

Lefort, Claude, 'La révolution comme religion nouvelle' in F. Furet and M. Ozouf (ed.), *The French Revolution and the creation of modern political culture* (Pergamon, 1987), iii, pp. 391-99.

Lecky, W. E. H. *A history of England in the eighteenth century* (London, 1879), 5 vols.

—— *A history of Ireland in the eighteenth century* (London, 1892), 5 vols.

Lenihan, M. *Limerick: its history and antiquities* (Cork, 1967).

McDowell, R. B. 'The personnel of the Dublin Society of United Irishmen' in *I.H.S.*, ii (1940), pp 12-53.

—— *Irish public opinion, 1750-1800* (London, 1944).

—— 'The Fitzwilliam episode' in *I.H.S.*, xv (1966), pp 115-30.

—— *Ireland in the age of imperialism and revolution, 1760-1801* (Oxford, 1979).

—— The age of the United Irishmen' in *N.H.I.*, iv, pp 339-70.

McEvoy, Brendan. 'The United Irishmen in Co. Tyrone' in *Seanchas Ard Mhacha*, iii (1959), pp 283-305; iv (1960-1), pp 1-32; v (1969), pp 37-65.

—— Father James Quigley', *Seanchas Ard Mhacha*, v (1970), pp 247-59.

—— 'The Peep of Day Boys and Defenders in County Armagh' in *Seanchas Ard Mhacha* (1986), pp 123-63; (1987), pp 60-127.

McSkimmin, Samuel. *Annals of Ulster, 1790-1798* (1849, E.J. Crum, ed., Belfast, 1906).

MacDermot, Frank. *Theobald Wolfe Tone: a biographcal study* (Tralee, 1969).

——'The Church and ninety-eight' in *Ireland Today*, iii, (January, 1938) pp 41-44.

Mac Giolla Phádraig, Brian. 'Dr. John Carpenter, Archbishop of Dublin (1760-86)' in *Dublin Hist. Rec.*, xxx (1976), pp 2-17.

Mac Grath, Kevin. 'Two Wexford priests and 1798' in *I.E.R.*, (1948) pp 1,092-1,098.

Mac Suibhne, Peadar. *'98 in Carlow* (Carlow, 1974).

Madden, R. R. *Lives of the United Irishmen* (Dublin, 1842-6), 7 vols.

Mahoney, T. H. *Edmund Burke and Ireland* (Oxford, 1960).

Malcomson, A. P. *John Foster. The politics of the Anglo-Irish ascendancy* (Oxford, 1978).

Meagher, J. 'Fr. Nicholas Kearns and state prisoners' in *Rep. Novum* (1955), pp 197-212.

—— 'Glimpses of eighteenth-century Dublin priests' in *Rep. Novum*, ii (1958), pp 129-47.

Miller, David. 'The Armagh troubles, 1784-95' in Clark and Donnelly (ed.), *Irish Peasants*, pp 155-91.

Mitchell, James. 'Laurence Nihell (1726-95), Bishop of Kilfenora and Kilmacduagh in *Galway Arch. Soc. Jn.*, xxxiv (1975), pp 58-87.

Moody, T. W. and Vaughan, W. E. (ed.), *A new history of Ireland, iv, eighteenth-century Ireland 1690-1800* (Oxford, 1986).

Moran, P. F. *History of the Catholic archbishops of Dublin* (Dublin, 1864).

Morton, R. G. 'The rise of the yeomanry', *Irish Sword*, vii (1967-8), pp 58-64.

Murphy, J. A. 'The support of the Catholic clergy in Ireland, 1750-1850' in *Hist. Studies*, v (1965), pp 103-21.

Murphy, N. 'Archbishop Troy' in *I.E.R.* (1898), pp 232-43.

Newman, Jeremiah. *Maynooth and Georgian Ireland* (Galway, 1979).

Noakes, R. 'Cardinal Erskine's mission, 1793-1801' in *Dublin Review* (1934), pp 353-88

O'Brien, C. Cruise. *The great melody* (Dublin, 1992).

O'Brien, Gerard. 'The beginning of the veto controversy in Ireland' in *Journal of Ecclesiastical History* (Jan. 1987), pp 80-94.

—— (ed.) *Parliament, politics and people: essays in eighteenth-century Irish history* (Dublin, 1989).

—— (ed.) *Catholic Ireland in the eighteenth century: the collected essays of Maureen Wall* (Dublin, 1989).

O'Connell, M. R. The political background to the establishment of Maynooth College' in *I.E.R.* (May, 1956) pp 325-34, (June, 1956), pp 406-15: (July, 1956), pp 1-16.

—— *Irish politics and social conflict in the age of the American Revolution* (Philadelphia, 1965).

O'Donoghue, Patrick. 'The Holy See and Ireland' in *Archiv. Hib.*, xxxiv (1976-7), pp 99-108.

O'Farrell, Patrick. 'Millenarianism, messianism and utopianism in Irish history' in *Anglo-Irish Studies*, ii (1976), pp 45-68.

Ó Fearghail, F. *St Kieran's College 1782-1982* (Kilkenny, 1982).

—— 'The Catholic Church in County Kilkenny, 1600-1800' in W. Nolan and K. Whelan (ed.), *Kilkenny: history and society* (Dublin, 1990), pp 197-25.

O'Ferrall, Fergus. 'The only lever ... '? The Catholic priest in Irish politics' in *Studies*, lxx, 280 (1981), pp 308-24.

O'Flaherty, Eamonn. 'The Catholic Convention and Anglo-Irish politics, 1791-3' in *Archiv. Hib.*, xl (1985), pp 14-34.

—— 'Ecclesiastical politics and the dismantling of the penal laws in Ireland, 1774-82' in *I.H.S.*, xxvi (May, 1988), pp 33-50.

O'Laverty, James. *An historical account of the Diocese of Down and Conor, ancient and modern* (Dublin, 1878-95).

Ó Muirí, R. (ed.) *Irish Church history today* (Armagh, 1991).

—— 'The killing of Thomas Birch, United Irishman, March 1797, and the meeting of the Armagh freeholders, 19 April 1797', *Seanchas Ard Mhacha*. (1982) pp 267-320.

Osborough, W. N. 'Catholics, land and the Popery Acts of Anne' in Power and Whelan, *Endurance and emergence*, pp 21-56.

Ó Snodaigh, P. 'Class and the Irish Volunteers' in *Irish Sword*, xvi (1986), pp 165-84.

Pakenham, Thomas. *The year of liberty: the story of the great Irish Rebellion of 1798* (London, 1969).

Peel, H.E. 'The appointment of Dr. Troy to the See of Dublin' in *Rep. Novum*, iv (1971), pp 5-16.

Power, Thomas. ''Converts' in Power and Whelan (ed.), *Endurance and emergence*, pp 101-28.

—— and Whelan, Kevin (ed.), *Endurance and emergence: Catholics in eighteenth-century Ireland* (Dublin, 1990).

—— (ed.) *Waterford: history & society* (Dublin, 1992).

Power, T. R. 'The Most Rev. James Butler, D.D., Archbishop of Cashel, 1774-1791' in *I.E.R.*, (1892), pp 302-18, 522-38.

Purcell, Mary. 'Archbishop John Thomas Troy, 1739-1823' in *Dublin Hist. Rec.*, xxxi (1978), pp 42-52.

Renehan, L. F. *Collections in Irish Church history* (Dublin, 1861).

Rogers, Patrick. *The Irish Volunteers and Catholic emancipation, 1778-93: a neglected phase of Irish history* (London, 1934).

Scholfield, P. 'British politicians and French arms: the ideological war 1793-5' in *History*, lxxvii (June, 1992) pp 183-202.

Senior, Hereward. *Orangeism in Britain and Ireland, 1795-1836* (London, 1966).

Silke, John. 'The Irish College Seville' in *Arch. Hib.*, xxiv (1961).

Simms, J. G. 'The making of a penal law (2 Anne, c. 6), 1703-5' in *I.H.S.*, xii (1960), pp 105-18.

—— 'The case of Ireland stated' in Brian Farrell (ed.), The *Irish parliamentary tradition* (Dublin, 1973), pp 128-38.

Simms, Samuel. *Rev. James O'Coigly, United Irishman* (Belfast, 1937).

Smith, E.A. *Whig principles and party management: Earl Fitzwilliam and the Whig party* (Manchester, 1975).

Smyth, James. 'Popular politicisation, Defenderism and the Catholic question' in Gough and Dickson, *French Revolution*, pp 109-16.

—— 'Dublin's political underground in the 1790s' in G. O'Brien (ed.), *Parliament, politics and people* , pp 129-49.

—— *The Men of No Property*, (London, 1992).

Smyth, Peter. '''Our cloud-cap't Grenadiers'': the Volunteers as a military force' in *Irish Sword*, xiii (1978-9), pp.185-207.

—— 'The Volunteers and parliament' in Thomas Bartlett and David Hayton (ed.), *Penal era and golden age*, pp 115-36.

Stewart, A. T. Q., *A deeper silence*, (London, 1993).

Swords, L. *The green cockade: the Irish in the French Revolution 1789-1815* (Dublin, 1989).

Tohall, Patrick. 'The Diamond fight of 1795 and the resultant expulsions' in *Seanchas Ard Mhacha*, no. 3 (1958-9), pp 17-50.

Trainor, Brian, and Crawford, W. H. (ed.), *Aspects of Irish social history* (Belfast, 1969).

Wall, Maureen [MacGeehin]. 'The Catholics of the towns and the quarterage dispute in eighteenth-century Ireland' in *I.H.S.*, viii (1952), pp 91-114.

—— 'The rise of a Catholic middle class in eighteenth-century Ireland' in *I.H.S.*, xi (1958), pp 91-115.

—— *The penal laws* (Dundalk, 1965).

—— 'John Keogh and the Catholic Committee' in G. O'Brien (ed.), *Catholic Ireland in the eighteenth century: the collected essays of Maureen Wall* (Dublin, 1989), pp 163-71.

Wallace, Patrick. 'Archbishop James Butler II: catechist to generations at home and abroad' in Wm. Nolan (ed.), *Thurles: the cathedral town* (Dublin, 1989), pp 47-54.

Walsh, T. J. 'Francis Moylan, Bishop of Cork 1735-1815' in *Cork Hist. Soc. Jn.*, lv (1949), pp 98-110.

Whelan, Kevin. 'The Catholic parish, the Catholic chapel and village development in Ireland' in *Irish Geography*, xvi (1983), pp 1-16.

—— 'The Catholic Church in Tipperary, 1700-1900' in W. Nolan (ed.), *Tipperary: history and society* (Dublin, 1985), pp 215-55.

—— 'The religious factor in the 1798 Rebellion in County Wexford' in O'Flanagan, Ferguson and Whelan, *Rural Ireland*, pp 62-85.

—— 'The role of the Catholic priest in the 1798 Rebellion in County Wexford' in Whelan, *Wexford*, pp 296-315.

—— 'The regional impact of Irish Catholicism 1700-1850' in W. Smyth and K. Whelan (ed.), *Common Ground: essays on the historical geography of Ireland* (Cork, 1988), pp 253-77.

—— 'Politicisation in County Wexford and the origins of the 1798 Rebellion' in Gough and Dickson (ed.), *French Revolution*, pp 156-78.

—— 'The Catholic community in eighteenth-century County Wexford' in Power and Whelan, *Endurance and emergence*, pp 129-70.

——'Catholics, politicisation and the 1798 Rebellion,' in R. ÓMuirí (ed), *Irish Church history today* (Armagh, 1990), pp 63-84.

——'Catholic mobilisation, 1750-1850' in P. Bergeron and L. M. Cullen (ed.) *Culture et pratiques politique en France et en Irlande XVIe-XVIIIe Siécle* (Paris, 1991), pp 235-58.

Whelan, Patrick. 'Anthony Blake, Archbishop of Armagh 1758-87' in *Seanchas Ard Mhacha* (1970), pp 289-323.

Zimmerman, G. D. *Irish political street ballads 1780-1900* (Geneve, 1966).

UNPUBLISHED DISSERTATIONS

Curtin, Nancy. 'The origins of Irish Republicanism: The United Irishmen in Dublin and Ulster, 1791-8' (Ph. D., University of Wisconsin, 1988).

Graham, Thomas. 'The Dublin United Irish Organisation,' (Ph.D., University of Dublin, forthcoming).

O'Donoghue, Patrick. 'The Catholic Church and Ireland in an age of imperialism and rebellion, 1782-1803' (Ph.D., UCD, 1975).

Murphy, W. G. 'The life of Dr. Thomas Hussey (1746-1803), Bishop of Waterford and Lismore (M.A., UCC, 1968).

McNally, Vincent. 'Archbishop John Thomas Troy and the Catholic Church in Ireland, 1787-1817' (Ph.D., University of Dublin, 1976).

O'Flaherty, Eamon, 'The Catholic question in Irish politics, 1774-95' (M.A., UCD, 1981).

Power, Thomas. 'Land, Politics and Society in Eighteenth-Century Tipperary' (Ph.D., University of Dublin, 1987).

Wallace, Patrick. 'Irish Catechesis–the heritage from James Butler II, Archbishop of Cashel 1774-1791' (Ph.D. Catholic University of America, 1975).

Whelan, Margaret. 'Edward Hay; styled Mr. Secretary Hay and Catholic politics 1792-1822,' (M.A., U.C.G., 1991)

Index